THE DRUNKEN DUCHESS OF VASSAR

With — with love + best wishes

Chris

8.2019

THE DRUNKEN DUCHESS OF VASSAR

*Grace Harriet Macurdy, Pioneering
Feminist Classical Scholar*

BARBARA McMANUS

Foreword by Judith P. Hallett and Christopher Stray

THE OHIO STATE UNIVERSITY PRESS

COLUMBUS

Library of Congress Cataloging-in-Publication Data

Names: McManus, Barbara F., 1942– author. | Hallett, Judith P., 1944– writer of foreword. | Stray, Christopher, writer of foreword.
Title: The Drunken Duchess of Vassar : Grace Harriet Macurdy, pioneering feminist classical scholar / Barbara McManus ; foreword by Judith P. Hallett and Christopher Stray.
Description: Columbus : The Ohio State University Press, [2017] | Includes bibliographical references and index.
Identifiers: LCCN 2016043813 | ISBN 9780814213278 (cloth ; alk. paper) | ISBN 0814213278 (cloth ; alk. paper)
Subjects: LCSH: Macurdy, Grace Harriet. | Women classicists—United States—Biography.
Classification: LCC PA85.M278 M36 2017 | DDC 880.09—dc23
LC record available at https://lccn.loc.gov/2016043813

Cover design by Susan Zucker
Text design by Juliet Williams
Type set in Adobe Minion Pro

9 8 7 6 5 4 3 2 1

*To the memory of Allan Macurdy (1960–2008),
courageous disability-rights advocate, kindred spirit of
his great-great-aunt Grace Macurdy*

CONTENTS

❧

Illustrations follow page 122.

FOREWORD

Introductions to scholarly books customarily conclude with thanks *by* their author. Sadly, this preface begins with our thanks *to* its author, Barbara Frances Wismer McManus, who died on June 19, 2015, only hours after putting the finishing touches to the manuscript. The extraordinary caregiving of Barbara's sister-in-law, Dorothy McManus, and devoted colleague Ann R. Raia, professor emerita of classics at The College of New Rochelle, made Barbara's efforts in the last weeks of her life possible. We would like to express our special gratitude to them; to Barbara's daughter Prentice Clark; to Dorothy Helly, professor emerita of history and women's studies at Hunter College and the Graduate School, City University of New York; and to several others with whom we have had the privilege of working since Barbara submitted the book to The Ohio State University Press in March 2015, entrusting its future to the two of us.

Eugene O'Connor of the press has shepherded Barbara's manuscript through the refereeing process with sensitivity and alacrity. The final version has greatly profited from the insightful suggestions of Elizabeth D. Carney, professor of history and Carol K. Brown Endowed Scholar in Humanities at Clemson University, and Donald G. Lateiner, John R. Wright Professor of Humanities–Classics emeritus at Ohio Wesleyan University, the two referees for the press. In addition to those named in Barbara's acknowledgments, we would like to thank Barbara's former student Maria Marsilio, professor of classics at Saint Joseph's University, for her invaluable help.

Introductions of this kind, moreover, ordinarily begin by accounting for the book's genesis, outlining its development as an intellectual project over time, and defining its contribution to one or more fields of specialist study. Sadly, too, we do not know exactly *how* Barbara first became aware of and interested in the life and work of Grace Harriet Macurdy. She did not herself attend Vassar College, where Grace Macurdy taught from 1893 until 1937. Barbara's training in classics and comparative literature foregrounded Latin texts and German and American literature. She did not publish in the field of Greek tragedy, the topic of Macurdy's 1903 Columbia University doctoral dissertation and early publications. Nor did she work in the area of Macurdy's best-known and best-remembered research, Hellenistic and Roman political history. According to Dorothy Helly, a fellow member of both the New York Women Writing Women's Lives Biography Seminar and the Family History Group, Barbara believed that Macurdy deserved greater recognition as a woman classicist because the male-dominated field of classics, especially in the United States, had overlooked Macurdy's scholarly contributions. Still, how Macurdy initially came to Barbara's attention remains unclear.

Yet Barbara's many scholarly presentations and publications about Macurdy, culminating in this full-length biography, also illuminate *why* this fascinating academic figure caught her attention and captured her interest. To be sure, their lives barely overlapped: Macurdy died in 1946, four years after Barbara was born. In addition, like other women academics of her generation, Barbara enjoyed far more opportunities as a teacher and scholar in the field of classics than those afforded Macurdy. Nevertheless, these two pioneering feminist classical scholars had a great deal in common.

Macurdy studied at Harvard University as an undergraduate in its all-female Annex, earning her bachelor of arts with honors in classics; Barbara also studied there, receiving both her master of arts in 1965 and her doctorate in 1976 in comparative literature, writing her Harvard doctoral dissertation on a classical topic, "*Inreparabile Tempus*: A Study of Time in Vergil's *Aeneid*." Like Macurdy, Barbara taught at a women's college in New York State for her entire academic career: The College of New Rochelle, her own undergraduate alma mater—the college's alumnae association recognized her with its Ursula Laurus award in 1994, and its Woman of Achievement award in 2014. In addition, Macurdy taught—as its first female faculty member—in the summer session at Columbia University while earning her doctorate there, and shouldering a full teaching load at Vassar; Barbara taught at The College of New Rochelle full-time while earning her Harvard doctorate.

During the years when she studied and taught at Columbia, Macurdy occupied a prominent position in the New York City classics community. Barbara, long-time resident in the New York City suburbs, held leadership positions in two New York City professional and scholarly organizations: the New York Classical Club and the aforementioned Women Writing Women's Lives Biography Seminar. Within the mid-Atlantic region where the two women worked, both played a major role in its regional professional organization, the Classical Association of the Atlantic States. Macurdy presented a paper at its first meeting, held at Columbia University in 1907. Barbara, who served the organization as president, webmaster, and member of several key committees, co-coordinated the organization's centennial celebration in 2007. Upon her retirement from teaching in 2001, CAAS celebrated Barbara's achievements with a Latin *ovatio*. Ten years later, in 2011, it recognized her rare combination of dedication and vision by establishing the Barbara F. McManus Leadership Award, which recognizes pedagogical and scholarly advocacy for women and minorities, a focus on gender in both teaching and research, and the incorporation of technology into the study of the classical world.

Both women grappled with formidable physical challenges. Macurdy coped heroically with deafness for the last twenty-eight years of her life, Barbara with polio and its aftereffects for most of hers. Both also took immense pleasure in family life, investing time and energy in sustaining strong relationships with partners and children, balancing these responsibilities with those required of them as teachers and scholars. In addition, Helly points out that both women enjoyed not only doing scholarly research but also imparting its results to those around them, friends as well as students.

Barbara's own scholarly research includes two earlier books. Both resemble this biography in exploring later engagements with the study of classical antiquity by women, as well as by men who sought to judge the public and intellectual activities of such women. *Half Humankind: Contexts and Texts of the Controversy about Women in England 1540–1640*, coauthored with Katharine Usher Henderson, was published by the University of Illinois Press in 1985. *Choice* nominated *Classics and Feminism: Gendering the Classics*, which was published by Twayne in 1997, as an Outstanding Academic Book of that year. Barbara also published book chapters and articles on a wide variety of classical texts and professional issues in learned journals, and gave many invited lectures and refereed papers at conferences in the United States and abroad. Like this biography, her publications and public presentations are noteworthy for their innovative, interdisciplinary, and feminist approaches to a diversely constituted body of evidence.

Perhaps the most memorable of those presentations took place at the spring 2000 CAAS meeting in Princeton, when Barbara and two of her undergraduate honors students reenacted a scene from Grace Harriet Macurdy's own life: her self-defense when threatened with dismissal from her teaching post at Vassar by her department chair Abby Leach. McManus performed as the college's male president James Monroe Taylor, "the voice of reason." In 2012, the Women's Classical Caucus, which Barbara served as co-chair and secretary-treasurer, inaugurated the Barbara McManus award—for the best article published in gender studies each year—to recognize her scholarly achievements. They include monumental efforts in the area of digital humanities, among them major grants from the National Endowment for the Humanities: her NEH-funded Teaching with Technology Initiative developed into the *VRoma* project, a virtual city and community for classics students and teachers worldwide, on which she closely collaborated with her College of New Rochelle classics colleague Ann Raia. On January 6, 2016, the Women's Classical Caucus honored her, posthumously, with its first award in leadership, "in recognition of her tireless commitment to professional equity, her longstanding service to [this organization] and the field [of classics], her leadership in the study of women and gender in antiquity, her mentorship of those in the field, and her ability to inspire those around her."

On the morning that Barbara died, Adam Blistein, executive director of the Society for Classical Studies, formerly the American Philological Association (APA), paid moving tribute to Barbara's labors for that organization from 1983 onwards. Her contributions included service on its Committee on the Status of Women and Minority Groups, its ad-hoc Committee on Outreach and the Outreach Prize, as well as on its board of directors. Blistein singled out, however, her extraordinary work as its Vice-President for Professional Matters, creating the APA census on classics-department staffing and enrollments in North America. In 2009 the APA presented her with its Distinguished Service award for her extraordinary achievements on behalf of the discipline and profession. A century ago, this same organization benefitted immensely from Grace Harriet Macurdy's endeavors and energies; in addition to serving on its executive committee, Macurdy presented a series of papers at its annual meetings, appearing on its program more than any other female scholar at that time.

On multiple occasions, as cofounder of the "Representing Our Ancestors" project, Barbara McManus impersonated Grace Harriet Macurdy herself. Joining colleagues who performed the roles of other illustrious nineteenth- and twentieth-century classicists, she shared Macurdy's story, illustrating the impact of Macurdy's life and work upon classical studies in the United States and abroad. Her performance endowed the figure of Macurdy with her own distinctive traits of personality and character: a powerful and searching intellect; disciplined, meticulous work habits; a principled, ethical, and inclusive approach to dealing with professional duties and fellow professionals; caring support of colleagues, especially as mentor to younger scholars and teachers; and generosity of spirit, unforgettably evinced in her sharing of her knowledge, time, and talents. What Barbara McManus has uncovered and shared about Grace Harriet Macurdy in this volume richly explains her decision to identify so closely with the object of her research. We hope that what we have shared about her will provide readers with a fuller appreciation of both the author and her subject.

Judith P. Hallett and Christopher Stray

ACKNOWLEDGMENTS

I have received help from many people in the eighteen years I have worked on researching and writing this biography. Two of Grace Macurdy's great-nieces, Caroline Skinner O'Neil and June Macurdy Landin, have generously shared with me letters, photographs, and family reminiscences; they have given me permission to use all of these and to quote freely from Grace's letters. James Griffith Macurdy, Grace's first cousin twice removed, has sent me letters relating to Grace's genealogical research and the manuscript of Grace's poem. Alexander Murray has given me permission to quote from the letters of his grandfather, Gilbert Murray, and has helped in my ultimately unsuccessful search for a photograph of J. A. K. Thomson. I have received advice and research help from librarians and archivists, most notably Natalia Vogeikoff-Brogan, Doreen Canaday Spitzer Archivist at the American School of Classical Studies at Athens; Nancy MacKechnie, former Curator of Rare Books and Manuscripts at Vassar College, and Dean M. Rogers, Library Specialist, Vassar Archives and Special Collections; Jane S. Knowles, former Radcliffe College Archivist; Eloise M. Lyman, librarian at the Watertown Free Public Library. My daughter, Prentice Clark, has read the narrative and offered valuable suggestions from the perspective of a non-classicist. Ann R. Raia and Christopher Stray have perused the entire manuscript with the careful eyes of classical scholars. I am also grateful to members of my Family History Group, who have read and commented on portions of the book: Sarah B. Pomeroy,

Dorothy O. Helly, Nancy Reagin, Martha W. Driver, Alison Smith, Jo Ann Kay McNamara, Miriam Schneir, and Camille Trentacosta. Members of the Women Writing Women's Lives Biography Seminar (www.writingwomenslives .org) welcomed me warmly into their association and taught me a great deal about the craft of writing biography. Many thanks as well for the love and support of my husband, John J. McManus. I am especially grateful to Judith P. Hallett and Christopher Stray for volunteering to see this manuscript through to publication should my health prevent me from doing so.

ABBREVIATIONS FOR FREQUENTLY CITED ARCHIVAL COLLECTIONS

Blegen Library	Blegen Library Archives, American School of Classical Studies at Athens
Bodleian	Bodleian Library, Oxford University
Rockefeller Archive	Rockefeller Archive Center
Schlesinger	Schlesinger Library, Radcliffe Institute, Harvard University, Cambridge, Mass.
Vassar Archives	Archives and Special Collections Library, Vassar College Libraries
Yale Library	Humanities and Fine Arts Collection. Manuscripts and Archives, Yale University Library

PROLOGUE

Women at the Well

"A Black-Figured Attic Vase in the
Classical Museum of Vassar College"

Archaic, lovely, at the well they stand,
  Girls who were living centuries ago,
Each with her shapely pitcher in her hand,
  Waiting her turn to catch the water's flow.
Perchance the painter passed them on his way
  Up to the workshop near the Maiden's Hill,
And on the vase which he must paint that day
  Painted their beauty, quaint, majestic, still.
The golden girls he painted all are dust—
  Dust and a shadow, as their poets say—
And yet they live and neither moth nor rust
  Has spoiled the beauty that was caught that day.
His work shall perish, but the artist's soul,
  Imaging beauty changing endlessly,
Shapes still new visions of the Eternal Whole
  And finds for beauty immortality.

  —Grace H. Macurdy

On that late-October day in 1946, Elizabeth Hazelton Haight (Hazel) set about the mournful task of cleaning out the desk of her dear friend Grace Harriet Macurdy, who had recently died in Vassar Brothers Hospital. Hazel herself had retired from the Department of Latin only four years previously, and she was feeling her own mortality as she sorted through the papers. One small sheet of stationery caught her eye. It was a poem, copied out in a careful hand whose unsteadiness was revealed by the differing shadings in the ink (see figure 1). Since the Classical Museum had been her own special preserve, she knew immediately which vase had inspired the poem, the lekythos that Grace had brought back from England in 1938, on what would prove to be her last trip overseas. Her eyes misted as she read the closing lines of the poem, for it seemed a final benediction from Grace to those who felt her loss so keenly. Hazel would later publish the poem in her 1949 article for the *Vassar Alumnae Magazine* about "The Macurdy Collection," Grace's bequest to the Classical Museum of more than two hundred Greek artifacts. But long before that article appeared, the final stanza of the poem would be quoted in numerous tributes to the late professor of Greek as a fitting epitaph for her own life and accomplishments.

These accomplishments were certainly formidable. When little "Hattie" came into this world in 1866 in a small rented cottage on the windswept coast of northeastern Maine, no one could have predicted that she would become an internationally known Greek scholar with a long list of publications and close friends as renowned as Gilbert Murray and John Masefield. But Grace Macurdy was always defying expectations. A pioneering woman in a man's world, she strove to make the lives of ancient women a respectable topic in classical scholarship.

Like the life of its author, the history of the manuscript of Grace's poem is surprising. In her last few years, Grace had been tracing her family's genealogy and had become friends with many distant relatives. These relatives carefully preserved the manuscript, passing it on from Poughkeepsie to England, New Haven, and finally Seattle. Eventually that sheet of paper, now spotted with age, was sent to me by a distant cousin too young to have known Grace himself. In the packet with the poem was a letter explaining the roundabout journey that finally brought it to the hands of Grace's biographer.[1] According to the letter, Hazel Haight had said that she found the poem "lying, just finished, on Grace's desk and that it was like a message from her."

Hazel tended toward the sentimental, and the poem could not have been "just finished," since Grace had been in the hospital for two months before she died; in fact, Grace might have written the poem any time after 1938. To my eyes, this poem was indeed a message from Grace Macurdy, but more like a challenge than a benediction: Grace was throwing down the gauntlet,

---

1. The letter had been sent to Horace Winslow McCurdy, grandson of one of Grace's uncles who had immigrated to Washington before Grace was born. It was written by Janet G. B. MacCurdy, widow of George Grant MacCurdy, prehistoric archaeologist and anthropologist of Yale University: "It is I who should have the copy—you must have the original, just as Grace wrote it, and fortunately I have it with me as my husband prized it highly and had put it with his family notes to show to some relatives we planned to visit this winter. He had it from Edward Alexander MacCurdy of Surrey who received it in a letter from Miss Haight. She said she found it lying, just finished, on Grace's desk and that it was like a message from her. Robert McCurdy Marsh was greatly interested in the poem and thought it should be published" (March 9, 1948). I received the letter and poem from Horace's son, James Griffith McCurdy.

confronting dismissive attitudes toward women as expressed, in this case, by John Keats. Her long life had been a journey toward achieving the status of a respected classical scholar who also spoke authoritatively as a woman. The fences and ditches she encountered along the way did not deter her progress, and she opened a new path by focusing her research on the lives of ancient women, disputing the claims of many eminent male scholars in the process. Since she was also extremely well read in English literature, there can be no doubt that she was deliberately invoking Keats's "Ode on a Grecian Urn" in this poem.

Although the stanza form is different, the meter is the same, iambic pentameter, and everything else in the poem offers a direct contrast to Keats's Ode. It is generally agreed that Keats was celebrating the aesthetic ideal advocated by Sir Joshua Reynolds and others that elevated the universal and general at the expense of the particular; his Grecian urn is a generic "Attic shape," an idealized composite that describes no specific work of art. In fact, most of the description of the carved scenes on the urn is rendered through rhetorical questions that emphasize their unknowability ("What men or gods are these? What maidens loth?"). Grace's poem, on the other hand, focuses on a particular vase in a specific museum, depicting women collecting water at a fountain who were seen by the painter in a specific place (near the Acropolis in Athens, evocatively called "the Maiden's Hill") at a specific time, "that day" when he saw and painted them. The first word of her poem, "archaic," not only focuses attention on the past, but also denotes the precise period in Greek history when the vase was produced.

Keats's urn is large and grand, made of carved marble and serving only an ornamental function, the sort of vessel that might decorate a garden. Grace's vase is a functional utensil, a small, painted vessel used to contain olive oil or perfume. The scenes on Keats's urn are mythological and pastoral, drawn from literature rather than life, and the standpoint is decidedly masculine; women appear only as the object of male desire, eternally beautiful because unobtainable. Grace's vase portrays a routine but essential scene from daily life, the quintessentially female task of drawing water from a fountain. The women first appear as subjects carrying out this task, and the painter is able to see and capture the beauty inherent even in such a mundane feminine activity (strikingly emphasized by the juxtaposition of "quaint" and "majestic"). Like Grace's publications, this poem underlines the importance of women and their work, which is worthy of the attention of artists and scholars alike.

The most dramatic contrast appears in the concluding stanzas of the two poems. However we interpret the punctuation of Keats's final two lines, his conclusion is static, emphasizing the immortality of the artwork ("Thou shalt remain") and its ability to freeze life and time into an unchanging object of beauty. In contrast, Grace notes that even a work of art is not immortal ("His work shall perish"); what persists in the face of constant change ("beauty changing endlessly") is human creativity and imagination ("the artist's soul"). Her emphasis is not on a static past but on the future; art finds immortality by continually shaping "new visions."

Thus I see this poem as a prologue rather than an epitaph, one that befits Grace Harriet Macurdy's pioneering life story. The framed manuscript of this poem hangs in my kitchen, reminding me every day of the importance of women's work and of Grace's role in promoting the study of ancient women. Like this poem, Grace Macurdy always looked forward, focusing on a future that she would help to create; her life and work provide a model for current women scholars that have not received sufficient recognition. How did the daughter of a struggling carpenter in nineteenth-century New England become a distinguished feminist scholar, one who gradually developed an authoritative, scholarly voice as a woman? This biography is my effort to answer that question, to make visible Grace Macurdy's footprints on the path that feminist classical scholars are walking today. In the process, I hope to shine the light of an individual life on a turning point in the history of women. Grace's story illuminates developments in higher education and the role of women's colleges, the struggle for professional careers, emerging feminism, and major changes in the discipline and profession of classics. As Virginia Nicholson points out, "The historians have documented how in the last century the doors for women were slowly but surely creaking open. . . . But we have to look in the Biography sections to find out what it felt like to live through those momentous times."[2]

---

2. Virginia Nicholson, *Singled Out*, 245.

CHAPTER 1

The Drunken Duchess

A Woman of Contrasts

Standing at the podium of the lecture theater in King's College London on May 25, 1925, Grace Macurdy looked out over the audience. She was satisfied to see the large, diverse crowd that had come to hear her speak, although she suspected that the novelty of a woman lecturer was for many the primary attraction. When she had asked President MacCracken of Vassar for permission to miss the final weeks of teaching to sail to England in time for this lecture, she had emphasized the great honor of being the first woman ever invited to deliver a public lecture in classics at King's College, and the trustees had gladly granted her leave.[1]

She was very pleased to see seated in the front row two classicists whom she counted among her good friends, the distinguished Gilbert Murray and the recently appointed chair of classics at King's College, J. A. K. Thomson, to whom she owed the invitation to speak that evening.[2] Thomson had written

---

1. Records in King's College London's archives indicate that Grace Macurdy was the first and only woman to deliver such a public lecture in classics before 1946; her name appears among such distinguished scholars as Gilbert Murray, Arnold Toynbee, H. J. Rose, Cyril Bailey, and E. R. Dodds. K/LEC5 Public Lecture Lists, Complete Series from 1924 to 1955 UL, KCL, & KCW, King's College London Archives.

2. For more information on Gilbert Murray, Regius Professor of Greek at Oxford, a well-known humanistic scholar, translator of Greek plays, man of letters, and active participant in the League of Nations, see Christopher Stray, s.v. "Murray, (George) Gilbert Aimé (1866–1957)," *Oxford Dictionary of National Biography*. James Alexander Kerr Thomson (1879–1959), always

to Murray that he hoped these lectures would promote his new department and classical studies in general:

> Classics there are badly in need of some kind of advertisement (not of course of a vulgar sort), and I really think there are some signs of a return to classical studies as being more interesting than people imagined. It is of course vital to the scheme that the lecturers themselves should be interesting. . . . I rather hope to get public attention gradually drawn to these lectures on Classical subjects—there is nothing else of the kind in London.[3]

She was sure of her topic and her ability to catch and hold the interest of the audience; she knew she would not let down her friend or herself. The audience may have come to hear "a woman," but they would leave remembering Grace Harriet Macurdy.

Since she had suffered a severe hearing loss several years earlier, she could not actually hear Thomson when he introduced her, but he had given her a copy of his remarks and she easily read his lips. After explaining her scholarly background—a degree from Radcliffe where she studied under notable Harvard classics professors, a year at the University of Berlin with well-known German professors including the great Greek scholar Wilamowitz, and a doctorate from Columbia University—and her current position as professor of Greek and head of the Greek Department at Vassar College, Thomson praised her new book on *Troy and Paeonia* as "a work of first-rate importance, full of curious and varied learning. There is in my belief hardly anyone at all who has contributed more to produce a new orientation of the whole question of prehistoric Greece." He noted that her subject for that evening's lecture, "Great Macedonian Women," marked a new direction in her scholarship, one that promised "a really important contribution to history." As the audience would hear, "Her statements of fact are exactly documented; her opinions are necessarily and delightfully her own."[4]

---

known as J. A. K., published numerous books and articles on classical topics, but there is very little information about his life in print; see Barbara F. McManus, "J. A. K. Thomson and Classical Reception Studies: American Influences and 'Classical Influences,'" in *British Classics outside England: The Academy and Beyond*, ed. Judith P. Hallett and Christopher Stray (Baylor University Press, 2008), 129–48 and "'*Macte nova virtute, puer!*': Gilbert Murray as Mentor and Friend to J. A. K. Thomson," in *Gilbert Murray Reassessed*, ed. Christopher Stray (Oxford: Oxford University Press, 2007), 181–99.

3. J. A. K. Thomson to Gilbert Murray, 30 January 1924, MSS Gilbert Murray 172, fols. 114–15, Bodleian.

4. The quoted statements of Thomson are very slightly adapted from a draft of his December 1923 letter to Columbia University Press in support of the publication of *Troy and Paeonia*

In her lecture, spoken with assurance since her deafness had not affected her delivery, Grace carefully unraveled the complex history and relationships of women in the royal houses of ancient Macedonia. She presented a strong and convincing argument that Macedonian queens played an active role in politics because of their own characters and personalities, rather than because of a Macedonian tradition that conferred power on women. This disputed a claim made by Edwyn Bevan,[5] who she knew would be in the audience, but she was confident that an unbiased consideration of the evidence supported her conclusions. She revealed how stereotypes about women could cloud scholars' reading of the ancient evidence; for example, calling Olympias (wife of Philip II and mother of Alexander the Great) "the Jezebel of a Queen," ascribed to her a sexual license that was totally unsupported by the ancient sources. Grace did not diminish the cruelties and murders perpetrated by Olympias but put them into a new context by arguing that she shared many qualities with her husband, Philip II, and her son, Alexander. As soldiers and conquerors, however, they had an outlet for their genius and desire for power, while she, as a woman, had a much more confined theater of operations, where her "weapons had chiefly to be intrigue, slander, and bursts of passion." As she spoke, Grace was pleased to see that she was leading the thoughts of her audience in a new direction, and she included humorous anecdotes to hold their interest, such as Olympias's witty rejoinder to her son's claim that Zeus was his father: "Will Alexander never stop getting me into trouble with Hera!"[6]

Exhilarated by the applause and compliments she received after the lecture, Grace reflected that this was the defining moment of her fifty-eight years. During her study at the Harvard Annex, she had determined to win international recognition as a classical scholar, and this lecture marked her first experience of such recognition. Heady and sweet as this appreciation was, she realized that her experience at Vassar had expanded her life's goal. She wanted to make a scholarly contribution as a woman, to be accepted by the scholarly fraternity as a classicist who wrote authoritatively in her own voice and from her own perspective, not as an honorary man. She realized that the King's

(MSS Gilbert Murray 175, fols. 252–53, Bodleian) and his "Tribute to Miss Macurdy" upon her retirement, published in *Vassar Alumnae Magazine* 23 (1937): 9.

5. Edwyn Robert Bevan (1870–1943) was at this time lecturer in Hellenistic history and literature at King's College London. In volume 2, 279 ff., of his book *The House of Seleucus* (London: Edward Arnold, 1902), Bevan had argued that the political activities of later queens such as Cleopatra VII stemmed from old Macedonian tradition whereby queens and princesses "mingled in the political game as openly as the men."

6. See the chapter on "Queenship in Macedonia" in Grace H. Macurdy, *Hellenistic Queens: A Study of Woman-Power in Macedonia, Seleucid Syria, and Ptolemaic Egypt* (Baltimore: Johns Hopkins Press, 1932), 13–76.

College lecture was a step toward achieving this goal. She would focus her scholarship on ancient women, developing a new approach that would liberate these women from the prejudices and stereotypes that had marred the work of other scholars, all of them male and all inclined to treat women as a "species" rather than as individuals. She had come of age at a time when women in the United States were just beginning to find opportunities for professional academic careers; now she would demonstrate her own individuality as "a woman and a scholar" by creating a new approach to the study of women.

The Drunken Duchess

Grace Harriet Macurdy (1866–1946) was a woman of surprising contrasts. The audience in the King's College lecture theater saw a woman of unprepossessing appearance whose gray hair was unfashionably piled on top of her head, yet her vitality and compelling presence made them attend to her words and respond to the force of her arguments. Her students at Vassar paid tribute to these contrasts by affectionately dubbing her "the Drunken Duchess," although everyone on campus knew that she was a teetotaler. There was something regal in her bearing and presence, yet she was famous for her infectious humor and effervescent joie de vivre. She was fond of large hats, jewelry, and dresses made of beautiful fabrics, yet her clothing was never in fashion and her appearance was always slightly disheveled, with hat or skirt askew and abundant hair forever escaping from the pins that vainly struggled to keep it in place (see figures 14 and 15). The nickname was so well-known around Vassar that some alumnae evidently asked Henry Noble MacCracken, president of Vassar from 1915 to 1946, why he had not alluded to this in his reminiscences about Vassar in *The Hickory Limb*, as he noted in a letter: "I suppressed 'drunken duchess,' though several have written to ask why. Evidently I wasn't frank enough!"[7]

Later in her career this nickname morphed into "the Mad Queen," a sobriquet explained by Theodore Erck, one of her successors in the Greek Department: "Often outspoken and sometimes a little outrageous, Miss Macurdy dearly loved and was loved dearly by most of Vassar. The students called her 'the Mad Queen,' because of her great mass of hair and her fondness for fan-

---

7. Henry Noble MacCracken to Bradford S. Skinner, 12 January 1951, private collection of Caroline Skinner O'Neil; Henry Noble MacCracken, *The Hickory Limb* (New York: Scribner, 1950).

tastic hats" (see figure 13 for Grace wearing an elaborate hat).[8] In 1936 the student newspaper *Vassar Miscellany News* printed a humorous spoof description of a faculty meeting called to determine whether there was a raging blizzard that would prevent students from making it back to Vassar at the end of a weekend. The article gives the faculty mock names such as "Miss Squellery" (Eloise Ellery, professor of history), "Miss Washboard" (Margaret Floy Washburn, professor of psychology), and "A Noble" (Henry Noble MacCracken, president of Vassar), while Grace Macurdy is called simply "the Queen" and "Queenie" and has the most sensible things to say:

> A NOBLE: (calls the meeting to order) I have been informed by the Miscellany News, har, har, har, that there has been a blizzard. (This is greeted by boos, hisses, and one timid anonymous cheer).
> MISS SQUELLERY: I don't want to interrupt but have you looked up the source, would you say it was written under stress? (Enter the Queen. Several fall on their knees, but whether from worship, fear, or housemaid's knee cannot be determined.)
> THE QUEEN: I wish to corroborate the News. It is more or less accurate.[9]

These affectionate nicknames testify to the many anomalies in Grace Macurdy's life, one of the most surprising of which was the way she managed the delicate balancing act between personal and professional life required of women. Like most academic women of her era, she remained single all her life, but she nevertheless experienced a kind of motherhood and also a sort of marriage. She was a pioneering feminist scholar, yet her career was almost destroyed by another feminist pioneer who waged a twelve-year campaign to have Grace Macurdy dismissed from Vassar. She experienced a severe hearing loss in her early fifties, yet her years of almost total deafness were rich with international friendships, adventurous travel, and productive teaching and scholarship. Public confrontations made her physically ill, but she led a far-reaching fight in the managing committee of the American School of Classical Studies in Athens against the dictatorial policies of its chair, Edward Capps of Princeton University. Though her academic training was in philology and literary studies, her most enduring contributions to scholarship were in the field of history. Finally, despite the poverty of her immediate family and the fact that she was the first member of her extended family in several generations to earn a college degree, she forged a successful academic career in an era when

8. Theodore H. Erck, s.v. "MACURDY, Grace Harriet," *Notable American Women, 1607–1950.*

9. "Campus Chat: Faculty Meeting," *Vassar Miscellany News,* 22 January 1936, 2.

professors, female as well as male, came from cultured families of the middle and upper classes. The woman who inspired such intriguing nicknames as the Drunken Duchess and the Mad Queen was, in actuality, neither drunk nor mad, but she *was* fascinating, a woman of contrasts who became one of the premier classical scholars of her generation.

CHAPTER 2

Family and Childhood

I should be in sack-cloth and ashes if I had a drop of German blood in me. I thank God that my ancestors were Scotch, Scotch-Irish, and (Tory) English![1]

Grace Macurdy was proud of her ancestry and devoted much of her time during the last years of her life to genealogical research.[2] The emphasis on the word "Tory" in her letter to Murray refers to the fact that four of her ancestors were British Loyalists during the American Revolution—Simon Baxter and Neil McCurdy on her father's side, and Benjamin Bradford and Dugald Thomson on her mother's—and explains why all of her great-grandparents were living in the new Canadian province of New Brunswick by 1784. In fact, her grandparents, parents, and older siblings were all born in New Brunswick (see appendix 1).

---

1. Grace H. Macurdy to Gilbert Murray, 13 June 1942, MSS Gilbert Murray 157, fols. 185–86, Bodleian.

2. At the behest of a distant cousin, Horace W. McCurdy of Seattle, Washington, she had prepared a 163-page typescript entitled *Pioneer Ancestors of an American Family, 1620–1857,* which traced the paternal McCurdy ancestry, and she was sending information on her maternal line to her nephew Ernest Macurdy up until her death. This typescript was later donated to the Seattle Public Library, where it is available in the reference section of the Central Library (R929.2 M139Mg).

Loyalist Background

Simon Baxter (grandfather of Harriet Hayes McCurdy, Grace's paternal grandmother) was the most colorful of her Loyalist ancestors; Grace describes him as "a vital, headstrong, tempestuous man, a stubborn Connecticut Yankee, who would not be deterred from obeying his conscience and his king by any kind of intimidation, though beaten, imprisoned, threatened with hanging, subjected to tortures that would have broken the spirit and determination of a lesser man."[3] He was captured and imprisoned several times, at one point allegedly making a dramatic escape to join Burgoyne's army with the hanging rope around his neck. Although all his property in New England was confiscated,[4] his was perhaps the first Loyalist family transported to Canada, where he received a Crown grant of five thousand acres in what is now Norton, New Brunswick.[5]

Benjamin Bradford (grandfather of Lydia Bradford Thomson, Grace's maternal grandmother) was a lineal descendant of Governor William Bradford of Plymouth Colony in the fourth generation. He also had an adventurous life. In 1758, during the French and Indian War, natives from the Penobscot tribe raided the settlement of Meduncook, Maine, killing and scalping his father, Joshua, and his mother, Hannah, before the eyes of the five-year-old Benjamin. The natives took Benjamin and his brother Joshua to Canada, and he was not returned to New England until after the fall of Quebec in 1759.[6] Bradford later became a pilot in the British navy; he and his family were among the Penobscot Loyalists transported across the Bay of Fundy and Passamaquoddy Bay to Canada and granted land in St. Andrews, New Brunswick.

---

3. Macurdy, *Pioneer Ancestors*, 135. See also John B. M. Baxter, *Simon Baxter: The First United Empire Loyalist to Settle in New Brunswick: His Ancestry and Descendants* (St. John, New Brunswick: The New Brunswick Museum, 1943).

4. During one of his imprisonments, when his property in Alstead, New Hampshire, was under threat of confiscation, his wife, Prudence, petitioned the state assembly on 14 December 1778 to spare his life, arguing (presumably without her husband's knowledge) that he wished to swear allegiance to the United States: "I Cair not how we Live or how we are fed, if he can but have authoritive Liberty to Live in this state, the small [property] that we did possess shall with pleasure go only spair him. . . . The arms of america has spread Terrow thro the world—o that their mercy might not be Confined or Limeted—I do in my husband name Lay myself and him att the foot stool of this state for mercy and if we must perish we must perish there." *Town Papers: Documents Relating to Towns in New Hampshire, "A" to "F" Inclusive*, ed. Isaac W. Hammond (Concord, N.H.: Parsons B. Cogswell, 1882), 11:24–25. The assembly was not convinced by her petition, since their property was confiscated and Baxter was not released for at least a year.

5. W. O. Raymond, "At Portland Point," *New Brunswick Magazine* 2 (1899): 314.

6. John Johnston, *A History of the Towns of Bristol and Bremen in the State of Maine, including the Pemaquid Settlement* (Albany, N.Y.: Joel Munsell, 1873), 2:318–19.

Dugald Thomson (father of Adam Duncan Thomson, Grace's maternal grandfather) was born in Scotland and immigrated to New England; he also was among the Penobscot Loyalists and land grantees of St. Andrews. Neil McCurdy (father of William Augustus McCurdy, Grace's paternal grandfather) and his brother Laughlin, descendants of Scottish Presbyterians from the Isle of Bute, were born on Rathlin Island off the coast of Ireland and made the dangerous Atlantic crossing to Maine. Although he was living in Halifax, Nova Scotia, as early as 1778, he was among the St. Andrews Crown grantees and was included in the "Return of Men, Women and Children of the Penobscot Loyalists Settled in the District of Passamaquoddy the 10th of June 1784."[7]

Having lost everything, the Loyalist families were forced to start over with little besides the lands they were granted. New Brunswick was a wilderness of pine forests from which the immigrants had to carve out farms to support their families. One of the first industries in St. Andrews was shipbuilding, and both Neil McCurdy and John Cook Hayes (who had emigrated from England to Canada and married Simon Baxter's daughter Dorothy) had been trained as shipwrights before leaving their native lands. However, the lack of infrastructure, particularly schools, made farming the most common occupation.[8]

Grace herself writes that "the McCurdy family in St. Andrews had not an extended formal education, such as we their descendants have enjoyed,"[9] and a glance at Neil McCurdy's descendants confirms the importance of farming and the close association and cooperation among family members in the small community of St. Andrews. Alexander "Captain Sandy" McCurdy, eldest son of Neil by his first wife, was a master mariner but settled in a farm lot in Bayside along the St. Croix River with his wife Charlotte Hayes, second daughter of John Cook Hayes and Dorothy Baxter. Neil sold adjacent farm lots to his second and third sons, George H. McCurdy and William Augustus McCurdy, who had married Charlotte's older sister Harriet Hayes; George conveyed part of his farm lot to his eldest brother, James, and when George died unmarried, the rest of his lot went to his brother William. On another adjacent farm lot

---

7. Robert C. Brooks, "Penobscot Loyalists," *Downeast Ancestry* 7.4 (December, 1983): 134–37, accessed 22 January 2011, http://freepages.genealogy.rootsweb.ancestry.com/~aek740/penobscot_loyalists.html.

8. For an overview of the early history of New Brunswick, see W. O. Raymond, "New Brunswick General History, 1758–1867" in *Atlantic Provinces*, vol. 13 of *Canada and Its Provinces: A History of the Canadian People and Their Institutions by One Hundred Associates*, ed. Adam Shortt and Arthur G. Doughty (Toronto: Publishers Association of Canada, 1914), 127–210. One comment is particularly telling: "Certainly, the lack of schools was a serious disadvantage to the rising generation, the greater part of which was growing up in ignorance. It was clear that the children of the loyalists were destined to be inferior to their parents in knowledge, if not in ability and force of character" (182).

9. Macurdy, *Pioneer Ancestors*, 145.

lived a cousin of these brothers, John, son of Laughlin McCurdy, who had married Prudence Hayes, youngest of the three daughters of John Cook Hayes.

Grandparents

William Augustus McCurdy and Harriet Hayes, Grace's paternal grand-parents (see figure 2), had five sons; see appendix 1 for detailed information about the descendants of both of Grace's grandparents. The eldest son, Captain James McCurdy, died at the age of twenty-five on his ship, Everton, while en route from Honduras to Boston; the youngest, Theodore Harding McCurdy, drowned a short distance from his father's farm at the age of eleven. The second and fourth sons, Hayes Warren and William Augustus McCurdy Jr., immigrated to the United States soon after James's death in 1846, settling near Boston to gain training in the trades of home building and shipbuilding, respectively. Only the third son, Grace's father, Simon Angus McCurdy (called Angus by his family), stayed with his father to work on the farm. By 1854 or 1855, Angus had married Rebecca Manning Thomson, daughter of the minister of the Baptist church at Bayside, and had immediately begun a family (the young couple is pictured in figure 3). When the 1861 census was taken they were still living on the farm, but by 1864 Angus, his parents, and his growing family had moved into the town of St. Andrews.[10] By this time William Augustus Sr. had become very lame, making farm work difficult, and Angus found work in St. Andrews as a ship's carpenter, though without benefit of the specialized training his brother William Augustus Jr. had received at the McKay Shipyard in Boston.

Education played a more significant role in Grace's maternal ancestry, however. Her great-grandfather Dugald Thomson prospered in New Brunswick; he began with three Crown grants (a town lot in St. Andrews, a 100-acre farm lot in St. David's, and a 270-acre farm lot in Pleasant Ridge, a rural area in the north of Charlotte County). According to his will, he also owned a store and wharf in St. Andrews.[11] Because of the lack of schools in New Brunswick, he sent his third son, Grace's grandfather Adam Duncan Thomson, to Scotland to be educated. Upon returning to St. Andrews, A. D. Thomson was licensed as a schoolmaster by the Charlotte County Court of General Sessions of the Peace on December 5, 1820, "being of good moral character and

---

10. *Hutchinson's New Brunswick Directory for 1865–66* (St. John, New Brunswick: Thomas Hutchinson, 1865), 532.

11. R. Wallace Hale, *Early New Brunswick Probate Records, 1785–1835* (Westminster, Md.: Heritage Books, 1989), 455.

in the opinion of the said Court highly qualified to keep a School." According to court records, he single-handedly maintained a school in the third district of the parish of St. Andrews for thirteen years,[12] until he became a deacon in the Baptist Church in 1833. Reportedly a "thrilling" speaker who made a "deep and powerful" impression on his congregations,[13] Thomson became the minister of St. Stephen's Baptist Church at the "Ledge" and in 1838 organized and built a new church in Bayside in the parish of St. Andrews (see figure 4). His handwritten records for this church are still extant and include an unusual anecdote that gives us a glimpse into his mind as well as revealing the sometimes harsh conditions under which these people practiced their faith. On April 2, 1837, nine people were scheduled for baptism by immersion in the St. Croix River:

> At this baptism a most remarkable interference of divine providence was manifested in behalf of his cause and people. When the congregation with the Elders and candidates repaired to the river, an immence [sic] quantity of ice that had broken up the night before was seen passing down the river with great swiftness and some lodging on the shore as it passed along. We however, believing our case was known and seen of God, repaired to a small nook in the river where we might attend to the ordnance [sic], but before singing and prayer was over we were completely shut from the water by ice. At this critical moment God appeared to interfere. Several of the largest cakes of ice stuck fast and remained immovable just above us, which formed a wall or breaker from both wind and tide. The ice below passed off and left us a most delightful baptistry. The ordnance [sic] was immediately attended to, and when the ninth or last candidate came out of the water the way immediately closed up with the floating ice which returned in the eddy of wall or breaker before mentioned.[14]

---

12. Adam Duncan Thompson, 1820, Petitions for Teachers Licenses & Payment, 1812–1882, RS655 (Provincial Archives of New Brunswick, Fredericton, New Brunswick). There are petitions for Thomson through 1833. See also the obituary for Adam Duncan Thomson in the *Christian Visitor*, 6 Oct 1870 (Daniel Fred Johnson, *Vital Statistics from New Brunswick Newspapers*, vol. 30, no. 131), accessed 15 July 2009, http://archives.gnb.ca/APPS/NewspaperVitalStats/Default.aspx?culture=en-CA.

13. I. E. Bill, *Fifty Years with the Baptist Ministers and Churches in the Maritime Provinces of Canada* (St. John, New Brunswick: Barnes and Company, 1880), 414, 587.

14. St. Stephens & First Baptist Church of Bayside Records, 10, St. Croix Library, St. Stephen, New Brunswick (punctuation and capitalization added). The lack of punctuation and capitalization in the original contribute to the breathless pace of the narrative.

Thomson was called to preach in many Baptist churches in the area (one man whose spelling was weak refers to Duncan as "Elder Dunking Thompson," perhaps associating his name with his baptismal duties[15]) and was noted for his support of education. He was instrumental in raising funds for Acadia University in Nova Scotia and served for many years on its Board of Governors. A history of the early Baptists in the maritime provinces of Canada lauds him as one of the "Fathers" of the church, "so extensively and favourably known in both Nova Scotia and New Brunswick. . . . His sermons, exhortations, and prayers, are remembered by thousands."[16]

Grace's maternal and paternal grandparents came together when A. D. Thomson converted and baptized Harriet and William Augustus McCurdy, as well as their eldest son, James, in 1836; their son Angus was baptized in 1853, a year or so before he married Thomson's daughter Rebecca (who had been baptized in 1851).[17] Indeed, all the McCurdys, Bradfords, and Thomsons with farms in the Bayside area eventually became members of this church. Because of his success as a preacher, Baptist missionary, and fundraiser, Thomson was frequently away from the family home, and the Thomsons experienced many of the same struggles and privations as the McCurdys. Their eldest daughter, Nancy, died at the age of twenty-five, and daughter Adelia (twenty-five) and youngest son, William, (thirteen) both died of diphtheria in March 1864.[18] By 1868, Thomson was seriously ill, confined to his house with dropsy until his death in 1870. His wife, Lydia, married the widower Samuel Kelly (seventy-five) at the age of sixty-two and moved with her remaining unmarried daughter, Elizabeth, to Calais, Maine, where Kelly was deacon of the First Baptist Church.[19] This marriage, only a year after her husband's death, offers mute testimony to the difficulties faced by the family after Thomson died.

Robbinston,   aine

Angus McCurdy, Grace's father, soon found that there was not enough work in St. Andrews to support his extended family. His brothers, Hayes Warren

---

15. St. Stephens & First Baptist Church of Bayside Records, 14, St. Croix Library, St. Stephen, New Brunswick.

16. Bill, *Fifty Years*, 496–97.

17. St. Stephens & First Baptist Church of Bayside Records, 8, 46, St. Croix Library, St. Stephen, New Brunswick.

18. The poignant group of five tombstones is located in Sandy Point Cemetery, on the banks of the St. Croix River north of the Bayside Baptist Church.

19. The marriage announcement appears in the *Christian Visitor,* 30 November 1871 (Johnson, *Vital Statistics,* vol. 30, no. 673).

and William Augustus Jr., had improved their prospects by immigrating to the United States many years earlier. By 1860, Warren had established himself as a successful homebuilder in Watertown, Massachusetts, while his more adventurous brother William had sailed to the Isthmus of Panama in 1857 and then traveled overland to the Territory of Washington, where he settled in Port Townsend. A letter William wrote to Warren on January 15, 1861, shows that the two brothers knew that Angus was struggling financially and thinking of moving to Maine: "I think Angus could do much better out here than down east. There is plenty of lumber business carried on. I think he could always demand $50 or $60 per month. I wish you would write to him, and let me know what he thinks about coming out here."[20] By this time, however, Angus had two children to support with another on the way, and he did not share his brothers' entrepreneurial spirit. Finally, early in 1865 (as indicated by records showing that they were all dismissed from the Bayside Baptist Church by January of that year), Angus and Rebecca packed up their meager belongings and crossed the St. Croix River to Maine. The family of four adults and four children (their first child, Eliza, had died in 1860 at the age of four) found lodgings in one of the small rented cottages near the tannery in South Robbinston. Here, on September 12, 1866, Rebecca gave birth to her sixth child in twelve years, lacking the comforting presence of her mother and sisters, with only her mother-in-law, Harriet, to help. The child, their first born in the United States, was named Grace Harriet, but called "Hattie" in honor of her grandmother.

Robbinston was a rural town stretched along the coast of the St. Croix River south of the more urban city of Calais and directly across the river from St. Andrews; it was a stop on the Calais–Eastport stagecoach route. In the mid-nineteenth century, Robbinston had been a busy river port and shipbuilding center, but by 1865 this trade had decreased precipitously, as it had in St. Andrews; the town's population fell from 1,028 in 1850 to 926 in 1870.[21] By 1865, the main industry in Robbinston was the tannery and associated machine mills.

For the McCurdys, life in Robbinston proved even more difficult than in St. Andrews, where they had had the support of many relatives and friends. The air was tainted by the noxious odors of the nearby tanning pits, and the climate was cold and rainy. The depressed shipbuilding industry had no work for Angus, and home carpentry was little better. Angus soon had to seek work in Massachusetts, leaving Rebecca and Harriet to manage alone for long

---

20. Quoted in Macurdy, *Pioneer Ancestors*, 148.

21. *Maine Register or State Year-Book and Legislative Manual* (Portland, Maine: G. M. Donham, 1891), 739–40; Walter Wells, *Provisional Report upon the Water-Power of Maine* (Augusta, Maine: Stevens & Sayward, 1868), 252–53.

stretches of time. Reading between the lines of a December 1867 letter from Rebecca to William Augustus Jr., we can see something of the difficult situation these two women faced, trying to hold the family together in a tiny cottage with five rambunctious young children; an elderly, lame patriarch; and no breadwinner:

> Dear Brother William:
> As your parents are writing to you, I thought I would put in a few lines. We were very glad indeed to hear from you once more. Angus is in Boston. He has received your letter and answered it. He was very much rejoiced to hear from you. We soon expect him home to spend Christmas, we wish you could be with us too, but that cannot be this year, you will say, though I hope you may be permitted to return and see your Father and Mother once while they live.
>
> You don't know the joy your letter gave them. Your Mother did not know whether to laugh or cry. I think she did both.
>
> You have all the news from the others about the family, which consists of Father, Mother, myself and five children. They are beautiful children and quite as noisy as I would wish for. While I write, I can scarcely hear my own ears. They all send love to Uncle Willy. I must close and wish you a happy New Year. Hoping to hear from you often
>   I remain your affectionate Sister
>   Rebecca McCurdy[22]

Another clue that Angus was not with his family for most of their time in Maine is the spacing of their children. Rebecca had borne a child every other year from 1856 to 1866, but she did not have another until 1873, after the family was settled in Massachusetts. When the 1870 federal census[23] was taken on August 5, 1870, Angus had returned to Maine to move his family to Water-

---

22. Quoted in Macurdy, *Pioneer Ancestors*, 149–50. Also quoted in H. W. McCurdy with Gordon Newell, *Don't Leave Any Holidays* (Portland, Ore.: Graphic Arts Center, 1981), 2:163–64.

23. U.S. Census Bureau, 1870 U.S. census, population schedule, Robbinston, Washington county, Maine, dwelling 157, family 165, Simon A. McCarty household; National Archives microfilm publication M593, roll 563; digital image, Ancestry.com, accessed 10 December 2006, http://www.ancestry.com. Despite the surname misspelling, this census reveals much useful information, including Grace's nickname. Angus lists himself as a home carpenter, a trade he would follow for the rest of his life. The family has no real estate or personal estate. Only the two older children, Theodosia and Maria, have attended school. Angus indicates that he is a U.S. citizen, despite the fact that he was never naturalized. Finally, by looking at the families residing around the McCurdys and comparing these with a 1881 map of Calais and Robbinston that contains the names and locations of residents, it is possible to pinpoint the location of the McCurdy lodging.

town, to join his brother Warren. The trip would not have been easy, especially with his infirm father and five children ranging in age from four to twelve. There was no direct rail connection to Boston at that time, so they probably traveled via some combination of stagecoach, steamship, and rail. The trip was also emotionally wrenching for Rebecca, who knew that she would never see her own parents again. Her beloved father was already seriously ill, and it is likely that the family left before he died on September 10, 1870.

Watertown, assachusetts

When the McCurdys arrived in Watertown, there was a happy reunion with Angus's older brother Warren, whom they had not seen for decades, and his American wife, Maria, whom they had never met. After the hugs and tears, Warren immediately warned them that they must now spell their surname *Macurdy*, as he did, or they would be taken for "dirty Irish," immigrants who had poured into Watertown since the 1840s; the new spelling would proclaim them as Scotch Protestants rather than Irish Catholics.[24] Warren owned his own home on Elm Street in East Watertown and had established a successful business as a builder and contractor; he helped Angus find a house to rent several blocks north on Arlington Street. The house was somewhat isolated, set in a rural area some distance from the town center amid the many market farms that grew fresh produce for Boston. This undoubtedly eased the transition of moving to a town more than five times as large as any they had seen before.[25]

The newly christened Macurdys found themselves in a town of contradictions, with the tradition and charm of old New England contrasting starkly with the rough and raucous bustle of a modern factory town. Located north of Boston on the Charles River between Waltham and Cambridge, Watertown was founded in 1630 by Sir Richard Saltonstall and had a strong New England tradition, including such nineteenth-century artists and intellectuals as the sculptors Harriet Hosmer and Anne Whitney, author and abolitionist activist

---

24. In a letter to her nephew Ernest H. Macurdy, Grace explained the spelling change, "Uncle Warren, with whom the old people lived opposite us on Elm St. East Watertown, was so afraid of being taken for Irish that he changed the spelling of our name. . . . It was very foolish of him and he made my poor father follow him in the spelling of the name" (24 September 1943, private collection of June Macurdy Landin). State census figures indicate that 25 percent of the population of Watertown in 1865 were born in Ireland. Charles T. Burke, *Watertown: Town on the Charles* (Watertown, Mass.: Town of Watertown 350th Anniversary Celebration Committee, 1980), 11.

25. According to *McCarty's Annual Statistician,* Watertown had a population of 5,426 in 1870 (San Francisco: L. P. McCarty, 1885), 214.

Lydia Maria Child, and Convers Francis, minister of the Unitarian Church and senior member of the Transcendental Club, who often brought intellectuals such as Ralph Waldo Emerson to meetings at his home in Watertown. Throughout the nineteenth century, governance remained as it had in the colonial period, with a town meeting that included all males over twenty-one as the appropriating and legislative body whose decisions were administered by three elected selectmen. The rich fields surrounding the town attracted not only commercial farmers, but also wealthy residents of Boston, gentleman farmers who established large estates with stately summer homes. Many kinds of shops stood along the wide, tree-lined streets, which were coated with gravel to mitigate the dust and mud, and the town meetings were held in an impressive town hall with a lofty colonnaded porch.

But Watertown was also a commercial manufacturing center whose industries were mostly located on or near the river, beginning with the massive U.S. Arsenal established in 1816 and including Aetna Mills (woolen goods), Pratt Foundry, Lewando's Dyeing and Cleansing, a gasworks, and many different types of mills by 1870. A branch of the Fitchburg Railroad ran through the town, next to which stood the Union Stockyards, lending a touch of the Wild West to Watertown every Tuesday, when huge herds of cattle were penned in the yards and later driven through the streets on their way to farms or the slaughter-house in nearby Brighton. All this industry brought large numbers of workers to Watertown in the second half of the century, many of them poor and uneducated Irish immigrants living in disreputable, clustered shacks or shanties.[26]

For the Macurdys, life on Arlington Street must have seemed like paradise compared to the hardships of Robbinston, even though their house was heated with a stove fired by wood, coal, or oil, lighting was by candlelight or kerosene, water had to be fetched from wells or the town pump, and there was a cold walk to the outhouse. Best of all, the family was together, and soon another child testified to the continuing presence of Angus. On July 25, 1873, a second son was born; at first named Charles J. L. Macurdy, his name was changed to John Ordway Macurdy sometime after 1880 (the Ordways were close friends of Adam Duncan Thomson, the child's grandfather). A third son,

---

26. For general background on Watertown, see Solon F. Whitney, "Watertown," in *History of Middlesex County, Massachusetts, with Biographical Sketches of Many of its Pioneers and Prominent Men*, ed. E. Hamilton Hurd (Philadelphia: J. W. Lewis & Co., 1890), 317–431; G. Frederick Robinson and Ruth Robinson Wheeler, *Great Little Watertown: A Tercentenary History* (Cambridge, Mass.: Riverside Press, 1930); Maude deLeigh Hodges, "The Story of Our Watertown" (unpublished typescript, 1956), Watertown Free Public Library, HIST 974.443 HOP1956.

Leigh Theodore Macurdy, followed on July 27, 1876, and both were healthy, lively boys (see figure 5 for a photo of all the Macurdy siblings).

These happy events were shadowed by the death of Grace's grandfather William Augustus in October 1878 at the age of eighty-five. Sometime after their arrival in Watertown, William and Harriet had moved in with their son Warren, who had a larger house and no children (though they took in and raised a boy, Arthur, born in 1876 and formally adopted only in Warren's will). Twelve-year-old Grace was very distressed by her grandfather's death, since she had spent a great deal of time in her early childhood with her grandparents. She described William as "a handsome tall old man, whose hair had been reddish and his eyes light blue" and who was happy to sit, "pleasantly silent," while his more voluble wife, Harriet, told Grace stories of her ancestors.[27] The birth of a fourth son, Ronald Thomson Macurdy, on May 30, 1879, raised everyone's spirits, but four months later the family was again plunged into grief when cholera carried off Rebecca's last baby.

Sometime before 1880, the family moved into a rented home opposite Warren's house on Elm Street. Grace fondly remembered this home, especially her time spent with her grandmother Harriet, "a woman of extraordinary strength of character and intellectual power":

> I am indebted to my grandmother, Harriet Hayes McCurdy, in whose company much of my childhood was passed. As I sat by her side making gay patchwork quilts and learning to knit, she quickened my childish imagination and instilled in me an interest in the past by her extraordinary gift of vivid narration. Born in 1798 in Norton, N. B. of colonial American and English parentage she was a woman of noble gifts and character and possessed in high degree that quality of endurance which I find in the best of our ancestors. I was too young to realise the historical value of what she told me in her stories about her ancestors, her childhood and youth, and the events of her later life, but I know now that I owe more to the impulse that she gave me than to years of formal education.[28]

Education

For young Grace, her grandmother and mother were strong influences and role models. She mentions her father in only one extant letter (referring to

---

27. Macurdy, *Pioneer Ancestors*, 18, 95.
28. Macurdy, *Pioneer Ancestors*, 145, i.

the change in spelling of their surname), but she credits her mother with the impetus for her education: "My mother had a large family, nine of us, and high ideals of education for her means. . . . My mother felt that her children must have college training, if possible."[29] With little money, but a passion to educate all her children, Rebecca was fortunate to reside in Watertown in this period. Because of its dual nature and town-meeting governance, public education was a contentious issue in Watertown, with the upper-class and intellectual segments of the population advocating for liberal education and the poor and working-class opposed to paying taxes for education beyond practical training. The former ultimately won the battles, helped by Watertown's proximity to Cambridge and Boston and by the growing prestige of Harvard College. The town established a public high school in 1853, which soon offered both a three-year course and a four-year college-preparatory course whose curriculum was geared to the Harvard entrance requirements. Annual reports of the school committee give a picture of the high school and its ongoing struggle to enroll pupils and keep them until graduation. In 1884, for example, the school superintendent noted that less than a fourth of the graduates of the grammar school entered the high school, and even fewer of these graduated: "The school has always been engaged in a battle with hostile influences, as the difference between the number in a class at the start and at graduation abundantly proves."[30] This was particularly true of boys, and female graduates of the four-year college-preparatory course greatly outnumbered males in the last decades of the nineteenth century. For example, there were only ten graduates of the four-year course in 1883, the year that Grace graduated, and eight of these were females.

Rebecca's father, Adam Duncan Thomson, had engendered in his daughter a respect for the power of an extended education, though this was not shared by Angus, who wanted his children to contribute to the family income as soon as possible. Rebecca's wishes evidently prevailed, however, for her older children all completed at least the three-year course at the high school, and Grace and her younger brothers completed the college-preparatory course. This is truly remarkable for a family who must have lived hand to mouth on Angus's earnings as a freelance carpenter (according to the town assessor's reports,

---

29. Grace Macurdy to Gilbert Murray, 4 February 1911, MSS Gilbert Murray 157, fols. 15–18, Bodleian.

30. George R. Dwelley, "Superintendent's Report," in *Forty-Sixth Annual Report of the School Committee of Watertown for 1883–84,* Watertown School Committee (Watertown, Mass.: Fred G. Barker, 1884), 14, 17.

Angus never owned real estate or had a taxable personal estate).[31] After her graduation from the three-year course in 1878, Grace's sister Maria immediately began teaching in the Centre Primary School No. 2, a position she held with distinction for six years. A look at the conditions under which she taught gives some idea of how difficult school teaching was in that period. In 1883, for example, for a salary of $425 she had fifty-five enrolled pupils with an average daily attendance of forty-six in a crowded classroom with poor ventilation heated by a wood or coal stove. When she married in 1886, she was forced to give up teaching, since Watertown law up to the 1940s prohibited married women from teaching. Furthermore, upper-class women apparently tended to look down upon female schoolteachers, since the school superintendent, George Dwelley, felt compelled to encourage more "recognition, appreciation, and courteous attentions" from these women: "Ladies in happy and beautiful homes sometimes forget to extend a welcome to those less fortunate who are their sisters by all laws of spiritual affinity, and their rivals in the graces that spring from refined associations and the cultivation of intellectual tastes."[32]

Grace's older brother William was already employed as a clerk at the Otis Brothers dry-goods store when he graduated from the three-year course. Her sister Edith may have graduated from the four-year course, since she was still listed as "at school" when the 1880 census was taken in June; she later taught mathematics at Wheaton Female Seminary, so she may have been the first of the children to continue study beyond high school, possibly at the Boston Normal School, though their records from that period no longer exist.

Grace was the first of the Macurdy children to attend college; she was fortunate to have older siblings contributing to the family finances and also to be the right age to take advantage of the burgeoning interest in higher education for women in Massachusetts.[33] After extensive lobbying by the Woman's Education Association of Boston, Harvard College began offering the Harvard Examinations for Women in 1874, designed at first to provide some certifica-

---

31. Watertown Assessors, *The Taxable Valuation of the Real and Personal Estates with the Amount of Tax in the Town of Watertown* (Watertown, Mass.: Fred G. Barker, 1898–1905).

32. George Dwelley, "Superintendent's Report," in *Forty-Seventh Annual Report of the School Committee,* Watertown School Committee (Watertown, Mass.: Fred G. Barker, 1885), 25.

33. In his school report for 1873, H. G. Edwards noted, "To-day, more than ever, the liberal minds of the community throughout the country at large are demanding that the doors of the higher universities of learning shall be as open to the girls as to the boys; that the co-education which is offered to them in the public schools shall be as free to them in the seminaries and the colleges." Unfortunately, he then asked parents to consider whether Watertown's system of coeducation was a mistake, citing Edward H. Clarke's stringent objections to higher education for women and identical coeducation for girls and boys in *Sex in Education* (1873). "School Report," in *Thirty-Sixth Annual Report of the School Committee,* Watertown School Committee (Watertown, Mass.: Fred G. Barker, 1874), 15–17.

tion of educational accomplishments already attained by women. However, in 1879 the "Harvard Annex," a private program offering women the equivalent of collegiate instruction by Harvard professors, opened, and by 1881 women were allowed to take Harvard's standard entrance examinations in order to gain admission to the Annex (which was officially called the Society for the Collegiate Instruction of Women after 1882 and was chartered as Radcliffe College in 1894). With this goal in mind, Grace enrolled in Watertown High School's college-preparatory course in 1879. Along with English, French, history, mathematics, and science, the most motivated students were offered four years of Latin and special courses in Greek, and Grace distinguished herself in the latter subjects, absorbing an abiding love for ancient languages and classical antiquity. As she wrote much later, "It is to me a daily thanksgiving that I have had the privilege of being a student of Greek from my twelfth year and a teacher of it for more than forty years. I would not change this lot for any other if I were to live my life over."[34]

The Watertown Town Hall was the scene of commencement exercises, preceded by exhibitions of student accomplishments in the form of poetry recitations, declamations, dramatic readings, and musical performances. At her commencement on March 30, 1883, Grace recited a poem and read the part of Antonio in a selection from Shakespeare's *Merchant of Venice*. The ceremony closed rather differently than the usual Watertown commencement, however, for after the awarding of diplomas Grace recited an ode of her own composition:

> 'Tis here with willing fingers deft,
> > The busy threads we ply;
> And see with joy the warp and weft
> > Grow as the moments fly.
> Yet these dear scenes we now must leave—
> > 'Round which dwell memories bright—
> Shall in the pattern each must weave
> > Be wrought in flowers of light.
> Each year we sing our song and part,
> > Each year our place is filled;
> And each old truth in some young heart
> > With fresh delight instilled.
> Then weave now threads with choicest care,

---

34. Grace H. Macurdy, Report of the Greek Department 1935–36, 27 April 1936, Annual Reports R.36 S.5, Vassar Archives.

> Which later shall unfold
> A texture rare, with symbols fair,
> The perfect Cloth of Gold.[35]

It is interesting to note that Grace's first poem, though unsophisticated, shares some characteristics with her last—most notably the core metaphor of a typical woman's task and the emphasis on time, continuity, and the future.

Grace then embarked on an intensive year of additional study, an indispensable benefit offered by the high-school teachers, since her family would never have been able to afford private tutoring. Superintendent George Dwelley explained why the school offered such an unusual program:

> No graduate of this school within the last seven years has entered college, university, or the Institute of Technology, without post-graduate help from the teachers. . . . Special instruction has been needful—because impossible to be crowded into the regular course—in the sight-reading of Latin and Greek, in Latin and Greek composition, in advanced problem work in Algebra and Geometry, and in experiments in Physics and Chemistry.[36]

Her diligent study paid off handsomely, since Grace passed the three-day Harvard examinations in 1884 without conditions of any kind, earning honors in classics. These examinations included thirteen subjects—Latin (Caesar and Vergil), Latin sight translation, Latin composition (Cicero), Greek (Xenophon and Homer), Greek sight translation, Greek composition (Herodotus), ancient history and geography, arithmetic, algebra, plane geometry, physics, English composition, and French sight translation. A classmate, Abby Fitz, also passed these examinations, winning honors in mathematics, but she did not enroll in the Annex until 1886, making Grace the first student of Watertown High School to enter the Annex (see figure 7 for a photo of Annex students in 1885). In fact, of the seventeen candidates accepted for admission to the full four-year program in 1884 based on their examination scores, only four actually enrolled in the Annex, perhaps because of inability to pay the $200 tuition.[37] For the Macurdy family, this was a very steep investment to make in their

---

35. "The High School Exhibition," *Watertown Enterprise,* 4 April 1883, 4.

36. George Dwelley, "Superintendent's Report," in *Fiftieth Annual Report of the School Committee,* Watertown School Committee (Watertown, Mass.: Fred G. Barker, 1888), 13.

37. Arthur Gilman, "Secretary's Annual Report, Sixth Year," in *Annual Reports,* Society for the Collegiate Instruction of Women (1885), 7, accessed 15 December 2006, http://iiif.lib.harvard .edu/manifests/view/drs:2573644$17i. As Sally Schwager points out, this tuition was higher than that of Harvard at $150, Smith and Vassar at $100, or Wellesley at $60. "'Harvard Women': A History of the Founding of Radcliffe College" (EdD diss., Harvard University, 1982), 244.

youngest daughter, and it is difficult to know how they afforded it. At that time the Annex had no official scholarship program, but some wealthy Massachusetts women privately paid some or all of the fees for promising young women who would otherwise be unable to attend the Annex, and this may have been the case for Grace, though there are no extant records to prove it. Even if she did receive some financial aid, her determination to attend college and her mother's support were quite remarkable and can only be explained by Grace's character and the respect for education instilled in Rebecca by her minister father.

CHAPTER 3

From the Annex to Vassar

G race was consumed with excitement when she climbed aboard the Cambridge Railroad horse car (see figure 6) in September of 1884 for her first day at the Annex.[1] On this day the crisp autumn air dissipated the dust and the smell of the piles of manure in the street, and the rhythmic clatter of the wheels on the iron rails throughout the nearly hour-long journey helped her conquer her nervousness. She was embarking on the greatest adventure of her young life; soon she would be studying with some of the best professors at Harvard. Remembering the poem she had written for her high-school commencement, she told herself that the golden cloth she wove would shine new light on the ancient world she had come to love. When she arrived at Harvard Square, she carefully held up her long skirt so that the hem would not trail in the dusty streets as she walked to the Annex rooms on Appian Way, thinking to herself that the residents of Cambridge who opposed paving the streets (or at least using a coating of gravel as Watertown did) in order to preserve their city's "rural" character were indeed foolish. The board-

---

1. Grace Macurdy herself did not leave any descriptions of her time at the Harvard Annex. The following account has been created from documents in the Radcliffe Archives at the Schlesinger Library, including reminiscences left by other students during this time period, Grace's transcript, and Annex annual reports and catalogues. See also Sally Schwager, "'Harvard Women': A History of the Founding of Radcliffe College" (EdD diss., Harvard University, 1982).

walks placed in the center of main streets from late fall to spring did little to protect shoes and skirts from the mud and snow.

From her high school experience, she was used to small classes with male instructors, so she soon settled into the rigorous routine of classes and studying. Each of her five courses, held in rooms used for classes at Carret House on 6 Appian Way, met for two hours per week during the year, except for her half-course in Latin Composition, which met once a week. Most of her classes that first year were taught by younger men, instructors and assistant professors, and enrolled five to eight students, except for English Composition, with twenty-three students. Despite her lack of private-school training, Grace achieved excellent marks in all her courses:

- 98% in Greek 1, taught by James Greenleaf Croswell and including Lysias, Plato, and Homer;
- 98% in Latin 1, taught by Henry Preble and including Livy, Horace, and Cicero;
- 92% in Latin Composition, taught by Henry Preble;
- 91% in English Composition, taught by Le Baron Russell Briggs;
- 97% in Elementary German, taught by Edward Stevens Sheldon.

When she learned that the famous professor of Latin, James Bradstreet Greenough, was offering a voluntary series of readings in Latin from Cicero, Vergil, and Plautus, she eagerly signed up for these sessions as well, even though they added more hours to her already long days in Cambridge.

Encouraged by her success, Grace took on a more demanding course load in her second year, with five full courses and two half courses, Latin and Greek Composition; class sizes ranged from five to ten students and some were held in the Annex's new, more spacious quarters, Fay House on Garden Street. Again, she did very well in all her language courses, showing only a slight weakness in essay writing:

- 91% in Greek 2, taught by Louis Dyer and Harold North Fowler, including Aristophanes, Thucydides, Sophocles, Euripides, and Greek history;
- 100% in Greek Composition, taught by James Greenleaf Croswell;
- 95% in Latin 2, taught by James Bradstreet Greenough and including Tacitus, Pliny, Terence, and sight reading;
- 97% in Latin Composition, taught by Henry Preble;
- 85% in English Themes, taught by Le Baron Russell Briggs;
- 92% in German 2, taught by George Alonzo Bartlett and including Schiller and German prose;

- 97% in French 2, taught by Adolphe Cohn and including La Fontaine's Fables, modern prose, grammar, and composition.

On May 15, 1886, Grace lost her beloved grandmother, Harriet Hayes Macurdy. Looking back at that sad time as she was approaching her own eightieth year, Grace wrote:

> She retained her vigor of mind almost to the end of her eighty-eighth year. In that year, in her last days she conversed, as she believed with her dead son, Capt. James McCurdy, and he, she said, revealed to her that her son William, from whom she had not heard for years, was living and had four sons. This I do not explain, but can testify to the fact.[2]

Later that year Grace's family moved away from her uncle Warren to be closer to the center of Watertown, renting a home on Riverside in an industrial section near the Charles River.

These disruptions in her family life made her third year even more challenging. Because she was required to take mathematics and science, not her strongest subjects, she took four full courses and two half courses, Latin Composition and Physics. Except for the latter, with nineteen students, these classes were very small; two had only four students, one had five, and one had eight. Results were now recorded in letter grades instead of percentages, although her highest and lowest grades that year also included percentages:

- A (98%) in Greek 5, taught by William Watson Goodwin and including Aeschines, Demosthenes, Sophocles, and Aristophanes;
- A in Latin 4, taught by Clement Lawrence Smith and including Tacitus, Juvenal, Martial, sight reading, and Roman history;
- A in Latin Composition, taught by Henry Preble;
- B in English Forensics, taught by Le Baron Russell Briggs;
- B in Analytic Geometry and Differential Calculus, taught by Benjamin Osgood Peirce;
- C (67%) in Experimental Physics with lab work, taught by Edwin Herbert Hall.

She was at last able to take a class with the much-admired Professor Goodwin, who met his Annex students in his own library. Since Greek was her favorite subject and she felt immensely privileged to be studying with

---

2. Macurdy, *Pioneer Ancestors*, 145.

him, Grace did not experience the problem described by another student of the time: "Professor W. W. Goodwin's course was memorable in retrospect because of the difficulty of keeping on the alert in the deep, upholstered chairs of his library at the P. M. sessions just after dinner."[3] The evening classes, however, made her commute home more difficult, especially in the winter months, when she stood on the corner waiting for the horse car so paralyzed with cold that she had to ask the conductor to wait until her fingers thawed out so she could take the nickel from her purse to pay the fare.

Her achievements in Greek and Latin were so outstanding that her professors encouraged her to apply for Second-Year Honors in Classics, which required excellent performance in at least four classical courses plus passing with distinction a special examination near the end of the academic year in translating Greek and Latin at sight, writing Greek and Latin prose, and demonstrating knowledge of ancient history, literature, culture, and Greek and Latin grammar. At the 1887 commencement exercises, Grace proudly accepted a certificate for Highest Second-Year Honors in Classics.

In her final year, as in her first, Grace achieved solid A grades in four full courses, plus a half course in Latin Composition:

- A+ in Greek Composition, taught by John Henry Wright, with only three students;
- A in Greek 6, taught by William Watson Goodwin and including Plato and Aristotle;
- A in Latin 6, taught by James Bradstreet Greenough and including Plautus and Lucretius;
- A in Latin Composition, taught by Henry Preble;
- A in Philosophy: Lectures on Logic, taught by Josiah Royce.

On June 21, 1888, the eight women who were to receive BA certificates from the Annex for the full classical course were given the special privilege of a "Senior Day," receiving their friends and family for tea at Fay House. A simple commencement was held the following Monday, June 25. Elizabeth Agassiz, President of the Society for the Collegiate Instruction of Women, gave out the certificates, each with a small bouquet of flowers to be worn by the graduate. Grace was the only one of the eight women to be awarded Final Honors in Classics, a remarkable achievement for the first person in her fam-

---

3. Catharine Bird Runkle '86 to Annie Ware Winsor Allen, 7 November 1942, Papers of Annie Ware Winsor Allen, 1884–1950, SC 35, box 2, folder 10, Radcliffe College Archives, Schlesinger.

ily for generations to earn a college degree (after Radcliffe was chartered in 1894, Grace was retroactively granted a Radcliffe BA).

Unlike many alumnae of that period, Grace did not write about her years at the Annex, except for remarking in 1913, "Much is vague and misty in my thought of those early days at the Annex on Appian Way, a time of strenuous study and work."[4] It is not surprising that what she did associate with this time was effort, determination, and focus. Although the Annex was beginning to offer some social events and extracurricular activities, Grace had neither the time nor the social background to participate in these. These words of Catharine Bird Runkle, class of 1886, could have been written by Grace:

> As, during two of those years, I commuted practically every weekday from Brookline, you can see that I had little chance to form lasting friendships, or take part in extracurricular activities. Besides this, my attitude of mind was then narrowly academic. I was so much interested in the subject matter of my courses that nothing else mattered. In fact I was a typical "blue stocking."[5]

Professional Ambition

Grace had developed a different sort of ambition from that of most of the women at the Annex, who were planning to teach or were already teaching in the schools. She was determined to win recognition as a classical scholar with a professional career like her Harvard mentors. Although she had no female role models for this ambition, she was apparently not plagued with the kind of self-doubt and lack of self-confidence that afflicted classmates like Annie Ware Winsor Allen, who gave up her early ambition to pursue graduate study at Bryn Mawr and become an English professor. Instead, Allen taught in secondary school and "suffered intermittently from deep depressions and conflicts about her intellectual and professional ambitions and the role she was expected to fulfill as a woman."[6] The attitude of the Harvard professors toward

---

4. Grace H. Macurdy, "A Tribute to Mary Coes," 10 November 1913, Mary Coes Papers, 1880–1958 (inclusive), 1880–1913 (bulk), SC 22, box 1, folder 37, Radcliffe College Archives, Schlesinger.

5. Catharine Bird Runkle to Annie Ware Winsor Allen, 7 November 1942.

6. Schwager, "Harvard Women," 282. Schwager hypothesizes that the lofty reputation of the university and of the Harvard professors, combined with their ambivalent attitudes toward the higher education of women, was responsible for the lack of self-confidence and absence of driving professional ambition in many of the Annex students (262–91). She quotes a remi-

their female students was at best paternalistic, and some were disparaging or even hostile. Helen A. Stuart, class of 1891, describes the situation:

> It was always impressed upon us that we must be inconspicuous, and must *never* cross the Harvard Yard, unless we were attending some special lecture or reading (such as Prof. Palmer's translations of Homer). As to the relations between Harvard and the Annex, it was borne in upon us very frequently that the University as a whole scorned us, and only the broad-minded professors were really interested in our success. The students in general thought of us as unattractive blue-stockings and compared us unfavorably with the Wellesley girls.[7]

Another reminiscence provides a telling example of the attitude of one of the "broad-minded professors," the greatly admired Latin professor James Bradstreet Greenough:

> But of all the men who taught me, Professor James B. Greenough impressed me most. He seemed a reincarnation of some noble Roman whose profound grasp of the Latin language had been born with him, not merely acquired by study. He turned a speech by Theodore Roosevelt into Ciceronian Latin as easily as Professor Francke might have turned it into German, and did us the honor of allowing us to read it, but the responsibility of teaching girls weighed on his conscience, for once in class he stopped suddenly and remarked, with reference to the text, that for the life of him he couldn't construe it so as to help us to become better wives and mothers.[8]

In her analysis of internal conflicts and self-doubt among the first generation of women faculty at Wellesley, Patricia Palmieri believes that a genteel, middle-class social background was also a contributing factor:

> Being female weighed heavily upon the Wellesley women scholars; in spite of numerous supports from family, class, and new educational and career opportunities, many of them complained of depression or devalued their own professional contributions. . . . The Wellesley academic women combined a progressive spirit that valued science, rationalism, and public

niscence of Leslie W. Hopkinson, "As I look back on those times, what strikes me most is the *bigness* of the men who gave their time to that tiny little group of girls." (264).

7. Helen A. Stuart, to Annie Ware Winsor Allen, 20 November 1942; Papers of Annie Ware Winsor Allen, 1884–1950, SC 35, box 2, folder 10, Radcliffe College Archives, Schlesinger.

8. Catharine Bird Runkle to Annie Ware Winsor Allen, 7 November 1942.

achievement with a commitment to the romantic, genteel life. Yet to be a professor at Wellesley during this period entailed costs: individuals were made to feel guilty if they considered leaving; in a climate that both praised and plundered a person's achievement, many gifted women succumbed to self-disparagement, unable to overcome their ambivalence toward success; and too often, homes, gardens, and summer trips compensated for stalled careers.[9]

Ironically, Grace Macurdy's social background helped her to withstand this kind of self-doubt and ambivalence, since she had never experienced a "romantic, genteel" life. She grew up in a family waging an unremitting struggle for economic survival; through hard work and tremendous determination, she was able to master the Harvard examinations and persuade her parents to allow her to attend college. She could not afford ambivalence; she had been given an advantage unavailable to her older siblings, and success was her only option. She aimed for the highest success, a professional academic career and recognition as a classical scholar. In Grace's family, there were no separate spheres or pedestals for women; everyone pitched in, and the women worked as hard as the men. In high school, Grace had discovered her talent for languages and research, and she saw her male professors at the Annex as representatives of the scholarly life she intended to make her own. Their paternalism, benign neglect, or negative attitudes did not undermine her confidence that she could achieve this goal. Many years later, noted Columbia professor Carolyn Heilbrun experienced the same sort of aspiration prompted by Clifton Fadiman, Lionel Trilling, and Jacques Barzun:

> Although one of them never knew of my existence, the second ignored it, and the third treated me with formal kindness, without them I would have had no concrete model in my youth of what I wanted to become. . . . Theirs was the universe in which I wished to have my being. When I first encountered them, however, the fact that no woman could have her being in the world where they prevailed evaded my consciousness; the impossibility of that particular dream did not present itself to me as an inexorable fact. Like women before me, I hoped against all evidence that I, an exception, might join that blessed circle. . . . If I wanted a prototype, an example of the sort

---

9. Patricia Ann Palmieri, *In Adamless Eden: The Community of Women Faculty at Wellesley* (New Haven, Conn.: Yale University Press, 1995), xix.

of career and accomplishment I sought, where was there to look except at men?"[10]

Cambridge School for Girls

After receiving her degree, Grace was immediately hired by Arthur Gilman to teach in the Cambridge School for Girls, which he and his wife Stella had founded in 1886 to educate girls and young women from twelve to twenty-five years of age, including those preparing for college (especially at the Annex, since the school offered special courses related to the Harvard Examinations). Grace taught both Greek and Latin at this school for five years, from 1888 to 1893, continuing her long commute from Watertown on the horse cars (electric trolleys did not operate from Watertown until 1894). All classes were taught in the mornings, but teachers were expected to remain at the school in the afternoons to meet with students and have conferences with parents. The school was expensive and highly regarded, classes were small, and the students were drawn mostly from wealthy families in Cambridge and the Boston area.[11]

Although her goal was an academic position on a college faculty, Grace had to begin earning money to contribute to the family finances as soon as she had completed her four precious years of study, so she accepted the high-school position. She rationalized this in part by viewing it as a sacrifice she would make so that her younger brothers could receive a college education: "I educated the two youngest brothers as a sort of sacred task, because my mother felt that her children must have college training, if possible. So I gave up all sorts of things for them, as we all did."[12] Because of these sacrifices, her brother John was able to attend the Lawrence Scientific School at Harvard from 1892 to 1895 to prepare for a career as a civil engineer, while the youngest, Leigh, received a bachelor of arts from Harvard College in 1899 and a bachelor of law from Boston University in 1902.

10. Carolyn G. Heilbrun, *When Men Were the Only Models We Had: My Teachers Barzun, Fadiman, Trilling* (Philadelphia: University of Pennsylvania Press, 2002), 1–3.

11. *Manual of the Cambridge School for Girls* (Cambridge, Massachusetts, 1898). In 1918 the school was named the Cambridge-Haskell School after merging with the Haskell School; in 1931 the school left Cambridge to become a coeducational boarding school named The Cambridge School of Weston.

12. Grace Macurdy to Gilbert Murray, 4 February 1911, MSS Gilbert Murray 157, fols. 15–18, Bodleian.

Family Cooperation

The Macurdy children had to contribute to the family income as soon as possible because their father, Angus, never moved beyond work as a freelance carpenter. In contrast, his brother Warren established a successful building firm, with employees and contracts for constructing some of the finest homes in Watertown. Solon Whitney's 1890 history of Watertown names him as one of the foremost builders of the area: "Among the builders whose honorable record has been made during the past fifty years should be mentioned H. W. Macurday [*sic*], who has erected in this and the adjoining towns more than a hundred buildings of the best class."[13] Warren was even elected as one of the three town selectmen, serving from 1872 to 1876. At the least, Angus must have envied if not resented his brother's economic success, which stood in such stark contrast with his own constant struggle to earn enough to support his large family. Warren never took his younger brother into his firm, and there is no evidence of the kind of cooperation and mutual support that would later mark the relations of Angus's children and their spouses, enabling them to move up the social and economic scale.

Because they had all completed at least a high school education, the Macurdy children were able to obtain white-collar jobs and ultimately respected positions in the Watertown community. As already mentioned, Maria began teaching primary school in Watertown in 1878, moving to a higher-paying teaching position in Somerville in 1885 but leaving teaching when she married George Herbert Tarleton on October 4, 1886. Tarleton began work as a jeweler but rose to the position of town auditor in 1890, then justice of the peace and postmaster, and finally manager of a boiler company. In 1879, William began working as a clerk in Otis Brothers, the major dry-goods/shoe store in Watertown, even before he had graduated from the three-year high school course. He swiftly rose to treasurer then eventual owner of the store; he also became a trustee of the Watertown Savings Bank and clerk and deacon of the First Baptist Church. On August 31, 1886, he married Anna Louise Richardson of Cambridge, and he bought a home on Chester Street in a new development begun in 1888 and popularly called "Otisville" after the land company also owned by Horace and Ward Otis.

Theodosia, the eldest of Grace's siblings and the only other who never married, began work as an assistant librarian in the Watertown Public Library in 1889; the following year she took a position in the Boston Public Library,

---

13. Solon F. Whitney, "Watertown," in *History of Middlesex County, Massachusetts, with Biographical Sketches of Many of its Pioneers and Prominent Men,* ed. E. Hamilton Hurd (Philadelphia: J. W. Lewis & Co., 1890), 393.

where she remained until her retirement, rising through the ranks to become the highly respected head of the ordering department. As mentioned earlier, Edith taught mathematics at Wheaton Female Seminary from 1889 to 1892; during the school year she lived in the Wheaton dormitories. She also served as editor of *Rushlight*, the school newspaper. Like Maria, she had to relinquish her position when she married Henry Reuben Skinner on October 6, 1892. Skinner was a Phi Beta Kappa graduate of Brown University who became a successful lawyer with offices in both Boston and Watertown; he was elected to the Massachusetts Senate in 1899. Skinner's youngest sister, Lillian, was introduced to her future husband, Truman S. Richardson, by Grace's brother William when the young Richardson was boarding at his house and working as a clerk in Macurdy's dry-goods store, providing an example of the close interaction between these families. Truman was the younger brother of William Macurdy's wife, Anna Louise Richardson.

This diligence and cooperation greatly benefited the two youngest Macurdys, John and Leigh. However, in an action that would foreshadow events in his later life, Leigh disappointed his family by stealing money from those who were working so hard to give him an education. When the theft was discovered, Grace, William, and Theodosia witnessed a document handwritten by William and signed by the fourteen-year-old Leigh on September 24, 1890:

> Whereas I, Leigh T. Macurdy of Watertown, have the past year done wrong in many ways, among which I have taken money wrongfully from my father, sister, and the firm of Otis Brothers, and have deceived these said people about said money, and having been detected in said wrong doings by aforsaid [sic] relatives and Otis Brothers and they having been very lenient with me, agreeing to drop the matter, which is a State Prison offense, where it is providing I refund all money taken, and promise never to lie or steal as long as I live: I do repent of my wrong-doing, and do promise to refund the money as soon as I can possibly *earn* it to Otis Bros. $2.50, to my sister $1.50, to my father $1.00 and I do solemnly promise before God, and my sister Docia & Grace & my brother Willie never to steal one cent or any other thing as long as I live, neither to deceive anyone by wrong doing—but will try to behave my self and make amends for what I have done in the past and try to make my mother (whom it would perhaps kill if she knew of my wrongs) still be able to love and cherish me as her son.[14]

---

14. Manuscript in the private collection of June Macurdy Landin.

It is interesting to note that Angus is not a part of this proceeding and that Rebecca's role as the emotional center of the family is highlighted.

The Macurdy family continued their practice of moving into a different rented house every few years: in 1889, they moved to Center Street, near the home recently purchased by William, and in 1893, they moved to Fayette Street on the corner of Pearl Street. Within a year, Henry Skinner and Edith purchased a home on Pearl Street, and some years later George Tarleton and Maria settled on this street as well. The new Macurdy homes were also closer to the horse-car lines on Mt. Auburn Street, since all the children living at home were commuting to Cambridge or Boston. Theodosia and Grace continued to board with their parents, and the two youngest sons lived at home while attending college.

Most of the family worshipped at the First Baptist Church on Mt. Auburn Street, though Maria had switched to her husband's religion and become a Congregationalist. William was especially devoted to the Baptist church, serving first as clerk and later as deacon. The *Memorial History of the First Baptist Church* lists four church members who were "moulders of life in the century," and the first three are part of the family:

> Time would fail us to record the extent of such christian [*sic*] influence as that exerted by Grace H. Macurdy, baptized by Pastor Capen in 1881, a Vassar Alumna of culture, identified with the Department of Greek at her Alma Mater [*sic*] for thirty-five years and now its honored head. Deacon W. T. Macurdy, her devoted brother, now laid aside by failing health, has helped to keep untarnished the reputation of a century old Watertown firm, while his judgment and coöperation have been "above par assets" of the Watertown Church. Think of Henry R. Skinner, a Watertown boy, a member of the First Baptist Church, High School orator, Brown Alumnus, trustworthy lawyer, dependable town official and representation to the General Court.[15]

Ironically, Grace, who is listed first, soon ceased to practice any organized religion under the influence of the liberal progressive ideas she had absorbed through her education.

While she was contributing to the family income by teaching in the Cambridge School, Grace made herself more attractive for a college position by taking graduate courses at the Annex. She earned grades of A in all these courses, including Greek and Latin Comparative Philology, taught by James

15. Rev. James E. Norcross, *A Memorial History of the First Baptist Church, Watertown, Massachusetts 1830–1930* (Cambridge, Mass.: Hampshire Press, 1930), 152–53.

B. Greenough (1889–90); Early English 1200–1450, taught by George Lyman Kittredge (1891–92); The Seminary of Classical Philology, taught by Clement L. Smith and John H. Wright (1892–93); and Catullus and the Elegiac Poets (1892–93), a Latin course offered by Clement L. Smith at Harvard that she received special permission to attend. This preparation paid off handsomely in 1893, when she was hired by Abby Leach as an instructor of Greek in Vassar College.

Grace was finally advancing toward her life's goal; she had secured a professional academic position in a college that claimed to provide women with an education equal to that offered by Harvard and Yale.[16] It was difficult to leave the family with whom she had lived for all of her twenty-seven years, but excitement and hopes for the future sustained her through the long train journey from Boston to Poughkeepsie. When she alighted from the horse car that had taken her from the station to Vassar, she marveled at the beauty of the campus, so different from the urban environment of Watertown. As she walked up the wide, tree-lined drive, she gazed in wonderment at the massive red-brick structure where she would live, dine, and teach. Main Building, modeled on the Tuileries Palace in Paris, had a five-story central pavilion surmounted by a mansard roof with a grand dome in the center (see figure 8). Two long wings led to pavilions on each side as tall as the central structure. All around stretched sweeping lawns studded with trees. Although she could not know it at the time, Vassar was to be her home for the next fifty-three years, and she never lost her delight in the beauty of the place. Later she would write a song loved by generations of Vassar students, "Vassar in Beauty Dwelling":

Vassar in beauty dwelling
   Through all the changing year,
Hail to thee, mighty mother,
   Lovely, serene, austere.

Praise we thy blooming springtime,
   Rose-red thy June we praise,

---

16. When Grace began teaching at Vassar, the college was already well established since its founding in 1861, and it is not my intention to review its purpose and nature here. Interested readers can find a straightforward description in James Monroe Taylor and Elizabeth Hazelton Haight, *Vassar,* American College and University Series (New York: Oxford University Press, 1915). For comparison with other women's colleges in the United States, see Helen Lefkowitz Horowitz, *Alma Mater: Design and Experimentation in the Women's Colleges from Their Nineteenth Century Beginnings to the 1930s,* 2nd ed. (Amherst: University of Massachusetts Press, 1993).

Crimson and gold thy autumns,
    Crystal thy winter days.

Vassar enthroned in beauty,
    Glad at thy gates we throng,
Mother of all our dreaming,
    Lift we to thee our song.

Grace's original lyrics, submitted for a competition in Vassar's fiftieth anniversary year (1915), were longer; by 1917 she had reduced the number of stanzas and slightly changed the lyrics, presumably to facilitate singing. The original third and fourth stanzas made clear her belief that Vassar's chief glory was the elevation of women through education:

But not for these we greet thee,
    The mother of our dreams,
Thy spirit high and holy
    In rarer beauty gleams.

Thou art our vision splendid
    Of womanhood to be,
In knowledge pure, from bondage
    Of vanity set free.[17]

---

17. *Vassar Miscellany News*, 4 June 1915, 6; *New Alma Mater Songs* (New York: G. Schirmer, 1917) MacCracken Papers 75.43, Vassar Archives. The music was composed by Donald N. Tweedy, instructor of music.

CHAPTER 4

Teacher and Scholar

When Grace Macurdy climbed the stairs to her room at the end of one of the long student corridors in the Main Building, the students she passed saw a slim young woman in a long-skirted dress whose fabric and cut signaled serviceability rather than style. Her thick, dark hair was parted at the center and wound into coils on the top of her head; her oval face was pleasant, but rather plain, with a broad forehead and long nose. The fact that Grace herself had no illusions about her appearance is evident in her self-description for a passport application in 1898:

Stature: *5 feet, 5 inches, Eng.*
Forehead: *low and broad*
Eyes: *grey*
Nose: *long, blunt*
Mouth: *thin-lipped, straight*
Chin: *straight*
Hair: *heavy, brown*
Complexion: *medium*
Face: *somewhat large*[1]

---

1. Passport Application No. 10059, Macurdy, G. H., 12 July 1899, *Registers and Indexes for Passport Applications, 1810–1906* (National Archives Microfilm Publication M1371, roll 7),

What Grace couldn't see, but the students soon observed, was the way her ready smile animated her face and her eyes shone with intelligence, humor, and sympathetic interest in the people around her (see figure 9 for a studio photograph of Grace taken during her first years at Vassar). As they quickly learned, her head was often in the intellectual clouds, and she was anything but a strict taskmaster.

Grace was pleasantly surprised by the large size of the single room that would serve as her home and office for the coming year. Having grown up amid a large family living in straitened circumstances, she was thrilled to have a space all her own where she could work undisturbed (so long as she had the "engaged" sign on her door, which indicated that knocking was forbidden). Given her background, she did not consider it unreasonable that her salary of "$800 plus home for the college year" included not only teaching but also social responsibilities like corridor supervision and presiding over a student table during all meals in the dining room. This arrangement was popular with many students, "The teachers are so lovely. One comes into so much closer contact with them in living all under the same roof,"[2] but was resented by some of the instructors.

Abby Leach and Her Greek Department

Before beginning her courses, Grace met with Professor Abby Leach, the head of the Greek Department. She saw a beautifully dressed, imposing woman with brown hair softly waved around her face; although she was only two inches taller than Grace, her upright carriage gave the impression of even greater height (see figure 10 for a studio photograph of Abby Leach). Her gracious, welcoming smile did not lessen the awe Grace felt in the presence of this distinguished woman, whose history was well known at the Harvard Annex. Grace remembered that she had come from a prosperous merchant family in Brockton, Massachusetts, and had so excelled in her studies at the Oread Collegiate Institute that she had not only taught there after graduation but had been named preceptress at the tender age of twenty-one. Two years later she had courageously approached Harvard's Eliot Professor of Greek Literature, William Watson Goodwin, and requested that he give her private tuition in Greek. Seeing her now, Grace was not surprised that Goodwin had reversed

General Records of the Department of State, Record Group 59; National Archives and Records Administration (NARA).

2. Winifred Kirkland '97 to Jennie S. Liebmann, 1 October 1893, Vassar College Student Materials Collection, Vassar Archives.

his original refusal after hearing her construe a difficult passage of Greek at sight and had subsequently recommended her for private studies in Latin with Professor James Bradstreet Greenough and in English literature with Professor Francis James Child. All the later students at the Annex had heard repeatedly that Abby Leach's determination and linguistic skill had won over the Harvard professors to support the proposal to found the Society for Collegiate Instruction of Women in Cambridge, so that Leach was popularly known as the "nucleus" of the Annex. Without Abby Leach, Grace realized, she might never have received a college education. And now, a college teacher herself, she would be privileged to work with this remarkable woman at Vassar.

Professor Leach (Grace soon learned that she preferred this method of address over the "Miss" used by most of the female faculty) explained to Grace the background of the Greek department. When Leach had been hired as a teacher of Latin and Greek in 1883, there was a Department of Ancient Languages headed by Charles J. Hinkel, the Matthew Vassar Jr. Professor of Greek and Latin Languages and Literature,[3] with Abby Moore Goodwin serving as the other teacher. Applicants for admission to the freshman class were required to demonstrate by examination or certificate proficiency in Latin and one other language (Greek, German, or French) and then to take prescribed courses in those two languages throughout their freshman and sophomore years. The Department of Ancient Languages, however, concentrated mostly on the Latin courses, and Leach had originally spent most of her time teaching Latin (in her first year, for example, only eleven students had taken Greek). She had devoted herself to increasing the number of Greek courses and students, so that she had taught fifty students in five Greek courses in 1885–86, including six students who began studying elementary Greek in their junior year. In 1885, Vassar had conferred on her the degrees of bachelor and master of arts by examination, based on her work as a special student at the Harvard Annex, and in 1886 she was promoted to assistant professor of the Greek language, while Abby Goodwin was made assistant professor of the Latin language. After a year-long sabbatical in Europe, traveling and studying Greek at the University of Leipzig, Leach taught all the Greek courses, and she confided to Grace that she never intended to teach Latin again, regarding it as inferior to her beloved Greek. In 1888, she and Goodwin were promoted to associate professors; since Professor Hinkel was scheduled to retire in 1890, Abby Leach pressed her case for dividing the Department of Ancient Languages into separate departments of Greek and Latin. Her persistence and determination once

---

3. The 1882 bequest of Matthew Vassar Jr., a nephew of the founder of Vassar who was not in sympathy with the more feminist ideals of his uncle, had endowed this chair with the condition that it be restricted in perpetuity to men.

again paid off, as she was promoted to professor of the Greek language and made head of the new Greek Department in 1889. Abby Goodwin was at the same time promoted to professor of the Latin language, but she died suddenly in April of 1890, and in 1891 John Leverett Moore was hired as the new Matthew Vassar Jr. Professor and head of the Latin Department.

Since 1889–90, Professor Leach had been managing the Greek Department and teaching the courses almost single-handedly, having only the assistance of Ella Catherine Greene (Vassar BA 1887), whom she shared with the Latin Department. She told Grace that she was delighted to have a graduate of the Annex as the first Instructor in Greek; Grace's presence would enable the department to offer two new courses this year. By the time Professor Leach finished her story of the genesis of the Vassar Greek Department, Grace was not at all surprised by the possessive note that crept into her voice as she spoke about "my" department.

Learning to Teach

Grace was assigned a fourteen-hour teaching schedule with three course preparations, including all the required Greek courses for freshmen and sophomores,[4] plus one elective, a new one-hour course in the Greek New Testament. Professor Leach taught the other new course that Grace's hiring had made possible, an elective in Aristophanes. This was a heavy teaching load, because all the required courses included weekly assignments in which the students rendered English passages into Greek, necessitating careful reading and correction of the Greek. In her annual departmental report, Abby Leach reflected that this was an appropriate schedule for an instructor, indicating that she planned to continue this division of work as a general principle:

> I think that fourteen hours is a fair requirement [for a teacher]. This means at the most two classes as far as preparation is concerned and the lower classes besides, which never make as heavy demands upon a teacher. If not considered irrelevant, this suggestion occurs to me just here. If teachers are

---

4. The freshmen read the orator Lysias plus Plato's *Apology* in the fall and Homer's *Odyssey* plus selections from Herodotus in the spring; the sophomores read the orations Demosthenes's *On the Crown* and Aeschines' *Against Ctesiphon* in the fall and Plato's *Protagoras* in the spring. Besides translation and composition, these courses included lectures on background material relevant to the various topics; when teaching the *Odyssey*, for example, Grace lectured on the Homeric Question, Mycenean society and artifacts, and Homeric forms and syntax in relation to Attic Greek.

given elective work of an advanced grade, dissatisfaction is likely to ensue. The distinction in title should carry with it distinction in the line of work.[5]

Here Leach is looking at the schedule solely from her own perspective as the one with "distinction in title." She is not considering the point of view of her new instructor, who would certainly not feel "dissatisfaction" at being allowed to teach an advanced elective and might not be so sure of the fairness of a fourteen-hour schedule.

In fact, Grace taught fourteen or fifteen credits throughout her first six years at Vassar. Instead of the two preparations envisaged by Professor Leach, after her first year she taught at least four preparations and five in the fall of 1894, when she added Course B (second semester of the short course in Greek for students beginning the language in college) and Course D (Demosthenes' *Orations against Philip* and other Attic orators, an elective which also included weekly English–Greek compositions and was a prerequisite for all other Greek electives). After her first few years, at least most of her courses were repeats, with smaller enrollments after 1895, when the requirement of two years for a second language was reduced to two semesters freshman year, a reduction strongly opposed by Abby Leach, who wrote in 1896, "Protests are useless I suppose, but please do not hold me responsible for the decadence of my department."[6]

Intellectually, Grace was very well prepared to teach these courses, but she struggled in the beginning to find a pedagogical approach appropriate for her students. At the Harvard Annex she had focused with single-minded intensity on classical scholarship, and the Cambridge School for Girls, with its small classes, homogeneous student body, and close ties to the Annex, had done little to challenge that rarefied atmosphere of high erudition. She wanted to impress Abby Leach and quite naturally assumed that she would approve of teaching methods modeled on those of the Annex. However, the classes at Vassar were larger than any Grace had encountered, and the students had much more diverse backgrounds and interests. Excerpts from the letters of two of Grace's first students (Adelaide Claflin and Madeline Traver, both of the class of 1897) bear witness to Grace's initial difficulty in adapting to the Vassar student:

---

5. Abby Leach, Report of the Greek Department 1893–94, 8 May 1894, box 3, folder 53, Vassar Archives.

6. Abby Leach, Report of the Greek Department 1895–96, 15 May 1896, box 3, folder 53, Vassar Archives.

Our Greek teacher (I think she is Miss McCurdy but I am not sure) is very nice too, but she expects us to know an awful lot, and she pronounces some vowels differently from what we have been used to so that we can hardly understand her.[7]

I find I have forgotten a great deal of my Greek, and shall have to grind, for a time at least. That teacher, Miss McCurdy, . . . doesn't inspire me with a particle of enthusiasm, and yet she expects a great deal of us. Still she is very pleasant.[8]

Miss Macurdy told us to learn the names and subjects of Plato's *thirty-six* dialogues, for next lesson,—a sample of the crazy things she has us do.[9]

And of all fearful examinations that I ever had the pleasure of taking, that Greek was by far the *fearfullest*. The exam was on Lysias, and Ed [her sister Edith] will appreciate it when I tell her that one of the *minor* questions was to give in Greek Aristotle's opinion of Theramenes; another to give a brief description of Lysias' style, using Greek words to describe it, and giving illustrations from his speeches; another to name the rhetorical figures which Lysias uses, citing examples (in Greek) from his speeches. I got about half through the exam, but I think I passed. Miss Macurdy expects every body to be able, like herself, to have at her tongue's end every thing she ever heard or read. But still she told Ray [her roommate Rachel Schauffler] that most of the class did very well, and that Ray handed in one of the best papers that she ever saw.[10]

One of these students was from the Midwest and found Grace's Greek pronunciation difficult to understand; both thought she expected more of them than they were accustomed to but considered her personally very pleasant. The reference to her first examination shows both her high expectations and her lavish use of encouragement; indeed, throughout her career Grace never

7. Adelaide Claflin '97 to "Bess," 8 November 1893, Vassar College Student Materials Collection, Vassar Archives.

8. Madeline "Maidee" Traver '97 (beginning of letter lost), September 1893, Vassar College Student Materials Collection, Vassar Archives.

9. Adelaide Claflin '97 to "My dear Mother," 19 May 1895, Vassar College Student Materials Collection, Vassar Archives.

10. Adelaide Claflin '97 to "Mamma," 4 February 1894, Vassar College Student Materials Collection, Vassar Archives.

graded punitively. Adelaide Claflin, who found this exam so fearful, termed Grace's exam questions "fair and pleasant" the following year.[11]

As her own interests and experiences broadened, Grace gradually evolved a teaching method more in line with her naturally outgoing, warm personality, an approach that linked ancient to modern literature and culture and drew on her love of humor and good storytelling. Professor Leach visited only one class, in the fall of 1893, and never discussed teaching methods with her, choosing to leave her to her own devices. Grace later came to see this as a benefit, since she could not help but notice Leach's rather top-down, authoritative approach to teaching. Indeed, one of Leach's favorite type of questions was to quote the opinion of an authority and ask the students to prove it (rather than asking them to evaluate it or work out their own interpretation). Here is an example from her 1896 examination on the Greek lyric poet Pindar:

> Confirm this by reference to the poems: "He shows the epic heroes in a new light, as of a fair sunset, which the lay of the minstrel shed around them in the palace of Alcinous, nor yet that searching sunshine of noontide which fell upon them in the theatre of Dionysus."[12]

---

11. Adelaide Claflin '97 to "My dear Mother," 3 February 1895; and Scrapbook, Vassar College Student Materials Collection, Vassar Archives. Claflin pasted Grace's examination in sophomore Greek into her scrapbook: I. Translate: Dem. XVIII., 208. Comment on the rhetoric and give technical names of the figures used. II. Translate: Dem. XVIII., 62 to 66. What is the argument and how does Demosthenes use it to defend his policy? III. What services does Demosthenes claim to have rendered his country in XVIII., 300 to 303? Compare 230, 240, 241. IV. Translate into Greek: Today the Commons of Great Britain prosecute the delinquents of India. Tomorrow the delinquents of India may be the Commons of Great Britain. We know, I say, and feel the power of money, and we now call upon your lordships for justice in the cause of money. We call upon you for our national character. We call upon you for our liberties and hope that the freedom of the Commons will be preserved by the justice of the Lords. V. Give the argument in Dem. XVIII., 199 to 202 in connection with 96 to 98.

12. Adelaide Claflin '97 Scrapbook, Vassar College Student Materials Collection, Vassar Archives. Claflin's scrapbook contains four of Leach's examinations, and two others include this type of question:

> Prove this: No purely personal and exclusive passions animate the ancient tragedy. (1896 Sophocles examination)

> Cite and translate passages that illustrate these words of the French critic: "The idea of impending chastisement is incessantly repeated; it mingles with the joy of victory; a dark cloud, big with the storm, covers the gloomy scene, till the dream, so weary and so terrible, filled with visions so fearful and mysterious, ends with a peal of thunder." (1897 Aeschylus examination)

Christopher Stray has recognized the sources of the two quotations. The quotation in the 1896 Pindar exam is from Sir. Richard Claverhouse Jebb, *The Growth and Influence of Classical Greek Poetry: Lectures Delivered in 1892 on the Percy Turnbull Memorial Foundation in the Johns Hop-*

Interaction with Students Outside the Classroom

Because she taught all the required Greek courses, Grace came into close contact with freshmen and sophomore students. She also served as advisor for some of her Greek students. Comments in letters show affection coupled with a tolerant amusement at her single-minded focus on the world of the mind.

I took Miss Macurdy, our Greek teacher [to a piano concert]. You see, there being no gentlemen here, the girls have to act in that capacity, both with other girls and with teachers.[13]

I should have thought that as Miss Macurdy is my adviser and as she is spending her vacation here and knew that I was to do the same she might have asked me over for tea or something instead of saying with a far away Grecian expression "Yes—oh yes are you going to be here Miss Shipp—ah— well, come and see me." She's awfully sweet but I wish she'd come down to earth now and then. She doesn't do half as much for her charges as other instructors do.[14]

To-day I went to see Miss Macurdy [after receiving a flunk-note in algebra] and she was a perfect dear! I think she is just about as fond of mathematics as I am. She told me not to worry, and since I didn't like math, merely to try to pass the exam so I'd be through with algebra for good and all. She said (ahem!) that I did so well in everything else she was sure I wouldn't flunk. Well that's all she knows about it, but she was mighty nice, and said she would go see Miss Smith and tell her how hard I worked over it.[15]

Yesterday we did an extravagant thing. We went to see "Buffalo Bill," who is in town. We were talking about him at the table at lunch yesterday and some

---

kins University (Boston: Houghton Mifflin, 1893), 156. This type of florid writing appealed to Leach, but it is difficult to imagine what the students made of this quotation, especially since Leach has omitted its beginning, in which Jebb indicates he is talking about Pindar's place in the history of Greek literature. The "French critic" in the second quotation is Henri Joseph Guillaume Patin; Leach is borrowing the translation of Arthur Sidgwick in the introduction to his edition of Aeschylus's *Agamemnon* (Oxford: Clarendon Press, 1881), xiii.

13. Adelaide Claflin '97 to "Mamma," 21 January 1894, Vassar College Student Materials Collection, Vassar Archives.

14. Margaret M. Shipp '05 to "Dearest Mamie," 5 April 1902, Vassar College Student Materials Collection, Vassar Archives.

15. Margaret M. Shipp '05 to "Dearest Mamie," 7 March 1902, Vassar College Student Materials Collection, Vassar Archives.

of the girls were describing the glories of his exhibition to Miss Macurdy. She listened with a great deal of contempt at first. She has never even been to a circus in her life, her taste running chiefly to Latin and Greek plays and Boston lectures. But she really became interested in Buffalo Bill's career, and said she really believed she would like to go. I think she was most induced by the fact that Buffalo Bill is the brother of Mrs. Irvine, the President of Wellesley College. . . . Miss Macurdy amuses us so much sometimes—I used to read jokes about Boston people in the newspapers, and thought them all very much exaggerated, of course. But Miss Macurdy certainly goes far ahead of anything I ever read about Boston intellectuality.[16]

The students were certainly jesting about the President of Wellesley College, since Julia Irvine[17] was not related to William Frederick Cody ("Buffalo Bill"); they had cleverly chosen a strategy calculated to appeal to Grace's interests. One wonders, however, whether they ever suspected that this paragon of "Boston intellectuality" was the first member of her family to attend college and came from a socioeconomic class that would hardly be recognized by the Brahmins of that city.

Grace's head wasn't completely in the clouds, however, since she showed an avid interest in politics: "Though we don't hear much talk about outside things here as a rule, there was a great deal of interest in the [1894] elections. Miss Macurdy talked about them with more interest than I ever ~~heard~~ saw her show anything not connected with Greek. She talked politics at every meal for three weeks beforehand."[18] Although both faculty and students were prohibited from participating in the suffrage movement by Vassar's president, James Monroe Taylor, the students staged a full-fledged political campaign during every presidential election year, at the end of which the entire college community voted for the candidates. Grace helped the students with their elaborate preparations for various campaign events, one of which is described in detail by Adelaide Claflin:

---

16. Adelaide Claflin '97 to "My dear Mother," 19 May 1895, Vassar College Student Materials Collection, Vassar Archives. Claflin's scrapbook contains a ticket stub dated 18 May on which she has written Miss Macurdy plus the names of eight students.

17. Julia Josephine Thomas Irvine (Cornell BA 1875 and MA 1876), professor of Greek at Wellesley College, served as president of the college from 1894 to 1899.

18. Adelaide Claflin '97 to "Ed," 11 November 1894, Vassar College Student Materials Collection, Vassar Archives. Claflin states that Grace was a Republican, like most of the students, although many of the faculty were Democrats. Grace apparently changed parties later, since she indicated on a 1928 Radcliffe alumnae questionnaire that she was a "Registered but not faithful Democrat." *Notable American Women* files, MC 230, box 54, Schlesinger.

Friday evening we had another campaign demonstration. Mr. McKinley received four delegations at his home. That is, we had a girl dressed up as Mr. McKinley, another as his wife, and a corner of the Lecture Room fixed up as the porch of his house. . . . Of course the Lecture Room was crowded, so we had to have police to clear a path for the delegations. There were two delegations of workingmen, who were dressed up in old coats, overalls, old straw hats, etc. and they carried implements such as the hods that bricklayers use for carrying bricks, etc.—where they managed to get them I do not know. The head of each delegation made a short speech to Mr. McKinley, and then he replied, and afterwards invited them to shake hands with him and his wife. Another delegation was composed of dudes,—"Young Men's McKinley Club from Chappieville." They were splendid—You would not believe that intelligent girls could look so much like inane dudes. Of course most of them wore eye-glasses, and cork mustaches, and parted their hair in the middle, and for canes they carried short window-poles, with brass ends, which they held in their mouths a good part of the time. The last delegation was the "New Woman's Gold Standard Brigade," which they asked me to see to. I got Mary MacColl to make the speech, and she was fine—dressed up in the most severe and strong minded fashion, with her hair twisted into a tight knot, and big spectacles on. She made a fierce and emphatic speech in the regular old Woman's Rights style, jerking her head and continually taking off her spectacles and using them in gesturing. After her speech I read an "ode." . . . I was entirely a different type from Mary—the high-faluten [*sic*] simpering type of the New Woman. . . . Some of our delegation were rigged out in swell things and others—the strong-minded species wore bicycle suits. . . .

Last night the Gold Democrats had a mass-meeting. They are few in number but they happen to have in their ranks some fine speakers, so they had a very entertaining time. Republicans were invited to the meeting, on the ground that "there is yet time to reform." Secretary Whitney, Grover Cleveland, Col. Breckinridge and others made speeches—very bright ones. The girl who represented Grover Cleveland was made to look pretty much like him, and wore a stove pipe hat, which greatly added to the impression. A novel feature was the presence of the "shades of the old 'true' Democratic party"—Jefferson and three or four others. They were entirely covered by sheets and [carried placards] which said, "The True Democracy, present in spirit."[19]

---

19. Adelaide Claflin '97 to "My own dear Father," 18 October 1896, Vassar College Student Materials Collection, Vassar Archives. At this time, the word "dude" was used to describe men who were fops or dandies, overly fastidious about their clothes.

Anita Hemmings

When Grace befriended a student in her Greek B course, she inadvertently became involved in a cause célèbre that hit the newspapers in August 1897. Anita Hemmings was an attractive, olive-skinned young woman with black hair and dark eyes who enrolled as a freshman at Vassar in 1893. Popular with her fellow students, she was involved in a number of extra-curricular activities, including glee club; she was also intelligent and studious, with an excellent academic record. In her junior year she had taken Professor Leach's Greek A, the short course for those students who had not studied Greek in secondary school, and she enrolled in Grace's Greek B course in the fall of her senior year. Grace took a special interest in this enthusiastic student from Boston, and Anita chose to confide in Grace when her world was about to fall apart.

Anita's roommate had apparently become suspicious about her origins and had asked her father to look into Anita's family background. The detective hired by her father easily discovered that Dora Logan and Robert W. Hemmings, Anita's parents, were both of mixed racial heritage, and Anita had grown up among the Black community in the Roxbury neighborhood of Boston. When her roommate, outraged, moved out of their room, Anita told her story to Grace, explaining how her high educational aspirations had been recognized by a wealthy Back Bay woman who had become a kind of patroness, paying for Anita to attend Dwight L. Moody's Northfield Seminary after graduating from the Girls' English School in Boston so that she could prepare for college. When Anita applied to Vassar, she had not mentioned her racial heritage, recognizing that she would not be admitted if this were known.

Although Grace was far from a bigot, she had not wholly escaped her society's unthinking racial prejudices.[20] This girl's plight, however, cried out for justice. Grace saw in Anita her own passionate desire for an education; she herself had come from a poor background that had nearly kept her from attending college. Most importantly, Anita had earned her degree by dedication and hard work, and it should not be withheld now because of an accident of birth. Vassar's records are silent about what happened next, but the outcome is revealed in the flurry of newspaper articles that appeared after the story broke in August:

---

20. For example, this is the way Grace described one of her summer session classes at Columbia in a letter to Gilbert Murray: "I had my usual strange collection of Jews, Catholics, a negro, and usual Americans of a pleasant type, in my beginning class." 30 August 1913, MSS Gilbert Murray 157, fols. 185–86, Bodleian.

The kind-hearted professor, a woman, wiped away the girl's tears and spoke words of encouragement. Then she went to President Taylor with the story and pleaded with him not to deprive the girl of commencement honors and a diploma. The faculty considered the matter gravely. Never had a colored girl been a student at aristocratic Vassar, and professors were at a loss to foresee the effect upon the future if this one were allowed to graduate. Yet there was nothing in the college rules that prohibited a colored woman from entering Vassar. Commencement was but a few days off and the girl would soon be gone and forgotten. So it was decided to conceal the facts and to allow her to graduate with her classmates. On class day and commencement the young woman took a prominent part in the exercises, and of all the hundred or more girls in the class of '97 none looked more attractive or acted more becomingly than this girl of negro birth.[21]

After graduation, Anita began working in the Catalog Department of the Boston Public Library, where Grace's sister Theodosia, head of the Ordering Department, had perhaps helped her to obtain this position.

Family atters

Grace went back to the family home on Fayette Avenue in Watertown in the summers (see figure 11 for photos of Rebecca and Angus in the 1890s). Although a portion of Main Building, where Grace lived, remained open during holidays in the school year, the building was closed completely over the summer. It was good to spend time with her family, all of whom were still living in Watertown, but the summer of 1895 was very draining due to her mother's serious illness. A lifetime of hard work had taken its toll on Rebecca, who was dying of chronic kidney disease at the relatively young age of 58. Grace did her best to ease her mother's suffering, but there was little she could do as her mother's legs swelled and twitched, her skin itched fiercely, and she grew progressively weaker, seeming to struggle for every breath. Grace did not return to Vassar for the opening of school that fall, and on September 22 Rebecca died, surrounded by the family she had loved and cared for so tirelessly. As soon as the funeral was over, Grace returned to Vassar, where Profes-

---

21. "Negro Girl at Vassar," *The World*, 16 August 1897, 1. This New York newspaper, owned by Joseph Pulitzer and known for its liberal leanings, published in its Sunday Magazine section a sympathetic full-page spread, complete with numerous drawings, purporting to tell "the true story" of Anita Hemmings: "How a Negro Girl Slipped Through Vassar College," *The World*, 22 August 1897, 25.

sor Leach and new instructor Lida Shaw King were covering her courses. Her sense of loss, however, was profound and difficult to alleviate, though she was touched by the sympathy and concern shown by her students.

With Rebecca gone, summers at the house in Watertown were less inviting. In 1896, Theodosia Macurdy and her friend Helen G. Cushing, a school teacher who was boarding at the Macurdy home, each purchased an undivided half share in a parcel of land in North Falmouth on Cape Cod, where Grace's brother William T. Macurdy had also purchased a cottage for his family.[22] They engaged a carpenter in 1897 to build a two-story shingled house with wrap-around porch (see figure 12) on what is now Garnet Avenue. Since Grace planned to spend her summers with Theodosia in North Falmouth, she became acquainted with the carpenter. To her surprise, after he had completed work on the house he asked her to marry him. Although flattered by the proposal, Grace turned him down gently but firmly; she had resolved never to marry, realizing full well that for a woman, marriage would present a nearly insurmountable obstacle to fulfilling her life's ambition to become a Greek professor and acknowledged classical scholar. Grace never referred to this proposal in any of her extant letters; for her, this was evidently not as momentous a decision as it would have been for many other women of the period. Rather, she told the story as a humorous anecdote associated with the house when she sold it to her nephew Ernest Macurdy in 1945.[23] Theodosia, Grace, and Helen enjoyed summers at the "beach house" until 1907, when the sisters decided that they wanted to pursue other activities; from 1908 to 1918, Grace would spend her summers in New York City, teaching in the Columbia University summer session.[24]

Grace's family in Watertown suffered more losses over the next ten years. Sister Edith's first child, Rebecca Elizabeth Skinner, a bright, attractive little girl named after her grandmother, began to sicken inexplicably in the middle of her fourth year, dying on September 15, 1898. An autopsy revealed that

---

22. Helen Cushing later worked as assistant to Theodosia in the Ordering Department of the Boston Public Library, and the two women lived in adjacent apartments at 175 Dartmouth Street in Boston.

23. Information about this comes from Grace's great-niece June Macurdy Landin, daughter of William T. Macurdy's only son Ernest, who purchased the house from Grace and whose family summered there for many years. There is thus no documentary evidence for the proposal, but this type of family lore is generally reliable.

24. In 1907, Theodosia sold her half-interest in the house and property to Helen Cushing, who subsequently increased the property by small purchases of land around the house. When Cushing died in 1929, she left the house to Theodosia, and Grace and Theodosia purchased the surrounding land. Grace became sole owner after Theodosia's death in 1933. Since she did not use the house often and was in need of money for an operation, she sold the house to her nephew Ernest Macurdy in 1945 (see chapter 11). The house still stands at 49 Garnet Avenue.

she had died of clear-cell sarcoma of the kidney, a rare disease that primarily afflicts children between the ages of one and four. Sister Maria, whose own first child, George Herbert Tarleton Jr., had died during childbirth (January 19, 1889), became increasingly ill at the young age of forty-three, dying of sarcoma on September 6, 1903, leaving two young children ages seven and eleven.[25] Meanwhile, Angus Macurdy, Grace's father, was becoming a difficult trial for those still living in the family house in Watertown. As he lapsed into dementia, his irascible temper and unpredictable behavior forced Theodosia and her brothers to commit him to the Westborough Insane Hospital in Worcester, Massachusetts, where he died on May 12, 1905, at the age of seventy-five.[26] Finally, brother William's third daughter, Harriet Thomson Macurdy, a promising girl of sixteen greatly loved by all the family, died of sarcoma of the femur on December 16, 1907.[27]

Becoming a Scholar

In 1893, the Society for the Collegiate Instruction of Women had attempted to merge the Annex with Harvard College; when these negotiations failed, the Society applied to the Commonwealth of Massachusetts for a charter as a degree-granting institution to be named Radcliffe College. Grace had maintained her ties with the Annex and her fellow alumnae, but in January of 1894 she was disturbed by an Annex-Alumnae petition requesting that the Society stop all efforts to obtain a charter for Radcliffe College. The petition maintained that this was a betrayal of the Society's founding purpose to integrate the Annex into Harvard College and to obtain Harvard degrees for women. Grace immediately wrote to Elizabeth Briggs, former president of the Annex Alumnae Association, that she was "not prepared to sign the petition without deliberation." Although she admitted that the increasing opposition to Radcliffe College had recently changed her opinion on the matter, she still hesitated to sign the petition for two reasons: "I fear it will be unavailing and again because in my conversation with Mrs Agassiz [president of the Society]

---

25. Maria's husband married again a few years after her death and moved away from Watertown; their children, Russell and Rosamund, did not remain part of the close-knit Macurdy clan.

26. His death certificate lists senile dementia as the primary cause of death, with lobar pneumonia relegated to contributory cause. Death certificates for all the Watertown Macurdys are available on microfilm at the Watertown Free Public Library.

27. Sarcoma is a rare form of cancer, much less common than carcinoma; the fact that three Macurdy family members died of this form of cancer within the space of ten years is highly unusual.

I committed myself to the other view, honestly believing then that the change was a good one." Several days later, after carefully considering her position, she returned the petition unsigned, explaining her reasons in a second letter to Elizabeth Briggs:

> Although I agree with the petition in thinking that our certificate is better than a Radcliffe degree, there are many considerations which prevent my criticising the Society in public. I believe that they are as anxious for the full Harvard degree as we are and that they regard Radcliffe as a step only. I think a private expression of our views better than the public one which will only sharpen the weapons of the numerous enemies of the Annex. Miss Leach is in sympathy with the petition and was much disappointed at the result of "Radcliffe College."[28]

In the end, forty-eight alumnae signed the petition and nineteen did not. Although she was in the minority, Grace's decision reflected her strong distaste for public confrontation, a characteristic that Abby Leach did not share. Leach, however, was not qualified to sign the petition since, though she had been a special student at the Annex, she had not taken the full course and earned an Annex certificate.

In 1896, the alumnae nominated Grace to serve as an associate of Radcliffe College, and she was unanimously elected to a three-year term by the board of associates (equivalent to a board of trustees). Other members of the board at this time included not only the presidents of Radcliffe and Harvard, but also her revered classics professors William Watson Goodwin and James Bradstreet Greenough. This contact rekindled her passion to gain recognition as a Greek scholar, a desire that had been temporarily suspended due to her heavy schedule of classes and her struggle to become an effective teacher. In Cambridge, she learned that the Woman's Education Association (WEA) of Boston was offering fellowships of $500 for study abroad to women "who give promise of actual distinction in the subject to which they are devoting themselves . . . through original gifts, previous training, energy, power of endurance and health." To apply, she was required to submit her college diploma, testimonials of "superior ability and high character" from her professors or other qualified judges, evidence of excellent health, a statement of proposed scholarly work after the year of study, and examples of papers or articles already completed.[29]

---

28. Grace H. Macurdy to Elizabeth Briggs, 16 January and 21 January 1894; Elizabeth Briggs Papers, 1883–1937, SC 3, box 1, folder 3, Radcliffe College Archives, Schlesinger.

29. *Fellowships and Graduate Scholarships Offered to Women by Colleges, Universities, and Societies in the United States,* Publications of the Association of Collegiate Alumnae, series III,

Excited by the prospect of a year of study and scholarship, especially in Europe, Grace carefully considered her options. She sought the advice of Abby Leach, who explained that if she won the fellowship, she would have to resign from her position at Vassar, but she assured Grace that she would be hired again after the year abroad. Grace knew if she lived frugally, the $500 plus her meager savings would cover her expenses, but she also needed the blessing of her family, since she would not be able to send money home that year to contribute to the college fund for her younger brothers. In preparing her application, she worked very hard on the essay describing her scholarly ambitions, since as yet she had no papers or articles to submit. She also asked for testimonials from her Harvard professors, and probably from Abby Leach as well. James Bradstreet Greenough, her Latin professor at the Annex, later sent her a letter describing his testimonial:

> I have already written to Mrs. Hallowell [Chair of the WEA Committee on Fellowships] a recommendation to the effect that 'you were one of our favorite pupils at Radcliffe and an excellent specimen of the finished product, a lady of fine strong character, excellent abilities and superior attainments.' And further that 'I could hardly imagine a better place for educational investment being sure that you would well repay any such outlay.' I am so confident of the truth of all this that I am willing to say it to your face. If you prefer to have me send this in any other form pray let me know and I will do so.[30]

Grace was overjoyed when she was awarded a WEA foreign fellowship for 1899–1900. Since she had the highest aspirations for scholarly achievement in classical philology, she knew that she must go to Germany, specifically to the University of Berlin, where the most famous Greek scholar of the time, Ulrich von Wilamowitz-Moellendorff, taught along with many other distinguished classicists. The University of Berlin did not allow women to matriculate, but they might attend lectures and occasionally seminars as *Hospitantinnen* (auditors) after obtaining the written consent of the Prussian Minister of Education, the Rector of the University, and the professor of each course. Grace had

---

number 2 (July 1899): 20.

30. J. B. Greenough to Grace H. Macurdy, 19 January 1899, Biographical Files: Macurdy, Grace Harriet, folder 2, Vassar Archives. This may strike a modern reader as both unduly vague and paternalistic, but it was evidently the kind of "testimonial" the committee was seeking. Grace herself may have cherished this letter, since it was found among her papers when she died. In any case, Grace's scholarly career certainly bore out Greenough's prediction about the payoff for the Association's "educational investment."

the benefit of advice from Winifred Warren, who had studied for a semester at Berlin before teaching Latin at Vassar, and Susan Braley Franklin, who had begun teaching at Vassar at the same time as Grace and was spending 1898–99 at the University of Berlin. Since the University required a passport, Grace applied for one in June 1899. Her application was complicated by the fact that she had no birth certificate to prove that she was born in the United States, but fortunately the Justice of the Peace receiving her oath was her brother-in-law Henry Skinner, and his sister Lillian testified to the truth of her statements on the application.[31]

Grace was nervous about her German, since she had not begun study of the language until entering the Annex and had had only two years training there. Though she had achieved excellent grades and had subsequently acquired a good reading knowledge of the language, she was hardly fluent in speaking and writing German. Moreover, though she was now thirty-three years old, she had never traveled farther from her home than Poughkeepsie. So it was with some trepidation that she boarded the ship that would take her to Germany, though her courage was bolstered by her determination to succeed and by the knowledge that this year of study would significantly advance her progress toward her life's goal of achieving recognition as a Greek scholar.

After completing nearly a semester of study at Berlin, at the request of the recently founded alumnae journal *The Radcliffe Magazine* Grace wrote an article on "Women at the University of Berlin," dated February 12, 1900. Characteristically, she says little about her personal situation and includes light, humorous touches. For example, after giving a breakdown of the 406 women currently attending the university according to national origin (240 from Germany, 110 from Russia, 42 from America, 5 from England, etc.), she comments on the listing of one woman from Siam:

> My curiosity was so aroused with regard to the so-called Siamese that I asked the university-secretary about her and learned the comparatively unexciting fact that she was German, had taught in Siam, and was now in Berlin with her husband, a German officer. We are quite used to Japanese college girls

---

31. Grace's second passport application, in 1922, presented more difficulties, since she was asked about her father's naturalization. She first wrote "before the Watertown, Mass. Court," then crossed that out and wrote "(probably Watertown, Mass.)," then crossed that out and wrote "(do not know)." Her confusion is understandable, since it is probable that Angus was never naturalized. Mary Frances Macurdy, her brother John's wife, testified to the truth of her statements but had to attach a detailed letter explaining her relationship to Grace and how she knew that Grace was a native-born citizen.

now-a-days, but a Siamese in that capacity seemed so unique that I was sorry to have the illusion dispelled.[32]

Grace notes that the "women students are by no means a unity." She describes a special room for women students where they can, upon payment of a mark each month (22 cents at 2016 prices), rest between classes and obtain tea or a snack, but she notes that no more than forty women use this facility (from her description it appears that she was one of the forty). She says she has heard of a movement "to promote the common interests of the women students" but doubts whether it could succeed because the women are so isolated and diverse that they have few interests in common and even less leisure to pursue such a cause.[33]

Grace was admitted to the lectures of three great classical philologists. She had high praise for the renowned Ulrich von Wilamowitz-Moellendorff: "All that he says is stamped with individuality and full of vitality. . . . I have never heard a more eloquent speaker." She was also enthusiastic about Hermann Diels, noting that his lectures on the development of Greek religion "are most suggestive and valuable." Her comment about Adolf Kirchhoff— "Professor Kirchhoff's work is characteristically German in its thoroughness and exhaustiveness"—suggest that his lectures may have been less invigorating than the others. She also haunted the great museums of Berlin and attended the lectures of three well-known classical archaeologists: Reinhard Kekulé von Stradonitz, Hermann Winnefeld, and Erich Pernice: "Professor Kekulé von Stradonitz lectures in the Museum every Wednesday morning on Greek sculpture, and Drs. Winnefeldt [*sic*] and Pernice often hold their lectures on Greek Vase-painting and Topography of Athens in the antiquarium and Museum." Grace also received the less-common privilege of attending the Greek section

---

32. Grace H. Macurdy, "Women at the University of Berlin," *The Radcliffe Magazine* 2 (1900): 135–38. It is unlikely that very many Japanese girls attended American colleges by 1900, but Grace was doubtless thinking of Yamakawa Sutematsu (later Princess Oyama), who graduated with honors from Vassar in 1882 and was the first Japanese woman to receive a bachelor-of-arts degree, and her friend Shigeko Nagai (later Baroness Uriu), who completed a three-year course in Vassar's School of Music in 1881.

33. Sandra L. Singer has compiled a database of over 1,350 women from the United States and Canada who studied at German-speaking universities: *Adventures Abroad: North American Women at German-Speaking Universities, 1868–1915* (Westport, Conn.: Praeger Publishers, 2003). Although Grace Macurdy is included in this database, Singer's text focuses primarily on the women who obtained degrees from these foreign universities. Macurdy shared some of the characteristics of the women discussed by Singer, notably their "search for knowledge, prestige, and women's advancement," but she emphatically did not come from the same socio-economic background shown by Singer's breakdown of the professions of their fathers, which "clearly situated these women in the upper and middle classes" (xiv–xvi).

of the proseminar, conducted by Diels: "There one sees the teacher born, not made, in the way in which he deals with the students' work,—full of sympathy for all good effort, but unsparing in criticism when occasion demands it." Since the proseminar required student recitation, presumably Grace's work was classified as "good effort."

Never one to complain, Grace mentions only a few disadvantages: "Lack of ventilation in the lecture-rooms, short days without the sun in winter, and slowness in the matter of getting books from the Königliche Bibliothek. But on the whole the pleasure and profit far outweigh the inconveniences." Indeed, the pleasure of uninterrupted study with these giants in her field, even if only as a *Hospitantinnen*, seemed like paradise to Grace, and when the university was not in session she visited classical sites and museums in Italy and Greece, savoring the special thrill felt by every classicist upon the first personal contact with these ancient lands. She also returned to the United States with a new fluency in the German language.

Earning the Credentials

When she returned to Vassar in the fall of 1900, Grace was immediately rehired as instructor of Greek with the same salary and teaching schedule. However, Abby Leach was taking a sabbatical in the spring of 1901, and Grace would be acting head of the department for that semester. Professor Leach was taking a well-deserved break after her 1899–1900 term as the first female president of the American Philological Association, an honor she had earned after two terms as vice president (at the time, all officers were selected by a three-person committee of officers rather than elected by the general membership). Leach was also serving as president of the Association of Collegiate Alumnae from 1899 to 1901, so she was at the peak of her career and national recognition. Grace herself was elected to a second three-year term as an associate of Radcliffe College in 1900, but of course this did not compare with the lofty offices held by Abby Leach.

In the fall semester Grace taught sixteen hours, including weekly English–Greek compositions from three classes, but in the spring she was at last able to teach some advanced electives with an eleven-hour schedule: Sophocles (*Antigone* and *Oedipus the King*), Aeschylus (*Agamemnon*), Advanced Composition, and a small graduate course on Euripides, as well as directing a master's thesis on "The Diction of Euripides." Although these were all new preparations for her, she was delighted to be able to teach at an advanced level subjects which she had studied so thoroughly.

After her year in Berlin, Grace was determined to secure the credential that would enable promotion to a higher rank and status as a fully-fledged Greek scholar. On the advice of Abby Leach, she decided to enroll in the graduate program at Columbia University, which had authorized the awarding of humanities doctorates to women in 1891. She was accepted as a doctoral candidate in the Department of Greek Language and Literature and began commuting to classes in New York City by train, although she was still teaching a full schedule at Vassar.[34]

Despite her teaching responsibilities and graduate courses, Grace enthusiastically accepted the invitation of John Leverett Moore, head of the Latin Department at Vassar, to become a charter member of the Latin Journal Club, a new group designed to keep members abreast of the latest articles on Latin literature and Roman culture published in classical journals. Each member was assigned several journals and asked to present periodic reports at the group's weekly meetings (the first meeting was held on March 6, 1902). Although Abby Leach and Ida Carleton Thallon (a new instructor in Greek) did not join the group, Grace's vision of classical studies encompassed both Greek and Latin, and she saw the club as a way to hone her scholarship while also forging closer ties with other classicists at Vassar. She also correctly surmised that reports and discussion would soon incorporate Greek topics as well. In her department report of 1891, Abby Leach had requested subscription to more classical journals, noting that these are "of the utmost importance, for from them I learn the latest results of classical study, of course, and as I rarely see any who are interested in similar lines of work with myself, they are almost my only source of knowledge about what others are doing."[35] However, Abby's disparagement of Latin prevented her from perceiving that this new club would help to resolve those issues. Grace, on the other hand, became a very active member of the club, never missing a meeting and regularly reporting on German and British journals.

---

34. Unfortunately, Columbia University has not preserved graduate transcripts earlier than 1910, so it is not possible to document the dates and titles of Grace's courses. She received her degree in June 1903, and Leach mentions that Grace was taking graduate courses at Columbia in 1901–2 in her department report for that year. She may have begun classes the previous year, but it seems unlikely given her exceptionally heavy teaching schedule in 1900–1901. In the "Life" published with her dissertation, Grace states that she studied primarily with Edward Delavan Perry, James Rignall Wheeler, and Mortimer Lamson Earle, her dissertation director.

35. Abby Leach, Report of the Greek Department 1890–91, box 3, folder 53, Vassar Archives. Handwritten minutes of the Latin Journal Club detail 382 meetings of the group from 1902 to 1935, when the name was officially changed to the Classical Journal Club, presenting a fascinating picture of the evolution of an unusual and innovative volunteer organization of classicists within a liberal arts college. Multiple Collections, box 1: VC Latin Journal Club, Vassar Archives.

During her two years at Columbia, Grace took the Greek Seminar, focusing on the dramas of Euripides and taught by Mortimer Lamson Earle (who frequently lectured in Latin) in 1901–2 and James Rignall Wheeler in 1902–3. She also took at least one other course in her major field (Greek language and literature) each semester, possibly Greek Lyric and Bucolic Poets, Demosthenes and Thucydides, Plato, or Aristotle. She was required to take one course each semester in two minor fields, probably Greek Archaeology and Latin (since one field had to be in a different department). Because of her excellent work in Greek at Columbia, Grace was invited to serve in June 1902 as a reader in Greek, grading examinations for the College Entrance Examination Board, a service she was to perform for fifteen years, acting also as examiner (designing the examinations) for three years.

Grace probably took fewer courses in her second year at Columbia, since she was writing her dissertation on *The Chronology of the Extant Plays of Euripides* under the direction of Mortimer Lamson Earle, known to be a meticulous and exacting scholar (he himself wrote his 1889 Columbia dissertation entirely in Latin). After her dissertation was approved, Grace had to pass oral examinations in her major and minor subjects and defend her dissertation before the Classics faculty. Columbia also required publication of the dissertation in bound and printed form, but Grace's dissertation was not printed until 1905, although she received her degree in 1903.[36] The reason for this delay is not clear; it may well have been due to the expense of typesetting a lengthy work with a great deal of Greek, German, French, and Latin (at 127 printed pages, her work was considerably longer than most classics dissertations of the time).[37] Since the candidate was wholly responsible for paying for this printing, it may have taken Grace some time to save enough from her meager salary to defray the cost.

At the age of thirty-six, Grace proudly received her doctorate on June 10, 1903, at the 149th annual commencement of Columbia University. She was one of thirty-nine recipients of the doctoral degree; the only other woman, Ida Helen Ogilvie (a graduate of Bryn Mawr), was a geologist. Reporting on

---

36. Grace Harriet Macurdy, *The Chronology of the Extant Plays of Euripides* (Lancaster, Pa.: New Era Printing Company, 1905).

37. In his survey of 46 American doctoral dissertations in Classics between 1899 and 1906, W. A. Heidel notes that the average length is 80 pages and that nearly 25 per cent of the 46 were written by women: "In quality their work averages well with that of the men, and their subjects cover almost the same range. This is significant for the higher education of women, which is having a growth in the United States without precedent. . . . [I]t is comforting to know that there is an increasing number of women admirably prepared to assume the office of instruction in the classics." "American Doctoral Dissertations in Classical Philology," *Classical Quarterly* 1 (1907): 242–48.

this commencement, the New York *Sun* noted, "The applause for the women graduates was very enthusiastic." Grace was the third woman, and the first American woman, to receive a doctorate in classics at Columbia.[38] The first, Lucia Catherine Graeme Grieve (PhD 1898), was born in Dublin and graduated from Wellesley in 1883; she did not teach after receiving her degree. The second, Gertrude Mary Hirst (PhD 1902), was born in Yorkshire, England, and educated at Newnham College in Cambridge; she taught at Barnard College from 1900 to 1943. She met Grace in the 1901–2 Greek seminar, and the two women became lifelong friends. Hirst published her dissertation in the *Journal of Hellenic Studies* under the name G. M. Hirst, in the British fashion; when her work was discussed in the *American Journal of Archaeology*, the use of masculine pronouns indicates that the author immediately assumed she was a man.[39]

The Chronology of the Extant Plays of Euripides

After receiving her doctorate, Grace was immediately promoted to associate professor of Greek. (Vassar had eliminated the rank of assistant professor in 1893; it was not reinstated until 1913.) Her salary was increased to $1,100, and she was able to obtain a suite of rooms (349 Main) that would serve as her home during the academic year until 1919. She made sure that she would not be mistaken for a man by having her full name, Grace Harriet Macurdy, and rank printed on the front cover of her dissertation. Nevertheless, a 1907 review of her book gives most of the credit to her male professor. Although the reviewer notes that the author presents her own "discriminating and sensible" judgment about the dating of each play, he states, "It was written under the direction of the late Professor Earle, and reflects in large measure his views upon the subject treated. One would expect a scholarly paper from such a source, and so it is."[40] It is hard to see where in this book the reviewer found Earle's views, since Grace writes with a strong and decisive first-person voice which should leave no doubt that she is expressing conclusions that she has reached through her own research and reasoning. In fact, when Earle

38. "Gov. Odell a Columbia LL. D.: One of a Notable Gathering Honored at Commencement," *The Sun*, 11 June 1903, 5. See also Charles Knapp, "Doctoral Dissertations in Classics, Columbia University, 1885–1933," *Classical Weekly* 27 (1934): 164–68.

39. G. M. Hirst, "The Cults of Olbia," *Journal of Hellenic Studies* 21 (1902): 245–67; 22 (1903): 24–53; and "Archaeological Discussions: Summaries of Original Articles Chiefly in Current Periodicals," *American Journal of Archaeology* 7 (1903): 230, 452.

40. C. F. Castle, review of *The Chronology of the Extant Plays of Euripides, Classical Journal* 2 (1907): 185.

presented his chronology and rationale in the introduction to his edition of *Medea* (published after Grace had completed her dissertation), his dating differs from Grace's in four instances, two of them significantly (*Andromache* and *Ion*). Interestingly, in both of these cases he includes another possibility that must have been suggested to him by Grace's work, though he does not acknowledge this.[41]

Grace's tone in this book is sober and scholarly. After a general introduction to the problem of dating the eighteen extant plays of Euripides, Grace presents in outline form her proposed chronology. She then discusses each play in turn, beginning with an exhaustive review of dates proposed by previous scholars, many of them French and German. She explains where she is in agreement with these scholars and points out what she sees as the flaws in their arguments (including many criticisms of the views of the revered Wilamowitz). She then thoroughly describes the evidence upon which she bases her own dating of the play. Finally, she concludes each section with a summary recapitulation of her reasons for rejecting other views and supporting her own. Her evidence is both internal (changes in poetic structure, metrics, choral odes—primarily technical and textual, not aesthetic) and external (later scholia, verbal echoes or parodies in Aristophanes, references to historical events). She is careful to avoid an over mechanical use of changes in meter for precise dating, but does acknowledge that these are "valuable, when due care is exercised, in indicating the period of composition."[42] Some of her strongest arguments, in fact, draw upon historical evidence, as expressed, for example, in the summary that concludes her discussion of the *Children of Heracles*:

> I hold, therefore, that Euripides wrote his Heraclidae in the first year of the Peloponnesian war, after the affair at Plataeae, to which I see undoubted reference in the play, after the first invasion of the Spartans under Archidamus, which is reproduced in the Argive invasion in the Heraclidae, and probably after the funeral oration pronounced by Pericles in the winter of 431. The play is most truly a "Gelegenheitsstück" [play prompted by a specific event or situation].[43]

Although scholars are no longer sure that we can (or should try to) establish an exact chronology for these plays, and although one may disagree with

---

41. Mortimer Lamson Earle, ed., *The Medea of Euripides* (New York, Cincinnati, Chicago: American Book Company, 1904).

42. Macurdy, *Chronology*, 106.

43. Macurdy, *Chronology*, 36.

some of the conclusions that Grace draws in this book, it is a remarkable piece of scholarship for a woman just establishing herself in the world of academe, demonstrating a high degree of maturity in her confident approach and carefully argued premises.

Grace immediately began to produce new scholarship based upon her dissertational work. Selecting a topic she had mentioned in passing in the book, she constructed an erudite argument against the view advanced by Wilamowitz that the extant text of Euripides' drama *The Children of Heracles* had been significantly revised in the fourth century; she submitted this piece to the British *Classical Quarterly*, which published her first article in the fall of 1907. She also published book reviews in the British *Educational Review* (1905) and the new American *Classical Weekly* (1907).[44] Grace wrote a paper on "The Two Electras" that she presented at the first meeting of the newly established Classical Association of the Middle States and Maryland, held at Columbia on April 26, 1907. Proud of her scholarship and anxious to promote her work, Grace mailed copies of her book to a number of major scholars with expertise on Greek tragedy, among them the British classicist Gilbert Murray, who had at that time published two volumes of Euripides' plays for the Oxford Classical Texts and several verse translations of Euripides, some of which had been produced on the London stage. Murray wrote to thank her for her treatise, "which I shall carefully consult before publishing the third volume of my text" (the letter eventually reached her, though addressed to Vassar College, "Lancaster, Pa," the location of the book's printer).[45] When Murray came to the United States in 1907 to deliver a series of lectures at Harvard University on the rise of the Greek epic, he accepted an invitation to visit Vassar in May with his wife, the former Lady Mary Howard, and to lecture on "Greece and Progress." This visit, during which Grace hosted in her rooms a meeting of the Journal Club in honor of the Murrays, began a lifelong friendship and transatlantic correspondence that was to play a meaningful role in Grace's life.

Paradoxically, these scholarly achievements precipitated a major crisis that nearly destroyed Grace's academic career before it was fully launched. To her amazement, Grace now had to combat a stubborn campaign by her department chair to oust her from her position at Vassar. This battle would persist for more than a decade and involve not only Abby Leach but also two succes-

---

44. Grace H. Macurdy, "The *Heraclidae* of Euripides. Has Our Text of This Play Been Mutilated or Revised?" *Classical Quarterly* 1 (1907): 299–303; review of *An Abridged History of Greek Literature,* by Alfred and Maurice Croiset. *Educational Review* 29 (1905): 314–17; review of *Euripides and the Spirit of His Dramas,* by Paul Decharme, *Classical Weekly* 1 (1907): 5–6.

45. Gilbert Murray to Grace H. Macurdy, 29 January 1906, MSS Gilbert Murray 157, fols. 185–86, Bodleian.

sive presidents of Vassar College, as well as the many other faculty members and students who were witnesses to this extraordinary conflict. Since none of the protagonists in this epic struggle knew the whole story, the following narrative will unfold through the perspectives of Abby Leach, Grace Macurdy, and Vassar presidents James Monroe Taylor and Henry Noble MacCracken.[46]

---

46. Leach's ongoing efforts to undermine and fire Macurdy are copiously documented through hundreds of letters in a large box in the Taylor Papers entitled "The Leach-Macurdy Conflict," as well as in the early MacCracken Papers. In the next chapter I will sometimes quote directly from these documents but often simply describe the individual attitudes as they are presented in the letters.

CHAPTER 5

Embattled

Abby Leach: "I do not trust iss acurdy"[1]

Abby Leach felt increasing distrust and suspicion as Grace gained scholarly credentials and connections. Although she had initially encouraged her to pursue a doctorate, Grace's attainment of the degree now seemed pretentious and her promotion to associate professor appeared to challenge Abby's supremacy in the department. Greek was *her* department; she had built it up from nothing and needed only loyal assistants to keep it running smoothly. Grace was becoming too independent; her enthusiastic participation in the Latin Journal Club, for example, smacked of disloyalty when Abby had refused to join, and her younger instructors, Ida Carleton Thallon (1901–3) and Leila Clement Spaulding (1903–7), had followed Abby's lead. She had allowed Grace to employ her own teaching methods until she began to suspect that, after her doctorate, Grace was seeking to impress students rather than to train them. At that point, Abby had begun to investigate Grace's work and found a 1904 student paper in Greek prose composition with flagrant errors that were merely underlined rather than corrected. When confronted with the paper, Grace had offered the feeble excuse that she felt students learned better by having

---

1. Abby Leach to James Monroe Taylor, undated [January 1907], Taylor Papers, box 8, folder 33, Vassar Archives.

to correct their own mistakes. Abby had told her that she must make all the corrections herself, since students would just fall into worse errors. Feeling that she could no longer rely on Grace's teaching methods, Abby herself took over the senior course in advanced prose composition in the spring of 1905, even though Grace had taught that course since 1900 and it was listed in the catalog under her name.

Abby decided that she had lost all confidence in Grace; for the sake of the Greek department, she would have to be dismissed. She first spoke to Ida Thallon, Vassar alumna and former instructor of Greek who was teaching in the Latin Department from 1906 to 1907, offering her Grace's position and explaining that she intended to make things so difficult for Grace that she would resign. Thallon, however, declined, stating that she had accepted an instructorship in the History Department. In January of 1907, Abby notified Vassar's president, James Monroe Taylor, that she intended to request the dismissal of Grace Macurdy in 1908. Meanwhile, she planned to hire Florence Mary Bennett (Vassar BA 1903) as an instructor in Greek in 1907 to replace Leila Spaulding, who was leaving to pursue graduate studies at Columbia. Abby confided her plans to Spaulding and Elizabeth Hatch Palmer, associate professor of Latin, justifying these with strong criticisms of Grace's teaching and scholarship.

Grace   acurdy: Annus Horribilis (1907)

Grace had been totally unprepared when Abby Leach suddenly waved a student prose paper in her face in the fall of 1904 and used it to attack her teaching methods in the freshman Greek class, since her department chair had previously left her to her own devices during all her years of teaching at Vassar. Because of the fierceness of the attack, Grace did not feel that she could protest when Abby subsequently took the course in advanced prose composition away from her. She was somewhat reassured when things quieted down after that, though she could not help but notice Abby's increasing coolness toward her.

Early in 1907, however, she was deeply troubled to learn from Ida Thallon, Leila Spaulding, and Elizabeth Palmer that Abby Leach was actively seeking Grace's resignation or dismissal from Vassar. It was lucky for her that Abby was so caught up in her own indignant planning that she was apparently completely unaware that her three confidants were all strong friends and supporters of Grace. Although Grace had heard nothing official, she decided that it

would be wise to put her own side of the case on record, and she accordingly
sent President Taylor the following letter:

> It is very far from being my wish to burden you in any way now and I do not
> ask you even to read the statement which I send you under another cover if
> you have no desire to do so at present. I have tried in this statement to tell
> you of certain facts which are known to others here and elsewhere as objec-
> tively as possible. . . .
>
> Miss Spaulding, who is not to be here next year, has shown great loy-
> alty to me under hard conditions and has repeatedly urged me to use her
> testimony even if that should bring her a loss of the Babbott fellowship [for
> graduate study]. This of course I could not think of doing at the time when
> her prospects could have been imperilled and I have the greatest reluctance
> to involve any of my informants in unpleasant relations with Miss Leach. I
> much prefer peace for them and for myself, "*sub libertate quietem*" as the
> motto of my own state has it, and I do not ask you to take any action, or, as
> I said, even to read the statement now, if you do not wish it.
>
> I shall feel more comfortable, however, with the knowledge that that [*sic*]
> you have in your possession—even if unread—a statement of facts which,
> unfortunately, are known here and elsewhere to some extent.

Her statement, which referred to "an alumna" and "a faculty member"
rather than naming individuals, contained nine points, including the job
offer to Thallon, attacks on Grace's work and scholarship, the recruitment of
a freshman student to spy on Grace, pressure on a student to drop an elective course with Grace in favor of one of Abby Leach's courses, arrangement
of courses in ways that kept students away from Grace's electives, and refusal
to assign any graduate courses to Grace despite her rank and credentials. She
concluded by asking "above all to be able to plan and carry on my own courses
according to my own methods."[2]

Besides this serious threat to her academic position and career, Grace was
also facing major turmoil in her family. Early in the year her youngest brother,
Leigh Theodore Macurdy, a lawyer with offices in Watertown and Boston, had
abandoned his fiancée and his profession, running away to another state and
leaving his sisters, predominantly Grace, to settle his many debts. This is the
same brother whom his family caught stealing money from Grace and his

---

2. Grace Macurdy to James Monroe Taylor, 6 June 1907, Taylor Papers, box 8, folder 33,
Vassar Archives. It is interesting that Grace's first move in 1907 adopted the technique most
recommended today for targets of academic bullying and harassment—make and file a record
of abuses.

brother's store when he was a boy (see chapter 3). Grace described the situation in a later letter to Gilbert Murray:

> I would like to tell you something of my really great sorrow—not the bother with Miss Leach of which I told you last summer, but things that go back to my young womanhood. My mother had a large family, nine of us, and high ideals of education for her means. I educated the two youngest brothers as a sort of sacred task, because my mother felt that her children must have college training, if possible. So I gave up all sorts of things for them, as we all did. But both of them drank. They were splendid physically and the youngest brilliant in his studies. The older one has given it up after many years of a sort of dissipation, has become a Catholic and married. He is a civil engineer and has always been good at his work. That is all very well. But the youngest one, who entered the law with brilliant promise, went to pieces absolutely from drink and nearly four years ago went to a western city, leaving us to settle his obligations as well as we might, and lives there under an assumed name and now will not write to or communicate in any way with us. I have made many efforts in vain to meet him. This is a very sordid story to tell you, but you will understand why I hate men's vices with such bitterness. My younger brothers, whom I remember as such lovely little boys of extraordinary beauty, have been a prey to them. My oldest brother, I must say, has always been a splendid man in his narrow Christian life, full of good works and my sisters are wonderful. But these two and the youngest above all have broken ~~my~~ our hearts. I hope that you will pardon my telling you all this and do not write anything about it. I do not wish that you should take any of your time that is so full to write to me. But I have wanted you to hear this about my life which has happened to go deepest, and to stand before other things.[3]

More tragically, Grace's niece, sixteen-year-old Harriet Thomson Macurdy, daughter of Grace's older brother William, was stricken with osteosarcoma of the femur, which metastasized to her abdomen. She was a lovely, sweet-natured girl beloved by the whole family, who helplessly watched her suffering great pain as the disease progressed to its inevitably fatal conclusion on December 16, 1907.

As this drama was playing out, Grace was very surprised to receive a note from the dean, Ella McCaleb, asking her to bring to the office a list of the stu-

---

3. Grace Macurdy to Gilbert Murray, 4 February 1911, MSS Gilbert Murray 157, fols. 15–18, Bodleian.

dents in her section of freshman Greek so that they could all be transferred to Florence Bennett's section for the spring semester. Abby Leach was, in the middle of the year and in a very public way, removing Grace from a course she had taught for fourteen years, with no consultation or advance warning. Abby later justified this lack of communication by saying that she did not want to trouble Grace on account of the illness of her niece, but of course the lack of warning gave Grace no chance to prepare a defense and only heightened the shock. It is little wonder that Grace later characterized 1907 as "a time which for many reasons has been the hardest through which I have been yet called to go."[4]

James   onroe Taylor: "We want peace and we want a fair division of work."[5]

President Taylor was deeply disturbed when Abby Leach informed him in January 1907 that she intended to petition the Committee on Faculty and Studies to dismiss Grace Macurdy from the faculty at the end of the following academic year. Although he respected Abby Leach for all that she had accomplished and contributed to Vassar, he was well aware of her inability to appreciate any perspectives other than her own. He winced when he remembered how she had accused him of persistent lack of support and unfriendliness toward her when he had refused one of her demands, so that he had been forced to write a rather severe response:

> Your charges of indifference to your work and bias against you are too absurd for belief. They grow out of your habit of measuring one's fidelity to duty by one's agreement with you. I am sorry, indeed, that you have come to test friendship by conformity to your own views of policy or theory.[6]

Unfortunately, this statement had had no perceptible impact on her attitudes or behavior, and he dreaded the battle that would ensue if she persisted in her efforts to dismiss Grace Macurdy. As he explained in a long private letter to Abby Leach, it was a matter of simple justice: Grace Macurdy had been

---

4. Grace Macurdy to James Monroe Taylor, 12 February 1908, Taylor Papers, box 8, folder 33, Vassar Archives.

5. James Monroe Taylor to Abby Leach, 11 February 1908, Taylor Papers, box 8, folder 33, Vassar Archives.

6. James Monroe Taylor, draft of letter to Abby Leach, 28 May 1897, Taylor Papers, box 8, folder 33, Vassar Archives.

appointed by the board of trustees as associate professor of Greek and had shown herself worthy of the appointment through her scholarship and teaching, so she should be given a fair share of the work of the department in accordance with her rank, and both professors should endeavor to cooperate for the good of the department and the college. He was saddened but not surprised by her response: "Nothing that you can do or say would change this position of affairs when I lose confidence in a person."[7]

When he learned about the transfer of Grace Macurdy's freshman students to Florence Bennett's class in the middle of the year without consultation, he wrote Abby Leach that he deplored "the effect of it on the general mind of the college or questions it must raise as to what a Board means by an Associate Professor" and notified her that he would have to bring the matter before the trustees' Committee on Faculty and Studies. He pointed out that the rift had escalated from small beginnings and that he could not discount personal motives: "So here, it is not the mere act, but the manner of it. It has never seemed to me that arbitrary power can work among college men & women to secure any independent teaching & scholarship."[8] In response, Abby Leach wrote a series of long letters formally requesting that the Associate Professor position in Greek be withdrawn and that Florence Bennett be retained as her assistant. She vehemently denied any personal motivation, claiming that she was acting from a disinterested wish for the best interests of the department and trying to save money for the college by substituting a lower-paid faculty member for "an Associate Professor for whom there is no legitimate work." Taylor, however, found it quite telling when Abby maintained that it was a mistake for Grace to get a doctorate: "She can not do acceptably the work that I need and she would not do willingly the work that I require. In fact the work is better suited to a younger teacher for it must be to a large extent supplementary. In a small department the work must have a homogeneity if the best results are to be obtained." He was dismayed that she had even considered taking her grievances to the students or to professors outside the college: "I might have taken Miss M's thesis and riddled it with my graduate students this year or last had I chosen but I did not. Neither did I take up some of the points and ask Prof. Perry [of Columbia University] as I might have done, how he could let such things pass." Her repeated attacks on his own motivation were, he felt, an insult to his position as president: "In view of the smallness of the department, I ask for what will conduce to its best good and you seem to disregard

7. Abby Leach to James Monroe Taylor, undated [January 1907], Taylor Papers, box 8, folder 33, Vassar Archives.

8. James Monroe Taylor, handwritten notes for letters to Abby Leach, 11 December 1907 and 30 January 1908, Taylor Papers, box 8, folder 33, Vassar Archives.

that and fix your thought only on one thing whether Miss M. will be denied any thing that she wishes. It is beyond my comprehension."[9]

In preparation for the committee meeting, Taylor wrestled mightily with the issue, making several lists of claims on both sides, seeking a resolution that would promote the best interests of the college and yet be fair to both parties. When he asked Grace Macurdy to write a letter stating her side of the case, she described her distress at the abrupt mid-year cancellation of her section of freshman Greek with no reason given except an accusation of "disloyalty" to Abby Leach. She described her graduate work at Radcliffe, Berlin, and Columbia and noted with pride that she was to be the first woman to give courses in the academic program at Columbia: "In the coming summer I am to give by invitation of Columbia University courses which are counted for the bachelor's degree and the higher degrees in arts in Columbia." Her published work had met with approval by men eminent in the field, such as Edward D. Perry and James R. Wheeler of Columbia and Gilbert Murray of Oxford University. In support of this, she enclosed two personal letters from Gilbert Murray with statements praising her work on Euripides:

> Your letter, which happened to come at a time when I was depressed & rather disgusted with my work, gave me the greatest pleasure & encouragement. Besides caring for the poetry and the meaning of the plays, you are a real scholar and an understander of Euripides, which makes it that much the more valuable to me that you should like my work.
>
> It is a great pleasure to me to hear from you, and whenever you send me anything you have written, you may be sure of my reading it with keen interest. I have read your Heraclidae article before, and thought it made a very strong case.[10]

That so eminent an international scholar as Gilbert Murray should have such praise for one of his faculty strongly impressed Taylor; this was exactly the kind of recognition that Vassar needed to bolster its claim to provide women with an education equivalent to that offered to men at Harvard and Yale.

After the committee met, the chairman sent a copy of its decision to both Abby Leach and Grace Macurdy:

---

9. Abby Leach to James Monroe Taylor, 17 and 24 January 1908; 4 and 6 February 1908, Taylor Papers, box 8, folder 33, Vassar Archives.

10. Grace H. Macurdy to James Monroe Taylor, 28 January 1908; Gilbert Murray to Grace H. Macurdy, 15 August and 7 December 1907, Taylor Papers, box 8, folder 33, Vassar Archives.

The Committee on Faculty and Studies has taken under full consideration the statements of both parties to the controversy unhappily existing in the department of Greek.

The committee is in entire accord in the view that Associate Professor Macurdy has a definite appointment from the Board of Trustees and has the right to her present position in the department and to a fair share in its work:

It is the judgment of the committee that Professor Leach, as head of the department of Greek, is to be recognized as having the right to the first choice of classes and studies; and further that Associate Professor Macurdy has the privilege of offering any electives which she may prefer; and it is enjoined upon both to consult together and to co-operate in the work of the department:

The interest of the committee in the department leads it to feel willing to re-appoint Miss Bennett if Professor Leach finds room for the employment of both the associate professor and the instructor.

Taylor's cover letter to Abby acknowledged that she would be displeased with this result but tried to mitigate her disappointment by emphasizing the retention of Florence Bennett despite economic considerations. He also argued that "if talk can be quieted and a good outward appearance, at least, maintained, the department will be in a far better position before the college and the world than it could be if we were able to carry out your recommendation."[11] He felt that the contrasting responses that he received from Grace and Abby underlined the validity of the committee's decision:

I wish to express to you and the Committee on Faculty and Studies my heartfelt thanks for your action in my case. I cannot tell you what a burden the realization that you and they have not thought me unworthy has lifted from me. . . . I am desirous of cooperation with Miss Leach for the good of the Greek Department. It shall be my endeavor to prove worthy of the action which the Committee has taken. (Grace Macurdy)

I have seen Miss Macurdy and *as far as I can judge*, the matter of courses has been pacifically arranged. I think that you will not need to adjudicate the

---

11. Committee on Faculty and Studies to Abby Leach and Grace H. Macurdy, 11 February 1908; James Monroe Taylor to Abby Leach, 11 February 1908, Taylor Papers, box 8, folder 33, Vassar Archives.

matter and *up to my light* [heavily underlined] I shall try not to give grounds for offence. (Abby Leach)[12]

He was quickly to realize, however, that Abby's rage would drive her to more offensive behavior. Less than two weeks after the committee's decision, he received a disturbing letter from two graduate students in the Greek Department, Sarah Morris and Ruth Andrus:

An incident has recently occurred of which, it seemed to us, you should know. For a long time we have known something of the atmosphere in the Greek Department. The general management and changing of the courses have given and strengthened this idea in the minds of those students who have worked under the department.

Tuesday, February eighteenth, we met in the evening for our Greek Seminar in Miss Leach's room. She then expressed her feeling towards Miss Macurdy, to us as a class, giving as her reason the statement that five years ago she thought one of Miss Macurdy's prose papers poorly done, and from that time on Miss Macurdy's work had pulled down the department. This she intended to remedy by taking the Freshman work herself next year.

In connection with her criticism of Miss Macurdy's work, Miss Leach warned us against an exaggerated idea of Miss Macurdy's mental ability, taking up minor details of her Doctor's thesis and showing them untenable to prove her point.

Then Miss Leach requested that whatever we might hear in regard to the matter, we should give her the benefit of the doubt.

Our relations with the Greek Department have made the whole situation an extremely difficult one, both as regards our informing you and our work for the remainder of the year. For while if necessary we are willing that Miss Leach should know of our writing to you, still in view of our work under her, we wish that you might consider it confidential.

As graduate students we feel an added responsibility and need of advice in a rather difficult position.[13]

---

12. Grace H. Macurdy to James Monroe Taylor, 12 February 1908; Abby Leach to James Monroe Taylor, undated [February 1908], Taylor Papers, box 8, folder 33, Vassar Archives.

13. Sarah Morris and Ruth Andrus to James Monroe Taylor, 22 February 1908, Taylor Papers, box 8, folder 33, Vassar Archives. Sarah Morris (Vassar BA 1906, MA 1908) had a distinguished career as classics teacher and director of studies at the Baldwin School in Bryn Mawr, Pennsylvania. Ruth Andrus (Vassar BA 1907; Columbia PhD 1924) became a professor of education at Columbia Teachers College and acting director of the Institute of Child Welfare Research.

He assured the students that he would not speak to Professor Leach about their letter, but he had no such constraints when Abby herself boasted in a letter to him that she had also involved a Columbia professor in the matter. She related that she had had lunch with Professor James R. Wheeler of Columbia and had criticized Grace's thesis (he "thought the theory untenable"), had shown him the prose paper from 1904 ("he was shocked"), and had even told him about the transfer of the freshman Greek class: "He gave me much cheer and comfort by his ready appreciation of the situation." Taylor remembered that she had earlier patted herself on the back for not involving her students or professors from another institution but had now done just that. Amazed that she was so convinced of her own righteousness that she was totally oblivious of her own breach of professional ethics, he had no confidence that his own rebuke would have any effect:

> I am sorry that you felt it necessary to discuss her standing and her work with a professor of another institution. . . . Why, since she is here and is a member of this Faculty, should you care to attack her reputation outside? I confess to a feeling of sadness as I read what you tell me of this matter because, while I have felt all along that you need no defence as to your own standing and ability, this looks like a determination to force matters as far as possible against the express judgment of the committee which has in charge the Faculty and curriculum. The committee's vote was unanimous, and I am sure that its expressions are definite and I cannot think that you wish with your eyes open to expressly antagonize the committee of the Trustees.[14]

Grace   acurdy: "I am ready to be quoted."

On Saturday, May 16, 1908, Gertrude Hirst of Barnard College visited Grace; the disturbing news she brought prompted Grace to send three separate letters, with increasing shock and anger, to President Taylor that afternoon. Abby Leach had written "insulting" and "abusive" letters about her to several classics professors at Columbia (Charles Knapp, Edward D. Perry, and James Chidester Egbert Jr., director of the summer session) and even to Nicholas Murray Butler, president of the university. Up to this point Grace had taken a rational and conciliatory tone in regard to her department head, but she could not tolerate such an unconscionable attack on her scholarly standing

---

14. Abby Leach to James Monroe Taylor, 16 March 1908; James Monroe Taylor to Abby Leach, 16 March 1908, Taylor Papers, box 8, folder 34, Vassar Archives.

outside of Vassar: "This is regarded in Columbia as an academic scandal and I feel that I must protest to you and to the trustees against such conduct. . . . I am ready to be quoted." She obtained the letters and sent them to Taylor with the recipients' permission, though she specified that they "prefer not to have her [Leach] cognizant of the fact, as they wish no further controversy with her" (not surprising, Grace felt, considering her own experience of the results of "controversy" with Abby Leach). Grace was very dispirited by Taylor's response to these letters, however, since he minimized the attack on her, maintaining that Abby was primarily objecting to what she termed the "false" claim that Grace Macurdy was to teach a graduate as well as an undergraduate course at Columbia, and closing with the bromide, "She has hurt herself, not you." Grace had, in fact, been engaged to teach a graduate course in Greek drama during Columbia's summer session, and she wanted Abby Leach to be called to account for her unprofessional and hurtful behavior, but Taylor was clearly unwilling to take the matter any further. Protesting more strongly had not helped her case; she was still expected to be patient and accommodating in the face of Abby's rampage. Her response to Taylor's letter was restrained, but she could not suppress a hint of sarcasm in her final words: "I should be glad to accept your interpretation of the matter if it were possible. I will let the affair rest, regretting to have felt obliged to trouble you with it."[15]

Grace was acutely aware that her contract as associate professor was up for renewal in the spring of 1910, and she quickly realized that her department head was attempting to freeze her out of the department through attrition of courses and students. Ignoring the injunction of the Committee on Faculty and Studies, Abby refused to allow Grace to teach any new electives, not even the one course in Herodotus that she had requested. She would not allow Grace to move her Thucydides course to second semester, where it had a better chance of election, and she surreptitiously channeled students away from the courses Grace was allowed to offer. In contrast, the new instructor, Florence Bennett, was assigned a full schedule of Greek and archaeology courses, including graduate courses, although her highest degree was a BA in Greek. Grace, despite her superior training and degrees, had never been allowed to teach the graduates except in the spring of 1901, when Abby Leach was on sabbatical.

Fortunately, Grace had strong ties of friendship with all the faculty in the Latin department, including its head, John Leverett Moore, forged through long association in the Latin Journal Club. She remembered that Abby, with

15. Grace H. Macurdy to James Monroe Taylor, 16, 23, and 26 May 1908; James Monroe Taylor to Grace H. Macurdy, 26 May 1908, Taylor Papers, box 8, folder 34, Vassar Archives.

Florence Bennett in tow, had joined the Latin Journal Club in the fall of 1907 despite her earlier scornful dismissals of its value; Grace suspected that this was a belated effort to win over the Latin faculty. If so, it had backfired, and Abby had withdrawn from the club by February, with Florence joining her by the end of the year. John Moore was shrewd enough to see through the ploy and was determined to support Grace in any way he could. Besides offering Latin courses to Grace, which she taught very successfully, he also included her scholarly activities in his annual department reports, even though they were not strictly relevant: "the articles mentioned below belong properly in the report of the department of Greek and are given here in case they might be omitted from that report; they are all by Associate Professor Macurdy."[16] Professor Moore always offered her enough Latin courses to fill out her schedule, and the larger classes in that language meant that she was teaching more students than Abby Leach or Florence Bennett. Although she found it particularly pleasant and refreshing to teach in the welcoming atmosphere of the Latin department, she worried that this might look odd to the trustees when they considered the renewal of her contract; in the fall semester of 1909, for example, she had taught only three hours of Greek and nine hours of Latin. As she later wrote to President Taylor:

> I have been treated as a stranger in the Greek department for five years and more and I think you have no conception of the kind and amount of influence that has been used against my courses. I have heard it directly from students and also through friends in and out of the college. . . . I believe that with fair conditions I could make my Greek courses here as successful as I have my work in Latin here and my Greek work in Columbia. I know that you are very weary of all this, but so long as Miss Leach has refused me the privileges granted me by you and the trustees, my work has been hampered and hurt.[17]

Grace realized that her entire professional career was hovering in the balance; if she lost her position now, she would never achieve her goal of winning national and international recognition as a Greek scholar. Academic positions for women were still almost exclusively confined to the women's colleges, and none—with the possible exception of Bryn Mawr—was as good as Vassar. She was well aware that Bryn Mawr's president, M. Carey Thomas, favored male

---

16. John L. Moore, Report of the Latin Department 1907–8, box 3, folder 91, Vassar Archives.

17. Grace H. Macurdy to James Monroe Taylor, 18 October 1910, Taylor Papers, box 8, folder 36, Vassar Archives.

classicists, plus she strongly suspected that her lower-class social background would work against her in that quarter. Moreover, any college would look askance at a faculty member who had been dismissed from Vassar after sixteen years of teaching. Leaving Vassar would also be emotionally wrenching. She had made her life at this college, putting down strong roots of friendship and familiarity; she even loved the beauty of the place, so different from her early life in Robbinston and Watertown. As she wrote to President Taylor, "Next to the ties of home there is no place in the world so dear to me."[18] Since the initial challenge by Abby Leach, she had tried to keep her head down and carry out successfully as much teaching as she was permitted to do. She had published two reviews and four scholarly articles in three American classical journals, *Classical Weekly*, *Classical Philology*, and *Transactions of the American Philological Association*, and two articles in British journals, *Classical Quarterly* and *Classical Review* (see appendix 2). She had continued to serve as a reader for the College Entrance Examination Board and had earned an excellent reputation teaching in the summer sessions of Columbia University. She felt she had done as much as she could, but would it be enough?

Abby Leach: "It has been bewildering to be charged with making attacks and dealing hard treatment."[19]

Abby was increasingly convinced that the problems she faced could be traced back to Grace Macurdy. Yes, the reduction in the language requirement had cut the number of students taking Greek, but she could build up the department again by teaching the freshmen herself, keeping Grace away from the serious Greek students on the one hand and the popular archaeology courses on the other. Grace claimed that she had had good training in these subjects in Berlin and Columbia, but Florence Bennett had a more aesthetic side to her nature that suited her for these courses. Furthermore, Florence was adaptable and happy to serve as her assistant; she would offer no challenge to Abby's methods or plans for the department.

Grace was being lionized for her scholarship and publications, but Abby didn't find them impressive. Abby was going to prepare an article for publication when she found the time, but she had so many other responsibilities; Grace had never given a fraction of the work and thought to the department

18. Grace H. Macurdy to James Monroe Taylor, 18 February 1910, Taylor Papers, box 8, folder 34, Vassar Archives.

19. Abby Leach to James Monroe Taylor, undated [27 February 1910], Taylor Papers, box 8, folder 34, Vassar Archives.

that she had. Why didn't people remember that she herself had been the first woman president of the American Philological Association and also had served as president of the Association of Collegiate Alumnae for two years? Professor Goodwin had always praised Abby's work in Greek at Harvard but never could remember Grace Macurdy; it was Professor Greenough in Latin who had recommended Grace to Abby.

Most hurtful was President Taylor's favoritism for Grace after all that Abby had done for Vassar. He kept emphasizing personal motivations on Abby's part, but all she was doing was trying to protect her department and save money for the college. As she explained to him, "I feel that you have built up a wall of prejudice against me that is impregnable to any assertions of mine and yet I can not discover any foundation in fact. . . . The truth as I know it is that more and more Miss Macurdy in view of her supporters assumed towards me a rudeness of manner and a chip on the shoulder defiance."[20] Abby knew herself to be frank and outspoken by nature, but she was never underhanded or scheming. However, there was a charmed circle of Grace's friends on the faculty who were spreading rumors about Abby, publicly snubbing her at the dinner table, and creating such an atmosphere of hostility in Main Hall that Abby had applied to build a house on Faculty Row on Raymond Street, though she could ill afford the expenditure.

Despite all she had suffered, Abby was confident that she would prevail when Grace's contract came up for renewal in the spring of 1910. Her letter to the Committee on Faculty and Studies strongly emphasized the economic argument:

> I most earnestly beg that you will re-appoint Miss F. M. Bennett to the position she now holds in the Greek Department and that you will not re-appoint Miss Macurdy as there is no longer work for the latter to do. This was my request 2 years ago but then your answer was that there was a contract and the contract must be kept, so though I had not known of the contract before, there was nothing else to do but yield. I have lived strictly according to the terms you laid down for me 2 years ago and can challenge any one freely to produce one concrete case of any violation on my part, though I felt then and still feel that you gravely misconceived the situation when you took such action. There has not been an adequate amount of work for Miss Macurdy so that she has drawn a salary that she has not earned. . . . What I wish and have always wished and worked for is the highest efficiency of my department,

20. Abby Leach to James Monroe Taylor, undated [27 February 1910], Taylor Papers, box 8, folder 34, Vassar Archives.

and the arrangement that I propose not only would secure this but secure it at less cost. With this sole end in view, to make the Greek Department in all ways a credit to the college in the outside world as well as here, I respectfully present my request.[21]

James Monroe Taylor: "We cannot be blind to the fact that the issue is largely personal."[22]

Anticipating Abby Leach's renewed request to dismiss Grace Macurdy, Taylor wrote a confidential letter to the members of the Committee on Faculty and Studies asking for their advice, giving this summary of the dilemma:

> The question we shall have to face, therefore, is this: Is the college to lose a woman of scholarship and repute and a good teacher because of this personal conflict in the department, and to retain in her place, since only one will be needed, a much younger woman, in every way personally acceptable, but without the background of the scholarship or experience of the associate professor? What would be the effect on the college, and its reputation with other colleges? I may add the very important question, what will be the effect on the college and on Professor Leach herself if she be allowed to dictate to us in this matter?

Their responses unanimously favored retaining Grace Macurdy, and they advised Taylor to notify Professor Leach of their sentiments and encourage her to adjust herself to the situation. Florence M. Cushing, however, the only female trustee at the time, expressed doubts that such an accommodation would be possible: "From the interview held with Miss Leach last year and my knowledge of her temperament, I should judge that harmony was hopeless under these conditions." Taylor struggled laboriously over his letter to Abby Leach, continually crossing out and revising his words, ending with a heartfelt appeal: "I wish you could be persuaded to see how a reversal of your ~~attitude~~ proposition would make for the better interests of all. I doubt your knowing how strong is the general feeling. Not that that should move you if you are

---

21. Abby Leach to the Members of the Committee on Faculty and Studies, 1 March 1910, Taylor Papers, box 8, folder 35, Vassar Archives.

22. James Monroe Taylor to Abby Leach (draft), 17 February 1910, Taylor Papers, box 8, folder 36, Vassar Archives. Taylor had originally written "chiefly personal" and then substituted "largely," perhaps considering it more tactful.

right,—but shouldn't it make one ask earnestly if one is *surely* right? A general opinion of knowing friends should count."[23]

When Abby remained inflexible in her purpose, Taylor requested that Grace Macurdy send him her reflections on the nature and distribution of the courses in the Greek department, and he found himself agreeing with all the points in her long and thoughtful response. She argued that the courses in Greek life, vases and coins, and sculpture should be subordinate to courses in Greek literature and would be better taught by specialists and offered to advanced students. Even a course on Greek literature in translation, she maintained, "would contribute more to knowledge of the humanities than one descriptive of the extrinsic side of Greek life." Remembering what Abby Leach had said about the need for "homogeneity" in her department, he was particularly struck by Grace's statement that "The Greek literature in other colleges affords material for courses given by several people and I believe that it is for the best good of the student to hear the interpretations of different teachers of the subject. A monopoly of any literature is a dangerous thing."[24] He presented these arguments at the meeting of the committee along with a letter from Columbia professor Edward Delavan Perry testifying to the scholarly standing of Grace Macurdy:

> I have always regarded Miss Macurdy (that is, always since I have had good opportunities of observing her work at close range) as one of the best classical scholars in this country. She was here as a graduate student some years ago, while holding an instructorship in Vassar, and took her doctor's degree here in 1903. Her dissertation, on the Chronological Order of the Plays of Euripides, was an extremely thorough and creditable piece of work.
>
> For the past three years she has given the Greek instruction in the Summer Session at Columbia, and is to do so again this year. In this she has ~~received~~ achieved most excellent results. She is a very quiet person, and never sets off any fireworks or blows her own trumpet, but the thorough training and knowledge are there and she knows how to use them. We are always glad when a student whom she has trained comes to us.[25]

---

23. James Monroe Taylor to Members of the Committee on Faculty and Studies, undated [February 1910]; Florence M. Cushing to James Monroe Taylor, 10 February 1910; James Monroe Taylor to Abby Leach (draft), 17 February 1910, Taylor Papers, box 8, folder 34, Vassar Archives.

24. Grace H. Macurdy to James Monroe Taylor, 18 February 1910, Taylor Papers, box 8, folder 34, Vassar Archives.

25. Edward D. Perry to Laura Gill ("sent to Miss Cushing at her request"), 1 March 1910, Taylor Papers, box 8, folder 35, Vassar Archives.

At its meeting in March, the Committee on Faculty and Studies declined to reappoint Florence Bennett but did reappoint Grace Macurdy as associate professor of Greek, insisting upon a fair division of the work in the department and instructing Abby Leach to submit her schedule of courses for next year to President Taylor for approval. At the meeting, Taylor had argued for the retention of Grace Macurdy on all grounds—"loyalty, scholarship, devotion to work, industry, respect of colleagues, reputation abroad"—and he was greatly relieved that the matter was now settled.[26] He was not, however, looking forward to haggling with Abby Leach over the schedule of Greek courses.

---

26. James Monroe Taylor, handwritten notes, undated [February 1910], Taylor Papers, box 8, folder 35, Vassar Archives.

CHAPTER 6

Soldiering On

Grace acurdy: "That sort of thing
I suppose *vincendum ferendo est!*
[must be conquered by enduring]"[1]

Grace received the news of her reappointment with great joy, although her pleasure was somewhat tempered by the fact that the committee had set no term for the contract, letting it rest upon "the due consideration of our common interests."[2] She realized that if Abby kept restricting and undermining her courses, she might eventually convince the trustees that it was in their "common interest" to dismiss Grace on economic grounds. Thus Grace immediately wrote President Taylor noting that Abby Leach had scheduled seventeen hours of Greek for herself during the 1910–11 year but only five hours for Grace. Grace suggested a slight rearrangement of the schedule that would give her a place in the regular succession of courses in Greek literature: "Under the circumstances it appears to me reasonable to ask for one new course open, without the present discrimination against my work, to sophomores and

1. Grace H. Macurdy to James Monroe Taylor, 24 April 1910, Taylor Papers, box 8, folder 35, Vassar Archives.

2. James Monroe Taylor to Grace H. Macurdy, 8 March 1910, Taylor Papers, box 8, folder 35, Vassar Archives.

upper class-men and for a slight re-arrangement of my courses to make them consecutive and more likely to attract students, a motive which I believe is not reprehensible."³ The new course was the elective in Herodotus that she had been unsuccessfully requesting for the last two years.

Grace was well aware that she was not asking for much and that her tone was almost excessively deferential. She realized, however, that this approach had contributed to her success with the president and trustees, who welcomed it in contrast to the dictatorial demands of Abby Leach. Conciliation rather than conflict was her natural mode; verbal confrontation affected her like physical violence. She felt that her best strategy was to prove her merit through her work rather than trying to fight fire with fire. Besides, when she had taken a more assertive stance after Abby had written against her to the Columbia professors, Taylor had disparaged her protest, and he was always advising her to be "as patient as possible and as quiet."⁴

Recognizing that she had won a battle but the war was still raging, Grace did not change her tactics or insist on more prerogatives. With characteristic self-deprecatory wit, she coined a Latin phrase to explain to President Taylor that she would ultimately prevail through endurance: "I shall do my best to teach whatever courses you and the trustees think it desirable that I should undertake. . . . Miss Leach, of course, still denounces my scholarship in and out of the college. It has its annoying, but also its humorous side. She so often makes so poor a selection for her confidences. . . . But that sort of thing I suppose *vincendum ferendo est!*"⁵

James onroe Taylor:
"The breach shall be closed up"⁶

Taylor himself soon realized that the committee's decision did not bring an end to his troubles, for Abby Leach flatly refused to allow the Herodotus elective that Grace had requested. In fact, she wrote Taylor a letter which he later described to the Committee on Faculty and Studies as highly offensive: "It abounds in charges against my fairness, accusations of defamation of her to

---

3. Grace H. Macurdy to James Monroe Taylor, 16 March 1910, Taylor Papers, box 8, folder 35, Vassar Archives.

4. James Monroe Taylor to Grace H. Macurdy, 11 April 1910, Taylor Papers, box 8, folder 35, Vassar Archives.

5. Grace H. Macurdy to James Monroe Taylor, 24 April 1910, Taylor Papers, box 8, folder 35, Vassar Archives.

6. James Monroe Taylor to Abby Leach (draft), 18 October 1910, Taylor Papers, box 8, folder 36, Vassar Archives.

the trustees, & of 'my' purposes, having appointed an incompetent person, to adjust the work to her necessities. There is no hint of adjustment or compromise." Feeling that the situation was out of control, he asked for the committee's advice, concluding "Miss Leach's attitude convinces me that she must be made to see that she is dealing with her superiors. On the other hand I am counselling patience & moderate demands on the part of Miss Macurdy."[7] The committee unanimously judged that this was deliberate insubordination on the part of Abby Leach and insisted that she must allow the Herodotus elective. Taylor was exasperated, but not really surprised, when Abby still managed to thwart the committee's purpose by insisting upon an old prerequisite that prevented students in the Herodotus course from subsequently taking any other Greek courses, so Grace had to teach the course with only two students in the fall of 1910.

Amid this turmoil, Taylor was pleased to receive a letter from alumna Leila Spaulding, former instructor of Greek and currently graduate student at Columbia, that strengthened his support of Grace Macurdy. She wrote:

> A letter received from Professor Leach yesterday refers to the Associate Professor of Greek in such a manner that I wish to make clear my own relation to Miss Macurdy. Aside from my personal attachment to her which is of some fifteen years' standing, I have always admired her thorough scholarship and breadth of information.
>
> This conviction has been strengthened not only by the outspoken praise of her teaching from many undergraduates, but especially by the sincere regard for her ability and acquirements expressed by the members of the Classical faculty at Columbia. Only today I learned that a woman had been appointed Extension Teacher of Latin in Columbia largely because of "the scholarly work done by Dr. Macurdy in the Summer sessions which has gone far to remove the prejudice against women as teachers in the University."
>
> It is a source of genuine regret to me that Vassar cannot have the benefit of Miss Macurdy's training in Euripides. One who has been called "the best Euripidean scholar in the States" might do much with both graduates and undergraduates. However, anything that Miss Macurdy undertakes will be well done, whether it be archaeology or literature.[8]

---

7. James Monroe Taylor to Members of the Committee on Faculty and Studies, 15 April 1910, Taylor Papers, box 8, folder 35, Vassar Archives.

8. Leila Spaulding to James Monroe Taylor, 3 April 1910, Taylor Papers, box 8, folder 35, Vassar Archives.

Meanwhile, however, another crisis was brewing, as the master's thesis of Abby Leach's only graduate student at the time, Vara Whitehead, was rejected by two members of the thesis committee that was composed of Grace Macurdy and John Leverett Moore in addition to Abby herself. After Grace and Moore, head of the Department of Latin, refused to accept her thesis without revision, the Vassar faculty voted not to grant Whitehead the degree unless she presented an appropriately revised thesis in September. Taylor knew that the grounds for rejection of the thesis were fair and objective, but he was very disturbed by letters from Vara's mother and sister claiming that the thesis was not accepted because of "faculty jars & jealousies":

> You are convinced that the thesis was judged by a perfectly just committee, but it would be idle now for me to pretend that my sister and I know nothing of the friction in the department of the classics, friction which might extend to such lengths that it would sacrifice a student to gain its ends.[9]

Taylor could see the ripples created by the conflict in the Greek Department extending farther and farther afield, and he was at the end of his patience when he received a letter from Abby Leach saying that she had written to Wayland Spaulding, a distinguished Congregationalist minister and author, demanding to see his daughter Leila's letter "charging me with treating Miss Macurdy with indignity." He felt compelled to write to Reverend Spaulding apologizing for Abby's "extraordinary" demand, concluding with an expression of his own aggravation: "I am tired, even to the point of extinction, of the talk and exaggeration there has been in connection with this whole matter. If both sides to it and all their friends would keep still, there would be some hope for a comfortable solution of it."[10]

Despite his vexation with Abby Leach, he was moved by the tone of desperation in a letter she sent asking him to give Grace Macurdy a year's leave of absence with the understanding that she would not return in 1912:

> *I beg of you to do this.* If you have *any* regard for me, if you put *any* value on my work here, if you wish the dep't to be strong and efficient, I beg of you to do this. If you will, I will set a seal on my lips and let the sole reason be the smallness of electives. . . . I never dreamed you would re-appoint her for this year. You had emphasized *contract* and I thought when the 2 yrs. ended as

---

9. Vara G. Whitehead to James Monroe Taylor, 8 June 1910; Helen Whitehead to James Monroe Taylor, 3 June 1910, Taylor Papers, box 17, folder 72, Vassar Archives.

10. Abby Leach to James Monroe Taylor, undated; James Monroe Taylor to Wayland Spaulding, 7 June 1910, Taylor Papers, box 8, folder 36, Vassar Archives.

she had not had her courses elected and Miss Bennett had, that she would be the one to go. . . . I have been here 27 years and 24 years in charge of the department. Is *nothing* due me?[11]

He realized that she truly did not see that she herself had engineered the "smallness of electives" for Grace, though this could be viewed as a deliberate blindness on her part, and that despite his best efforts to explain she did not understand why it was important for Vassar to retain Grace Macurdy. Her last words clearly indicated that she could view the situation only through the lens of her sense of righteousness and preoccupation with her own status. His sympathy, however, did not prevent him from finally cracking down the following fall, when Abby again took away a course that she had previously assigned to Grace. As he drafted a letter to Abby, he struggled to express a threat strong enough to bring about at least a surface resolution of the trouble:

> The trustees ~~are feeling~~ feel very ~~deeply~~ strongly ~~about this matter because of the extent of the talk~~ that the trouble of last year, ~~which reached~~ which was discussed in other colleges, ~~and which has~~ hurt the influence of Vassar. They ~~were very~~ are strong in their ~~expressions to me~~ resolution that ~~this matter must be closed up~~ the breach shall be closed up, that there ~~must~~ shall be no further talk that ~~could~~ can injure the college, and that rather than have it continue it would be better to remove ~~the whole trouble on both sides and start afresh~~ all parties to the trouble. I can give you no better conception of the extent to which the feeling has grown in the committee than to say just that. That means of course that *neither on one side nor the other* will the trustees countenance hostile work or talk.

His letter to Grace said essentially the same thing, though he also stated that she had suffered very unjustly and that he had the utmost respect for her scholarship and teaching.[12]

---

11. Abby Leach to James Monroe Taylor, undated [5 June 1910], Taylor Papers, box 8, folder 36, Vassar Archives.

12. James Monroe Taylor to Abby Leach (draft), 18 October 1910; James Monroe Taylor to Grace H. Macurdy, 19 October 1910, Taylor Papers, box 8, folder 36, Vassar Archives.

Henry Noble   acCracken: "Certain matters will require a careful treatment"

In February 1915, Henry Noble MacCracken was reviewing the reports that he had requested from all college departments to give him essential background information as he began his presidency of Vassar. Although he had taught at Harvard, Yale, and Smith and had already published textbooks on Chaucer and Shakespeare, he was well aware that his youth (he was thirty-four) and lack of administrative experience put him at a disadvantage with the trustees. Thus, he was dismayed to see a letter from Abby Leach in place of a formal report from the Greek Department. The letter began, "I have been slow in handing in my report because I dislike to write what I feel I ought to write in the interest of the Department. As I told you, the effect of the present arrangement is, as it was bound to be, disastrous for the Greek. There has been given me a colleague drawing a high salary whose one concern is to try to keep enough students to enable her to retain her present position." She went on to criticize Grace Macurdy's involvement with the Latin Department, which she claimed caused "much interference with my courses," and accused her of refusing to recognize the authority of the head of the Greek Department. She urged MacCracken to transfer Grace to the Latin Department and move Katherine M. Cochran, the new instructor in Latin, to the Greek Department. Since he had been informed about Taylor's problems with Abby Leach, he realized that he would have to proceed with caution, as he noted in a memo: "Recommendations previously presented to the trustees are now again urged with respect to this department. Certain matters will require a careful treatment."[13]

MacCracken spent some time investigating the situation and concluded that he would have to act decisively now in order to prevent himself from becoming embroiled in the quagmire that had plagued his predecessor. Accordingly, his response to Abby Leach was concise and definitive. Only the head of the Latin Department could request such a transfer of faculty. He had decided not to revisit any of Taylor's decisions regarding the Greek Department. Her criticisms of Grace Macurdy were "neither specific nor substantiated by appended testimony," and he would not consider any charges that were not confirmed by documentation. He was relieved when Abby did not contest his decisions further, though, as usual, she still needed to have the last word:

---

13. Abby Leach to Henry Noble MacCracken, 27 February 1915; Henry Noble MacCracken, memo, undated [February 1915], MacCracken Papers, box 21, folder 2, Vassar Archives.

I have given the matter of the Greek Department serious thought and have
decided it is best for you to do nothing, intolerable as the situation is for
me. To open up the subject again would be merely to set tongues wagging
and stir smouldering embers into flame, without accomplishing anything of
benefit for the department but quite the reverse. . . . The department that I
built up, unaided and with unsparing effort, I have had to see spoiled in part
by the Faculty in changing the curriculum, and in part by the action of the
President in the retention of Miss Macurdy. The case seems to be hopeless
and without remedy. I do not believe, however, there is another college in
the country that spends or would spend the amount Vassar spends on such
a supernumerary. It is left for me to go on enduring what I have endured,
plainly.[14]

As he grew to know and respect Grace Macurdy, MacCracken realized that
he would have to take the initiative to make her position at Vassar permanent.
Accordingly, he himself nominated her to the trustees for full professor, supporting the nomination with an enthusiastic letter from the head of Latin,
John Leverett Moore, instead of her own department chair, whom he kept
in the dark until the promotion was a fait accompli by vote of the board on
February 8, 1916 (see figure 15 for a professional photo of Grace that may have
been taken at the time of her promotion). Many years later, while writing a
book about his thirty-one years as president of Vassar, MacCracken felt these
events were significant enough to include, though his wit and love of storytelling prompted an embellished version:

On the second day of my term there entered my office Miss Abbie Leach,
Professor of Greek, bearing a satchel which she emptied upon my desk.
"These documents," she said, "constitute the basis of my charges against Miss
Macurdy, the other member of my department." . . .

I stood up, gathered the papers solemnly, replaced them in Miss Leach's
bag, and placed it by her side. "Miss Leach, take back these papers, and never
let me see or hear of them again. My administration began yesterday. It will
never review what happened yesterday or the day before that. Any attempt
to the contrary will entail the most serious consequences."

There was a moment tense with electric frequencies in the academic air.
Miss Leach looked ready to explode. Then the air cleared, and ozone could
be sensed.

---

14. Henry Noble MacCracken to Abby Leach, 4 March 1915; Abby Leach to Henry Noble
MacCracken, 6 March 1915, MacCracken Papers, box 21, folder 1, Vassar Archives.

"At least we know where we stand," she said, and departed. I never heard the subject mentioned again by her.

Not that the matter was ended. When I recommended Grace Macurdy for promotion, as I did at the end of the semester, it was without Miss Leach's approval. In its place, I had a dozen letters from scholars of equal eminence in the faculty. Miss Macurdy won her way to eminence as a scholar, writer, and teacher, and today is remembered as one of the most distinguished professors in Vassar's long list.[15]

Grace   acurdy: "I do not know quite what iss Leach's object is"[16]

Grace was thrilled by her promotion to full professor and immensely relieved that her position at Vassar was now secure, though she was disappointed that the trustees had not granted her the full professor's salary of $3,200 but only $2,500, from which $700 would be deducted for room and board. She knew that Abby would continue to prevent her from teaching any of the main electives or advanced work in Greek, but she was always able to fill out her schedule by teaching at least one course per semester in the Latin Department. However, the ancient language requirement was changing as of the fall 1916 term; entering students could now substitute a year of Greek for the formerly required year of freshman Latin. Grace was surprised when Abby asked whether she would teach the new course of beginning Greek for freshman, but she agreed to do so. As she explained in a letter to President MacCracken:

> In this case I shall be obliged to give up my work in the department of Latin. This I regret, as I greatly prize my work in common with my colleagues of that department. I think it the part of prudence, however, to accept Miss Leach's suggestion for several reasons. The most important is that I think it would be unfortunate to have a new instructor come in the Greek department in consequence of this new arrangement while we have such good Greek scholars in the department of Latin who would be happy to teach Greek. I have gained so much myself from the opportunity which I have alone of the classical people enjoyed of teaching both languages and I am convinced that both departments would gain from this interchange. . . . I owe much to my Latin colleagues already in their encouragement of Greek

15. Henry Noble MacCracken, *The Hickory Limb* (New York: Scribner, 1950), 64–65.

16. Grace H. Macurdy to Henry Noble MacCracken, 15 May 1917, MacCracken Papers, box 23, folder 38, Vassar Archives.

studies here and if there could be a real rapprochement of the departments it would be a ~~real~~ renaissance for classics here, I firmly believe.[17]

When the fall arrived, however, Grace was chagrined to find that Abby took the new freshman Greek herself, leaving Grace with twelve hours in the fall but only eight in the spring, since she had given up her usual Latin course, while Abby was teaching fourteen hours (five courses) in the spring. She realized that this was a classic bait and switch, and she should have recognized that Abby had never intended to give her the class.

When Cynthia Wiley, one of her student advisees, came to Grace and told her directly that she had been pressured by Abby Leach to change from a Greek elective taught by Grace to one taught by Abby, Grace wrote a letter of protest to President MacCracken. Although this had happened many times before, she now had concrete evidence of Abby's tactics, especially since Abby had written to Cynthia's father, who had been a good friend of Grace's Columbia mentor, Mortimer Lamson Earle, and had sent Cynthia to Vassar expressly to study with Grace. As she wrote MacCracken, "I do not know quite what Miss Leach's object is in attempting to detach from me all the girls who would be eligible to take my elective courses. It is a procedure which is extremely bad in its effect on the students and brings contempt on the department. . . . She has apparently been even more active than usual and it has created much comment among the faculty and students." Grace was pleased to learn that MacCracken had investigated the situation further, had heard from members of the Latin faculty about more cases of this kind of pressuring of students, and had sent Abby a strong rebuke for this "highly reprehensible" behavior.[18]

Emboldened by MacCracken's support, so much more effective than Taylor's had been, Grace strongly seconded John Leverett Moore's proposal that the Greek and Latin Departments be consolidated:

With regard to the matter of amalgamating the departments of Greek and Latin at some future time I wish to say that I am thoroughly in sympathy with and believe that we could arrange a classical course that would be of greater service to the College if united than in our present state. I have had intimate relations with the department of Latin for many years and have taught in it with great pleasure. I feel sure of the harmonious working of such arrangement as that of which Professor Moore spoke to you. . . . The

---

17. Grace H. Macurdy to Henry Noble MacCracken, 28 May 1916, MacCracken Papers, box 21, folder 5, Vassar Archives.

18. Grace H. Macurdy to Henry Noble MacCracken, 15 May 1917; Henry Noble MacCracken to Abby Leach, 25 May 1917, MacCracken Papers, box 23, folder 38, Vassar Archives.

other members of the Latin department would hail enthusiastically the opportunity to teach Greek and there would in the end be a financial saving for the College.[19]

The opportunity for serious consideration of this proposal came sooner than anyone had suspected, with a dramatic change that occurred in December, 1918.

Abby Leach: "Greek has no need of Latin"

Abby was surprised by the rebuke from President MacCracken. In advising these students, she had not been "interfering"; she had merely been considering what was best for them and for her department. Since Grace's position was secure, surely the number of students in her courses did not matter. A much more important issue was claiming her attention—all this talk about grouping Greek and Latin in students' programs of study. She immediately wrote a letter to the president deploring such a plan: "If a group plan is adopted, I hope fervently that Greek will not be fast bound to Latin. . . . Many who will not take Latin wish Greek and they should not be hindered from this study from a mediaeval notion that the two must stand together. Latin needs Greek but she does not recognize the need but Greek has no need of Latin for she borrowed nothing from them."[20]

Even more disturbing were the rumors she had heard about a proposal to consolidate the Greek and Latin Departments. Because of Grace's years of fraternizing with the members of the Latin Department, Abby should have suspected that she would betray the Greek Department the minute she was promoted to full professor. Abby had sacrificed her own time and energy by taking on more than fourteen hours of work during the spring semester to extricate Grace from teaching in the Latin Department, but clearly it hadn't been enough. She would have to husband her strength and fight alone to preserve the autonomy of the Greek Department.

She knew this would not be easy, for she had recently been plagued with increasing bouts of fatigue even though she was only sixty-three years old. More worrisome was the blood she had seen in her urine and the recurring pain in her lower back. When she finally consulted a doctor before the fall

19. Grace H. Macurdy to Henry Noble MacCracken, 30 November 1918, MacCracken Papers, box 24, folder 20, Vassar Archives.

20. Abby Leach to Henry Noble MacCracken, 2 May 1917, MacCracken Papers, box 23, folder 38, Vassar Archives.

term began, she was shocked to learn that she had cancer of the bladder. She was determined to hide the seriousness of her illness from her colleagues. Fortunately, her long skirts hid her swollen legs and ankles, and the house she had been forced to build by the hostility of other faculty members enabled her to keep her suffering private. She would continue to teach as usual and show no sign of weakness that might endanger the future of her department.

Grace   acurdy: "   iss   acurdy should receive the dignity of the direction of the Department of Greek"[21]

Abby Leach died in her home on the morning of December 29, 1918; the cause was bladder cancer complicated by anuria (failure of the kidneys to produce urine). She had completed all but two weeks of the term. The news stunned the campus because no one had realized the extent of her illness. Grace wrote MacCracken immediately, offering to finish Abby's courses and to help Abby's sisters collect her possessions; in contrast, the first response of one of the members of the Latin Department, Elizabeth Hazelton Haight, was to request that she be allowed to teach Greek the following semester.

Grace's closeness with the Latin Department enabled her to cover all the Greek courses in the spring without any disruption or new faculty, and she continued this policy for the following year with great success, noting that "there has been a steady increase in the numbers of students in the department for the past two years. . . . Interest in Greek literature and thought appears to have quickened. The department can never be one of the larger departments of the college, but it is the hope and intention of those working in it to make its contribution to the humanitarian side of education increase."[22]

All the classical faculty therefore expected that the two departments would be merged, and Grace was surprised but secretly delighted when President MacCracken notified her of the action of the board of trustees in February 1919: "The Trustees acted upon the recommendation of the Committee on Faculty and Studies in not approving the plan submitted by yourself and Professor Moore for the amalgamation of the Greek and Latin Departments. It was felt by the Committee and by the Board that after so many years of service

---

21. Minutes of the Committee on Faculty and Studies, 4 February 1919, box 7, folder 12, Vassar Archives.

22. Grace H. Macurdy, Report of the Greek Department 1919–20, 19 April 1920, MacCracken Papers, box 24, folder 21, Vassar Archives.

you should have the honor of administering the teaching of Greek at the college, as the head of the Greek Department."[23]

Although she was gratified that her salary was finally raised to the full-professor level of $3,200, Grace recognized that chairing the department was much more significant for her life and career. She suspected that MacCracken had insisted on this as some slight compensation for all the indignities that she had suffered over the last twelve years, and she never forgot his kindness. Years later, when she wrote MacCracken to notify him that she was about to retire, she eloquently expressed her gratitude: "Those years under your presidency have been my happy and fruitful years. I cannot be thankful enough that you came to Vassar College when you did. It meant for me liberation of my work and of my spirit."[24]

Epitaph: "Could I really grow if I had to suppress every idea I had that disagreed a little with what Abby thought?"[25]

When choosing faculty to prepare the faculty minute honoring Abby Leach, President MacCracken tactfully bypassed the Vassar classicists, instead asking Ida Thallon, associate professor of history, to write and present the tribute; he also chose Florence Bennett, now married to Louis F. Anderson of Whitman College in Washington, to write the obituary published in the *Vassar Quarterly*.[26] He himself struggled to write a tribute that would recognize her many accomplishments but avoid any undeserved praise, as testified by the numerous cross-outs in his drafts. This statement, later published in the local newspaper's article about the death of Abby Leach, best sums up his attitude: "In the death of Miss Leach education loses one of the leaders among women of this generation, and a pioneer in higher study—Miss Leach was of heroic mould, and exemplified the Greek ideals of heroism and ~~self-control~~ self-development which she taught in her class."[27] In this passage he recognizes

23. Henry Noble MacCracken to Grace H. Macurdy, 13 February 1919, MacCracken Papers, box 24, folder 20, Vassar Archives.

24. Grace H. Macurdy to Henry Noble MacCracken, 26 October 1936, MacCracken Papers, box 43, folder 46, Vassar Archives.

25. Helen Drusilla Lockwood to family, 17 May 1910, Helen Drusilla Lockwood Papers, box 1, folder 15B, Vassar Archives.

26. Florence Mary Bennett Anderson, "In Memory of Professor Leach, May 18, 1855–December 29, 1918," *Vassar Quarterly* 4 (1919): 81–83.

27. Henry Noble MacCracken, memo, undated [February 1915], MacCracken Papers, box 50, folder 66, Vassar Archives. Quoted in "Abby Leach Died Sunday at her Home," *Poughkeepsie*

the courage of her pathbreaking effort to study with the Harvard classics professors without exaggerating its significance; he acknowledges that her most
important contributions were to the education of women (such as her role in
the Association of Collegiate Alumnae), while omitting any reference to classical scholarship; and his use of *heroic* and *heroism* tacitly alludes to the larger-
than-life persona that she adopted. He could not, however, bring himself to
attribute to her the quality of self-control.

It is clear from her correspondence and behavior during her campaign
against Grace Macurdy that Abby Leach did not possess the Greek quality of
self-knowledge either. Abby's summation of Grace's scholarship would much
more appropriately describe her own: "I always thought Miss Macurdy was
fond of books and study but she is very dependent upon authorities and lacks
originality and power of initiative."[28] One of her students, Sarah Morris (Vassar BA 1906, MA 1908), later observed that Abby was always quoting other
scholars in her classes, especially German ones, often to the detriment of "the
essentials" of the subject matter: "It was a question of what Wilamowitz-Moellendorff thought, and what some critic had to say about some line."[29] This
statement is substantiated by the surviving copies of her examinations (see
chapter 4).

Abby Leach was a talented linguist and had a broad knowledge and command of Greek literature, but her mind was narrow and rigid, and she had
little insight into the depth and complexity of literary works, as illustrated by
the following simplistic misinterpretation of Sophocles in a letter she wrote
to Gilbert Murray: "I am inclined to agree with you in dating the Electra
of Sophocles later than that of Euripides but think you hardly do justice to
Sophocles. God's in the heaven, all's right with the world is the doctrine of his
serene spirit."[30] She published only two classical articles, both of which began
as speeches. "The Athenian Democracy in the Light of Greek Literature," her
presidential address to the American Philological Association, overwhelms
the reader with quotations from Greek historians and philosophers, which
constitute nearly three-quarters of the article, making it difficult to discern a

---

Eagle-News, 30 December 1918, 5. It is likely that MacCracken had been reading Leach's article
"Fatalism of the Greeks" (*American Journal of Philology* 36 [1915]: 373–401), since the phrase
"heroic mould" appears twice in that article, including the British spelling, which the newspaper changed to "mold."

28. Abby Leach to Members of the Committee on Faculty and Studies, 1 March 1910, Taylor
Papers, box 8, folder 35, Vassar Archives.

29. Sarah Morris, interview by Elizabeth Daniels, taped 23 October 1980, transcribed by
Barbara F. McManus, VC Audio Tapes, Vassar Archives.

30. Abby Leach to Gilbert Murray, 25 February 1907, MSS Gilbert Murray 12, fols. 79–82,
Bodleian.

thesis or organized argument. The few parallels that she draws between the ancient and modern democracies illuminate neither, but they do reveal something about her own intolerant attitudes:

> While, then, economic conditions were somewhat affected by slavery, in general there seems little difference between slaves as we find them at Athens, mildly treated and with the hope of freedom before them, and a large class of our own laborers, who are ignorant foreigners without any interest in our country beyond the gaining a mere livelihood.[31]

The testimony of students reveals a great deal about Abby's personality and temperament. In an oral interview, Sarah Morris described her as "an entirely different character" from Grace Macurdy: "Miss Leach had been the first student at the Harvard Annex, which later developed into Radcliffe College, and she never let anyone forget it! [in a pretentious voice] 'I have opened doors, and they have not been shut behind me.' It's too bad when somebody might have developed into a good teacher but was so absorbed in herself and what happened to her."[32] A number of letters written home by students at the college support this estimation. While Adelaide Claflin (Vassar BA 1897) wrote, "Miss Leach is such a fine teacher and makes the recitations very interesting," Margaret M. Shipp (Vassar BA 1905) had the opposite experience:

> Miss Leach may know a lot and be very famous, but she is absolutely the most uninteresting instructor I ever came across. She is all right out of class but in class she is the limit! She is about as flexible as a wooden post, [and] she says the most squelching things with a "smile that won't come off." She is invaluable to the college however as a figurehead to introduce lectures

---

31. "The Athenian Democracy in the Light of Greek Literature," *American Journal of Philology* 21 (1900): 362. Her later article on the "Fatalism of the Greeks" does have a clear thesis, that the ancient Greeks were not fatalists as currently claimed by many writers, but she is actually arguing against a straw man, since she does not produce a single example of a creditable classical scholar who makes such a claim, though she cites many scholars who express the opposite opinion. Once again the majority of the article consists of quotations from ancient Greek sources, and her florid style and abundance of rhetorical questions suggest a speech before an interested but non-specialist audience rather than a scholarly article.

32. Sarah Morris, interview by Elizabeth Daniels. Morris was one of the graduate students who wrote to President Taylor about Leach's criticism of Grace Macurdy in the graduate student seminar. While a graduate student at Columbia, Morris shared an apartment there with Grace during the summers, and the two women became lifelong friends. Although her later opinion of Leach may have been somewhat biased by this friendship, other student reports say substantially the same thing.

etc, for she is remarkably handsome and fine looking, and her clothes are perfect.[33]

The most fascinating view of Abby Leach as a teacher, however, comes from the letters of Helen Drusilla Lockwood, who attended Vassar from 1908 to 1912 during the height of Abby Leach's campaign against Grace Macurdy and later became a distinguished member of Vassar's English Department. During her four years at Vassar, she wrote several letters to her family every week, constituting a kind of journal of her entire student experience at Vassar and a chronicle of her intellectual maturation. Her mother, Mary E. Lamson (Vassar BA 1890) had studied Greek with Abby Leach, and Helen, who originally planned to become a Latin teacher, followed in her footsteps. She was initially critical of Abby, especially her handling of the freshman Greek class, astutely noting that it seemed that she had not taught freshmen recently (Grace had taught that class for fourteen years). She stated that Abby did most of the translating herself and then asked the class to answer grammar questions, and she wryly observed that Abby insisted that students call her "Professor Leach" though most of the faculty were known as "Miss." She complained about Abby's sarcasm and particularly about her "eternal grin." After her mother wrote to Abby, however, Helen felt that she was becoming a favorite and observed that flattery was the way to Abby's heart:

> I flattered [her] a little and left her in smiles so I guess I will call again soon and flatter her a little more. As I have often said before, you have got to work every teacher and some you work by your own good work and others you work by jollying them up and so on and the sooner you discover how to work them and reconcile yourself to it and act accordingly, the sooner you are going to get on with them.[34]

By the end of the first year Abby Leach had completely won over Helen with her "at home" parties (including ice cream, quite an unusual treat at the time),

---

33. Adelaide Claflin '97 to "My dear Mother," 10 February 1895; Margaret M. Shipp '05 to "Dearest Mamie," Sunday morning [25 October 1903], Vassar College Student Materials Collection, Vassar Archives. Two biographers of Abby Leach include only the phrase "remarkably handsome and fine looking" from this letter, inadvertently demonstrating how misleading it can be to take a quotation out of context: Ann Townsend Zwart, s.v. "Leach, Abby," in *Notable American Women, 1607–1950*; Ward W. Briggs, "Abby Leach (1855–1918)," *Classical World* 90 (1996–97): 101.

34. Helen Drusilla Lockwood to family, 27–28 October 1908, Helen Drusilla Lockwood Papers, box 1, folder 13B, Vassar Archives.

her "perfectly splendid" rooms, the gold cup awarded to her by the Emperor of Japan, and her impressive background and contacts:

> Miss Leach called me over to see her this morning about "my future." She said that she had been watching my work with great interest all through the year and especially in Greek last semester when she had the class and that I had really done remarkably good work in Greek. . . . What she wants me to do, is to take it all through and do advanced work in it and then come back and do graduate work under her and help in her department and then study at some university or in Athens. . . . She gave example after example of Vassar graduates who are now holding remarkably good positions purely because they took Greek. She is the one to get you a good position too for she knows everybody. All her girls do get fine positions and, many of them, [Elizabeth] Hazelton Haight for instance, get fellowships through her. . . . Miss Leach is culture from head to toes and believes that a college should stand for culture. What is more she has traveled so much and as I say knows everybody so much that she knows of opportunities all over the country and it seems to me just as well to make her a friend on my side. . . . And here at the beginning of the year I didn't like her at all and was scared to death to go into her class but I can't see how I ever could be frightened of her.[35]

Although she had not intended to take sophomore Greek, Helen did continue, clearly enjoying all the attention she was getting from Abby. She wrote that all her friends would be dropping Greek for the second semester, though she would probably take it because she had "such a great pull with Abby that it would be a mistake for me to drop it." During the second semester, however, Helen began to show increasing disillusionment with Abby as her own intellectual horizons expanded through her argumentation course in English and especially through participation in Qui Vive, the debate society:

> All the girls seem to think that Abby is terribly narrow and doesn't see things very clearly. I have found out that she has absolutely no use for anything bordering on science so I guess you have to take what she says with a grain of salt.
>
> All the nice people have dropped Greek so the class isn't very interesting and what is more I think we have very nearly gotten to Abby's limit. Anyway

---

35. Helen Drusilla Lockwood to family, 29 May 1909, Helen Drusilla Lockwood Papers, box 1, folder 14B, Vassar Archives.

she keeps saying the same old things over and over so that aside from reading the Greek we don't get very much.[36]

Abby wanted Helen to do some work for the Hellenic Society and to be
in the chorus of a play that Abby was performing in Greek. Helen turned
her down because of her debate preparations, and Abby first badgered her to
drop debate and then reported her to the lady principal, Georgia Avery Ken-
drick, for overwork. Helen was infuriated at this interference and very anxious about how Abby would react when she told her she was not planning to
take any more Greek courses: "From the way that woman spoke the other day
she evidently fully expects me to continue Greek the rest of my natural life. I
am wondering what will happen to me when she finds out I am dropping it."
When Helen finally told Abby, she "raked me over in great style" and was not
placated when Helen said that she would be continuing in Latin. Helen gave
the excuse that she wanted to earn some money by tutoring in Latin, but she
couldn't tell her the real reason:

> You see in Latin I don't have to devote much energy to translation but can
> give practically all my attention to the thought and the life represented and
> what is more if I have an idea I don't have to cover it up as I do in Greek. I
> have thought I would like to read Plato and Aristotle but could I really grow
> if I had to suppress every idea I had that disagreed a little with what Abby
> thought?[37]

It is important to take into consideration Abby Leach's personality and
temperament when attempting to understand why a committed suffragist and
strong advocate for women's education, a woman who boasted of opening
doors for others, would try to slam one of those doors in the face of a younger
woman scholar.[38] The trouble began when Grace received her doctorate from

36. Helen Drusilla Lockwood to family, 30 January and 13 February 1910, Helen Drusilla
Lockwood Papers, box 1, folder 15B, Vassar Archives.

37. Helen Drusilla Lockwood to family, 6 March, 17 April, and 17 May 1910, Helen Drusilla
Lockwood Papers, box 1, folder 15B, Vassar Archives. Because of Leach's monopoly of the Greek
courses during this period, Helen never took a course with Grace Macurdy, and she mentions
her only once in her letters, saying that she gave a "dry old Latin lecture on Roman historians"
(19–20 November 1908, box 1, folder 13B).

38. Leach's biographers seriously downplay this part of her life. Briggs calls it "the single,
if minor, blemish" of Leach's life and career (Briggs, "Abby Leach," 105). Halporn relegates the
whole conflict to a footnote. Although he notes Leach's "strong personal animus" toward Macurdy, he lists her academic charges against Macurdy as though they were true. J. W. Halporn,
"Women and Classical Archaeology at the Turn of the Century: Abby Leach of Vassar College,"
in *Assembling the Past: Studies in the Professionalism of Archaeology*, ed. A. B. Kehoe and M. B.

Columbia University and came to a head when she was hired to teach Greek in the Columbia summer session, making Grace the first woman to teach in Columbia's academic program. Grace was also building a solid record of publication in classical journals. Instead of taking pride in her younger colleague's accomplishments, Abby was clearly threatened by them, though she displaced the threat from herself to "her" department, claiming that Grace's presence was weakening the Greek department. There may have been an element of class bias as well. Abby cultivated students and alumnae of the higher social classes (note her remark about "ignorant immigrants"), and she may well have believed that a person with Grace's background did not belong in the top ranks of the professoriate.

From her youth, Abby had always gone her own way and created her own rules. Although she could have attended one of the women's colleges, she did not consider these good enough for her; she felt that she must be privately tutored by eminent Harvard professors. Even after the Harvard Annex was established, she would not take the regular certificate program but continued to study as a special student. When she received disproportionate praise and fame for her independence and persistence, even being called the "nucleus" of Radcliffe, this solidified these traits to the extent that she could not break free of them later, when they became liabilities rather than assets. Thus she did not pursue a formal program of study leading to a doctorate but rather studied informally at the University of Leipzig and also attended some lectures of Basil Lanneau Gildersleeve at Johns Hopkins University. When a formal degree and publications became increasingly significant in the academic profession, Abby found it more difficult to sustain her sense of specialness, which apparently needed continual buttressing (hence her insistence on being called "Professor Leach" and her boasting about Harvard and all her professional connections). Grace's presence in the department was a constant irritant to Abby simply because of what Grace had already achieved. When Abby complained that Grace could not give her what she required, she spoke truly, because Abby required an acolyte, not an equal.

What seems most remarkable about Abby's attempt to remove Grace—that she went to such lengths and continued for so long despite clear evidence that she could not succeed—can be understood in this context. The fame and praise she won in Cambridge accentuated her self-absorption and made her unable to question her own motivations or the correctness of her opinions.

Emmerichs (Albuquerque: University of New Mexico Press, 1999), 130, n. 6. Zwart actually read the correspondence, but she chose to minimize the conflict by calling it an "inability to get along," though she acknowledges that Leach "could be distressingly inflexible" (Zwart, "Leach, Abby," 380).

Having been lauded so highly for her persistence, Abby was convinced that she would prevail if she just kept on trying. Every defeat only escalated her attempts, so that her behavior became increasingly unprofessional and alienated most of her friends on the faculty. Although she certainly caused Grace a great deal of anxiety and distress, Abby ultimately injured herself the most. Ann Townsend Zwart, who wrote the biographical sketch of Abby Leach for *Notable American Women* and expressed great admiration for her, nevertheless described Abby as "an unhappy & disturbed woman—obsessed with GH Macurdy issue" in her notes on the Leach/Macurdy papers.[39]

Ironically, Abby's groundbreaking role in the foundation of the Harvard Annex, exacerbating tendencies in her own personality, set the stage for her attempt to impede the progress of another pioneering woman scholar. Without the hindrance of Abby's enmity, Grace Macurdy's career, launched through the doors of that very Annex, would now begin to soar.

---

39. Notes of A. T. Zwart on Leach-Macurdy-Taylor correspondence, *Notable American Women* files, MC 230, box 52, Schlesinger.

CHAPTER 7

৵◎৴

Setting a Course

S oon after joining the Vassar faculty, Grace became a member of the American Philological Association (APA), the principal learned society for classical scholars in North America.[1] Founded in 1869, this association was masculine to the core. Although a few women had been members since its inception, the APA took little note of their presence. The official history of the first fifty years of the APA consistently refers to members as "men" and "gentlemen" and does not mention women at all.[2] Grace attended her first APA annual meeting in July 1894 at Williamstown, Massachusetts. She and Abby Leach were the only women among the sixty-three attendees, and all the papers were presented by men. Abby, however, was beginning her fourth year as a member of the APA executive committee (equivalent to a board of directors), the first woman to serve as an officer of the association. The nominating committee would later select her as vice president (1897–99) and president of the association (1899–1900).

Grace's initial awe at the position of honor her department chair had attained gradually diminished as she came to realize that this advancement had nothing to do with scholarship. Abby Leach was strikingly different from

---

1. In 2014, the association changed its name to the Society for Classical Studies.

2. Frank Gardner Moore, "A History of the American Philological Association," *Transactions and Proceedings of the American Philological Association* 50 (1919): 5–32. The first printed APA membership list names eight women among the 164 members.

the small number of men who controlled the APA offices—not so much because she was a woman, but rather because, unlike these eminent scholars, she had never published a single article nor delivered a paper at a classical conference until she gave her APA presidential address. She was the "prodigy" of William Watson Goodwin, the Harvard Greek professor whom she had persuaded to give her private tuition. Goodwin had twice served as APA president, had been selected for the executive committee at the same time as Abby Leach, and had appointed her to serve on the APA Committee of Twelve, which he chaired, tasked with preparing a rationale for requiring three years of Greek in secondary schools for admission into the classical course in college. To Goodwin and others, Abby Leach was a fine figurehead, an imposing and attractive woman who was a skilled classical linguist but posed no threat to male hegemony in the association.[3] Hers was not the path that Grace would follow.

In the Footsteps of (ale) Scholars

Like the ambitious male scholars of the period, Grace studied for a year in Germany and earned a doctorate from a major university. She then began to submit papers to classical conferences and articles to classical journals. Slowed at first by the necessity of fighting to keep her position at Vassar, she soon became the most indefatigable female presenter at the APA annual meetings. From 1910 to 1918, she delivered papers at eight APA conferences (missing only 1916), and in four of these years (1910, 1911, 1913, and 1917) she also had a paper "read by title" (i.e., listed in the program and printed in the abstracts but not delivered orally). During this period few women gave papers at all; the only other women who presented more than one paper were Grace's Vassar colleagues Catharine Saunders (three), Cornelia Coulter (two), Elizabeth Hazelton Haight (two), and Mary Bradford Peaks (two), and her friend Gertrude Hirst from Barnard (two).[4] Grace published ten of her twelve APA

---

3. The report of the Committee of Twelve, of which she was a member, described the best classical teachers as "men of taste and cultivation." "Address of the Committee of Twelve," *Transactions and Proceedings of the American Philological Association* 26 (1895): xxxiv.

4. Before 1910, almost no women gave papers at the APA annual meeting, and women never exceeded 13 percent of conference attendees (with percentages usually much lower) up to 1917, when the APA stopped printing the names of attendees in *Transactions and Proceedings of the American Philological Association*. With such statistics, it is not surprising that the *New York Evening Telegram* listed Grace Macurdy's name among "the eminent men of letters" assembled in Pittsburgh for the 1911 APA annual meeting (27 December 1911, 1), since there were only four women among the ninety-seven attendees that year.

papers in classical journals. During this time she also gave three papers at regional classical conferences, two of which were published (see appendix 2 for a chronological list of Grace's scholarly publications). In order to bring attention to her work, Grace assiduously mailed offprints of her articles to scholars in the United States and especially in England.

Grace was also diligent in professional networking. Her service for the College Entrance Examination Board (reader in Greek, 1902–16, as well as examiner, 1913–15) brought her into contact with many other Greek scholars, but her eleven years as faculty member in the Columbia summer school were even more beneficial in this respect. Not only did these summers provide her with the opportunity, long denied her at Vassar, to teach graduate Greek courses in major authors such as Euripides, Sophocles, Aristophanes, Plato, Pindar, and Theocritus, but her residence on the Columbia campus also enabled a lively social interaction with New York City classicists. When Grace's former student Sarah Morris was a Columbia graduate student, Grace included her in these activities, which Sarah later described in an oral interview:

> This was the way it was when I was with Miss Macurdy there in the summer. I went to all the classical dinners, and the classical dinners in summer were quite interesting because of the visiting professors. We went around wherever these people lived, and they would write something [in Greek] and then it would be passed around so you would have to answer in kind. . . . We knew all these people in this marvelous way. It was this kind of *alive* thing, the people you knew, interesting and alive.[5]

Sarah gave an example of how she and Grace had composed a short parody of the *Odyssey* in Greek hexameters when Columbia professor Edward Delavan Perry's cat, Pippin, had gotten lost and was eventually found on Broadway, ending with a line meaning "going to destruction on the Great White Way, the shameless Pippin," with a humorous footnote in Latin that this line was a recent interpolation. Through her Columbia courses, Grace also impressed her predominantly male students. For example, the 1933 printed catalog of William H. Allen Bookseller states, "One of my most beloved teachers!" under the entry for Grace's book *Hellenistic Queens* (Allen received his BA and MA from Columbia).[6]

---

5. Sarah Morris, interview by Elizabeth Daniels, taped October 23, 1980, transcribed by Barbara F. McManus, VC Audio Tapes, Vassar Archives.

6. William H. Allen Bookseller catalogue, 1933, Biographical Files: Macurdy, Grace Harriet, folder 1, Vassar Archives.

Grace was proud that she had earned the honor of teaching at Columbia solely through her scholarship and teaching ability. One of the many articles she wrote during this period, however, reveals hints that she would ultimately diverge from the traditional path of male classical scholars.

Her 1911 article "The *Andromache* and the *Trachinians*"[7] opens conventionally, arguing that Euripides's *Andromache* preceded Sophocles' *Trachinians* (*Women of Trachis*) and influenced both the structure and plot motifs of the latter play. However, when Grace moves to her second point, "to show to what an extent Euripides' interest in and conception of feminine character has affected Sophocles," her authorial voice changes as she assesses the characterization of Andromache as heroine. She finds herself "compelled to differ" with Gilbert Murray's positive evaluation of Andromache's character:

> Andromache in her various long speeches of self-praise in the *Andromache* and the *Troades* [*The Trojan Women*] upholds a single virtue that has made her great among women, that of absolute obedience to Hector and of self-effacement for his sake, carried to an extent which is horrifying from the point of view of Occidental morality. Her bitterness toward women is not surpassed by that of Menelaus, who, one would grant, had some grounds for hatred of womenkind. So I fail to perceive the wonderfully studied character which Professor Murray finds in the Euripidean *Andromache*. We have rather Euripides' conventional picture of the Periclean ideal woman as she is often described in the dramas of this poet.[8]

Although she does not explicitly mention her own sex, it is clear that Grace is speaking from her own perspective, as an independent professional woman who has challenged the social conventions of her own time and thus finds "horrifying" Andromache's expression of the age-old concept that women's natural inferiority requires unquestioning submission to men. The article's conclusion, that the artistry of Sophocles was able "to make from this pattern a living character" in his heroine, Deianira, does not diminish the resonance of the word "horrifying." Before this article was published, Grace privately wrote Gilbert Murray twice about it, attempting to soften her public disagreement with his analysis:

---

7. Grace H. Macurdy, "The *Andromache* and the *Trachinians*," *Classical Review* 25 (1911): 97–101.

8. Macurdy, "The *Andromache*," 99–100.

I send you part of a paper in which I dispute you about the character of Andromache. I cannot really like her, in spite of the Troades. I love what you say about her, but I think she is not worthy of it.

I think that Andromache *is* different in the two plays and it may be that she is noble about her husband's *nothoi* [Hector's illegitimate children]. She need not have put it quite so badly. I think it is her rhetoric that I mind so much and I think Euripides saw woman's faults too plainly. I hope that we shall lose most of them some time, but it will take a long time. We are still very feminine.[9]

Clearly, Grace did not find it easy to differ with Murray in print, but she felt that her perceptions as a woman as well as a scholar gave her a meaningful insight into the problematic nature of the "femininity" that Andromache was espousing.

In December 1915, the APA Nominating Committee named Grace to the association's executive committee, the second woman (after Abby Leach) to serve on this committee. Although she had won this position like the male officers, through her scholarship, she described the honor to Gilbert Murray in broad terms, as an acknowledgment of women in the profession: "They made me a member of the Executive Committee, which we women hailed as a recognition of us as the Philological Association has been so conservative about us."[10] However, the APA was not yet ready to treat a female scholar as the equal of a man. Grace served only two more years on the committee and was not nominated to higher office, as was typical for male committee members.

Gilbert   urray and World War I

During the years when her faculty position at Vassar was under attack, Grace developed her scholarship with fierce determination, publishing twenty-one scholarly articles and six reviews from 1907 to 1918 (more articles than any other female classical scholar in the United States or Europe during that period). The intensity and persistence of the assault, however, left her vulnerable to bouts of insecurity. Thus the approbation and support of the eminent British scholar Gilbert Murray, Regius Professor of Greek at Oxford and cele-

---

9. Grace H. Macurdy to Gilbert Murray, 4 February and 30 April 1911, MSS Gilbert Murray 157, fols. 15–22, Bodleian.

10. Grace H. Macurdy to Gilbert Murray, 23 January 1916, MSS Gilbert Murray 157, fols. 104–5, Bodleian.

brated "man of letters," were extremely important to Grace during this difficult time in her life, not only as concrete evidence against Abby Leach's charges, but also as psychological validation for Grace herself.

On her first trip to England, in June 1910, Grace stayed with the Murrays at their home on Woodstock Road in Oxford for a few days; their second son, eight-year-old Basil, took her around Oxford, and she later sent him small gifts and remembered him frequently in her letters to his father. During the period from 1907 to 1918, Grace sent Murray thirty-six letters, letters which reveal a certain amount of dependency and hero worship, though she displaced this from his person to his work. The strength of these emotions made her uneasy, and she wryly acknowledged this with German phrases:

> It is so hard to tell you all that your work means to me without seeming "übertrieben" [exaggerated, excessive], but it is so much that I must say it once in a while!
>
> I feel so inadequate to thank you for a book like this. If I say what I think of it, it sounds so like "Schwärmerei" [oversentimental enthusiasm] when written down in my poor words. But I get an understanding of things from you unlike anything else.[11]

Despite her admiration for German scholarship, with the outbreak of World War I Grace turned against Germany and vehemently favored American intervention. In her letters she consistently identified Murray with England itself, adding a strong emotional component to her anti-German sentiments:

> I inundate you with letters, but I hope that you will forgive me. Not a day passes that I am not reading or referring my classes to some thing of yours and I cannot tell you how absolutely supernatural it seems that you who have written these things should be in a state of things more savage than any of the times you have interpreted, which seemed brought near by your genius. I say it badly as always, but it is dreadfully real to me. You have come to mean to me and many others the summing up of what we ~~mean~~ think of when we think what English ethics and spiritualness mean for us and it is sorrowful to think that all that is in peril and that you and yours are in peril.[12]

---

11. Grace H. Macurdy to Gilbert Murray, 28 April 1912 and 13 April 1913 MSS Gilbert Murray 157, fols. 34–35, 42–45, Bodleian.

12. Grace H. Macurdy to Gilbert Murray, 24 February [1915], MSS Gilbert Murray 157, fol. 51, Bodleian. The letter is dated 1914, but this must be an error since war was declared August 4, 1914, and in the letter Grace says she has received Jane Ellen Harrison's pamphlet, "Epilogue to War: Peace with Patriotism," which was not published until 1915.

When Grace wrote Murray to thank him for sending her a copy of his book *The Four Stages of Greek Religion*, she said, "I am ashamed of emphasizing always what your work is to me in a *religious* way. I can think of no other name for it, but of course I do not mean 'religious' but the thing that takes the place of it when all religion goes." In calling her attitude toward Murray's work "religious," Grace was also acknowledging the development of her own position on religion. Although she had been raised as a strict immersionist Baptist, her classical studies, plus her admiration for Murray, had led her to eschew organized religion in favor of liberal progressivism; as she wrote Murray, "It seems dreadful that people who have studied and thought can still believe in bartering with God."[13] However, during World War I her anxiety made her nostalgic for the consolation of a religion in which she could no longer believe:

> I do not dare to ask how you all are. It would be a comfort to me to be able to use the terminology of my childhood and say I pray for you. Whatever is the equivalent of that I do. I wish always that you and your family and your country may be safe.[14]

This emotional investment in Murray as England-under-threat continued throughout the war and inspired Grace to various types of war work—knitting jackets for babies (an activity for which she had little talent), raising money for refugee relief, including contributions from her own meager funds, and collecting clothing to send overseas. In addition, after the United States entered the war Grace volunteered her time in the Barnard Canteen serving American and Allied soldiers during her seven weeks of teaching in the 1918 Columbia summer school.

The war brought Grace into contact with another distinguished Englishman when the poet John Masefield spoke at Vassar in January 1916 as part of his three-month lecture tour across the United States, designed partly to assess the temper of the American people with regard to the war. Grace impressed him with her support for the British cause, and they struck up a warm friendship that led to a frequent correspondence. In fact, Masefield wrote her from the ship taking him back to England, "I hope that I may often hear from you when you are not too busy, for you will always be one of the most charming of the many delightful memories which I carry home." Grace had given him

13. Grace H. Macurdy to Gilbert Murray, 13 April 1913 and 25 November 1910, MSS Gilbert Murray 157, fols. 42–45, 13–14, Bodleian.

14. Grace H. Macurdy to Gilbert Murray, 5 November 1914, MSS Gilbert Murray 157, fols. 87–90, Bodleian.

an international money order for one of his causes (wounded French soldiers), though he had written her, "I do not at all like to think of your selling your jewel. That is an act of generosity not really called for by the wounded." Ironically, Masefield's wife, Constance, later confessed to Grace that her husband had given her the money order to send to the soldiers, but she had left it on a table "one terrifically windy day" and Grace's "little cheque" must have blown out the window or into the fire.[15] Despite her distress at this cavalier treatment of a donation that, however small, represented a real sacrifice on her part, Grace continued her correspondence with John Masefield and visited the Masefields after the war whenever she was in Oxford.

Grace's more lasting contributions toward the war effort were made with her formidable intellect. On December 11, 1914, the *New York Times* published a poem she had written, "To Melos, Pomegranate Isle," drawing a comparison between the German invasion of Belgium and the Athenian destruction of Melos in 416 BCE because of its stance of neutrality:

O thou Pomegranate of the Sea,
    Sweet Melian Isle, across the years
Thy Belgian sister calls to thee
    In anguished sweat of blood and tears.

Her fate like thine—a ruthless band
    Hath ravaged all her loveliness.
How Athens spoiled thy prosperous land,
    Athenian lips with shame confess.

Thou, too, a land of lovely arts,
    Of potter's and of sculptor's skill—
Thy folk of high undaunted hearts
    As those that throb in Belgium still.

Within thy harbor's circling rim
    The warships long, with banners bright,
Sailed bearing Athens' message grim—
    "God hates the weak. Respect our Might."

The flame within thy fanes grew cold,
    Stilled by the foeman's swarming hordes.

---

15. John Masefield to Grace H. Macurdy, 20 March and 12 March 1916; Constance Masefield to Grace Macurdy, 18 March 1917, Autograph Files, Vassar Archives.

Thy sons were slain, thy daughters sold
　　To serve the lusts of stranger lords.

For Attic might thou didst defy,
　　Thy folk the foeman slew as sheep.
Across the years hear Belgium's cry—
　　"O sister, of the wine-dark deep,

"Whose cliffs gleam seaward roseate,
　　Not one of all my martyr roll
But keeps his faith inviolate.
　　Man kills our body, not our soul."

According to the *Poughkeepsie Daily Eagle*, this poem received "many glowing comments . . . by editorial writers all over the country." It was reprinted in the *Washington Post* and anthologized in a number of collections of war poetry.[16] Grace published an article in the *Radcliffe Quarterly* on "Gilbert Murray in War Work," in which she strongly defended Murray against accusations of inconsistency because of his support of the war:

> Gilbert Murray, pacifist and pro-German in the sense of those words as we used them before the Great War, was ready after the invasion of Belgium to sacrifice himself and all that was humanly dearest to himself to "prevent this religion of Blood and Iron over-running Europe."

Using many quotations from Murray's writings, she also refuted American charges that Murray was a self-eulogist or chauvinistic eulogist of England: "Personally I know of no finer political creed than his."[17] In a talk on "The Classical Scholar in War Times" during a 1919 classical conference, she discussed the wartime activities of scholars from many countries. With a bit of distance from the immediacies of war, she was able to include a humorous perspective, quoting some irreverent verses composed by Oxford undergraduates about the morning military drills practiced by their professors:

---

16. *New York Times*, 11 December 1914, 12; *Poughkeepsie Daily Eagle*, 17 December 1914, 6; *Washington Post*, 24 December 1914, 6. Grace later published a poem celebrating the liberation of France, "The Doves of Amiens," though this was not based on a classical comparison (*New York Tribune*, 31 August 1918, 6).

17. Grace H. Macurdy, "Gilbert Murray in War Work," *Radcliffe Quarterly* 3 (1918): 4–9.

Seen in the foremost rank,
His brow with *sudor* dank,
His gown unpipeclayed in his loyal hurry,
Private Professor Gilbert Murray.[18]

The newspapers that she avidly consumed occasionally provoked Grace to send letters to the editors, and one of these landed her in hot water with President MacCracken. Her letter to the *New York Evening Post* had castigated the American Sinn Fein for their pro-German position, denouncing "those who are afflicted with the provincial egotism which has no thought for the world beyond Ireland, and the Germany which deludes them with hope of independence as pay for their treachery to civilization." She had signed the letter "A Lover of Ireland," but the place read "Vassar College." MacCracken wrote to ask whether she had sent an anonymous letter to the editor from Vassar College. "If this is true I fear I cannot quite approve the practice." Grace hastened to explain that she had not used her name for fear of disagreeable letters from "violent Sinn Feiners" but had included her card as an indication of her bona fides; the editor had taken the address from the card and appended it to the letter, much to her surprise. "I am very sorry indeed that the name of Vassar appeared in an anonymous communication. It shall not happen again so far as I am concerned."[19] Grace was chagrined, but this did not deter her from continuing to express her opinion in letters to editors and political figures, though she was now careful about the way she signed them.

Grace referred to Gilbert Murray and used his translations frequently in her classes. She was not above name-dropping even as late as the 1930s, as the writer Mary McCarthy (Vassar BA 1933), who studied Latin but said in her memoir that she later regretted the omission of Greek, rather wickedly observed, "It was afterwards that I grew sorry. Old Miss MacCurdy, with her ear trumpet, friend of 'dear Gilbert' (Murray), was a saltier personality than gracious Miss Haight." McCarthy goes on to relate an anecdote about her friend Frani Blough, who did take Greek. Frani and some friends had

---

18. "Latin Conference Held at Vassar. The War and the Classics was the Subject of Discussion by an Enthusiastic Gathering," *Vassar Miscellany News*, 15 November 1919, 1, 3. During the war Gilbert Murray carried out military drills with the Oxford Volunteer Training Corps. The students' verses are playing with the incongruity between the academic and the military. The Latin word *sudor* (sweat) would of course not be used by ordinary soldiers, and Murray would not be wearing his academic gown during drills (pipe clay was used to whiten the leather parts of military uniforms).

19. "Irish Humor Missing," *New York Evening Post*, 27 May 1918, 8; Henry Noble MacCracken to Grace H. Macurdy, 6 June 1918; Grace H. Macurdy to Henry Noble MacCracken, 8 June 1918, MacCracken Papers, box 23, folder 38, Vassar Archives.

removed the plaster casts of the statues of Venus and Minerva from Avery Hall and staged some bacchanalian revels on the lawn:

> The next day a letter from Elizabeth Hazelton Haight was on the desk of our Chief Justice. "I regret to be obliged to report to you the rape of Venus and Minerva from the Classics Department." If she had not gone on to demand the immediate return of the statues and the punishment of the culprits, Miss Haight might have been felt to be horsing around herself on some old steed of parody. But she did not get the benefit of the doubt, and it was noted that Miss MacCurdy, dear Gilbert's friend, had not added her voice to the denunciation—the rape of *Roman* statues was outside her department.[20]

However, Grace found that some students were taking her emphasis on Murray's work too much to heart, as she wrote Murray in 1914:

> I have had a repetition of an odd experience lately—that of protesting against an article in our college magazine, absorbed from you. The same thing happened four or five years ago when a girl in the same way borrowed the introduction to the Troades. The poor little ostriches did not mean harm and did not realize what they were doing. The last one was a most absurd "Misch-Masch" of many of your fine things, interspersed with shocking original errors. But they had both caught the feeling and had a spurious inspiration. It made me think and I can see that you say things in your own unforgettable way, but so reasonably that one thinks that one could have said it so, or at least thought it so.[21]

She was referring to articles in Vassar's literary magazine, *The Vassar Miscellany*, by Louise Seaman, class of 1915, and Ruth Fulton, class of 1909. The latter student became the noted anthropologist Ruth Fulton Benedict, and one of Benedict's biographers points to Fulton's *Miscellany* essay, "The Trojan Women of Euripides," as an example of "the struggle of individuals touched by insanity to achieve self-control—a topic with resonance in her own life. . . . Benedict concluded that personal salvation lies in suffering, for the experience of pain has a 'splendor and beauty' that can inspire self-understanding." However, as Grace had immediately recognized, this essay is highly derivative in both content and language from the introduction and notes to Murray's 1905 translation of *The Trojan Women*, which had described "the inmost theme of

---

20. Mary McCarthy, *How I Grew* (New York: Harcourt Brace Jovanovich, 1987), 224–25.

21. Grace H. Macurdy to Gilbert Murray, 24 February 1914, MSS Gilbert Murray 157, fols. 52–57, Bodleian.

the whole play, a search for an answer to the injustice of suffering in the very splendour and beauty of suffering."[22]

Jane Ellen Harrison

Grace was proud of the distinction of being the first woman to teach in Columbia's academic program, but when she wrote Gilbert Murray about this honor, she was careful to couch her success in praise for the books of his which she used in her classes:

> This summer I had a most interesting class in Epic poetry in Columbia. For the last two summers I have given the courses in Greek there and this summer your book on the Greek Epic was daily in my hands and those of my students. It was such a delight to introduce them to it. My students in that class were mostly men and of a very good sort, graduated from college and teaching in New York or thereabout. I was the only "lady-professor," as the janitor called me and had some fears about a new kind of work. But with last year, in the drama, and this year, in the Epic and Plato, every thing went well and in both years my students thanked me again and again for their acquaintance with your work.

Murray responded by drawing a comparison with Jane Ellen Harrison: "It is very interesting that you have been lecturing to a class chiefly of men. Miss Harrison has sometimes done that over here, but very few other women scholars. It is all good for the cause."[23] The situation of these two women classicists, each a pioneer in her own country, was not really so similar, however, though Murray was correct in claiming that both were "good for the cause" of women in higher education. A key difference lay in their professional status, for Grace Macurdy had earned a doctoral degree from a major university, had a recognized professional position carrying the academic rank of associate professor and later professor (albeit in a women's college), and was teaching credit-bearing courses to mostly male students at Columbia University (albeit

---

22. Louise Seaman, "The First Romantic Tragedian," *The Vassar Miscellany* 43 (1914): 245–48; Ruth Fulton, "*The Trojan Women* of Euripides," *The Vassar Miscellany* 37 (1907): 53–57; Lois W. Banner, *Intertwined Lives: Margaret Mead, Ruth Benedict, and Their Circle* (New York: Knopf, 2003), 111–12; Gilbert Murray, *The Trojan Women of Euripides, Translated into English Rhyming Verse with Explanatory Notes* (London: George Allen, 1905), 93.

23. Grace H. Macurdy to Gilbert Murray, 25 September 1909, MSS Gilbert Murray 157, fols. 7–10, Bodleian; Gilbert Murray to Grace H. Macurdy, 6 October 1909, Autograph Files, Vassar Archives.

in the summer program). Jane Ellen Harrison, in contrast, did not have professional academic credentials, was never a full member of the university at which she taught, and never lectured to men as part of their regular academic program.

Although British classicist Mary Beard has recently said of Harrison, "in a way, she was the first female professional 'career academic' in the country," the operative phrase is "in a way."[24] Jane Ellen Harrison (1850–1928) devoted her life to writing, lecturing, and scholarship on Greek art and archaeology, and especially on the origins of Greek ritual and religion, but she lived at a time when British higher education for women was determinedly nonprofessional. Her early education was spotty; she had learned Greek mostly through self-study, aided by tutors. She won a scholarship to the recently opened Newnham College for women at Cambridge University and passed the Tripos examinations at the top of the second class, though the degree she earned was not recognized by Cambridge University, which did not award formal degrees to women until 1948. She applied twice for the Yates Professorship of Classical Archaeology at the University of London, but lost both times to males with more conventional credentials and scholarship. In 1898, Newnham College offered her a research fellowship tailored to her particular needs and talents, and she remained on the staff at Newnham until 1922. Her two most influential books, *Prolegomena to the Study of Greek Religion* (1903) and *Themis* (1912), were studies of early Greek religion and ritual—brilliant, innovative, creative, and highly controversial. She had close personal ties with a number of Greek scholars who sometimes collaborated in her work, most notably Gilbert Murray of Oxford and Francis M. Cornford of Cambridge (see figure 16).[25]

Although Grace viewed Gilbert Murray as the ideal classical scholar, she knew that she could never pattern herself after him: he had attained a Regius professorship at Oxford; he had married into the English aristocracy; his translations of Greek dramas were produced on the London stage. So Murray's influence on Grace's scholarly development was indirect. Grace did, however, initially adopt Jane Ellen Harrison as a role model. She chose to do so partly because of Harrison's close association with Murray, but more significantly

24. Mary Beard, "Living with Jane Harrison," *A Don's Life* (blog), *Times Literary Supplement*, 22 May 2009, accessed September 30, 2014, http://timesonline.typepad.com/dons_life/2009/05/living-with-jane-harrison.html.

25. For more information on Harrison, see Annabel Robinson, *The Life and Work of Jane Ellen Harrison* (Oxford: Oxford University Press, 2002); Mary Beard, *The Invention of Jane Harrison* (Cambridge, Massachusetts: Harvard University Press, 2000); Hugh Lloyd-Jones, s.v. "Harrison, Jane Ellen," *The Oxford Dictionary of National Biography*, ed. H. C. G. Matthew and B. Harrison (Oxford: Oxford University Press, 2004).

because Harrison was a woman, the only female classical scholar who had achieved any kind of international recognition by the beginning of the twentieth century. Grace had begun her career following the well-trodden paths of male classical scholars, but she had quickly learned that these paths were strewn with obstacles for ambitious female scholars. The recognition granted to Abby Leach was not for scholarship, since she had never set foot on those paths, and her vindictive treatment of a younger colleague certainly disqualified her as any kind of role model. Harrison, on the other hand, was boldly creating her own path, one that brought her distinction as a female scholar, if only in certain quarters.

Inspired by Harrison's example and dispirited by her struggles at Vassar, Grace increasingly turned her scholarly focus to Harrison's field of study. Grace plunged into this new field with enthusiasm and intense energy. A glance at the titles in appendix 2 indicates that her first eight articles (from 1907 to 1911) were straightforwardly philological, but nineteen of the twenty-five scholarly articles she published between 1912 and 1926 dealt with etymology of names, mythic and religious origins, and ethnology. Characteristically, when writing to Gilbert Murray she linked her interest in Harrison with praise for *his* work: "I have just been reading *Themis*. It is a wonderful book. Of course I think your chapter the most splendid. Miss Harrison's work is so stimulating and this seems to me to be the best of her books."[26]

Grace soon began corresponding with Harrison, sending her drafts of articles for suggestions and critique. Harrison must have been delighted to have such an enthusiastic female scholar following in her footsteps, and she went out of her way to introduce Grace's work to a British audience in *The Year's Work in Classical Studies*, discussing five of Macurdy's articles:

> We welcome from America a new worker of high originality. Prof. Grace Macurdy won her spurs by an article on Paean and Paeonia. The path she then cleared has broadened to a veritable highway. . . . Prof. Macurdy is, like most good enquirers, so hot on the immediate trail that she scarcely seems to see whither the hunt is drifting, but her vivid paper on 'Rainbow, Sky, and Stars' is, if unconsciously, all alive with the new mythological movement. . . . Here, as in the paper on the 'Water-gods' illumination is cast on Homer from quite a new quarter. Vassar College is much to be congratulated on its professor, the new *Chorizousa*.[27]

---

26. Grace H. Macurdy to Gilbert Murray, 7 July 1912, MSS Gilbert Murray 157, fols. 36–39, Bodleian.

27. J. E. Harrison, "Greek Religion and Mythology," *The Year's Work in Classical Studies* 10 (1915): 75–76. Harrison has coined a feminine singular form of the Greek word *Chorizontes*

During the planning for Vassar's celebration of its fiftieth anniversary in 1915, Grace was on the committee seeking distinguished women speakers to "mark the advance in the feminist movement in that time," and she secured an invitation for Harrison to speak, though Harrison was unable to accept the invitation.[28] When Grace began traveling to England on a regular basis, she met with Harrison on a number of occasions, seeking her advice as she revised and expanded her articles into a book, published in 1925 as *Troy and Paeonia, with Glimpses of Ancient Balkan History and Religion.*

When Murray began taking a young Scottish classicist named J. A. K. Thomson under his wing, he encouraged both Harrison and Grace Macurdy to befriend him. In 1912, Grace began corresponding with Thomson at Murray's behest, and she brought him to speak at Vassar in 1920, during his term as a visiting lecturer at Harvard. Murray enlisted Harrison to help Thomson complete his first book, *Studies in the Odyssey*, published through Murray's influence by the Clarendon Press in 1914. When Thomson spent a year teaching at Bryn Mawr College in 1921–22, Grace developed a close friendship with him, and she asked Harrison, Murray, and Thomson, all of whom had read parts of *Troy and Paeonia* in manuscript, to write letters to Columbia University Press recommending publication: "I am only a gleaner after you all, but I do wish to get the book done and out."[29] However, she chose to dedicate the book to Harrison alone, and the dedicatory inscription prefigures Grace's concept of the woman scholar as an individual who does not have to suppress her personal qualities in order to be accepted as an intellectual: "I dedicate this work to Jane Ellen Harrison, one of the greatest of living scholars, the splendor of whose intellect is equalled by the candor and generosity of her spirit"[30] Harrison's response, written less than three years before her death, indicates her delight with the book and the tribute:

> At last the long looked for book has come! How can I tell you the intense pleasure you have given me. I feel it a great great honour to have such a book dedicated to me. I sat up late last night to read it right thru & was filled with fresh wonder at the vigour and originality of yr mind. . . . I have only one serious fault to find & and that is that is [*sic*] that in yr generous way

---

(Separators), a masculine plural term used to characterize ancient Homeric scholars from Alexandria who argued for separate authorship of the *Iliad* and *Odyssey.*

28. Grace H. Macurdy to Gilbert Murray, 24 February 1914, MSS Gilbert Murray 157, fols. 52–57, Bodleian.

29. Grace H. Macurdy to Gilbert Murray, 8 December 1923, MSS Gilbert Murray 157, fols. 138–39, Bodleian.

30. Grace H. Macurdy, *Troy and Paeonia, with Glimpses of Ancient Balkan History and Religion* (New York: Columbia University Press, 1925), v.

you have made much too ample acknowledgment of my help. It makes me ashamed tho it delights me. Dear Miss Macurdy you have given me one of the greatest pleasures in my life & I thank you from my heart.[31]

Troy and Paeonia

Grace was finally able to begin her first sabbatical, a fifteen-month sojourn in Europe, in May of 1922. She had originally planned to devote part of her sabbatical to travel in the Balkans as part of her research for *Troy and Paeonia*, but she ended up spending the majority of her time "writing furiously" on her book in Oxford's Bodleian Library and the British Museum Reading Room (though she managed to visit Scotland, Denmark, and France as well). As she explained in a letter to President MacCracken, "My reason for giving up the trip to the Near East was that Jane Harrison, Gilbert Murray and the other scholars who are most interested in my work said strongly that I must write it in England, either in London, Oxford or Cambridge."[32] She did visit Harrison while she was in Paris, and conferred with both Murray and Thomson on this trip and her trip to Europe the following summer.

Although her three advisors did write letters to Columbia University Press urging publication of Grace's manuscript, the press has not preserved these in its archives. The dust jacket of the book quotes from Murray's letter: "Out of some fifty books on Homeric subjects which have been published in the last few years, I should put this among the first half dozen," and he told Grace that he had written that the press would be "disgraced forever if they do not jump at it."[33] Thomson sent Murray a draft of his recommendation, which began as follows:

> I feel it a special privilege and pleasure to recommend to you for publication the *Troy and Paeonia* of Professor Grace Harriet Macurdy of Vassar College. I ~~know the manuscript~~ have read the work in manuscript and in print and have discussed it at length with the author. It seems to me a work of first-rate importance. I think I am familiar with everything, or nearly everything, of genuine merit that has been written on the 'Homeric Question' in the last ten

31. Jane Ellen Harrison to Grace H. Macurdy, 30 December 1925, Biographical Files: Macurdy, Grace Harriet, folder 2. Vassar Archives.

32. Grace H. Macurdy to Henry Noble MacCracken, 16 February 1923, MacCracken Papers, box 29, folder 15, Vassar Archives.

33. Grace H. Macurdy to Henry Noble MacCracken, 11 January 1924, MacCracken Papers, box 29, folder 18, Vassar Archives.

years or so. Professor Macurdy's studies in that and kindred ~~studies~~ subjects have long seemed to me easily the most original and suggestive, in many ways also the most learned, that have ~~appeared~~ come from an American scholar during those years.[34]

The book contains fifteen discrete chapters connected primarily by their focus on the prehistoric culture and religion of tribes from the Balkan and Danubian regions of Europe, tribes that lived in and around the city we call Troy and left traces of their civilization in the Homeric epics. The first seven chapters are fairly closely linked by an emphasis on the *Iliad* and the *Odyssey*; Grace analyzes passages and allusions in the two epics from which she deduces information about the prehistoric background of various tribes that constituted the Trojans and their allies. The following eight chapters deal with various aspects of the nature worship of the tribes discussed in the earlier sections. Although many chapters were based on earlier articles, all the material was reworked and expanded for inclusion in the book.

Troy and Paeonia was widely reviewed, with nine substantial assessments in major academic journals, including not only classical journals but also the *Journal of Philosophy*, the *American Journal of Archaeology*, and *Man* (the journal of the Royal Anthropological Institute), but none of the reviews were uniformly positive. Almost all the reviewers praised the amount of material gathered in the book, pointing out "the great number of new and striking ideas," and summarizing the merits of this "brilliant and stimulating work" as "originality, abundant learning, sound reasoning, and clarity of statement."[35] Even one of her detractors acknowledged her "great and accurate learning and wide reading," though another commented that her "book research" should have been supplemented with travel and archaeological research in the lands she discusses.[36]

Reviewers recognized the book's inspiration: "In the school of Greek religion which is represented by Gilbert Murray, Jane Harrison, J. A. K. Thomson, F. M. Cornford, and other British scholars, Professor Macurdy, of Vassar

---

34. J. A. K. Thomson to Gilbert Murray, 15 December 1923, MSS Gilbert Murray 175, fols. 252–53, Bodleian. See also chapter 1.

35. Samuel E. Bassett, review of *Troy and Paeonia*, *Classical Weekly* 19 (1926): 203; J. G. Winter, review of *Troy and Paeonia*, *Classical Journal* 22 (1927): 696, 698.

36. John A. Scott, "Origins and Etymologies," *The Nation* 122 (1926): 614; S. C. [Stanley Casson], review of *Troy and Paeonia*, *Journal of Hellenic Studies* 46 (1926): 276–78. Thanks to Christopher Stray for the identification of Stanley Casson as the *JHS* reviewer. Casson was a classical archaeologist who had conducted excavations in Macedonia.

College, is the most distinguished American member."[37] Ironically, however, *Troy and Paeonia* was largely praised for the sections that were most different from Harrison's work, the opening chapters on Homer: "Miss Macurdy finds the solution to many hitherto puzzling Homeric questions"; "It will scarcely be possible ever again to hold that the peoples of Troy were Asiatics or Athenians or anything but immigrants from Thrace or Macedonia. . . . All who take an interest in the civilization and history that lies behind the Homeric story will find this book suggestive and altogether delightful."[38] Even when reviewers were cautious about the book's heavy reliance on etymology, they were impressed by the depth and breadth of Grace's knowledge and interpretation of Homer, as in this judicious summation by J. L. Myres, who noted an uneasy feeling that "there must be a catch somewhere":

> But to detect where that catch is, one must know one's Homer, and a good deal besides, as well as Dr. Macurdy does; and be prepared, probably, to go a long way with her, on this adventurous quest, before parting company at a real *impasse*. Even where one hesitates to agree, it is worth while to read and ponder.[39]

However, the book came in for a great deal of criticism in the later chapters that were more directly influenced by Jane Harrison's approach and ideas, with comments ranging from moderate to scathing:

> In general the reader will find more of profit in the chapters which deal with ethnological relations, folk-customs, and place-names than in the interpretations of myth and religion. In the former field the author has added to our knowledge; in the latter her methods are too much like those of her admired fellow-worker, Miss Harrison, to gain the assent of cautious readers.[40]
>
> The remaining chapters are confined to religious topics. They lead us into a strange land where nothing is as it seems, where conflation leads to inflation, and a single word is the spark that sets vast haystacks aflame, with the consequent loss of the needle which lurked there. . . . Research on etymologico-religious lines tends to warp the judgment.[41]

---

37. Bassett, review of *Troy and Paeonia*, 203. Oddly, Robert Ackerman's book *The Myth and Ritual School: J. G. Frazer and the Cambridge Ritualists* (New York: Garland, 1991), which argues for Harrison's central role in this movement, never mentions Grace Macurdy.

38. H. T. Westbrook, review of *Troy and Paeonia*, *Journal of Philosophy* 23 (1926): 362; E. H. Sturtevant, review of *Troy and Paeonia*, *American Journal of Archaeology* 30 (1926): 95.

39. J. L. Myres, review of *Troy and Paeonia*, *Man* 27 (1927): 36.

40. Campbell Bonner, review of *Troy and Paeonia*, *Classical Philology* 22 (1927): 438.

41. Casson, review of *Troy and Paeonia*, 277.

Finally, many reviewers noted problems with proofreading, particularly in the many citations. Samuel Bassett's long and balanced review devotes several pages to what he terms "a most regrettable treatment of the necessary documentation." Although Bassett maintained that these shortcomings were "a matter of book-making rather than scholarship," in the hands of a hostile reviewer like Alexander Shewan, the "many *errata*, some of them . . . real monstrosities," became the basis of a scornful dismissal of the book as a whole.[42]

Although chagrined by some of the reviews, Grace was not surprised, since she was well aware of the antagonism Jane Harrison had encountered: "What a most unkind and unfair review of Miss Harrison's work Professor Farnell wrote in the Hibbert Journal! He seems to have no appreciation of her genius. I cannot understand how he could write with such curious fury."[43] When she found an inaccurate claim in Alexander Shewan's review she did write a feisty letter to the editor of *Classical Review* noting that she had never identified Hector with Hades but had indicated that a number of Trojan princes bore the names of chthonian deities, just as people who are named after saints are not identified with those saints: "A statement of my position which is absolutely incorrect in point of fact should, I think be brought to the attention of the same public as that which the review reaches."[44]

Grace did, however, learn from these reviews. For all her subsequent books she enlisted expert help on proofreading, particularly from her friend and former student Sarah Morris, who later explained:

> Grace Macurdy became my very close friend, and I took everything she had to give. She was a very remarkable woman. . . . I had a habit later of going up to do the proof for her and to put the bibliography in shape and also used to have some sentence structure, because she was fluent and rambled on.[45]

Even before *Troy and Paeonia* was published, Grace had begun moving away from the field of primitive myth and religion, and these reviews confirmed her decision to find a different scholarly focus. Although her admiration for Jane Harrison never diminished, Grace realized that she needed

---

42. Bassett, review of *Troy and Paeonia*, 203; A. Shewan, review of *Troy and Paeonia*, *Classical Review* 41 (1927): 37.

43. Grace H. Macurdy to Gilbert Murray, 13 April 1913, MSS Gilbert Murray 157, fols. 42–45, Bodleian.

44. Grace H. Macurdy, "Correspondence," *Classical Review* 41 (1927): 157–58.

45. Sarah Morris interview by Elizabeth Daniels, taped 23 October 1980, transcribed by Barbara F. McManus, VC Audio Tapes, Vassar Archives.

to create a place for herself as a woman on the scholarly path traditionally reserved for men (see chapters 1 and 10).

Deafness

Although Grace's postponement of her much-needed sabbatical from 1920 to 1922 was primarily due to the need to reorganize and revitalize the Greek Department after the death of Abby Leach, a new and serious physical problem also contributed to the delay. The "liberation of her work and her spirit" that she experienced after the death of Abby Leach coincided with a rapid and severe loss of hearing in both ears. In the summer of 1919, she had been treated by a hearing specialist in New York City with no discernible improvement; although retaining some residual hearing, Grace Macurdy became, for all practical purposes, deaf at the age of fifty-three. There is no evidence as to the cause of this hearing loss, but it was totally unexpected and very difficult to accept. Deafness threatened the core of Grace's life and livelihood, the ability to communicate with others. As a scholar, she could of course continue to write, but she had no means of support beyond her Vassar salary, and her faculty position was essential for her professional standing in the academic community. Losing this position was not an idle fear. The mere possibility that she would lose her hearing was enough to deny Catharine Saunders, Grace's colleague in the Latin department, promotion to a permanent appointment as full professor for several years: "Without assurance of the removal of what, in the light of their present information, seemed to them likely to become a permanent handicap, [the trustees] were unwilling to consider the recommendation."[46] Moreover, Vassar was her home; Grace could not imagine leaving the community to which she was bound with so many close ties of friendship.

At this time the deaf were stigmatized and shamed; even the manufacturers of mechanical devices claiming to aid residual hearing used these negative emotions to sell their products. The 1920 Acousticon manual began with the warning, "Good hearing is essential to your happiness and welfare. Without it you are at a disadvantage wherever you go and whatever you do. You stand on an unequal footing with other men and women, and this fact is emphasized a dozen times a day." The 1895 Hawksley catalog scolded, "A deaf person is always more or less a tax upon the kindness and forbearance of friends. It

---

46. Henry Noble MacCracken to Catharine Saunders, 26 February 1923 MacCracken Papers, box 29, folder 34, Vassar Archives. When this "permanent handicap" did not materialize, Saunders was finally promoted in 1928.

becomes a duty, therefore, to use any aid which will improve the hearing and the enjoyment of the utterances of others without any murmuring about its size or appearance."[47] While naturally disturbed and frightened by her disability, Grace was able to surmount the depression and isolation that often afflicts the newly deaf through her own drive and determination as well as through the supportive fellowship of her Vassar colleagues and students. Grace had earned the highest academic credentials despite early poverty and social disadvantage; she had survived the enmity of Abby Leach and was winning distinction as a classical scholar. She would not be stopped now because of the loss of her hearing. Her outgoing personality, generous nature, and obvious care for others had won her many strong friends at Vassar, who now formed a protective circle within which she could learn to cope with this new situation.

So Grace, highly motivated and supported by sympathetic friends, made use of every possible means to enhance her ability to communicate. Devices available to aid hearing at the time all relied on amplification of sound. Grace used the ear trumpet for many years, despite its old-fashioned, comical associations. This was the most portable device; inadequate as it was, at least it did not distort the sound, and it was helpful for one-on-one conversation. With her quick mind and linguistic ability, Grace also learned to lip-read, so that she became reasonably proficient in conversation. Her ear trumpet became a well-known sight on campus, an occasion for good-natured banter. Mary McCarthy tells an amusing story involving the ear trumpet when President MacCracken played the role of Theseus in Vassar's 1931 Greek production of *Hippolytus*:

> Prexy forgot his lines. But he was a born actor, full of resource: in his head he hastily translated "to be or not to be," which was about the right length, into Greek, spoke the resulting lines, and nobody noticed a thing. Except old Miss MacCurdy, whose ear trumpet could not be fooled by *Hamlet*, in Greek or English. She did not let on till after the performance was over and Prexy was receiving congratulations. Then she added her own.[48]

The classroom was a more difficult arena, and here Grace utilized a new "electrical" device based on the carbon microphone, the Multi-Acousticon, claimed by its manufacturer as "the most powerful hearing device ever constructed." This device consisted of a black box measuring seven by seven by

---

47. *Directions and Helpful Suggestions for the Use of the Acousticon*, (New York: Dictograph Products Corporation, 1920), 5. The Hawksley catalog is quoted in Mara Mills, "When Mobile Communication Technologies Were New," *Endeavour* 33 (2009): 145.

48. McCarthy, *How I Grew*, 225.

three and a half inches, weighing three pounds with its batteries, connected by wires to a large earpiece that could be held with a detachable handle or fastened to a headband.[49] Despite the manufacturer's claims, the device was noisy and scratchy because of the movement of the tiny carbon balls in the microphone. Although it probably helped to some degree, Grace's success in the classroom was due to her own enthusiasm and humorous, lively lectures plus a joint effort by the students to mitigate the effects of her deafness. "There was just so much good will toward her," explained Evalyn Clark, who took some of Grace's classes during the first years of her deafness:

> She was much better conversing one-on-one than any other way. I mean what was always difficult was in class, because it would have been very difficult to have any sort of adequate question-and-response type of thing. We all learned that very soon. . . . But anyhow the students were *very* careful to try to recognize what her problems were. But I mean sometimes it wouldn't work, despite perfectly good intentions and therefore you would sort of have to spell it out or write it out or something of that sort, write it on the board or something. But everyone was trying very hard not to have it come to that, you know. Because everybody thought she was the most wonderful thing in the universe. She was such a character—I mean, not only appearance but everything about her. You know she was obviously sort of in love with Classics, and the human beings in general, and the students, and everybody reciprocated, you know. The whole atmosphere was an entirely different atmosphere from anything I've ever seen in class before. The students usually tried to answer—well to sort of shift the ground—not to ask questions that would mean *she* had to answer. She could ask a question and you could answer it, but you didn't ask questions of her if you could help it. She wouldn't understand what you were saying. It was a pretty interesting example of sort of a group nurturing *her*. And at turns you know she just thought we were the most wonderful things in the universe too. It was a very interesting example of sort of cooperation on the part of the faculty and the students. And everybody had a great time in the process, too.[50]

Grace also had an Acousticon that could be carried; it was similar to the larger version but the battery and transmitter could be fastened to clothing with harnesses or clips. This was much more portable than the tabletop Acousticon but was obviously more cumbersome than an ear trumpet. How-

---

49. *Directions and Helpful Suggestions for the Use of the Acousticon*, 29.

50. Interview with Evalyn Clark by Barbara F. McManus, 6 December 1997. Clark was a classics major at Vassar from 1920 to 1924 and returned in 1939 to teach history.

ever, by May 1922 Grace was ready to embark on her sabbatical in Europe, fifteen months of study, travel, and writing that took her to Scotland, England, France, and Denmark.

Grace had clearly adjusted to her loss of hearing, though for a period of time she retained some hope of reversing it. On the advice of Lady Mary Murray, she repeatedly went for treatments to the fashionable London physician Ivo Geikie Cobb, author of *A Manual of Neurasthenia* (1920), and she wrote to Gilbert Murray about her hopes for improvement: "I go every week to Dr. Geikie Cobb and though he may not cure my deafness he has made me much better on my raw fruit diet. I have always been inclined to vegetarian diet and now I have foresworn all meat forever!"[51] Unfortunately, all that fruit did nothing to restore her hearing. Upon her return to Vassar, Grace gave up the search for a cure and instead focused her energy on achieving her personal and professional goals.

Colleague and   entor

Though still struggling with her unexpected loss of hearing, Grace reveled in her new position as chair of the Greek Department, vowing to carry out her responsibilities very differently than her predecessor had. Close collaboration with the Latin Department was the most immediate change—some Latin faculty members were finally given the long-desired opportunity to teach a Greek course; the Hellenic Society was renamed the Classical Society; joint activities and conferences were planned. Under Grace's leadership, the number and quality of Greek students steadily increased. Explaining some of the reasons for this growth in her department report for 1921–22, Grace was unable to refrain from some subtle criticism of Abby Leach's regime:

> Much has been gained in the study of Greek in shifting the emphasis from the purely grammatical to the cultural side and many girls delight in reading Homer's poetry who have no vivid interest in his Aeolic infinitives as such. I have never had more responsive classes in Greek literature. . . . We are very glad that with absolutely no propaganda in its favor and absolutely no suggestion to any student that she should continue with the subject we

---

51. Grace H. Macurdy to Gilbert Murray, 10 December 1922, MSS Gilbert Murray 157, fols. 135–36, Bodleian.

have a department that compares most favorably with Greek Departments
in other colleges.[52]

Although Grace herself had been barred from teaching advanced courses
for many years, she expressed regret in this report that she had been unable
to give her new Greek instructor, Cornelia Catlin Coulter, any advanced
courses because she did not want to put too much of a burden on her during
her first year in the department. However, Coulter would have nine hours
of advanced elective work and no elementary courses in the following year:
"This will give her opportunity to immerse herself in Greek Literature under
favorable circumstances." Grace repeatedly wrote to President MacCracken
praising Coulter's work and recommending a higher salary and promotion
to assistant professor. Later she did everything in her power to foster Coulter's career, even when it meant losing her to Mount Holyoke College. In fact,
Grace privately asked Mount Holyoke's president, Mary Woolley, to make sure
that Coulter did not "burden herself so heavily that she will have no time for
research and publication."[53]

Grace did not confine her mentoring to her colleagues in Greek. In 1922,
she wrote an unsolicited letter to MacCracken in support of Elizabeth Hazelton Haight's long-delayed promotion to full professor. Hazel Haight had begun
teaching in the Latin Department in 1902 and had been promoted to associate
professor in 1910 after earning her doctorate from Cornell, but the trustees
had been reluctant to advance her to professor. Grace felt strongly that Haight
had been treated unjustly after her long and dedicated service to Vassar, but
she would not seek to remedy that injustice through easy platitudes or inflated
claims. In her usual forthright manner, she wrote the truth as she saw it:

> I have known Miss Haight well, though not intimately, for many years. Her
> good points are so conspicuous that it is hardly necessary to set them down.
> She is a teacher whose enthusiasm and genuine love for her subject infect
> her classes, so that the "gospel" of the classics is spread through her. She is,
> in an entirely good sense of the word, a propagandist for her subject. That,
> in a sense, is her greatest gift and I know that no member of the two depart-
> ments would deny her pre-eminence over all the rest of us in that line. . . .
>
> She is distinguished for "executive ability" and you know still better than
> I her achievements in that way during the War. Her administration of the

52. Grace H. Macurdy, *Report of the Greek Department 1921–1922*, 20 May 1922, Mac-
Cracken Papers, box 27, folder 35, Vassar Archives.

53. Mary Woolley to Grace H. Macurdy, 15 March 1926, Autograph Files, Vassar Archives.

Department of Latin this year has been tactful and successful. In all our dealings I have found her fair and eager for the best good of both departments.

You know her indefatigable industry and the quality of her writing. I shall be untruthful if I said that I believe her to be distinguished in the line of pure research:—as for example, Professor Lily Taylor is distinguished. She has been too busy with other things for that and probably too the quality of her mind is not that, fine as her mental equipment is. I speak perhaps with too great frankness here, but it is in no spirit of derogation. I do not hold that pure research is, with the brief time allowed for it, a *sine qua non* for the full professorship in most of our American colleges.

Miss Haight would be a very great loss to the Department of Latin if she should resign because of a failure to receive promotion. I very sincerely second the request of my friends in the Latin Department that she be given the rank of full professor for next year.[54]

MacCracken no doubt recognized the validity of her assessment; in any case, Haight was finally promoted to full professor. Unlike Abby Leach, Grace put her feminist convictions into practice, serving as a friend, mentor, and strong supporter of all her younger colleagues. She never perceived the success of another as a diminishment of her own. Her genuine interest in others and delight in their triumphs drew people around her. In the words of Henry Noble MacCracken, "She was centric, a center of people always," and she was now to become the center of a new family.[55]

54. Grace H. Macurdy to Henry Noble MacCracken, 7 January 1922, MacCracken Papers, box 27, folder 47, Vassar Archives.

55. Quoted in Elizabeth Hazelton Haight, "The Macurdy Collection," *Vassar Alumnae Magazine* 34 (1949): 12.

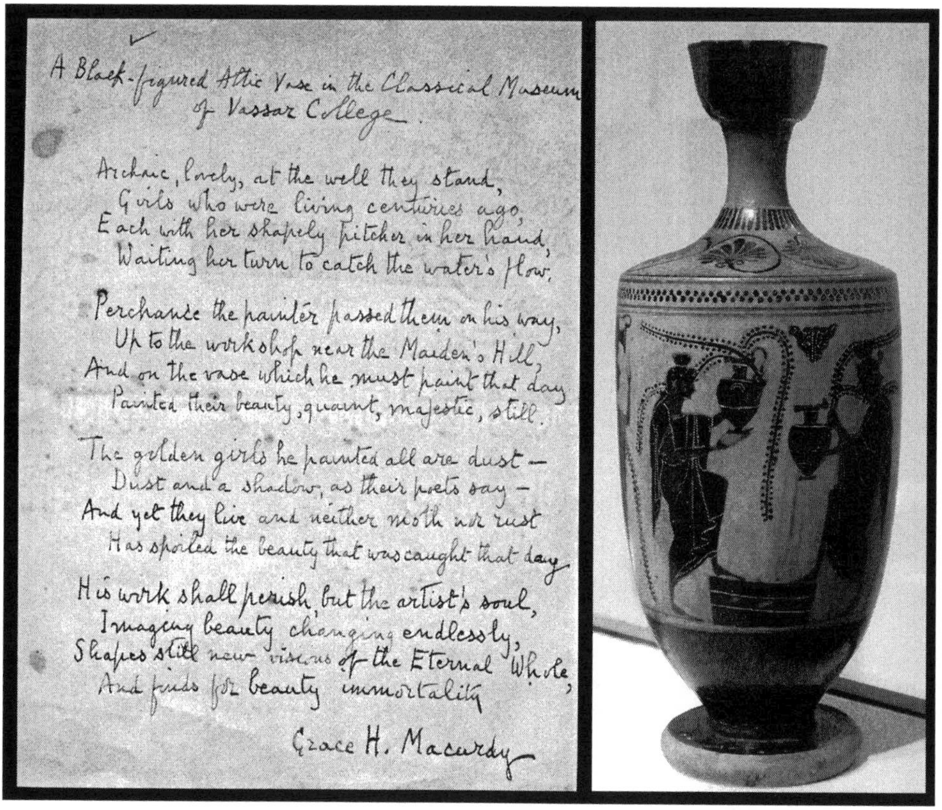

A Black-figured Attic Vase in the Classical Museum
of Vassar College.

Archaic, lovely, at the well they stand,
 Girls who were living centuries ago,
Each with her shapely pitcher in her hand,
 Waiting her turn to catch the water's flow;

Perchance the painter passed them on his way,
 Up to the workshop near the Maiden's Hill,
And on the vase which he must paint that day
 Painted their beauty, quaint, majestic, still.

The golden girls he painted all are dust —
 Dust and a shadow, as their poets say —
And yet they live and neither moth nor rust
 Has spoiled the beauty that was caught that day.

His work shall perish, but the artist's soul,
 Imaging beauty changing endlessly,
Shapes still new visions of the Eternal Whole,
 And finds for beauty immortality.

                              Grace H. Macurdy

FIGURE 1. Macurdy poem and Greek vase that inspired it. Photograph by Barbara F. McManus.

FIGURE 2. William Augustus McCurdy and Harriet Hayes.
Genealogical History of James Winslow McCurdy and Neil Barclay McCurdy.

FIGURE 3. Rebecca Manning Thomson and Simon Angus McCurdy.
Genealogical History of James Winslow McCurdy and Neil Barclay McCurdy.

FIGURE 4. Bayside Baptist church, originally built under
Adam Duncan Thomson as pastor. Photograph by Barbara F. McManus.

FIGURE 5. Grace Macurdy and her siblings with birth dates, ca. 1883.
Standing: Grace (1866), William (1864); seated, middle: Edith (1862),
Theodosia (1858), Maria (1860); seated, front: John (1873), Leigh (1876).
Private collection of June Macurdy Landin.

FIGURE 6. Watertown horse car on Mt. Auburn Street.
Watertown Free Public Library, figure 168.

FIGURE 7. Students at the Harvard Annex, 1885 (Grace Macurdy is circled).
Schlesinger Library, Radcliffe Institute, Harvard University, olvwork347152.

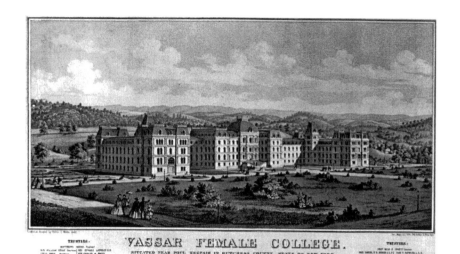

FIGURE 8. 1862 Vassar poster showing Main Hall.
Library of Congress, LC-USZ62-4194.

FIGURE 9. Grace Macurdy, ca. 1895.
Vassar Archives and Special Collections,
PhF 7.28, photo by Marshall Newton.

FIGURE 10. Abby Leach, ca. 1900.
Vassar Archives and Special Collections,
PhF 7.23.

FIGURE 11. Rebecca and Angus Macurdy, ca. 1890s.
Private collection of Barbara F. McManus.

FIGURE 12. Grace and Theodosia's house on Garnet Avenue in North Falmouth, Massachusetts.
Private collection of June Macurdy Landin.

FIGURE 13. Grace Macurdy (second from right
with elaborate hat) on Vassar Field Day, 1898.
Vassar Archives and Special Collections, PhF 9.1.1.

FIGURE 14. Grace Macurdy with her
nephew Jack, son of John Ordway
Macurdy, 1912. Private collection of
June Macurdy Landin.

FIGURE 15. Grace Macurdy, ca. 1916.
Vassar Archives and Special Collections,
PhF 7.28, photo by E. L. Wolven.

FIGURE 16. Jane Ellen Harrison, Hugh Stewart,
Gilbert Murray, and Francis Cornford in Cambridge Newnham
College, Cambridge University. The Principal and Fellows,
Newnham College, Cambridge, PP Harrison/3/2/1.

FIGURE 17. Ernest Macurdy, Theodosia Skinner (Fid),
Grace Macurdy, Helen Macurdy, with Ernest's and
Helen's children William and June, 1941.
Private collection of June Macurdy Landin.

FIGURE 18. Richard Skinner
(Dicky, circled) with the Jitney
Players, ca. 1920s. Billy Rose
Theatre Division, The New York
Public Library for the Performing
Arts, Astor, Lenox and Tilden
Foundations, TH-24192.

FIGURE 19. Bradford Skinner and Grace Macurdy, with Brad's
children Barbara (holding Mau) and Caroline, ca. 1945.
Private collection of Caroline Skinner O'Neil.

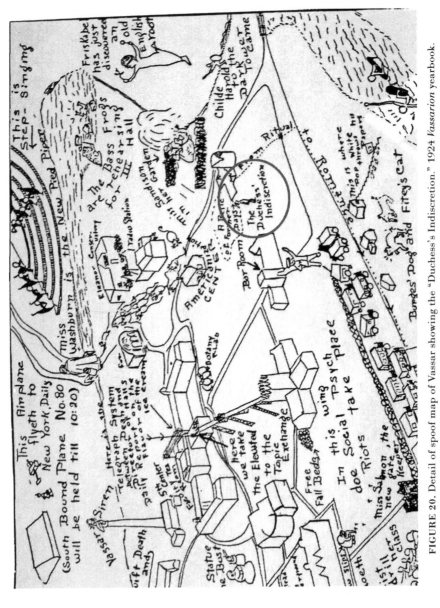

FIGURE 20. Detail of spoof map of Vassar showing the "Duchess's Indiscretion." 1924 *Vassarion* yearbook.

FIGURE 21. Grace with her cat Jason in front of Williams Hall, ca. 1932.
Vassar Archives and Special Collections, PhF 7.28, photo by Elizabeth Hazelton Haight.

FIGURE 22. Ida Thallon
Hill and Elizabeth Pierce
Blegen hiking. Blegen Library
Archives, American School of
Classical Studies at Athens,
Elizabeth Pierce Blegen
Papers, box 2, folder 5.

FIGURE 23. Grace Macurdy at her
summer house, ca. 1930. Private
collection of June Macurdy Landin.

FIGURE 24. Formal portrait of Grace Macurdy, ca. 1930s.
Vassar Archives and Special Collections, PhF 7.28,
photo by Margaret De Muth Brown.

FIGURE 25. Grace Macurdy at work in Vassar's Classical Museum, ca. 1940s.
Vassar Archives and Special Collections, PhF 7.28.

CHAPTER 8

❧

Unconventional Families

The years 1918–19 marked a time of prodigious change for Grace Mac-urdy. Not only did she assume the chairmanship of the Greek Department and experience a severe hearing loss, but she also took on new and life-changing family responsibilities that greatly enriched her emotional life while also making increasing demands on her time and financial resources. On June 23, 1918, Grace's sister Edith Macurdy Skinner died suddenly from acute appendicitis at the age of fifty-five. Edith had been raising her three children alone since the death of her husband, lawyer Henry Reuben Skinner, from a cerebral hemorrhage in 1912. Her eldest child, Theodosia, was just twenty-two when Edith died, and her two sons were still minors: Richard was eighteen and Bradford was twelve (the legal age of majority in Massachusetts at that time was 21). Grace's oldest sister, Theodosia Macurdy, was appointed administratrix of the estate, most of which was tied up in real estate, some of it heavily mortgaged. At her death, Edith had only $500 in personal funds.[1]

The family first thought that Edith's children could be cared for by Henry's sister, Anna Mabel Skinner, who had a large house on Hawthorne Street

---

1. All legal information about Edith's probate and the children's guardianship comes from the Massachusetts Trial Court Record Center, Probate File Papers, Edith M. Skinner docket number 117570 (AUD-A box 112248) and Bradford S. Skinner docket number 125337 (AUD-A box 112302). Thanks to Diane Rapaport of Quill Historical Consulting for her excellent work on obtaining and explaining this information.

a few doors from Edith's home. Anna was a successful physician who had received a medical degree from the Boston University School of Medicine and subsequently studied at the Rotunda Maternity Hospital in Ireland, affiliated with Trinity College Dublin. In 1896, Anna had married George B. Grocock, a widower with a four-year-old daughter, but the marriage ended in divorce after less than a year, and Anna legally changed her name back to Skinner. Although Anna would later make a name for herself as an adolescent psychiatrist in Boston at the Judge Baker Foundation for juvenile delinquents, her two lively nephews found her remarkably unsympathetic and the family turned to Grace for help. As early as November 1918, Grace wrote President MacCracken that she would soon be "a person with a family" (an eligibility requirement for renting a faculty house):

> I have just been appointed guardian of one of the minor children of my sister who died five months ago today. My responsibilities for the younger members of our family, which have always been considerable, are likely to be still great both financially and morally. The home in which these children live has been broken up again by sickness. I intrude upon you with these personal details reluctantly, but I should like to have my claim considered in the future in case one of the houses in the Faculty Row should be vacated.[2]

Vassar had purchased the three-story house Abby Leach had built on college property on Raymond Avenue after her death;[3] in an ironic twist of fate, this house was now assigned to Grace and her instant family. Theodosia, Richard, and Bradford came to live with Grace in this house in September 1919, although documents appointing Grace as the legal guardian of Richard and Bradford were not filed until January 1920. Suddenly Grace had an entire household to run with no previous experience of domestic responsibilities, since she had lived in her parents' home and then in dormitory rooms in Vassar's Main Hall. The house represented an unexpected drain on her finances as well, not only because of the increased rent, but especially because the furnace was defective. Despite the fact that Grace paid excessively high amounts for coal and wood, the family shivered through two winters before the college

---

2. Grace H. Macurdy to Henry Noble MacCracken, 23 November 1918, MacCracken Papers, box 17, folder 39, Vassar Archives.

3. When Abby Leach decided to leave Main Hall because she felt other faculty there were shunning her due to her treatment of Grace Macurdy, she was not eligible for a faculty house because she had no family members living with her. She was, however, allowed to build a house at her own expense on college property along Raymond Avenue with the proviso that the college would purchase the house at appraised value after she died.

agreed to renovate the furnace pipes. These costs were only slightly defrayed by the rent paid by German professor Marian P. Whitney, who was Grace's tenant for the first three years. Edith's estate did pay her children's major expenses, including Richard's tuition fees at Harvard.[4]

Grace accepted these new responsibilities with her usual good humor and positive attitude. She told President MacCracken that "she had prayed for a family when she was a girl, and the Lord had certainly responded!"[5] When discussing her instant family with the students, she jokingly proffered the maxim that "every woman, married or not, should be allowed one child, no questions asked."[6] A former student had observed that Grace "was always rather famous for her attachment to the family, especially all the young things coming along, and how she was helping them and how interested she was in that," but this was even more deeply personal; her sister's children were suddenly transformed into her own.[7]

" y Children"

Grace opened her heart as well as her home and her pocketbook to these three orphans, whom she liked to call "my children." They thrived under her loving, easygoing care. The eldest, Theodosia Frances Skinner (born August 1, 1895), was always called "Fid" by her family, apparently because her younger brother could not pronounce her name. When her mother died, Fid had just graduated from Simmons College in Boston with a bachelor of science in household economics. Her domestic skills were important to the new family, since Grace admittedly had none. Abby Leach had managed the large house with the help of a live-in Japanese butler, but Grace could not afford more than a maid who came in to clean. In April 1919, Fid was hired to manage an employee cafeteria established by the Dutchess Manufacturing Company, where she met Carl P. Immekus, a Poughkeepsie native working for this firm. Fid and Carl soon became a couple. Carl was Catholic, a religion that Grace

---

4. Legal documents indicate that the estate paid out $2,915.51 for the children during the years 1918–20.

5. Henry Noble MacCracken to Bradford S. Skinner, 12 January 1951, private collection of Caroline Skinner O'Neil.

6. In her research notes for her biographical sketch of Abby Leach, A. T. Zwart presents this as a serious quote from her 1969 interview with "Mrs. Allardyce." However, Margaret Middleditch Allardyce was a student at Vassar from 1920 to 1924, when Bradford was still a boy under Grace's care, and this statement has all the hallmarks of a typical Grace Macurdy witticism. *Notable American Women* files, MC 230, box 52, Schlesinger.

7. Evalyn Clark, interview by Barbara F. McManus, 6 December 1997.

did not quite approve of, but she had already accepted and come to love her brother John's Irish-Catholic wife, so she celebrated Fid and Carl's marriage in Poughkeepsie's Church of the Nativity on September 17, 1920. The young couple, who never had children, lived in Grace's house. This arrangement was invaluable for Grace, since she was able to spend her 1922–23 sabbatical year and subsequent summers abroad knowing that Fid and Carl would take good care of Bradford. In May 1926, Carl accepted a job in New York, and Fid and Carl moved to Jackson Heights, Queens. After their departure, Grace moved to a large apartment in the recently opened Williams Hall. Grace remained in close contact with Fid for the rest of her life (see figure 17 for a photo of Fid with Grace with the Ernest Macurdy family).

Richard Henry Leigh Skinner (born February 27, 1900) entered Harvard in the fall after his mother's death, graduating in 1922. Grace served as his legal guardian until his twenty-first birthday. He lived in Cambridge during the school year, but spent holidays with Grace. Dicky, as Grace always called him, was a talented actor and singer; he had been very active in the Harvard Dramatic Club and sang as a tenor in the Glee Club. After graduation he lived in Grace's house and worked for two years as a reporter on the local newspaper, the *Poughkeepsie Eagle-News*, where his "nose for news" involved Grace in an embarrassing contretemps. He published an article announcing that Vassar was opening a new department devoted to euthenics, which aimed at betterment of the human race through "the science of controllable environment." This multidisciplinary field, first promoted by Vassar alumnae Ellen Swallow Richards and Julia Lathrop, became a project heavily supported by President MacCracken, who was counting on a large donation by Vassar alumna Minnie Cumnock Blodgett to fund the construction of a special hall to house the Division of Euthenics. When Dicky published the article in 1923, the entire Vassar community was under strict orders of secrecy, and Mrs. Blodgett and the Vassar trustees were angered by the premature announcement. Grace, acutely conscientious about college matters, felt compelled to write to President MacCracken explaining her nephew's actions:

> My nephew, Richard Skinner, tells me that Professor Johnson [Burgess Johnson, head of Vassar's Bureau of Publication] has just acquainted him with the fact that an account which he gave the Eagle based on a pamphlet about Euthenics sent to me has been discussed by the trustees. Such a pamphlet never reached me. It was considered by my nephew as sent to him by Professor Johnson with whom he had been talking the matter over and from whom he was looking for a statement. The pamphlet which I have never seen came just after his request for information was made to Professor Johnson and he

not unnaturally thought the pamphlet which was not addressed to me was sent to him. I greatly regret the occurrence and assure you and the trustees that I never have given and never should think of giving any information to my nephew or any one else that came to me through the college or about the college without permission from the proper authorities.[8]

Despite his occasional impulsive behavior, Dicky was a popular figure on campus and often accompanied Grace to college events. He was lively and witty, an excellent storyteller, and always very good company. He was also flamboyantly gay at a time when this lifestyle was considered reprehensible, though never by Grace, who was notably broad minded and tolerant. By 1924, Dicky had left the newspaper for a life in the theater, first joining the Jitney Players, a repertory drama group that toured the northeast every summer performing on a collapsible stage mounted on a truck (see figure 18 for a photo of Dicky with the Jitney Players). He also studied for two years with Richard Boleslavsky and Maria Ouspenskaya at the American Laboratory Theater in New York. Besides his many summers with the Jitney Players, he won parts on Broadway and in other theaters in the metropolitan area, but he found his greatest success as a producer and company manager in New York City and especially in many summer-stock theaters. The *New York Times* summed up his career with a substantial obituary in 1971.[9]

Until her death, Grace provided a stable core of family and home in Dicky's peripatetic life, and he visited her often, especially on holidays, when he delighted her friends with stories of life in the theater. As a favor to Grace, he agreed in 1933 to direct a Vassar Alumnae Association production of Oscar Wilde's play *A Woman of No Importance* in which faculty played many of the major roles. When novelist Mary McCarthy, then a senior at Vassar, gave the play an acerbic review, she aimed most of her criticism at the playwright; her flippant remarks about the director offer backhanded testimony to Dicky's popularity on campus: "This blurring, this disharmony of interpretation seems to lie at the door of the director, Richard Skinner, who has had professional experience, and the Lord defend us from criticizing him!"[10]

8. "Vassar Starts New Department," *Poughkeepsie Eagle-News*, 17 December 1923, 5; Grace H. Macurdy to Henry Noble MacCracken, 17 January 1924, MacCracken Papers, box 29, folder 18, Vassar Archives.

9. "Richard Skinner, Stage Producer: Broadway Figure, Active in Summer Stock, Dies at 71," *New York Times*, 4 August 1971, 37.

10. Mary McCarthy, "Woman of No Importance is Condemned as Unimportant," *Vassar Miscellany News*, 12 April 1933, 5.

Bradford Swanton Skinner (born October 9, 1905) was most in need of "raising" when he came to live with Grace at the age of twelve, and he flourished under her loving, supportive, and lenient care. He quickly became a college pet among the students, who promptly nicknamed him "the Duchess's Indiscretion." A spoof campus map full of inside jokes drawn for the 1924 *Vassarion* yearbook shows him standing by the main gate of the college with the label "The Duchess' Indiscretion" (figure 20 shows a detail of this map). Brad did not learn about his nickname until some years after he had reached adulthood and moved to Springfield, as he explained in a letter to Henry Noble MacCracken:

> One evening we were entertaining among others Miss Grace Stebbins who graduated from Vassar in the early twenties. We were talking about mutual acquaintances when she remarked "Why you must be th[e] Duchess's Indiscretion." When I looked puzzled she explained that my aunt, who was fondly respected by the girls at that time, did have a certain regal appearance that she combined on occasion with a slightly askew hat or a slip that showed so that she was secretly known to the girls as "The Drunken Duchess." When a teen age [*sic*] boy appeared at her home and escorted her to church at the college and to other college affairs the girls promptly dubbed me the "Duchess's Indiscretion." That apparently was my title to that generation of Vassar girls.[11]

The pages of the *Poughkeepsie Eagle-News* are full of Brad's accomplishments in Poughkeepsie High School—he won honors in debating, served as editor of the school monthly magazine, was a member of the football team for three years, earned praise as star of a high-school play, and was elected president of the senior class. The entire school elected him to serve as Poughkeepsie's "Boy Mayor for a Day" in April 1924. During his term in office he mischievously proposed closing the schools at 2:00 p.m., a proposal swiftly vetoed by the school superintendent. A statement in one of his articles as high-school correspondent for the *Eagle* shows that he was not unaffected by Grace's academic interests: "That the advantages of athletics is [*sic*] recognized freely is shown by the growth of gymnasium work as connected with

---

11. Bradford S. Skinner to Henry Noble MacCracken, 8 January 1951, private collection of Caroline Skinner O'Neil. The map was part of a spoof 1923–24 Vassar catalog included in the 1924 *Vassarion*.

the school life, in the fashion of the old Greek civilization, and by the growth of athletics for girls."[12]

Like any proud mother, Grace attended school events, opened her home for Brad's activities and friends, and worried when he was out late. Her responsibilities did not end when he entered Amherst College in 1924, however. His skills in Latin were not strong, and he was in danger of flunking his required Latin course. Ever resourceful, he invited Grace to visit him at Amherst and arranged for his Latin instructor to meet his distinguished aunt, the classical scholar. As a result of that meeting, he was allowed to make up his deficiencies with an extra research paper on the aqueducts in Rome, though his instructor commented on his paper that he was a better engineer than the Romans, since he had constructed a twelfth aqueduct while they had managed only eleven.

After graduation from Amherst, Brad moved to Springfield, Massachusetts, and worked for some years as a reporter for the *Springfield Republican*. He married Dorothy Fitzgerald of Ohio, owned and ran the Bradford S. Skinner Insurance Agency, and had two daughters, Grace's "grandchildren," Barbara and Caroline (see figure 19).

Cats

When Grace moved to the house on Raymond Avenue, she was finally able to indulge her love for cats, adopting a black cat appropriately named Felix. The long-lived Felix became something of a legend on campus, inspiring the devotion not only of his mistress but also of Margaret Floy Washburn, professor of psychology at Vassar, author of *The Animal Mind*, and the second woman inducted into the National Academy of Science. His fame spread beyond Vassar, due to his mention in *Time* magazine: "Professor Washburn's great and good friend at Vassar was Felix, the Greek Department's old black cat. Felix knew all the stunts of the psychological laboratory and he helped out in a friendly way. He and she, she would half-seriously say, knew what each was thinking." When he died, hit by an automobile while crossing Raymond Avenue, the playwright Emmet Lavery published an obituary in a New York–area newspaper called "Felix, the Companionable, Leaves Vassar and Campus Is Shy One Who Mattered," that concluded, "Whether Felix will have an epitaph we do not know now. But visible or invisible, any epitaph that he might have would inevitably radiate from the thought that of all people and

---

12. Bradford Skinner, "School Athletics Have Advantages," *Poughkeepsie Eagle-News*, 23 November 1923, 9.

things Professor Macurdy had prized him extraordinarily well. To that degree he mattered."[13]

Grace was never without a cat once she moved out of Vassar's Main Hall. After Felix came Jason, then Mau (see figure 21 for a photo of Grace and Jason). As much as she loved her cats, however, she never let them interfere with her travels or her scholarship, though she always made provision for their care while she was away. The summer that Felix died, for example, she had offered her apartment in Williams Hall, where she had moved after Fid and Carl left her house, to a young instructor in psychology on condition that she would look after the cat while Grace was in England. A humorous poem that Grace wrote in 1937 thanking her friends for their parting gifts when she left for a year abroad after she retired concludes with a reference to her current cat:

> And all the members of Williams Hall
> My heart aches sorely to leave you now.
> I thank you and beg still another boon;
> I ask you all to be kind to Mau.[14]

A Sort of   arriage

Although she never married, Grace was a strong supporter of women's right to both a career and marriage. For example, when she was in England on her first sabbatical, her ire was aroused by an article in the *Pall Mall Gazette* by Charlotte Cowdroy, antifeminist headmistress of the Crouch End High School for Girls, arguing that women should give up paid employment after marrying. In support of this contention, Cowdroy cited the scandalous case of Edith Thompson, hanged for inciting her young lover to murder her husband, labeling her "an abnormal woman" because she continued to work outside the home after her marriage—even earning more than her husband—and did not want children.[15] Grace's reply, "Shall the Married Woman Work?" (signed "an American Woman"), presented a dramatic contrast to the article that pro-

---

13. "Science: Facts, Questions," *Time*, 11 May 1931, 42. The newspaper clipping of Felix's obituary, headed "Poughkeepsie, N. Y.," is located in Biographical Files: Macurdy, Grace Harriet, folder 2, Vassar Archives. The clipping does not name the newspaper or date the article.

14. Edward R. Linner, "As I Remember Them," *Vassar Alumnae Magazine* 55 (1969): 17.

15. Charlotte Cowdroy, "A Study of Mrs. Thompson," *Pall Mall Gazette*, 9 January 1923, 9. Cowdroy's article was published on the day of Thompson's hanging. I am grateful to Patricia Auspos for locating this article.

voked it. Avoiding all sensationalism and not even mentioning the Thompson case, Grace composed a judicious rebuttal of Cowdroy's position that drew on arguments ranging from Greek philosophers to modern class prejudices. Her conclusion reveals not only her conviction of the importance of employment for women, but also her belief in a woman's right to conduct her private life without societal interference:

> And if, as is terribly apparent, men degenerate by unemployment, the same is true of women, whether married or single. . . . It seems unfair that the teacher or gymnastic expert or physician should give up her work, which is as dear to her as a man's is to him. And I contend that the domestic arrangements should be a private and individual affair.[16]

Grace was, in the words of a former student, "her own type and she was going to go ahead and live that way. . . . She was very much her own person."[17] And so her unorthodox family life was not limited to her single motherhood; she also became part of an unconventional couple. Grace had first met the Scottish classicist J. A. K. Thomson when she invited him to lecture on "Greeks and Barbarians" at Vassar in the spring of 1920 when he was a visiting lecturer at Harvard. Thomson later wrote Murray that Grace had impressed him favorably: "I must say the atmosphere of classical study in America is far from stimulating. Really I think the most living person I met there was Miss Macurdy of Vassar. She may be a little mad about the Paeonian Apollo, but it is the right sort of madness."[18] When Thomson returned to America to teach as a sabbatical replacement at Bryn Mawr from 1921 to 1922, Grace invited him to visit her for a weekend in November at her house on Raymond Avenue. From that point, they quickly became very close friends despite the age difference (Grace was fifty-five, Thomson forty-two).

Their friendship was close enough that Thomson was able to confide to Grace his ongoing difficulties with finding academic employment. Grace suggested that he serve as her 1922–23 sabbatical replacement at Vassar. She then privately proposed to President MacCracken that she would make an anonymous gift of $600, nearly 20 percent of her own salary, so that Vassar could offer Thomson a salary of $2,000 instead of the usual $1,400 for an instructor. Despite the fact that this would put a strain on her own tight finances, she was excited about the prospect of secretly helping Thomson in this way,

---

16. "Shall the Married Woman Work?" *Pall Mall Gazette,* 11 January 1923, 9.

17. Evalyn Clark, interview by Barbara F. McManus, 6 December 1997.

18. J. A. K. Thomson to Gilbert Murray, 27 September 1921, MSS Gilbert Murray 172, fols. 23–24, Bodleian.

though she did acknowledge the eccentricity of this gesture. As she wrote MacCracken, "Mr. Thomson is such a fine young scholar and so fine in character and spirit that I would very much like to do this. . . . May I ask that no one except yourself and me should hear of this? My friends would think it quixotic and perhaps wrong in principle." The generosity and impracticality of Grace's offer emerges in a later letter when she has to petition Vassar to guarantee her salary for her sabbatical year so she can receive a letter of credit from her bank: "I had not contemplated this emergency and as I have no means of going abroad except the salary of next year I am in trouble about it. Owing to family service on my part extending over all the years of my working life I have no other resources."[19] Fortunately for her finances, Grace had to withdraw her proposal when she discovered that members of the Latin department did not want Thomson to come to Vassar because that would deprive them of the advanced electives in Greek they had been teaching. After his visiting appointment at Bryn Mawr, therefore, Thomson returned to his family in Scotland in June 1922 with no prospects of a faculty position.

Grace then threw herself into efforts to find another position for Thomson, recommending him unsuccessfully for faculty posts at New York University and Swarthmore College. When she departed for her sabbatical, instead of sailing from New York she traveled to Montreal so she could sail on the SS Tunisia directly to Glasgow and visit with Thomson before going to England. Thomson arranged for the two of them to meet with Gilbert Murray: "Since Miss Macurdy is in this country, it would be a great pity, I think, if she and you and I did not have a consultation together about Homer. I could come to Oxford for the purpose or to any other place more convenient for you."[20] While in England, Grace worked behind the scenes to help Murray secure a position for Thomson; as she wrote Murray, "I am very anxious indeed that our friend should have a position worthy of his talents. His sensitiveness is against his pushing, but he would fill any such post with honor and his great gifts would gradually be recognized." She collected testimonials from American scholars and provided valuable advice about whom not to ask, particularly M. Carey Thomas, president of Bryn Mawr, who was prejudiced against Thomson by one of her faculty and who was known to "hate men."[21] Grace's efforts on Thomson's behalf did not have much effect in Britain since she was

19. Grace H. Macurdy to Henry Noble MacCracken, 2 and 6 February 1922; 25 March 1922, MacCracken Papers, box 27, folder 34, Vassar Archives.

20. J. A. K. Thomson to Gilbert Murray, 28 June 1922, MSS Gilbert Murray 172, fols. 36–37, Bodleian.

21. Grace H. Macurdy to Gilbert Murray, 17 and 20 December 1922, MSS Gilbert Murray 157, fols. 53–58, Bodleian.

not only an American but also a woman in a male-dominated profession. However, she did have a great deal of influence in her own institution, so she was able to secure a fallback offer for Thomson—a two-year faculty position at Vassar—which he did not have to accept or decline until after he had exhausted all possible opportunities in England. In the end, Gilbert Murray was able to procure for Thomson the position of professor of classical literature and chair of the Classics Department at King's College London, which he assumed in the fall of 1923 and held until his retirement in 1945.[22]

Once Thomson was settled in London, Grace spent every summer from 1924 to 1936 there, plus her half-year sabbatical in 1930 and her postretirement year from spring 1937 to fall 1938. She always rented a flat right next to his, moving from Queensberry Place in South Kensington to Lexham Gardens in Kensington when he did. Grace and Thomson frequently traveled together to Italy, Greece, other parts of Europe, Scotland, and Wales. Over the years, they jointly collected a large number of Greek vases and other artifacts, which Thomson proudly displayed in his flat. Grace wrote with easy familiarity about Thomson, including issuing invitations on his behalf, as in a letter to Bert H. Hill:

> I have written J. A. K. Thomson that you and Carl [Blegen] are coming to London about Feb. 9. I do hope that you will give him the pleasure of seeing you. . . . J. A. K. T. would love to have you for dinner etc. and then you might like to look at our treasures of vases, of which his apartment is full. . . . And he will probably give you a detective story or two!"[23]

Besides their passion for all things Greek, Thomson and Grace shared a fascination with detective stories of the more intellectual sort. As Grace wrote her friend Ida, "I like my victims and my murderers to be gentlemen and scholars. These Crime Kate and Lefty Louie Crime Club stories I cannot read. . . . Well, I must buzz off, as Lord Peter Wimsey, the detective, would say."[24] Even when World War II prevented Grace from sailing to England, their relationship continued through letters. Grace fretted about Thomson's safety during the blitzes and sent him razor blades and other supplies still

---

22. All the efforts on Thomson's behalf, including the King's College London search stage-managed by Murray, are documented in a series of letters in MSS Gilbert Murray 172, fols. 51–98, Bodleian.

23. Grace H. Macurdy to Bert H. Hill, 19 January 1937, Bert Hodge Hill Papers, box 4 folder 2, Blegen Library.

24. Grace H. Macurdy to Ida Thallon Hill, 13 April 1929, Ida Thallon Hill Papers, box 2, folder 5, Blegen Library.

available in America. In the beginning of 1946, Grace and Thomson arranged
to loan their collection of Greek vases to Oxford's Ashmolean Museum, and
after Grace died later that year, Thomson offered them to the museum as a
permanent gift, with any that the Ashmolean did not want to go to Vassar.
Their joint collection was a symbol of their close relationship, and now that
she was gone he did not want to keep it. As he wrote to the museum's keeper
of the Department of Antiquities, "The only thing I really care about is that
her name should attach to the gift."[25]

Although both Grace and Thomson carefully saved their letters from Gilbert Murray, they (or their executors) did not preserve their many letters to
each other, perhaps because they seemed too personal. However, there are
many other forms of evidence that they considered themselves "a couple,"
and that their friends accepted them as such. When Grace was in London, she
and Thomson always entertained friends together, and if one was invited to
any event, the other would always be included in the invitation. As Grace and
Thomson were departing on a trip to Greece together, Grace's former student,
friend, and colleague Ida Thallon closely linked the two in a letter to the director of the American School of Classical Studies in Athens: "Miss Macurdy and
JAK Thomson are leaving for Athens in less than a week. Be good to them.
They are rare spirits."[26] Vassar psychology professor Margaret Floy Washburn
thought of Grace's summers in England when she wrote from the deck of a
Cunard ship, "The ship's food is vile beyond words . . . This is because the food
is English. Your affection for J. A. K. T. must indeed be great. I understand
now why you always come back so sylph-like in form."[27] This joke between
friends testifies to the easy acceptance of Macurdy's rather unorthodox relationship with Thomson. Gilbert Murray and his wife sent Thomson a photo of
Grace as a Christmas present, so they were aware that this was something he
would value. An odd illustration of the close association of Grace and Thomson in the minds of their friends appears in a letter of Peter Giles, master of
Emmanuel College in Cambridge, to Grace: "Your young relative Norman
Meldrum has settled down satisfactorily, I think. He was here on Sunday to
lunch; he was, as you told my wife, he would be, rather shy; but he will no

---

25. J. A. K. Thomson to D. B. Harden, 30 May 1947, Ashmolean Museum, Oxford University.
26. Ida Thallon to Bert H. Hill, 22 July 1924, Bert Hodge Hill Papers, box 7, folder 1, Blegen
Library.
27. Margaret Floy Washburn to Grace H. Macurdy, 10 April 1928, Autograph Files, Vassar
Archives.

doubt get over that."[28] But Meldrum was Thomson's nephew, no relation to Grace.

With Thomson, Grace forged an egalitarian, intellectual partnership that promoted the confidence and independence of both individuals, something neither could achieve with the Olympian Gilbert Murray, however supportive he undoubtedly was. In 1926 they even began writing a book together, "A Chapter in the History of Pity," a subject that Grace eventually incorporated in her book *The Quality of Mercy* (1940). At first glance their relationship appears similar to that of Jane Ellen Harrison and Francis M. Cornford because of the age disparity and the fact that the attraction was based on both parties' intense commitment to their shared subject and deep respect for each other's intellect and scholarship. The differences, however, are more significant than the similarities. Cornford and Harrison became friends when he was a fourth-year student at Trinity College in Cambridge; he was twenty-four, while she was forty-eight, literally twice his age (see figure 16). For the next ten years they were often together—bicycling, sharing long intellectual discussions, spending vacations together; Cornford proofread the text of *Prolegomena* and contributed a chapter to *Themis*. But Cornford fell in love with and married Frances Darwin in 1909, sending Harrison into a tailspin of jealousy, depression, and ill health and effectively ending their close relationship.[29] In contrast, Thomson saw Grace as a fellow scholar, never a mentor or teacher. Unlike Harrison, Grace showed no evidence of flirtatiousness, jealousy, or possessiveness toward Thomson. Their relationship was mutually satisfying and continued so until Grace's death.

There is, however, one major similarity—the likelihood that neither relationship was sexual. Grace and Thomson certainly loved each other, but there is no hard evidence to substantiate or disprove physical intimacy. Grace's nephew Brad Skinner, who as an adult took her to the ship on her annual sailings to England and met her when she returned, told his daughters that

---

28. Peter Giles to Grace H. Macurdy, 31 March 1929, Biographical Files: Macurdy, Grace Harriet, folder 2, Vassar Archives. Unfortunately, Meldrum did not ultimately settle down; while a chemistry student at Cambridge in 1933, he committed suicide by swallowing chemicals from the lab. There must have been a strain of psychosis inherited from his father, the noted Scottish chemist Andrew Meldrum, whose own suicide in 1934 was disguised as an accident, since his sister, Elizabeth Meldrum, was committed to a mental health institution in 1950 because of repeated suicide attempts, and his other sister, Margaret Meldrum, committed suicide in 1952 by taking sleeping pills and lying across train tracks at night.

29. For more information on Harrison's relationship with Cornford, see Annabel Robinson, *The Life and Work of Jane Ellen Harrison* (Oxford: Oxford University Press, 2002), 199–217; and Jessie Stuart, *Jane Ellen Harrison: A Portrait from Letters* (London: Merlin Press, 1959), 101–13.

the relationship "may or may not have been platonic."[30] Former student and colleague Evalyn Clark, however, said that it was widely known at Vassar that Grace was very attached to Thomson but this was not considered scandalous: "I don't think anybody was thinking of scandals looking at her. . . . Well in the first place because she had sort of a disarming approach—nobody would ever think that this was being sort of illicit or anything. They were perfectly frank and open. She had a kind of a charm about her and an innocence, an air of innocence."[31] Both Grace and Thomson were first and foremost scholars whose highest life was that of the mind, not the body; they both found in the relationship what they needed: the love and support of a kindred spirit, the steady companionship of an equal, the pleasure of challenging intellectual discussions.

Both were progressive and broad minded but not social radicals. Grace's approach to life was always straightforward and unsentimental, but Thomson had a streak of Victorian romanticism that appeared in the poetry and fiction he occasionally tried to write. For example, after his retirement in 1945 he submitted to Allen & Unwin, his long-time publisher, a volume of short stories, ultimately rejected by the press's readers as "completely out of touch with present day writing." Most of the stories are set in the distant past and full of fantasy, but one stands out for its quiet sentiment. "Miss Cristina," set in nineteenth-century Scotland, brings a young divinity student to aid a country vicar who has injured his leg. The vicar's middle-aged daughter, Cristina, serves as his housekeeper, and the student is drawn to her. One night they walk over the countryside together to see a brilliant display of the aurora borealis. As the student is departing upon the vicar's recovery, he suppresses a strong impulse to kiss Cristina, but he cannot resist looking back at her standing in the doorway. In the words of one of the readers, "The meaning of the story is implicit; Cristina was born fifteen years too soon."[32] This story may or may not have any bearing on his relationship with Grace, but it does shed light on Thomson's strong sense of propriety and restraint.

"The Four"

From her own experiences, Grace was used to nontraditional families, and friendship associated her with a four-person family that was unconventional

---

30. Caroline Skinner O'Neil, interview by Barbara F. McManus, 13 May 2005.

31. Evalyn Clark, interview by Barbara F. McManus, 6 December 1997.

32. AUC 325/7, Allen & Unwin Collection, Department of Special Collections, Reading University Library. The reader's reports are dated 1947.

indeed, a family that would have a profound effect on her life for the next several years.[33] Although Grace was certainly familiar with crushes and smashes among the students and with more long-lasting relationships sometimes forged between a female faculty member and former student, there is no evidence whatsoever that her own many close friendships with other women ever had a romantic component. However, her dear friend Ida Thallon, a former student and later colleague who had been the first to notify Grace that Abby Leach was planning to fire her, did form such a relationship with one of her students, Elizabeth Denny Pierce, usually called Lib or Libbie.[34] Lib enrolled in Vassar in 1906 and fell in love with her teacher Ida; she carefully preserved in her college scrapbook a card with a poem most likely written by Ida, who had a fondness for referring to people by three initials:

O E. D. P.
Come here to me.
I like thy violets and like thee!
Dost thou like me?
Then, don't you see?
No one must longer "bashful" be,
O E. D. P.[35]

Lib remained at Vassar to earn a master of arts in 1912 and returned to Vassar in 1915 to serve as an assistant in art history; she and Ida now lived in adjacent rooms in a Vassar residence hall. Grace was well aware of their close relationship and warmly accepted Lib into her circle of friends; Ida and Lib are the only people who called her "Gracie." Ida had been a student at the

---

33. I am grateful to Robert L. Pounder of Vassar College for encouraging me to consult the archives of the American School of Classical Studies at Athens for information about the Hills, Blegens, and their relationship to Grace Macurdy. Pounder has recently published an article on "The Blegens and the Hills: A Family Affair," in *Carl W. Blegen: Personal and Archaeological Narratives*, ed. Natalia Vogeikoff-Brogan, Jack L. Davis, Vasiliki Florou (Atlanta, Ga.: Lockwood Press, 2015), 85–98. Natalia Vogeikoff-Brogan, Doreen Canaday Spitzer archivist at ASCSA, gave me invaluable help accessing the archival material, without which this and the following chapter could not have been written.

34. Brief biographical sketches of both women can be found on the *Breaking Ground: Women in Old World Archaeology* website: Natalia Vogeikoff, "Ida Thallon Hill (1875–1954)," http://www.brown.edu/Research/Breaking_Ground/results.php?d=1&first=Ida%20Thallon&last =Hill; and Elizabeth Langridge-Noti, "Elizabeth Pierce Blegen (1888–1966)," accessed 22 January 2015, http://www.brown.edu/Research/Breaking_Ground/results.php?d=1&first=Elizabeth %20Pierce&last=Blegen.

35. Elizabeth Pierce Blegen Scrapbook, Vassar College Student Materials Collection, Vassar Archives. In a letter dated 8 May 1924, Lib told Bert Hodge Hill that she had loved Ida since her freshman year. Bert Hodge Hill Papers, box 8, folder 3, Blegen Library.

American School of Classical Studies in Athens (ASCSA) in 1899–1901 and earned a Columbia doctorate in 1905; following in Ida's footsteps, Lib earned a doctorate at Columbia and was an ASCSA student in 1922–23. During her year abroad, she wrote many letters to Ida that reveal the depth and passionate nature of their relationship:

> September 23, 1922:
> You do not know how much you have done for me, my own dearest one, for if these things had happened before I had your love, I should have been as blue as indigo but now they seem mere "flea bites" . . . beside the biggest thing in my life.

> November 29, 1922:
> I like that any how for you make everything so interesting, my own beloved-est. I wish I could kiss you 29 times right this minute!

> December 11, 1922:
> I love you so much and I know you didn't mean to hurt me but I want your arms around me tight and then I'd be so happy. But 5,000 miles is an awful long way for anyone's arms to reach![36]

A later letter to Ida, however, mentioned a complicating factor: "My 'personality' which I have been so assiduously cultivating may be having too powerful an effect on a certain person (C. W. B.) and I wish to avoid all 'entangling alliances.'"[37] At this time Bert Hodge Hill was director of the American School and Carl William Blegen was assistant director.[38] Lib was downplaying the seriousness of this issue, since Blegen had fallen deeply in love with her. In fact, he proposed marriage on January 27, just a few weeks after this letter, and Lib agreed to marry him. Ida was very distressed when she received a cable notifying her of this news, but she proceeded with her sabbatical plans to study in Greece and Italy, traveling with Lib and returning to New York

---

36. Ida Thallon Hill Papers, box 2, folders 6–7; box 3, folder 1, Blegen Library.

37. Elizabeth Pierce to Ida Thallon, 10 January 1923, Ida Thallon Hill Papers, box 3, folder 1, Blegen Library.

38. Bert Hodge Hill (1874–1958) and Carl William Blegen (1887–1971) were both classical archaeologists and excavators; Blegen, later a professor at the University of Cincinnati, became one of the foremost American archaeologists, most famous for his work on the Palace of Nestor in Pylos and the site of Troy. Neither has a full-length biography, but Vogeikoff-Brogan et al., *Carl W. Blegen*, gives an excellent portrayal of Blegen, and Hill to a lesser extent, in the context of the development of classical archaeology in Greece.

together. The reunion of the two women swayed Lib's affections, and she broke off her engagement with Carl in June 1923.

Ida was overjoyed, but Lib remained very conflicted, wavering back and forth between Ida and Carl, who continued to write urging his suit and came to New York in person at the beginning of the summer. When Lib finally decided that she would accept Carl's marriage proposal, she wrote poignantly to Bert Hill:

> I have already decided to marry Carl. The difficulty with making Ida understand the situation is that she will not recognize that there are two kinds of love and as she knows I love her she cannot realize that I also love Carl. After she hears I have married him she will be very much hurt and think that I have put him in her place, not realizing that I shall still love her just as much as before.[39]

Lib and Carl were married on June 11, 1924, keeping this a secret from Ida until after the fact. Carl wrote a triumphant letter to Bert predicting a "wonderful year coming for the triumvirate": "I couldn't possibly tell you in words how wonderful it is, and what a tremendous relief it is to both of us to have the problem finally definitely settled and settled right."[40] However, the triumvirate was soon to become a quartet, as Bert and Lib conspired to bring about what they jokingly called "the Pro Par," or professional partnership. Bert kept pressing Ida, who was staying at her family's summer home in England, to marry him. Feeling hurt and betrayed, Ida at first resisted but finally wrote Bert a long letter explaining that she was seriously considering such a partnership but only if all her conditions would be met, including her own freedom to come and go as she pleased and visit with family for part of the year. The most crucial condition, however, was that all four of them would have to live together always:

> With the various permutations and combinations there are several ways in which we should often be inclined to pair off, and I do not see how this would in any way interfere with your intimacy with Carl. . . . Of course, she [Lib] would always have first choice, for fond as I am of you I love her more than anything in the world. Carl has married her knowing she feels the same way about me.

39. Elizabeth Pierce to Bert H. Hill, 3 June 1924, Bert Hodge Hill Papers, box 8, folder 3, Blegen Library.

40. Carl W Blegen to Bert H. Hill, 15 July 1924, Carl William Blegen Papers, box 16, folder 3, Blegen Library.

Bert's reply, preserved in a carefully composed draft, accepted all her conditions in his characteristically humorous way. This letter seems to have won the day, for he and Ida married later that summer:

> While I could not conscientiously make quite so sweeping a statement I can say I d. n. l. you more than is reasonable. . . . All the possible pairings out of ~~the quartet~~ the four of us ~~they are not many~~ seem to me ~~most~~ quite satisfactory: (1) I + B, E + C; (2) I + E, B + C; (3) I + C, E + B. I ~~am~~ should not, however, be prepared to take oath *always* to prefer (2) to (1).[41]

They did fulfill these conditions to a remarkable extent, living together in the same residences for the rest of their lives, their only lengthy separation caused by World War II, during which Bert remained in Greece and the other three in America. Among close friends, they referred to themselves as "the Four" or "the family." They were all fiercely devoted to each other and to their union, and Ida and Lib continued their passionate relationship apparently without arousing jealousy in any quarter (see figure 22 for a photo of Ida Hill and Elizabeth Blegen). Their famous house at 9 Ploutarchou Street in Athens became a social and intellectual center for scholars and archaeologists from all over the world and contained a shared bedroom for Ida and Lib, while Carl and Bert each had a separate room. When the men's positions at the American School were under siege a year after their marriages, Lib and Carl went to Boston to attempt to ameliorate the situation. Comments from two letters Lib wrote Ida show that the intensity of their feelings for each other had not diminished:

> Belovedest my own. This is just another page added to tell you that nothing else in the world matters as long as I have you. And I'm going to keep you for ever and ever—nothing can part us now. . . . There is a lovely little sickle moon out now—how I want you! [last two words underlined three times]
>
> My sweet Bunny, if I could just have you all the time I'd never ask for anything else! I want to bury my face in your neck and kiss you and kiss you and put your eyelids to sleep and oh so many other loving-nesses.[42]

---

41. Ida Thallon to Bert H. Hill, 22 July 1924; Bert H. Hill to Ida Thallon, 30 July 1924, Bert Hodge Hill Papers, box 7, folder 1, Blegen Library. These letters are hole-punched and tied together with string. Robert Pounder's "The Blegens and the Hills" maintains that Carl's devotion to Bert was based only on close friendship and gratitude for his tutelage but that Bert may have harbored a stronger emotion, albeit one that was only hinted at in extant letters.

42. Elizabeth Pierce Blegen to Ida Thallon Hill, 21 August 1925 and 28 August 1925, Ida Thallon Hill Papers, box 3, folder 2, Blegen Library.

Grace had no difficulty accepting the unconventional domestic arrangements of "the Four," but she did occasionally struggle with terminology. In an early letter after their marriage, she referred in the traditional fashion to "Mr. Hill," but then added wryly "(very formal way of speaking of *your* husband!)." She sometimes opened letters with the salutation "Dearest Ida-and-Lib," but had more trouble with closings: "Give my love to Lib and, if proper, to B. H. H. and Carl"; "Give my love to Lib and whatever affectionate greeting is appropriate to B. H. H. and C. B." She finally settled on "Love to Lib and regards to the rest of the family."[43]

---

43. Ida Thallon Hill Papers, box 2, folder 5, Blegen Library.

CHAPTER 9

Fighting for Justice

G race's affection and admiration for "the Four" embroiled her in two major controversies involving the American School of Classical Studies in Athens during 1925–29. Once more, as with Abby Leach, she was plunged into conflict with an individual in a position of authority who used every resource to wrest away the job and diminish the dignity of a younger scholar. This time, however, her participation in the battle was voluntary, motivated not only by friendship, but especially by a strong sense of justice honed to a fine point by her past experiences. Her foe shared some similarities of temperament with Abby Leach but was much more powerful, a man with institutional prestige and notable administrative accomplishments in an academic world heavily dominated by men.

Princeton classicist Edward Capps served as chairman of the ASCSA managing committee from 1918 to 1939 and focused a great deal of his formidable energy on expanding the American School and on promoting American interests in Greece.[1] Grace was appointed to take the place of Abby Leach on the ASCSA managing committee in 1919, and this committee became the battleground for a fierce controversy over the actions and procedures of Capps. Despite her visceral aversion to public confrontation and the difficulties pre-

---

1. For a brief biographical sketch of Edward Capps (1866–1950), see William M. Calder III, s.v. "CAPPS, Edward," *Biographical Dictionary of North American Classicists*, ed. Ward W. Briggs (Westport, Conn., and London: Greenwood Press, 1994), 84–85.

sented by her deafness, Grace drew upon all her courage to combat what she perceived as an unjust abuse of power. As Ida later wrote to Grace:

> I do not know how to say what a perfect brick you have been about all this, and how I know what a terrible strain it must have been for you to go through it all. You are a darling and I love you for it. You also are accustomed to the ways of the unrighteous, having had much experience in that line, and you can neither be put upon nor fooled, nor intimidated by all the blustrings [*sic*] and fury of that great coward and bully and sneak [Edward Capps].[2]

The Capps-Hill Controversy[3]

The American School of Classical Studies at Athens, which opened in 1882, had no ties to the U.S. government but was an independent entity supported by subscriptions from cooperating colleges and cultural institutions. It was governed in the United States by a managing committee composed of representatives from the cooperating institutions and elected officers. In the interval between annual meetings of the managing committee, a much smaller

---

2. Ida T. Hill to Grace H. Macurdy, 29 January 1927, Ida Thallon Hill Papers, box 2, folder 5, Blegen Library.

3. Published accounts of this major controversy in ASCSA history are incomplete and sometimes even misleading. *A History of the American School of Classical Studies at Athens, 1882–1942: An Intercollegiate Project* (Cambridge, Mass.: Harvard University Press, 1947) was written by Louis E. Lord, who followed Capps as chairman of the Managing Committee from 1939 to 1950 and dedicated the book to Capps, whom he calls ASCSA's "second founder." Lord's information is presented without documentation, and his discussion of the controversy takes Capps's perspective, glossing over much of the hostility. David W. Rupp ("Mutually Antagonistic Philhellenes: Edward Capps and Bert Hodge Hill at the American School of Classical Studies and Athens College," *Hesperia* 82 [2013]: 67–99) analyzes the controversy as background for a study of the two men's roles in the foundation and development of Athens College. Rupp consulted extensive archival documents and presents a more balanced narrative, but his account is necessarily brief and contains some inaccuracies. Jack L. Davis also mined the archives for his discussions, presented as contextual background for other theses, including "The Birth of *Hesperia*: A View from the Archives," *Hesperia* 76 (2007): 21–35; and Jack L. Davis and Evi Gorogianni, "Embedding Aegean Prehistory in Institutional Practice: A View from One of Its North American Centers," in *Prehistorians Round the Pond: Reflections on Aegean Prehistory as a Discipline*, ed. J. F. Cherry, D. Margomenou, and L. E. Talalay (Ann Arbor: Kelsey Museum Publication 2, 2005), 93–113. A number of articles in *Carl W. Blegen: Personal and Archaeological Narratives*, ed. Natalia Vogeikoff-Brogan, Jack L. Davis, Vasiliki Florou (Atlanta, Ga.: Lockwood Press, 2015), refer to the controversy ("the most dramatic episode" in ASCSA history, 5) but do not discuss it in detail. My account, drawing particularly on letters from deeply engaged insiders supplemented by other archival documents, seeks to emphasize the human dimension of the controversy, particularly its impact on Grace Macurdy.

executive committee was empowered to act on issues requiring immediate action, subject to later ratification by the managing committee. The chair of the managing committee effectively controlled both committees, since the few members of the executive committee who were not ASCSA officers were nominated by the executive committee itself. The managing committee appointed the staff who actually ran the school in Athens, including a director, assistant director, and annual professors. However, communication between the officers in the United States and the staff in Athens was greatly complicated by the need to rely on letters that often took weeks to arrive and expensive, cryptic cablegrams that could be easily misunderstood. It would be many years before the telephone simplified transatlantic communication.

In 1906, Bert Hodge Hill was appointed to a five-year term as ASCSA director; he was reelected to another five-year term in 1910, and in 1916 the ASCSA managing committee voted that he be reelected as director and "that no term be fixed for the tenure of Mr. Hill." A letter dated May 14, 1916, by the chair of the managing committee at that time, James R. Wheeler, explained, "The Committee this time elects you without fixing any term, so you see you are on the 'good behavior' basis of a University professorial appointment."[4] Carl W. Blegen supported Hill in Athens as ASCSA secretary from 1913 to 1920, when he was promoted to assistant director. Because of World War I, the school accepted no students from 1916 to 1920, during which time both Hill and Blegen worked for American relief organizations in Greece. In 1921, a distinguished member of the managing committee, Edward Robinson, director of the Metropolitan Museum of Art, was sent to Athens to investigate the affairs of the school, and his positive report particularly praised the work of Hill: "The School has steadily maintained a high standard of scholarship. . . . So far as men are concerned, it was never better equipped for this work than it is at present. Mr. B. H. Hill is an exceptionally able Director on both the scholarly and the economic side."[5] Until 1916, Hill had continued the school's large-scale program of excavations at ancient Corinth, in the Peloponnese.

After assuming the chairmanship of the managing committee in 1918, Edward Capps had ambitious fundraising plans for the school, and he felt strongly that rapid publication of the results of ASCSA excavations was essential to further his plans. This put him at cross-purposes with Hill, who was a meticulous and exacting excavator but believed that publication should be delayed until field work was complete; in the words of Carl Blegen, Hill was "reluctant to have anything published until he could be sure that he had been

---

4. Quoted in B. H. Hill, "For the Further Information of the Managing Committee" (pamphlet), 8 April 1927, 2, Bert Hodge Hill Papers, box 12, folder 3, Blegen Library.

5. Quoted in Hill, "For the Further Information," 4.

able to find and interpret even the smallest wanting bit of evidence."[6] Hill's difficulty with writing went beyond philosophy, however; it was ingrained in his
temperament, as Lib noted in her letters to Ida as an ASCSA student, pointing
out that he had not received a PhD because "he hates to write" and would not
produce a dissertation. She also wrote that Hill was an excellent teacher and
superb diplomat and negotiator with Greek officials and was expected to do
the work of three men.[7] Hill's negotiating skills were crucial to bring to frui-
tion a major coup for ASCSA, what Capps termed "the most remarkable piece
of good fortune that has fallen to the lot of the School since its foundation—
the gift it has received of the Gennadius Library, of the building to house it,
and of the land in Athens on which to build it." Capps secured the funding to
build the library from the Carnegie Corporation, but he acknowledged Hill's
essential contribution in his 1921–22 annual report:

> The School is under the greatest obligations to Director Hill for his inex-
> haustible patience and resourcefulness in the conduct of this business, which
> he followed through changes of government, political and social distur-
> bances, and legal complications until the land was wholly ours to build the
> Gennadeion upon. Probably no other person, Greek or foreigner, could have
> succeeded in the circumstances, in spite of the utmost good will on the part
> of all the Greek authorities concerned.[8]

Despite his praise for Hill's work on the Gennadius Library, which consumed large amounts of Hill's time and energy from 1922 to the gala dedication on April 23, 1926, Capps kept pressing Hill for publications to support
the campaign to raise endowment funds from the Carnegie Corporation and
from John D. Rockefeller Jr. The internal strains flared up more visibly at the
managing committee meeting of May 10, 1924, when the committee refused to
grant Hill an increase in salary and appointed Harold North Fowler of West-
ern Reserve University as editor in chief of the Corinth publications. In his
letter reporting these actions to Hill, Capps used the occasion to raise more
general charges against Hill:

---

6. Carl W. Blegen, "Necrology: Bert Hodge Hill," *American Journal of Archaeology* 63
(1959): 193.

7. Elizabeth Pierce to Ida Thallon, 27 October and 14 November 1922, 14 January 1923, Ida
Thallon Hill Papers, box 3, folder 1, Blegen Library.

8. Edward Capps. "Forty-First Annual Report of the American School of Classical Studies
at Athens, 1921–1922," Extract from the *Bulletin of the Archaeological Institute of America*, 31, 37,
accessed 22 January 2015, http://www.ascsa.edu.gr/pdf/uploads/AR_41_1921-22.pdf

The greatest defect is an almost complete failure to cooperate with your Chairman in matters of administration. . . . I had to state this plainly to the Committee with respect to a number of matters, and to state that if there were not a radical reform on the part of our Athens staff the Committee could seek a new Chairman or else adopt effective measures of another kind. Our present condition is intolerable, as I suppose you and Blegen realize quite as well as I do.[9]

Although Grace Macurdy attended the May 1924 meeting, her vote on these resolutions is not recorded; Capps states that the resolutions were passed unanimously, but he used this term even if there were abstaining votes. Hill and Blegen may not have paid sufficient attention to the warning shot fired by Capps, since this was the summer when they negotiated their complex marital arrangements with Ida and Lib. They were certainly not prepared for Capps's rapid escalation of events, culminating in a resolution at the meeting of the managing committee on May 9, 1925 that suddenly reduced Hill's directorship without fixed term to a one-year appointment, from July 1, 1925, to June 30, 1926. Grace was unaware of the importance of this meeting for her friends' future since Capps did not send out agendas before managing committee meetings. Absorbed in preparations for her "Great Macedonian Women" lecture at King's College London, Grace did not attend this meeting. Nor did Capps notify Hill in advance about this dramatic change in his status. The resolution contained an important qualification, however:

That the Chairman be requested, in notifying the Director of this action, to state to him the Committee's intention of renewing the appointment for one year from July 1, 1926, if the administration of the School shall prove satisfactory during the coming year, and to express its earnest hope that such action may appear justified; but at the same time to make very clear, reiterating the views of the Committee as stated in the Chairman's letter of May 14, 1924, to the Director, its dissatisfaction with the Director's conduct of the School in recent years, including the current year, and its determination to correct the evils to which the Director's attention has repeatedly been called.[10]

---

9. Edward Capps to Bert H. Hill, 14 May 1924, quoted in Edward Capps and E. D. Perry, "For the Information of the Managing Committee" (pamphlet), 11 December 1926, 7, Mac-Cracken Papers, box 82, folder 31, Vassar Archives.

10. Quoted in Capps and Perry, "For the Information of the Managing Committee," 9. Rupp confuses the managing committee actions of 1924 and 1925 and completely omits the resolution changing Hill's term ("Mutually Antagonistic Philhellenes," 82).

In keeping with its call for reform, the managing committee also appointed a Greek archaeologist, George Mylonas, as ASCSA bursar in order to relieve Hill of many of the burdensome bookkeeping and accounting demands on his time. When Hill's friends on the managing committee who had not attended this meeting received the minutes, they were not so sanguine about the possibility of renewal. For example, Lacey D. Caskey, curator of classical antiquities in Boston's Museum of Fine Arts, wrote to Samuel E. Bassett of the University of Vermont, "as I see it, a noose was slipped around Hill's neck and he was warned that the trap might be sprung as part of the Gennadeion celebration next year."[11]

Meanwhile, the Four in Athens were working on the assumption that they could rectify the situation by making changes. The women gave a great deal of unpaid labor to school affairs, especially the superefficient Ida. In August, after the 1925 excavation season at Corinth had been completed, Ida wrote Hill a forceful letter urging him to join her in England so that she could help him write up a preliminary excavation report:

> Simply to ignore the thing seems extraordinary for anyone who is as thoughtful and considerate of other people as you are—as a general thing. I am not in the habit of having no attention paid to suggestions that I make. . . . Now if I don't stop, you'll soon begin to call me Mrs. Capps or Edwardina or some other such term, but you know perfectly well why I am trying to help get this old job safely done. I am more than willing to do a job of the sort popularly known as "dog work." . . . I don't think I ask you to do very many things, but *please please* hurry along with your suitcase full of documents—and let's get it written.[12]

The report did get written and was published promptly in the *American Journal of Archaeology*, as was the report for 1926.[13] Meanwhile, Lib and Carl Blegen met personally with Capps and another ASCSA officer in Massachusetts on August 20, 1925 to try to ascertain the reasons for the change in Hill's status. In a long and contentious meeting, they were assured that this was not an effort to make "a clean sweep out at the School." When pressed for reasons

---

11. Lacey Caskey to Samuel Bassett, 26 June 1925, Samuel E. Bassett Papers, box 2, folder 12, MS 590, Yale Library.

12. Ida T. Hill to Bert H. Hill, 15 August [1925], Bert Hodge Hill Papers, box 7, folder 1, Blegen Library.

13. B. H. Hill, "Excavations at Corinth 1925: Preliminary Report," *American Journal of Archaeology* 30 (1926): 44–49; "Excavations at Corinth 1926," *American Journal of Archaeology* 31 (1927): 70–79.

for his dissatisfaction with the management of ASCSA, however, Capps did
not raise the issue of delay in publication but rather complained about bookkeeping problems, failure to answer letters immediately, not enough individual attention to students, scheduling of two excavations simultaneously, and
"impudence" in Hill's letters to him. Lib described Capps as in "a most tow-
ering rage" and concluded her report of this meeting to Ida pessimistically:

> Altogether it was a most disgraceful session—I feel that I never can quite
> consider myself a lady again after that performance. I never heard such
> things said to each other by grownups except the Irish wicks. I would have
> walked out in the middle of it if I hadn't been fighting for you and Bert.
> There is no one else in the world I would have done it for! However, you'd
> love me still even if I am smeared with slime![14]

In fact, Capps had raised many of these same charges against Hill in a long
letter to Samuel Bassett soon after the managing committee meeting in May.
The letter concludes with a broad indictment of Hill that suggests Capps was
already determined to remove him from the directorship and that the promise
of renewal if changes were made was a ploy. In a subsequent letter, Capps's
claim, "my attitude I try to keep as impersonal as possible," is belied by the
derogatory comments he then makes about both Blegen and Hill:

> The "danger" to the School . . . is Hill unreformed, and that he should be
> supported in our Committee in his recalcitrancy and inefficiency. . . . The
> choice is his, to remain Director or to go. And we can help him if he will put
> himself in harmony with our purposes. If he refuses, I see no outcome except
> his retirement, and nothing more desirable for the future of the School.
>
> Blegen is a valuable man, but very inferior to let us say [Theodore W.]
> Heermance. . . . If he should choose to resign because of what happens to
> Hill, that is his choice, and itself would argue that he cannot take the large
> view. But it would not, in reality, be difficult to replace him. . . . As a scholar
> or even as an excavator [Hill] ranks low in Athens. This may surprise you,
> but it is true. And it is also justified. He has by no means, in his own field,
> made good as a scholar among scholars. . . . Hill is not a classical scholar

---

14. Elizabeth P. Blegen, "Report of Interview between Edward Capps, George Chase, Carl
and Elizabeth Blegen," 20–21 August 1925, Ida Thallon Hill Papers, box 3, folder 2, Blegen
Library.

either. He does not read books, ancient or modern, except for reference, and could exist happily for years to come without opening a new book.[15]

Although Capps claimed that he had no personal animosity toward Hill, his subsequent actions reveal a tenacious determination to undermine Hill, which goes far beyond his stated position simply to improve the operations of the school. Like Abby Leach, Capps apparently chose not to examine his own motivations. It is abundantly clear that he wished to micromanage affairs at ASCSA and wanted a director who would always defer to his authority and respond to his every command with alacrity. Hill did not owe his appointment to Capps and did not meet these requirements, managing the school on the basis of his own assessment of the situation in Athens and being known for deliberation rather than for speed. Furthermore, once the extent of Capps's scheming against Hill became public, he felt he had to denigrate Hill in order to justify his own actions. Capps's hostility toward Hill escalated after the two marriages, and his dismissive attitude toward "the ladies," particularly Ida, makes it clear that he was not happy with the women's involvement in the school. However, there is no direct evidence that conveys his opinion of the unconventional lifestyle of the Four.

Capps inadvertently revealed both his intentions and his methods in a letter he sent to Grace Macurdy on November 6, 1925, in an effort to turn her against Hill. He maintained that he had large files of complaints from Vassar about conditions at ASCSA which were still the same or worse: "The opposition to Mr. Hill was led, as I recall, from Vassar and I still stand most solemnly pledged to some of the most influential people to bring about reforms as the condition of Vassar's continued support of the School. You will remember that. And Mrs. Hill should not forget it, as I fear she does." Grace ascertained that Vassar had made no such complaints about the school or about Hill; Capps had invented the whole story. As Grace later wrote Hill, quoting this letter, "I do not know who the influential people are and no one else here knows. . . . It seems clear that your 'year of probation' was over in the mind of Professor Capps before the college year was more than six weeks along."[16]

Grace's conclusion was confirmed when Capps called a special meeting of the ASCSA executive committee on December 21, 1925, at which Hill's appointment as director was summarily terminated on June 30, 1926, with a grant of $3,500 for the following year as former director. The stated rationale

---

15. Edward Capps to Samuel Bassett, 24 June and 13 September 1925, Samuel E. Bassett Papers, box 2, folder 10, MS 590, Yale Library.

16. Grace H. Macurdy to Bert H. Hill, 16 December 1926, Bert Hodge Hill Papers, box 4, folder 2, Blegen Library.

for this action was that "the conditions laid down by the Managing Committee in Resolution 15, of May 9, 1925, for the reappointment of Mr. Hill as Director of the School have not been complied with, and it is clear to the members of the Executive Committee that they will not be complied with." This rationale was based solely on information provided by Capps; the committee was not made aware of the changes already occurring in Athens with the help of Ida, Lib, and bursar Mylonas. The termination of Hill's appointment was made without any consultation with the managing committee, which had indicated its intention to renew the appointment for another year "if the administration of the School shall prove satisfactory during the coming year." Significantly, Hill was not told about the termination of his appointment until May 11, 1926, nor were members of the managing committee notified until they assembled at a special meeting on June 5, 1926. Capps justified this silence with the argument that he did not want rumors of dissension to disrupt the April dedication of the Gennadius Library in Athens, after which he planned to speak with Hill personally.[17]

Letters from Hill to his friend and supporter William K. Prentice of Princeton, a member of the managing committee, clarify the piecemeal and misleading way that Capps communicated the executive committee's resolution to Hill and disprove the account Capps later gave to the managing committee. On May 8, 1925, after meeting with Capps on April 27 and May 1, Hill wrote to Prentice that "the Executive Committee had met last December and decided that I be given a leave of absence for next year, that [Benjamin Dean] Meritt be added to the staff with title and duties yet to be defined, and that the long period of my directorship of the School terminate June 30, 1927. Capps and [Edward Delavan] Perry both expressed much concern for my future and suggested that my services might be retained as director of excavations if the School undertakes the projected work in the Athenian Agora." However, after meeting with Capps on May 11, Hill wrote Prentice the following day, "I gather that it had been the intention of the ~~Ex. Com.~~ Chairman that my directorship should end June 30 of the present year, not of 1927 as I had at first understood. He seems to agree, however, that 1927 is the righter time. Certainly it is incredible that the M. C. should vote on June 5 that my term shall end with that same June—on twenty-five days' notice." He indicated that Capps had suggested that he resign as of June 1927, but told Prentice that he thought

---

17. Capps and Perry, "For the Information of the Managing Committee," 13–14; Samuel E. Bassett et al., "To the Managing Committee of the American School of Classical Studies at Athens," (minority report), April 1927, Bert Hodge Hill Papers, box 12, folder 3, Blegen Library; Edward Capps to Samuel Bassett, 10 June 1926, Samuel E. Bassett Papers, box 2, folder 10, MS 590, Yale Library.

it best simply to take a year's leave of absence with title, with Blegen serving as acting director for the 1926–27 year. After a final meeting on May 15, Hill wrote the following to Prentice:

> Capps agreed to invite a modification of the recommendation of the Executive Committee so that I should remain Director of the School through next year but be absent on leave the whole year. . . . Nothing more was said of the suggestion that I offer my resignation; and I certainly should not think of doing so unless Vote XV of last May had first been rescinded. Capps and Perry believed that the leave of absence could be managed more simply if I would make application for it, and this I have done in the following brief terms:

> Dear Mr. Chairman: Having had no sabbatical year in the course of my twenty years' service as Director of the School I should very much like a leave of absence for the whole of next season. Will you please consider this an application for action in this sense by the Managing Committee?[18]

Grace Macurdy was distressed to receive letters from Athens near the end of May informing her about the December executive-committee resolution, which had never been communicated to members of the managing committee. She immediately wrote other committee members suggesting that something should be done at the upcoming meeting on June 5. As she wrote Lacey Caskey, she faced the prospect of taking an active role in the proceedings with considerable trepidation: "I am so hampered by my deafness in so large a meeting, but I shall endeavor to say something June 5 for Mr. Hill's desire to have more time to prepare himself and get ready for a defence of his work." She was relieved that a later letter from Ida, describing the plan for a leave of absence, intimated that a battle would not be necessary.[19]

Meanwhile, Capps sent Hill another letter from Naples on May 19, again suggesting that Hill resign but agreeing to present the plain request for a leave:

---

18. Bert H. Hill to William K. Prentice, 8, 12 and 16 May 1926 (typed carbons), Bert Hodge Hill Papers, box 11, folder 1, Blegen Library. Since these letters were written and received at the time, they disprove the sequence of events later reported in Capps and Perry, "For the Information of the Managing Committee," 14–17.

19. Grace H. Macurdy to Lacey Caskey, 30 and 31 May 1926, Bert Hodge Hill Papers, box 12, folder 1, Blegen Library. See also Grace H. Macurdy to Samuel Bassett, 28 and 31 May 1926, Samuel E. Bassett Papers, box 2, folder 30, MS 590, Yale Library.

Perry and I talked over procedure, with your [May 15] letter before us. We had hoped, you know, that this letter would be so phrased that there would be no particular occasion for the discussion again of the main issue—this in your interest—but only of the manner of carrying out our plan. But your letter gives us no point d'appui, in that regard. So it may prove advisable not to present it to the Ex. Com. at all. If you do want it presented, you can cable me "present" and I will understand. On the voyage I shall draft our proposals in the form of a modification of the action of last December, as far as concerns your status from July 1, 1926, to June 30, 1927. Both the original action and this modification will have to come before the M. C., so far as we can see. If there had been, as suggested, a resignation as of June 30, 1927, attached to your request for a year's leave, we could have simply rescinded the action of December and brought in a substitute. Would not that have been better?[20]

The Hills had been writing to their American friends urging them to support the plan for a year's leave with title at the June 5 meeting of the managing committee, but Ida became suspicious when Hill received the May 19 letter from Capps, as she wrote Hazel Haight at Vassar:

I find I was mistaken when I suggested last week that with the departure of EC there would be nothing more to be done but to sit back peacefully and twirl one's thumbs until after the meeting of the MC. But he sure is a Shifty Lad if there ever was one and always thinks of something else and of how to sidestep. The agreement had been that B was to ask for leave of absence next year, and that recommendation was to be made by the Ex Com to the MC. He did just what EC suggested and wrote such a request. Now a letter has come from Naples saying he and Mr P . . . were disappointed because the request for leave did not say that B would resign in July 1927! . . . Of course what EC was after was for B to put himself on record as offering a resignation and then he could say it was a voluntary act. But he must have thought B was a goose not to see through him. He now says it would make it much easier for himself (you bet it would) if B would withdraw the request for leave, but the only safe thing is to send that official communication to the Ex Com, otherwise you cannot tell in what garbled form the Ch[airman] would present it.[21]

---

20. Quoted in Capps and Perry, "For the Information of the Managing Committee," 18.
21. Ida T. Hill to Elizabeth H. Haight, [undated, but included with letter dated 16 May 1926, so probably ca. 23 May], Ida Thallon Hill Papers, box 1, folder 8, Blegen Library.

Following the instructions in Capps's letter, Hill sent a cable with the single word "Present" on May 29, 1926, having posted a letter to Capps two days earlier in response to Capps's May 19 letter. This letter, which was not received until June 10, stated definitively that Hill was not resigning but simply requesting the leave of absence. On June 5, however, Hill's supporters were blindsided when Capps, holding Hill's cable, declared that Hill had resigned. As Prentice wrote Hill the day after the meeting, "Capps presented your resignation, to take effect in June 1927, and what he said was your request and the recommendation of the Ex. Com. that your resignation be accepted without discussion. Capps also said that you had admitted to him that all the charges against you were justified, and wished no defense." Grace, who had hoped to avoid confrontation, had to challenge Capps publicly, since letters from Ida had indicated that Hill was not resigning, and she insisted that her name be recorded among the six votes against accepting Hill's resignation. When Grace met Ida in England later in June, before the resignation issue had been clarified, Ida described Grace's distress in a letter to Hill: "She was fearfully upset over it all, as any form of violence nearly makes her ill and apparently both EC and CHY [Clarence H. Young of Columbia University] became most truculent. . . . She was so upset about the way that you were treated that she did not half take in what they offered Carl." [22]

Immediately after the June 5 meeting, Capps wrote Bassett deploring what he characterized as interference from the outside and revealing his dismissive attitude toward Ida Hill: "There were several members who come [*sic*] to the meeting with a view of the situation based, not upon the facts which are of record, but upon an excited lady's impressions and hopes. . . . There were those present who were there in response to the appeal from Mrs. Hill and armed with what they were mistakenly led by her to believe to be the facts." [23] However, events soon forced Capps to admit that Ida's facts were more accurate than his own.

When Hill received the minutes of the managing-committee meeting at the beginning of July, he immediately cabled Capps that he had not resigned, reminding him of the code that Capps had himself defined on May 19. Capps had to write to all the committee members present at the meeting explaining his "mistake." He claimed that when he saw the word "present," he had "without question assumed the not unnatural interpretation" that this referred to a

---

22. William K. Prentice to Bert H. Hill, 6 June 1926, Bert Hodge Hill Papers, box 11, folder 1; Ida T. Hill to Bert H. Hill, 29 June 1926, Bert Hodge Hill Papers, box 7, folder 1, Blegen Library.

23. Edward Capps to Samuel Bassett, 6 June 1926, Samuel E. Bassett Papers, box 2, folder 10, MS 590, Yale Library.

resignation, completely forgetting the instructions he had given Hill just ten days previously. He wrote that he and Perry were convinced that Hill preferred to resign, although Mrs. Hill and Mrs. Blegen were opposing the resignation. He closed his letter to Julia H. Caverno of Smith College with a telling word, referring to "those of us who believe that the School can be saved only by the amputation."[24]

Grace and others found it difficult to believe that there was no deliberate deception involved in Capps's "mistake." Prentice attributed it to self-absorption: "It seems to me that Capps is so intensely absorbed in his own opinions and plans that sometimes he is unable to distinguish in his mind between what was actually said or done & what he has persuaded himself to believe." Julia Caverno, however, suspected a more calculated design. Right after the meeting she had confided her misgivings to Bassett: "I am going to say to you what I don't in general intend to say. Up to this time I have always thought the difficulty an irrepressible conflict between two men so temperamentally different that they couldn't understand each other. But I came out of this with a sick feeling that there was underhand work all through." After receiving Capps's July letter, she concluded that deception was definitely involved:

> I wish I had the comfort of feeling as I did before that meeting that Mr. Capps however dominating and domineering, was incapable of "downright trickery." But when a man reads me from a telegraph blank a long dispatch, containing expressions of contrition and an explicit resignation and then writes me personally afterward that the dispatch contained "only the one word *Present*"—well I can't see an[y] possible "moral alibi." It makes me sick all through because I was really fond of Mr. Capps.[25]

Hill himself astutely observed later that if Capps had really expected him to change his mind and submit a resignation, he would have specified a cablegram code for that in his May 19 letter along with the code for the simple leave of absence.[26] Capps continued to press Hill for a resignation, and when none was forthcoming convened the executive committee in August, reinstating the termination of Hill's directorship as of June 30, 1926 after the fact, subject to

---

24. Edward Capps to Grace H. Macurdy, 17 July 1926, Ida Thallon Hill Papers, box 3, folder 4; Edward Capps to Samuel Bassett and Julia H. Caverno (copies), 17 July 1926, Bert Hodge Hill Papers, box 11, folder 1, Blegen Library.

25. William K. Prentice to Samuel Bassett, 5 October 1926, Samuel E. Bassett Papers, box 2, folder 33; Julia H. Caverno to Samuel Bassett, 7 June and 11 November 1926, Samuel E. Bassett Papers, box 2, folder 12, MS 590, Yale Library.

26. Hill, "For the Further Information," 24.

ratification at a special meeting of the managing committee on December 27, 1926. The punitive nature of this decision is clear, since the committee could have given Hill a leave of absence with title for 1926–27 without a resignation, as Hill had actually requested. Had they done this, it is likely that further controversy could have been avoided. As Hill wrote Bassett after giving Capps his request for leave with title, "If Capps carries out the program indicated in his last conversations with me, I shall be content."[27] But Capps was apparently determined to humiliate Hill and vindicate his own actions.[28]

The Four in Athens, now deeply angered by the treatment Hill had received over the last several months, prepared for the managing committee meeting in December, with Ida and Lib organizing documents, typing and retyping copies of letters and other communications, and writing long, detailed letters of instructions to their supporters in America. Since Grace was the only person on the managing committee whom Ida trusted absolutely, she sent most of her instructions to Grace, tasking her with sharing materials, ideas, and strategies with Julia Caverno of Smith, William Prentice of Princeton, Samuel Bassett of Vermont, and Lacey Caskey of the Boston Fine Arts Museum:

> This is going to be a terrible struggle. EC is bound to fight for all he is worth, and he will not fight fair but will do anything and everything to make his points. . . . We have the facts, and they are convincing ones, but they will have to be driven in so that the dullest and sleepiest person on the MC will get their real significance. I depend on such people as yourself and Miss Caverno, both of whom have such unferocious exteriors, to hammer and hammer for all you are worth and to keep asking question after question to pin him down to definite concrete statements instead of the utterly worthless generalizations of which he is so fond. . . . At this meeting he will have to prove every statement he makes. For heaven's sake do not let him get away with a single point without proof strong enough to serve in a law court. That is sur[e] to be an unpleasant process, he will lose his temper and be a sorry spectacle. . . . And if he begins to fling mud, have an umbrella and a mop handy an[d] never mind him.[29]

---

27. Bert H. Hill to Samuel Bassett, 16 May 1926, Samuel E. Bassett Papers, box 1, folder 22, MS 590, Yale Library.

28. Rupp incorrectly claims that Hill and the Managing Committee were maneuvered into accepting a leave of absence and resignation ("Mutually Antagonistic Philhellenes," 82).

29. Ida T. Hill to Grace H. Macurdy, 1 December 1926, Ida Thallon Hill Papers, box 2, folder 5, Blegen Library.

Fueled by Capps's admission of his "mistake" about the resignation, Ida and others believed that Hill's directorship might still be saved. They planned to emphasize Hill's election with no fixed term as equivalent to academic tenure, to request the resignation of Capps from the chairmanship of the managing committee because of his actions concerning the alleged resignation, and failing that, to have a committee appointed on which Capps did not serve to study the claims of both sides in the controversy. The pressure on "unferocious" Grace was intense. Besides conferring with Hill supporters, she wrote to President MacCracken explaining the course of events and was delighted to receive from him an official letter directing her to cast her vote "for the maintenance of the highest principles and dignity and security in the tenure of an academic office such as that of the Director of the School."[30] As one of only nine women among eighty-two committee members at the time, Grace was aware that her voice would not have the clout of men from more prestigious institutions. Still, she was prepared to go into battle, armed with her Acousticon and her strong sense of justice.

Hill's supporters did not foresee the tremendous advantages conferred by Capps's administrative position. On December 11, he mailed a twenty-four page printed pamphlet, "For the Information of the Managing Committee," to all committee members, with a request that they submit a straw vote in advance of the meeting on the executive committee's August resolution declaring that Hill's directorship had terminated on June 30, 1926. The tenor of the pamphlet is clear from the sweeping generalization on the first page: "For many years the Managing Committee has recognized that its most difficult and serious problem was Mr. Hill's administration of the School." The pamphlet devotes four pages to delays in publication, quoting from a number of personal letters Hill had written to Capps in which Hill's rather excessive expressions of regret reveal his self-reproach over his difficulties with writing: "The assumption on which this letter is written—that I am incapable of writing for publication anything whatever with a practicable expenditure of time—is unfortunately the truth; but I do not face it, even now, without extreme chagrin and humiliation; it is so thoroughly unintelligent, unreasonable, and almost immoral."[31] The next eight pages of the pamphlet, however, are devoted to wide-ranging and often unsupported complaints of every sort, indicating the more personal nature of Capps's animus against Hill.

---

30. Henry Noble MacCracken to Grace H. Macurdy, 13 December 1926, MacCracken Papers, box 82, folder 31, Vassar Archives.

31. Bert H. Hill to Edward Capps, 18 December 1923, quoted in Capps and Perry, "For the Information of the Managing Committee," 5.

Hill was already in New York when the pamphlet was received; Ida, Lib, and Blegen were in Athens. Hill wrote a letter to all members of the managing committee on December 14 requesting that they refrain from voting; Grace and Hazel Haight had these duplicated and mailed out from Poughkeepsie on December 19:

> I earnestly hope that you will postpone committing yourself upon the approval or disapproval of the resolutions of the Executive Committee of August 25th, until you are more fully informed as to the merits of the situation. It is my intention to send you shortly a statement by way of supplement and amendment to the pamphlet issued "For the Information of the Managing Committee." Meanwhile, I ask that all excerpts from letters from me to Dr. Capps be read as parts of a correspondence between particularly good friends—written with smiles at the right points (perhaps at some wrong ones), with complete freedom, with no thought that they might one day be "used in evidence" against me.

Hill's hastily prepared memorandum, "Documents Bearing on the Termination of Mr. Hill's Directorship," was not completed until December 23 and reached few, if any, of the committee members before the meeting.[32]

Grace and many others wrote letters to the ASCSA secretary objecting to this procedure and refusing to vote, with the result that the straw vote was not presented at the meeting. The response of Eugene P. Andrews of Cornell presented a particularly apposite and eloquent summary of the situation:

> I do not wish to vote either Aye or No on the resolution adopted by the Executive Committee last August. It has been known generally, of course, for a number of years that Mr. Hill was not satisfying several important and influential members of the Managing Committee. There may well have been ample ground for this dissatisfaction, but in all these years there has been abundant opportunity to let him get out gracefully, with no damage done, either to the School or to his career. I have wondered many times why it was not done. I cannot understand why an adjustment cannot yet be made that will avoid carrying this deplorable situation to a conclusion which must be disastrous. However far Mr. Hill may have fallen behind what some members of the Executive Committee felt was necessary, the Committee has, in

---

32. Bert H. Hill to members of the Managing Committee (copy), 14 December 1926, Mac-Cracken Papers, box 82, folder 31, Vassar Archives; Bert H. Hill, "Documents Bearing on the Termination of Mr. Hill's Directorship," 23 December 1926, Samuel E. Bassett Papers, box 1, folder 22, MS 590, Yale Library.

my opinion, put itself in a far worse position, first by keeping from him for four months notice of its action in ousting him from the Directorship a year ago, allowing the information, vital to him in every way, to reach him first in "certain rumors," secondly in Mr. Capps' misinterpretation of Hill's "Present," with Hill using a cable code that Mr. Capps had himself devised. This is really not the sort of thing, is it, that can be undone by excusing. It seems to me that, in these two things alone, the Executive Committee has put itself so far in the wrong that it better not attempt to force things through as proposed. Mr. Hill ought to be given opportunity to present his side, for the pamphlet you have sent out is manifestly ex parte. Or, better still by far, it seems to me an amicable adjustment should be arranged with Mr. Hill that will allow him to retire from a position which he must surely not wish to retain in the face of so much dissatisfaction. We can hardly afford to have this thing end as an apparent personal quarrel, and this is, I am sorry to say, the impression I got of it from the pamphlet I have mentioned. The selection of certain of the passages from Mr. Hill's letters suggest that this is the case. This thing must not come to a counting of votes, for and against. I think it is not too late to avoid splitting the School into two camps. It would hurt the school terribly. It would much more than offset the good that has been done recently. Mistakes have been made, but on both sides. Cannot we forget ourselves for the sake of the School and recognize that we have no right to let it become a matter of "sides" or of personal prestige?[33]

Andrews, however, did not attend the managing committee meeting in December, nor did he lend his name to any further protests against Capps. When Grace wrote later to question him about this, he told her he had "taken advice and does not feel justified in bringing himself and the University into 'the quarrel,'" which Grace attributed to "the far-reaching influence of the Chairman."[34] Moreover, she discovered that Capps had cabled Andrews's colleague at Cornell, Horace L. Jones, to attend the meeting, promising him an ASCSA annual professorship (which he received in 1929–30). As Grace observed, "It is not right that one man should hand out annual professorships etc. and get apotheosized for it. I have heard of others who have expressed their fear that Capps would use his influence against their getting grants etc. if they opposed them [*sic*] and I heard that Capps said that no one who signed

---

33. Eugene P. Andrews to Edward D. Perry (copy), 17 December 1926, Bert Hodge Hill Papers, box 11, folder 1, Blegen Library.

34. Grace H. Macurdy to Lacey Caskey, 4 May 1927, Bert Hodge Hill Papers, box 12, folder 1, Blegen Library.

any of the those petitions would henceforth be a friend of his."[35] These were not idle threats. In 1927 Capps accused his Princeton colleague Allan C. Johnson, not a member of the managing committee but a former ASCSA fellow who had protested the treatment of Hill, of improper publication and tampering regarding his book *Municipal Administration in the Roman Empire*. Princeton University Press, which had published the book, completely vindicated Johnson.[36] In the minds of many committee members, however, Capps did not need to offer incentives or threaten sanctions; what they cared about was his success at fundraising for the school. He had already raised endowment funds and was in the process of negotiating a much larger endowment grant from the Rockefeller Foundation.

Grace's two letters to Ida reporting on the meeting[37] reveal how heavily the cards were stacked against Hill, who was not allowed to address the managing committee at all. As chair, Capps arranged the order of business, and he first had every member of the executive committee make an individual speech in support of their resolution firing Hill as of June 30:

> It now seems impossible that the Chairman could have put it all over as he did, but it was like nothing but a *steam roller*. It was a life and death game with him and he played it for all he was worth, with the able assistance of his body guard the X Com. They were prepared, to the last man, with their ammunition and so used up the time and patience that only an absolute onslaught and almost *hand-to-hand fight* could have got our facts before the audience. . . . And the bully sat there, intent, outwardly smiling, but swift to down every decent man who put his head up.

When William Prentice began a speech claiming that Capps had praised Hill's work at a time when the pamphlet complained that Hill was not effectively administering the school, Capps's interruption, "Oh Prentice, you have a perfectly rotten memory, You never get anything straight," broke him and spoiled his speech. Grace immediately stood up and read from Capps's own letters proving the truth of Prentice's claims. She also showed that Capps had already determined to remove Hill as early as November 1925 and spoke about Hill's

35. Grace H. Macurdy to Lacey Caskey, 20 March 1927, Bert Hodge Hill Papers, box 12, folder 1, Blegen Library.

36. Frank Frost Abbott and Allan Chester Johnson, *Municipal Administration in the Roman Empire* (Princeton, N.J.: Princeton University Press, 1926). Documents relating to this case can be found in the Bert Hodge Hill Papers, box 12, folder 1, Blegen Library.

37. Grace H. Macurdy to Ida T. Hill, 1 January and 16 February 1927, Ida Thallon Hill Papers, box 2, folder 5, Blegen Library.

appointment as equivalent to academic tenure. When the resolution ousting Hill came to a vote, the tally was thirty-one in favor and fifteen against (three of these were women—Grace Macurdy of Vassar, Julia Caverno of Smith, and Alice Walton of Wellesley; Caroline Galt of Mount Holyoke was unable to attend the meeting). The next resolution, on which all the Hill supporters abstained, named Rhys Carpenter of Bryn Mawr as the new ASCSA director with Carl Blegen to serve as assistant director. Blegen, who was acting director of the school until July 1927, later declined this demotion when it was officially offered to him, and Benjamin Dean Meritt was appointed assistant director.

As Grace summarized the result, "There was no show of justice in that meeting. We were lucky to get 15 votes. Some of our voters were not there. . . . I told David Robinson [of Johns Hopkins University] that I was so thankful that he had come over to our side. He said that he had to, for there was for the first time a ring, a machine, in American Classical scholarship. It was a terrible thing to see those old men sitting [rig]ht there and ruining the career of younger men." Twenty-six former ASCSA students had sent in petitions supporting Hill, but Capps did not introduce these until the end of the meeting. He made a point of stating that five professors from the University of Pennsylvania had requested to have their names removed from the petition before the meeting, though Capps neglected to mention that he had written to them all saying that Hill was opposed to such movements on his behalf and regarded them as injurious to his situation.

No one reading Edward Capps's annual report for 1926–27 would have any idea of the actual events: "Dr. Bert Hodge Hill, who had served the School as Director since 1906, retired from this position at the end of the academic year 1925–1926. The best wishes of the Managing Committee, of the many students who have enjoyed his instruction, and of those who have been associated with him on the staff, go with him."[38]

Grace was deeply distressed at the outcome of the meeting, returning to Vassar with influenza and a relapse that left her "all in" for weeks afterward. As she wrote Ida, "I am bitterly *ashamed* to write to you after such a defeat and feel as if it ought to have been prevented. . . . All that I can say, dear Ida, is that I did what I could and it was not sufficient. But we shall not stop." Good historical scholar that she was, Grace realized that they had to do something to correct the record, even if they had lost the war. Capps's version of events could not be allowed to stand unchallenged.

---

38. Edward Capps, "Forty-Sixth Annual Report of the American School of Classical Studies at Athens, 1926–1927," extract from the *Bulletin of the Archaeological Institute of America*, 19, accessed 22 January 2015, http://www.ascsa.edu.gr/pdf/uploads/AR_46_1926-27.pdf.

"It would be unendurable for our side to be utterly silenced."[39]

Disheartened and ill as she was after the meeting, Grace immediately began plans with other Hill supporters to redress the injustice—first by expressing personal support for Hill, and second, by distributing information that would present Hill's side of the case. Grace herself spearheaded the initial effort, a banquet in Hill's honor held at the Town Hall Club in Manhattan on March 4, 1927, immediately before Hill sailed back to Athens. Grace plunged into preparations for this event, writing letter after letter asking for contributions to an excavation fund for Hill and inviting appropriate guests. As she wrote Ida, "At this dinner only *extreme partisans* are invited, so we can talk freely and use our watchword *Capsicum est delendum* [Capps must be destroyed] as much as we like!"[40] A report of this dinner, later sent to Athens, gives something of its flavor:

> The next speaker was Professor Macurdy whose toast was the Managing Committee. As a member of the minority of that Committee in re the Athens School, she spoke plainly about the way in which the majority had voted on the matter of the Directorship and of how they had failed to listen to or to weigh evidence. All this was presented with gentle irony and topped with a good story. The members of the Managing Committee, she said, reminded her of the demented African convert of whom an Anglican Bishop remarked "our poor brother has unfortunately lost his reason, but has kept his faith." That, she said, was the pitiable state of her colleagues, but they had kept their faith in their chairman. Miss Macurdy paid a glowing tribute to Mrs. Hill saying that all those who had known her brilliant scholarship at Vassar had rejoiced in her presence in the School and the devoted and unselfish work she had given to it. She spoke of the unwearying and loyal work contributed

---

39. Grace H. Macurdy to Samuel Bassett, 30 January 1927, Samuel E. Bassett Papers, box 2, folder 30, MS 590, Yale Library. The official ASCSA history comes close to utterly silencing Hill's side: "The close of the year 1926 witnessed the retirement from the directorate of Bert Hodge Hill, after twenty years of service. . . . The action of the Managing Committee was unavoidable. It was accepted by Hill as inevitable." Lord, *History of the American School*, 190–92). Later discussions persist in using the terms "retirement," "resignation," or "forced resignation." But Hill and his supporters wanted the world to know that there was nothing voluntary about his leaving the school. The executive committee resolution had used the word "terminate"; Capps himself, in his letter to Julia Caverno, had called it an "amputation."

40. Grace H. Macurdy to Ida T. Hill, 16 February 1927, Ida Thallon Hill Papers, box 2, folder 5, Blegen Library. The Latin watchword is a humorous reference to a phrase that the Roman statesman Cato the Elder allegedly used to shout at the end of his speeches, *Carthago delenda est*, calling for the destruction of the city of Carthage, Rome's enemy in the Punic Wars.

by both Mrs. Hill and Mrs. Blegen to making the opening of the Gennadeion a success, and after expressing great admiration of Mr. Blegen's work
for the School and his excavations and publications she voiced the regret of
all present that the School was losing four such devoted supporters as Mr.
and Mrs. Hill, Mr. and Mrs. Blegen. Miss Macurdy then told Mr. Hill that
devoted friends and admirers had wished to express in some objective form
their appreciation of his great work for the School and they have therefore
created the Hill Fund for Research and Publication. She had the honor of
presenting to him at that time $3,105 which he was to use for his own future
work and the hope was expressed that the fund would be a growing one. . . .
[After Hill thanked them for the fund,] he also assured them ironically that
he would never give them any report of how it was used. The charm, humour
and direct personal appeal of Mr. Hill's speech can hardly be reproduced. He
was speaking as a friend to friends and was at his best."[41]

This banquet also produced the first salvo in the struggle to disseminate
information. The toastmaster at the dinner, Leicester B. Holland of the University of Pennsylvania, who had been an ASCSA architectural fellow from 1920
to 1923, prepared a printed statement signed by twenty-one of the twenty-four
people at the dinner; this was mailed from Poughkeepsie to all members of
the managing committee and to the heads of all supporting institutions. This
"banquet letter" presented a strong protest against the unjust treatment of Hill
and Blegen and called for further investigation:

> It is with deep regret that we see Archaeology for a time deprived of the
> services of the two most expert and experienced American excavators, Dr.
> Hill and Dr. Blegen, by the severance of their connection with the School;
> we regret that the School is to lose the benefits of their wide scholarship and
> stimulating criticism; and we regret most profoundly that this severance has
> been forced upon them in a manner that may be considered unworthy of
> American institutions of learning. . . .
>   We do not believe that a wrong can ever be righted by ignoring it, or that
> any healthy growth can spring from smothered wrongs, but that fairness and
> openmindedness are essential to all scholarly developments. We therefore
> urge insistently that the members of the Managing Committee and the heads
> of the institutions they represent do not yield to inertia, nor prejudiced pro-
> nouncements, nor one sided evidence, but individually and collectively

41. "The Dinner for Dr. Bert Hodge Hill March 4, 1927," Ida Thallon Hill Papers, box 3,
folder 4, Blegen Library. The style of the piece and handwriting in the comments suggest that
the author was Elizabeth Hazelton Haight.

employ their utmost efforts, without fear or favor, to probe to the bottom of this whole affair, for the sake of America's position in the world of archaeology and classical studies, and for the fundamental ideal of fair-play.[42]

Unfortunately, although most of the signers had connections with the school as former students, only four were actually on the managing committee, and three of these were women (Macurdy of Vassar, Caverno of Smith, and Galt of Mount Holyoke). In fact, fifteen of the twenty-one signers were women. Grace recognized that something else was needed, a lucid and reasoned argument with evidence from members of the managing committee, and so she lobbied men such as Prentice, Bassett, and Caskey to produce a minority report:

> I think that we ought to be sending around for signatures some sort of minority report to be presented on the fourteenth of May [the next managing-committee meeting]. . . . I think that we ought to register our protest as we did not on December 27. . . . We want to get the strong points in a simple form before the Managing Committee, but I do not think that an enormous amount of matter is necessary and it tends to confuse *my* mind at least. . . . It is really disgraceful to give up at this moment and let Capps think that he can put it over without a dissenting voice from any one in future.[43]

Grace did not write the minority report but participated actively in the discussion and editing of its content; she also sent many letters urging the fifteen Hill supporters to sign the document. In the end, there were only ten signatures, three of which were of women: Samuel E. Bassett, P. V. C. Baur, L. D. Caskey, Julia H. Caverno, Sherwood O. Dickerman, Arthur Fairbanks, Caroline M. Galt, Grace H. Macurdy, Clarence W. Mendell, and William K. Prentice (Galt had been unable to attend the December meeting, but she did sign the report). Grace was surprised that David Robinson of Johns Hopkins did not sign; as she wrote Caskey, "He can really not hope to be on good terms with Capps now. He might just as well throw in his lot with us for good and all."[44] Robinson, however, wanted to excavate at Olynthus; though he was will-

---

42. Leicester B. Holland et al., "To the Managing Committee of the American School of Classical Studies in Athens and Others Concerned," undated [signed 4 March and mailed from Poughkeepsie before 20 March 1927], MacCracken Papers, box 82, folder 31, Vassar Archives.

43. Grace H. Macurdy to Lacey Caskey, 20 March and 2 and 11 April 1927, Bert Hodge Hill Papers, box 12, folder 1, Blegen Library.

44. Grace H. Macurdy to Lacey Caskey, 11 April 1927, Bert Hodge Hill Papers, box 12, folder 1, Blegen Library. The other minority voters who did not sign the report were Harold N. Fowler, George E. Howes, Austin M. Harmon, George D. Lord, and Alice Walton.

ing to vote against Capps in December, his signature on a document such as the minority report would be perceived as a more indelible offense.

As Grace recognized, the minority report was an admirable document. In only seven printed pages, it summarizes the background of the controversy, highlights the procedural problems involved in Hill's removal, and concludes with a constructive proposal. The language is strong but not exaggerated, and the statements are supported by brief but telling evidence. The introduction and conclusion give a good sense of the whole:

> While a minority may not re-open a question settled by a majority vote, they have always the privilege of a minority report, and when, in their judgment, the action of the majority is not only unjust to an individual, but has followed a line of procedure irregular and doubtful, at a time when the interests of the School required scrupulous care to avoid even an appearance of unfairness, a minority report becomes not a privilege, but a duty. . . .
>
> In conclusion we desire to reiterate our opinion that most of the difficulties in the School's management have been due to the attempt to carry out too many and too varied activities with inadequate resources. These activities are apparently soon to be increased by the excavation of the Athenian Agora. The obvious remedy is a division of duties—the association with the Director of the School of a Director of Excavations. And Mr. Hill is the logical candidate for such a post by reason of his long experience and proved ability as well as by reason of the confidence reposed in him by the archaeological world and the Greek authorities. We believe that Mr. Carpenter's position as Director of the School would not be injured by such an association. We believe also that such action would restore harmony in the Managing Committee, in the staff, and the student body, as well as among the classical scholars and friends of the School in America.[45]

One of the ASCSA trustees, Frederick P. Fish, wrote to Judge William Caleb Loring, the president of the trustees, that the minority report was coming; he asked whether Hill could not be involved in the Agora excavations in the interests of peace. Capps sent a copy of this letter to the executive committee along with the following note, which indicates that he was in no mood for compromise:

---

45. Samuel E. Bassett et al., "To the Managing Committee of the American School of Classical Studies at Athens" (minority report), undated but mailed at the beginning of May 1927], Bert Hodge Hill Papers, box 12, folder 3, Blegen Library.

From the above it appears that there will be an agitation at the May 14th meeting again. It is important that all the Executive Committee who can should be present. Those who cannot be there should, after receiving the Minority Report, sent [*sic*] Prof. Perry a letter expressing their views. . . . Excavations can be conducted in Greece by nationals of any country that maintains a School in Athens only through that School, according to a Law. Mr. Courouniotis [*sic*], head of the Archaeological Service of the Ministry of Education, assures me that he enforces this law. Hill has been assiduous, since his return to Athens, in trying to secure a standing with Courouniotis in the Agora matter, but without success.[46]

Meanwhile, the Four were considering their options after the defeat at the December meeting. Ida immediately wrote Hill, who was still in the United States, not to consider taking an academic job where he would be teaching verbs to freshmen "in the American wilds." They should all stay in Athens, where they could certainly manage since "Lib and I have a combined income of more than $10,000." Blegen's letter to Hill, however, was less sanguine:

Ida and Elizabeth have been taking the whole thing very well and pretty calmly, though there have been some slight explosions now and then. . . . The ladies both insist that they want to live permanently in Athens, and they think that you and I should stay here, too. . . . I don't like the plan ~~much~~ at all and have not agreed to it—of living in Athens, I mean. I am not going to have it said that I am living on my wife's money; I have got to get a job.[47]

He suggested that a faculty position where he could spend half the year in America and half in Greece with money for excavation would be the best solution. Ultimately, Blegen was able to negotiate just such an unprecedented arrangement with the University of Cincinnati, where he assumed the position of professor of classical archaeology and fellow of the graduate school in the fall of 1927.[48]

---

46. Edward Capps, "Copy for the Executive Committee," 28 April 1927, Bert Hodge Hill Papers, box 11, folder 2, Blegen Library.

47. Ida T. Hill to Bert H. Hill, 22 January 1927, Bert Hodge Hill Papers, box 7, folder 2; Carl W. Blegen to Bert H. Hill, 23 January 1927, Bert Hodge Hill Papers, box 11, folder 2, Blegen Library. At this time, $10,000 was a substantial sum; Blegen's salary as acting director for 1926–27 was only $3,500.

48. For more information on the negotiations with Cincinnati, see "'On His Feet and Ready to Dig': Carl William Blegen," Jack L. Davis and Natalia Vogeikoff-Brogan, in Vogeikoff-Brogan et al., *Carl W. Blegen*, 6–7.

While the negotiations with Cincinnati were proceeding and Blegen was still ASCSA acting director, he had to exercise caution in his dealings with Capps, but Ida and Lib were under no such obligation. They decided that it was imperative to print a pamphlet for the managing committee that would refute the charges against Hill put forward in Capps's pamphlet. They had been going through files and gathering materials since 1925, and they decided that their pamphlet should follow the structure of the first pamphlet, countering each charge with evidence in a step-by-step fashion. It was intended to be "all facts and very restrained in tone." Their materials were mailed on April 8, and they depended on Grace and other Vassar women to get everything printed and mailed as soon as possible before the meeting on May 14: "You are angels to do this deadly job."[49] Grace and Hazel Haight typed and formatted the pamphlet, several Latin faculty proofread it and addressed the envelopes after it was printed, and Grace mailed it to all members of the managing committee and ASCSA trustees on May 2, 1927.

The Hill pamphlet is lengthy, thirty-seven printed pages, including ten pages of appended documents. To be comprehended fully, it must be read in conjunction with the Capps pamphlet, to which it constantly refers. Unlike the latter, it documents its claims, presenting evidence that disproves or at least discredits the sweeping generalizations that mar the Capps pamphlet. However, it is doubtful that many committee members actually took the time and effort to read it carefully. As Grace had pointed out in connection with the minority report, "an enormous amount of matter" tends to confuse the mind.

Some of the information, in fact, had little to do with the controversy, instead spotlighting less savory aspects of Capps's management style. For example, the Hill pamphlet devotes over two pages, supported by six pages of quotations from letters, to the timing of the 1925 excavation of the Argive Heraeum, financed by a generous gift from Joseph Clark Hoppin, who had been prevented by serious illness from conducting the excavation himself. Capps had wanted to delay the excavation but had instructed Hill to withdraw the funds from Hoppin's bank at the end of 1924. When Hill expressed reluctance to collect the money before the excavation was definitely scheduled, Capps wrote "As to drawing the money, you had no right to feel reluctance or to imagine an obligation that was not thought by us to exist." When Hoppin died on January 20, 1925, Capps wrote that the excavation could now be postponed, since "the matter was simplified . . . by Hoppin's death." Hill, however, acting on the 1924 resolution authorizing the dig according to a time of his

---

49. Ida T. Hill to Grace H. Macurdy, 7 April [1927], Ida Thallon Hill Papers, box 2, folder 5, Blegen Library.

choosing, did have Blegen conduct the excavation in March 1925.[50] Although Capps had not referred to this incident in his pamphlet, the temptation to include these letters must have been irresistible to the Four, especially after the way Capps had used quotations from Hill's personal letters in *his* pamphlet. As Grace commented in a letter to Hill, "It is such an open revelation of callousness and arbitrariness. His telling you that you should have no scruple that is not rubber-stamped by Me and My Committee is one of the funniest things I have read. One thinks of Dickens. Such excerpts from letters as these show your rightness and sensitiveness and the Chairman's wrongness so plainly that I should think few could be hardened in their cult so firmly as not to be shaken."[51]

This pamphlet did present a comprehensive account of Hill's side of the story, an account that Capps had previously prevented from reaching the managing committee. But its length, detail, and complexity diluted its impact.

Grace, meanwhile, was preparing for the managing-committee meeting on May 14. Her objectives were to use the minority report and Hill pamphlet as catalysts for appointing an impartial committee to evaluate the evidence on both sides and to present a resolution to have Hill named ASCSA director of excavations. In pursuit of the second objective, she wrote Hill and asked him to sound out Rhys Carpenter's attitude about the Corinth excavations. Hill replied, "He gave me the impression that he does not care greatly for Corinth for its own sake and that he would not mind having the excavation there finished by me, providing his own standing as Director of the School is conserved." Carpenter said that he would prefer, however, that Hill have no titular connection with the school.[52] Grace also wrote to Blegen inquiring about the reasons for his decision not to accept the managing committee's offer that he remain at the school as assistant director under Carpenter. His response, which he authorized her to share with others, indicated that the offer itself was a kind of insult, "a subordinate position for one year under a new man who is my junior in age, and has had no experience in the kind of work which mainly occupies us here, who has never taken part in an excavation." His main objection, however, was Capps:

> I declined the appointment because the experience of these past many years
> has convinced me of the futility and impossibility of continuing to work

50. Hill, "For the Further Information," 10–12, 28–33.

51. Grace H. Macurdy to Bert H. Hill, 27 January 1927, Bert Hodge Hill Papers, box 4, folder 2, Blegen Library.

52. Bert H. Hill to Grace H. Macurdy (carbon), 1 May 1927, Bert Hodge Hill Papers, box 11, folder 2, Blegen Library.

under the present Chairman of the Managing Committee, Mr. Capps. . . . He
is certainly a man of unusual ability and power and has many outstanding
qualities of the highest excellence. But he has also some serious faults which,
in my opinion, make him absolutely unfitted for the position of Chairman
of the Managing Committee of the School. He is habitually inaccurate, dictatorial and arbitrary, and is quite without the judicial temperament or fair-
mindedness necessary to a man in high administrative office.[53]

Although Grace had many copies of this letter made, she decided in the
end to send it only to Hill supporters rather than to all the committee members, since she did not know the status of Blegen's negotiations with Cincinnati and was worried that Capps "will take vengeance by trying to stop the
Cincinnati plan." As she wrote Ida before the meeting, "I am feeling rather
downhearted tonight after writing many letters and trying to round up voters
on our side. . . . Caskey thinks we should resign *en masse* and detach the colleges from the School if we fail in this attempt. But Capps would only chuckle
to get rid of us." She concluded her "dark and depressing" letter, "Well, we
fight on: even though a little band, it is a determined one."[54]

Grace wrote four letters to Ida reporting on the May 14 managing-committee meeting.[55] She drew Capps's fire at the very beginning, when she asked
why there would be no representative from the women's colleges on the executive committee. Both the new nominees were men, and Katharine M. Edwards
of Wellesley, known to be personally hostile to Hill, had been given a second
consecutive term but was now leaving the committee. Capps replied that they
had considered the matter very carefully and all the women had served on
the executive committee in the last fifteen years except Grace. He added that
it was permitted for someone to nominate her from the floor. "It was a fright-
fully insulting thing to say. . . . The fact was that every woman present, except
the retiring Edwards and Mrs. [Wilmer Cave] Wright, had voted against
Capps at Christmas or signed the documents." Next, a letter from executive-
committee member Augustus T. Murray was read calling for a vote of censure
of those who had signed the banquet letter, and Clarence H. Young proposed
censure for those who had signed the minority report, saying that they knew
they were signing lies. Grace immediately rose to defend the documents, fol-

53. Carl W. Blegen to Grace H. Macurdy, 17 April 1927, MacCracken Papers, box 82, folder
31, Vassar Archives.

54. Grace H. Macurdy to Ida T. Hill, 7 May 1927, Ida Thallon Hill Papers, box 2, folder 5,
Blegen Library.

55. Grace H. Macurdy to Ida T. Hill, 14, 15, 21 May and 1 June 1927, Ida Thallon Hill Papers,
box 2, folder 5, Blegen Library. All the quotations in the paragraphs describing this meeting are
taken from these letters.

lowed by Clarence W. Mendell. Much to Grace's disappointment, the committee did not vote for censure: "It would have been a splendid thing for our side
if he and the followers of him had censured the Dean of Yale and a number
of respectable professors of Greek. I was eager to go home with a censure, but
it was denied me."

Grace then read her prepared speech proposing that Hill be named
ASCSA director of excavations; as she wrote Ida, "This time I was no *sheep!*"
Her motion, however, was not seconded. Later George Dana Lord of Dartmouth moved that Hill be put in charge of the projected Agora excavation, but
after lunch he withdrew his motion. Capps produced a "trump card," a cable
from Rhys Carpenter saying that he "would resign if given a director of excavations." At this point Capps demanded a vote of confidence, saying *he* would
resign if he did not get it: "Capps had said that our pamphlet called him a liar
and slandered him. He said he could not go to Greece with out [*sic*] that wiped
out by a vote. I reminded him that we of the Minority had been called liars by
Young in the morning!" Louis E. Lord of Oberlin moved that the managing
committee express its confidence in the executive committee and deplore the
sending of unsubstantiated information to those outside the committee. This
motion was not seconded, and several of Capps's supporters dissuaded him
from continuing to demand it.

Finally, Austin M. Harmon of Yale, who had voted for Hill in December but had not signed the minority report, presented a motion that Capps
accepted in lieu of the vote of confidence. Grace did not report this motion
accurately to Ida until she received the minutes of the meeting: "I am shocked
at Harmon. My acousticon got entangled and I never really heard the exact
wording of the final motion—that the Managing Committee see no reason
for taking up again the matter of Mr. Hill's connection with the School." The
motion passed with twenty-nine in favor and seven, including Grace, record-
ing their names as refusing to vote. Grace had pushed herself beyond her
limits, fighting in the front lines at this meeting, but this motion definitively
ended Hill's association with the school: "I came away feeling horribly beaten
and discouraged until Caskey in the eve[n]ing pointed out that it was very
important that EC did not succeed in forcing the vote of confidence. It is his
first rebuff." As Grace pointed out to Ida in her letter of June 1, the official minutes of this meeting were "cooked." Grace's unseconded motion was included,
but not Lord's unseconded motion for a vote of confidence. There was no
reference to Carpenter's cable, nor to Capps's claim that he would resign if he
did not get a vote of confidence.[56]

---

56. Copied excerpts from the clerk's transcription of the May 14 meeting (Bert Hodge Hill
Papers, box 11, folder 3) support Grace's account of the meeting.

Although Capps had succeeded in his objective, he was not yet finished with Hill. When Grace attended the next meeting of the managing committee on May 12, 1928, Capps singled her out by calling attention to her deafness: "I took a seat three seats away from Capps but at the table but [*sic*] he insisted on my coming up next to him in order to hear and we were cheek by jowl when the list of my misdemeanors against him were read out in the minutes [of the meeting May 14, 1927]. I did not mind in the least and was quite pleased at my bad eminence." However, most of the Hill supporters were not at this meeting, and Grace was worried about a new resolution proposed by Capps that she found "suspicious." Although in the past American archaeologists wishing to excavate in Greece had to do so under permits issued to ASCSA, in 1928 the Greek government passed a decree altering this procedure, so that a permit could be issued to a Greek archaeologist who could then excavate in cooperation with a foreign archaeologist outside the jurisdiction of his national school of archaeology in Athens. Capps was asking the managing committee to protest this decree and to restore the old law, "in accordance with which all excavations made by Americans must be conducted under the concessions granted to the School and subject to the School's control." Since no one else spoke up, Grace questioned Capps closely about it, though "he somewhat turned his back on me and was not cordial in his answers. . . . Neither Miss Galt nor [George E.] Howes foll[o]wed up my lead and I felt very inexpert and useless." In a postscript, Grace expressed her delight that J. P. Morgan had given Hill funds for excavation. "Capps did not refer to B. H. H. in any way and I think that he does not know about the Morgan gift for the Eleusis excavation, unless that was the secret spring of his anger about the new law." Capps's resolution passed easily, though Grace did not vote for it, since she still "felt very uneasy about this."[57]

Hill had received a permit for excavation and restoration at Eleusis in collaboration with Konstantinos Kourouniotis, director of the Greek Archaeological Service; J. P. Morgan had contributed $3,000 toward this excavation, thus doubling the amount Hill had been given through the fund raised by Grace and others. Capps's intervention, however, had now made the project impossible. As Hill explained the situation to Morgan, "In the course of his second session of negotiation concerning the proposed excavations in the Athenian Agora, Professor Capps urged modification of existing archaeological laws and decrees so that excavation in Greece shall be possible to Americans only

---

57. Grace H. Macurdy to Ida T. Hill, 13 May 1928, Ida Thallon Hill Papers, box 2, folder 5, Blegen Library; Edward Capps to Grace H. Macurdy, 5 January 1929; MacCracken Papers, box 82, folder 31, Vassar Archives.

under the auspices of the American School, and indicated that to permit me to work at Eleusis as planned would be particularly obnoxious—would in fact be construed as an act of hostility—to the School." He noted that the Greeks did not change their laws but were worried about withdrawal of the promised funds for the Agora excavation. On August 23, 1928, Kourouniotis notified Hill that he must yield to the pressure from Capps and withdraw from their planned collaboration at Eleusis. Hill did not wish to embarrass the Greeks or harm Kourouniotis, so he did not insist on the permit for Eleusis.[58]

Grace's suspicions were confirmed at the next managing-committee meeting on December 26, 1928, when Capps announced a decree by the executive committee that no American archaeologist should be allowed to excavate in Greece in partnership with Greek archaeologists but only under ASCSA control. Grace described to Ida her exchange with Capps:

> When he *lulled* for a moment, as no one else did anything, I got up and asked him plainly whether this new law would prevent Mr. Hill from excavating in Greece, *not* under the School. He snapped "It *will.*" I said "Is not that *unfortunate* to prevent the work of such an archaeologist as Mr. Hill?" He said "Unfortunate for *Mr. Hill*, if he has any such plan!" I said "I think Mr. Hill ~~expects~~ intends to excavate some time." He said "there *had* been such a plan for Mr. Hill, but it is no longer." "It is no longer?" repeated I, "*No longer*" said he with a glare and snapping of his wolf jaws. No one else commented,—though David Robinson and [Clarence] Mendell both said after that it was an *outrage* and that I did well to draw him into the open about it."[59]

Ida wrote to thank Grace for interrogating Capps about Hill, stating that she believed Capps's real objective was to prevent Hill and Blegen from excavating at all, and all other Americans from excavating in Greece except under the jurisdiction of the school.[60] Capps's insistence on ASCSA control over American excavators certainly arose from broader considerations, such as the fear of losing American sources of funding, but his obsessive need to demean Hill and justify his own actions did play a part. As before, he also found it convenient to shift the blame to Ida and Lib. In a 1929 letter to Rhys Carpenter about Blegen's refusal to excavate again under ASCSA, he stated,

58. Bert H. Hill to J. P. Morgan, 18 March 1929, Bert Hodge Hill Papers, box 11, folder 2, Blegen Library.

59. Grace H. Macurdy to Ida T. Hill, 27 December 1928, Ida Thallon Hill Papers, box 2, folder 5, Blegen Library.

60. Ida T. Hill to Grace H. Macurdy, 24–25 January 1929, Ida Thallon Hill Papers, box 2, folder 5, Blegen Library.

"Blegen is simply being sacrificed to the vindictiveness of women."[61] In the long run, Capps's own vindictiveness did no lasting damage to the archaeological careers of Blegen and Hill, particularly because of Blegen's association with the powerful and wealthy University of Cincinnati. Hill conducted excavations on Cyprus, then a British Crown colony, for the University of Pennsylvania.

Grace, however, had one last task to perform for her friends. When Harvard University Press mailed a brochure advertising ASCSA publications in 1929, Grace noticed immediately that Ida's name, and that of her collaborator, Lida Shaw King, had been omitted from the description of her book *Decorated Architectural Terracottas*, the first volume to appear in the series of publications planned for Corinth. Only the name of the general editor of the series, Harold North Fowler, was listed. She asked MacCracken to complain to the press, which apologized and corrected the error in their next brochure. When Grace wrote to thank MacCracken, she noted that she did not wish to suspect conspiracy everywhere, but she added, "I think it probable that the Chairman furnished [the press] the information in this form. He has succeeded in preventing Mr. Hill from taking any part in any excavation in Greece."[62] Significantly, Grace, whose entire term on the managing committee (1919–37) was served under the chairmanship of Capps, was never put on the executive committee, leaving Vassar as the only women's college without representation on that committee during this period.

The Women's Hostel Controversy[63]

When Grace was appointed to serve on a committee to erect a women's hostel in Athens in 1924, she did not expect that this would involve her in another

---

61. Quoted in Jack L. Davis, "Blegen and the Palace of Nestor: What Took So Long?" in Vogeikoff-Brogan et al., *Carl W. Blegen*, 225, n. 27. This article and two earlier articles (Davis, "The Birth of *Hesperia*," and Davis and Gorogianni, "Embedding Aegean Prehistory") analyze the long-term effects of the Capps-Hill controversy on American archaeology in Greece and the Mediterranean.

62. Grace H. Macurdy to Henry N. MacCracken, 13 October 1929, MacCracken Papers, box 82, folder 31, Vassar Archives.

63. The backroom story of this controversy has never been published. Lord (*History of the American School*) says almost nothing about the role played by women in his very brief account, and the 1927–28 annual report presents only Edward Capps's version of events: "Forty-Seventh Annual Report of the American School of Classical Studies at Athens, 1927–1928," Extract from the *Bulletin of the Archaeological Institute of America*, 14–19, accessed 2 February 2015, http://www.ascsa.edu.gr/pdf/uploads/AR_47_1927-28.pdf. A brief article by the ASCSA archivist, Natalia Vogeikoff-Brogan, "Loring Hall: Could It Have Been 'Thomas Hall'?," is the

ASCSA controversy, though one where she was content to play a subordinate role to the presidents of several women's colleges. During the chairmanship of Edward Capps, seven women's colleges were among the ASCSA cooperating institutions—five had joined within fifteen years of the school's founding (Bryn Mawr, Mount Holyoke, Smith, Vassar, and Wellesley) and two joined in the 1930s (Hunter and Radcliffe). From the early years, women had been enthusiastic ASCSA students, despite the difficult living conditions for them in Athens and the fact that female students were initially not allowed to participate in the ASCSA excavations at Corinth. While an ASCSA student from 1899 to 1901, Ida Thallon chafed under this restriction, and she was one of the first female students allowed to participate in an excavation, at the Vari Caves in Attica under Charles Weller.[64] The restriction on excavation was gradually relaxed, and after World War I the percentage of women students at the school rose steadily, from 29 percent of regular students in 1923–24 to 59 percent in 1928–29.[65] Women were also winning a significant number of ASCSA fellowships. During this same period, at least one school fellow was female every year except 1925–26, and both ASCSA fellows in 1928–29 were women. Capps was not pleased with this development and at one time contemplated proposing a ratio of fellowships based on sex, as he wrote to Samuel Bassett:

> I am seriously wondering if we should not modify the terms of our Fellowship competition so as to make the School adapted better to the academic situation in the country. There is a dearth of men archaeologists and a superfluity of women. The latter can't get jobs; we can supply the institutions that are on the watch for able men. The Roman School has in the past set limitations on male and [f]emale; does it still do so? We are wasting, to some extent, the resources of the School. At least one could argue that way. I should be inclined to divide the Fellowships in some ratio.[66]

---

only published account that gives any sense of the underlying tensions: *Akoue: Newsletter of the American School of Classical Studies at Athens* 62 (2010): 17, 25–26, accessed 3 February 2015, http://www.ascsa.edu.gr/pdf/uploads/akoue-spr2010-web.pdf.

64. Natalia Vogeikoff, "Ida Thallon Hill (1875–1954)," accessed 22 January 2015, http://www.brown.edu/Research/Breaking_Ground/results.php?d=1&first=Ida%20Thallon&last=Hill.

65. These statistics are based on information in the annual reports. The percentages of women students in the intervening years are 37 percent (1924–25), 47 percent (1925–26), 50 percent (1926–27), and 53 percent (1927–28).

66. Edward Capps to Samuel Bassett, 11 April 1931, Samuel E. Bassett Papers, box 2, folder 10, MS 590, Yale Library. In an earlier letter to Bassett (3 June 1926), Capps made a disparaging remark about Barbara Philippa McCarthy, ASCSA Institute Fellow 1926–27, that indicates his lack of respect for female scholars: "Those who have taught Miss McCarthy speak well of her intelligence. But she is queer looking."

Since a high proportion of ASCSA female students were graduates of women's colleges, these colleges were naturally concerned about the accommodations for women in Athens. The small number of student rooms provided by the school were not open to women until 1922 as an emergency measure when Athens was crowded with refugees, after which the school leased a nearby building as an annex where women students could be lodged temporarily. In 1916, ASCSA had sent an appeal to presidents of women's colleges asking for subscriptions to purchase a lot near the school that could in the future be used to house women students, and eight colleges (the five cooperating colleges plus Barnard, Radcliffe, and Women's College in Brown University) contributed $450 each. The total was raised to $6,800 by ten individuals who contributed solely for this purpose. On November 21, 1916, Allen Curtis wrote, "I will agree as Treasurer of the School, to accept this money to be used only for the purchase of land on which a Women's Hostel shall be erected. . . . I will also agree that the land, if bought, shall be held solely for the purpose of erecting a Women's Hostel."[67] With the cooperation of the Greek government, a lot across from the school was purchased on April 11, 1919, with one-third of the area purchased by the British School at Athens to build accommodations for their women students. Because of the disruptions of war, nothing further was done for the next five years.

M. Carey Thomas, who had retired from the presidency of Bryn Mawr in 1922, became the driving force in a campaign to erect this hostel for women in Athens.[68] Thomas organized a Women's Hostel Committee, with herself as chair, comprising eight distinguished women educators from the colleges who had contributed to the purchase of the lot in Athens—four presidents (Ada L. Comstock of Radcliffe, Marion E. Park of Bryn Mawr, Ellen F. Pendleton of Wellesley, and Mary E. Woolley of Mount Holyoke), two deans (Virginia C. Gildersleeve of Barnard and Margaret S. Morriss of Women's College in Brown University), and two Greek professors (Julia H. Caverno of Smith and Grace H. Macurdy of Vassar). At the committee's first meeting, held on May 8, 1924, it adopted a plan for an elaborate hostel which Thomas had obviously drawn up in advance of the meeting. Instead of the small, boarding-house unit originally conceived for about eight women, Thomas proposed buying

---

67. Quoted in M. Carey Thomas, "Historical Account," submitted with other documents to Abraham Flexner, secretary of the Rockefeller Foundation's General Education Board, on 4 March 1927 to supplement Capps's 17 December 1926 application for ASCSA endowment funds. International Education Board records, series 1.2, box 35, folder 493, Rockefeller Archive.

68. For more information about Thomas, see Helen Lefkowitz Horowitz, *The Power and Passion of M. Carey Thomas* (Urbana and Chicago: University of Illinois Press, 1999; New York, Alfred A. Knopf, 1994). As Horowitz notes, "It was the Athens hostel that captured Carey Thomas' imagination during her early retirement" (445).

the British portion of the lot and erecting a large building for approximately twenty women students, with a restaurant that would serve the whole school. The entire building would be managed by the Women's Hostel Committee, which would guarantee ASCSA against loss of revenue. This plan was on the same day approved in general by the executive committee and ratified by the managing committee on May 10, 1924. By May 14, the committee submitted an appeal for $150,000 to the Laura Spelman Rockefeller Memorial fund to erect the hostel. In the fall of 1924, Thomas traveled to Athens and participated in a number of meetings with Hill and W. Stuart Thompson, supervising architect for the Gennadius Library, then being constructed on a lot adjacent to the hostel lot. Although Hill had previously favored the erection of a smaller building, the managing committee had approved plans for a larger building, so the three hammered out a plan for a large hostel whose architecture would harmonize with the Gennadeion.

On November 26, 1924, the director of the memorial fund informed the committee that the appeal had been transferred to John D. Rockefeller Jr.'s personal interest; Raymond B. Fosdick, attorney and advisor to John D. Rockefeller Jr., asked Rockefeller's architect, William Welles Bosworth, to look at the plans for the hostel while he was in Athens. Meanwhile, behind the scenes, Capps instructed Hill to try to influence Bosworth against Thomas's current plan, apparently hoping that the ASCSA could get funding for a different plan should this appeal fail. He was particularly opposed to the provision of rooms exclusively for women and to the fact that the building would be managed by the Women's Hostel Committee, as is clear from two official letters sent to Hill:

December 23, 1924:
If the Rockefeller people give the money for such a building, there is no reason why the women should have more than the proper share in planning our building or in determining its uses, is there? And here you may do a good stroke for the School without impropriety (unless by your agreement with Miss T. you are tied up)—for I should think the Rockefellers would more gladly give us a building that would provide for the School's growth in students (of either sex) than one which, while more than providing for the female element, leaves the growth in men students quite unprovided for.

February 22, 1925:
If Mr. Bosworth has not yet visited Athens, please make clear to him that the women's lot can receive only a women's building, but that we shall be free if we acquire the British lot, to build on it for the general uses of the School. That distinction would naturally lead us to a separation of the buildings,

and the reversion to the old scheme of separate units. If such a scheme, providing for such needs as we can today clearly foresee, should appeal to the Rockefeller people as sensible, and they will provide us with the building, we can ourselves assume the responsibility for running the building as a dormitory-boarding house, and will not need the Women's Committee guarantee to meet the losses in management for a period of years. . . . If the Rockefellers decline to do anything, I doubt if Miss Thomas' undertaking will go further.[69]

This occurred during the period when Capps was working to remove Hill as ASCSA director, and he did not scruple to use the hostel issue to denigrate and betray Hill. Immediately after the May 9, 1925, managing-committee meeting that put Hill on a one-year term, Capps wrote Fosdick a letter stating that "the management of the School at Athens is in entire accord with Miss Thomas and her Committee as regards their plans for dormitory accommodations for women in Athens." He claimed that he had just learned at the managing-committee meeting that Hill had been speaking against those plans to Bosworth and that his opposition represented "a reactionary tendency" contrary to the actual mission of the school. Thus Capps deceptively presented himself as reasonable and accommodating, when in fact he had dictated to Hill the very opposition he now denounced. Hill, he said, wanted a "school of research in Archaeology" with only a small number of fellows in attendance, while the real purpose of the ASCSA was to provide an opportunity for as many qualified students as possible to pursue many aspects of classical study in Athens. Thomas's proposal was "heartily welcomed" by the executive committee, the managing committee, and the trustees. "The only opposition has come from Athens, and on grounds that are wholly untenable." Hill, he added, "does no research. He has never written an article or a book in the twenty years he has been in Athens."[70]

On July 13, 1925, Fosdick wrote Ellen Pendleton that Rockefeller had declined the appeal of the Women's Hostel Committee, on the grounds that "he always hesitates to assume entire responsibility for a particular project that is subsidiary to a larger program."[71] By the time the hostel committee met on October 9, 1925, Thomas was convinced that Hill was actively opposing

---

69. Quoted in Hill, "For the Further Information," 9.

70. Edward Capps to Raymond B. Fosdick (copy), 11 May 1925, in Thomas, "Historical Account."

71. Raymond B. Fosdick to Ellen F. Pendleton (copy), 13 July 1925, in Thomas, "Historical Account."

plans for the hostel and was thus responsible for the failure of their appeal for funding. Despite Grace's objections, Thomas spoke forcefully against Hill and persuaded the committee to pass a resolution "that it would be unwise at the present time to beg for money for a Women's Hostel to be operated in conjunction with the American School at Athens; and that nothing could be done until such time as the Trustees and Managing Committee of the School in the United States and the Director of the School in Athens should be in accord on the plan of a Hostel for women students. It was felt by the Committee that even if the Hostel were built, it could not be successfully operated under present conditions."[72] Capps embellished this resolution in a postscript to his letter to Julia Caverno explaining his "mistake" about Hill's alleged resignation, apparently still hoping to alienate her from Hill:

> I suppose you know that the Hostel Committee of which you are a member notified Judge Loring and our Trustees last fall that they would not go ahead with their plans while the management of the School remained as it was, citing chapter and verse to prove that your Committee had been "double-crossed"? Possibly Miss Thomas and Miss Pendleton did not consult the whole Committee before taking this step. I have the impression that both they and Dean Gildersleeve are strongly of this opinion.[73]

Meanwhile, the hostel committee agreed to a modification of their original plan that would allow men to fill any vacancies in the hostel after all the women students had been assigned rooms. The ASCSA trustees, at a special meeting held on February 9, 1926, passed a resolution making the Women's Hostel Committee a special committee of the trustees to raise funds to buy the British lot, to build and furnish a women's hostel on one or both lots, to establish a $5,000–$10,000 guarantee fund to insure the school against loss in the early years of hostel operations, and to pay back, if necessary, the subscriptions of the two individuals who had contributed to the fund on the understanding that the hostel would be confined to women only. A joint building

---

72. Julia H. Caverno to Bert H. Hill, 30 November 1926, Bert Hodge Hill Papers, box 11, folder 1, Blegen Library. In Thomas's report of this resolution, she alters the last sentence: "It was felt that the Hostel even if built could not be operated harmoniously under Mr. Hill as Director of the School" (Thomas, "Historical Account," 8). On 3 November 1925, Mary Woolley wrote Grace, "You were quite right that there was no vote that 'we would have nothing to do with the Hostel while Mr. Hill was Director of the School.' It may be that some member of the Committee said that it 'looked as if Hill must go,' but that should not be interpreted as a committee expression of opinion." Autograph Files, Vassar Archives.

73. Edward Capps to Julia H. Caverno (copy), 17 July 1926, Bert Hodge Hill Papers, box 11, folder 1, Blegen Library.

committee was appointed, consisting of Edward Capps, William B. Dinsmoor, M. Carey Thomas, Virginia C. Gildersleeve, Ellen F. Pendleton, and treasurer Allen Curtis. The trustees also agreed in substance to adopt a new bylaw after the money had been raised that would make the Women's Hostel Committee an official ASCSA committee to manage the hostel under the general control of the trustees, with the committee chair an ex officio member of the managing committee.[74]

In September, Thomas and Gildersleeve secured a three-year option to purchase the British portion of the lot, since the British School had decided not to build lodgings for their women students. In November, Thomas, Gildersleeve, and Pendleton were constituted as a subcommittee to raise funds for the hostel (known as "The Women's Hostel Begging Committee"). While they were planning to ask the Rockefeller Foundation's General Education Board for funds, they learned that Capps was in negotiations to ask the same organization for a large endowment fund for the school. Thomas traveled to Princeton to meet with Capps, who agreed to include $200,000 for the hostel in his statement of the needs of the school, which he sent to Abraham Flexner, secretary of the General Education Board, on December 17, 1926. On December 24, he sent a letter to Flexner including a statement prepared by Thomas: "President Thomas has prepared the enclosed statement at my request about the proposed Students' Hostel for the American School at Athens, which may supplement my own brief paragraph on the subject." After describing the plan for the Women's Hostel, Thomas's statement concluded:

> The above plan has been approved unanimously by the Trustees, Board of Managers, and the Executive Committee of the American School. The former Director, Mr Hill, is believed to be the only person officially connected with the management of the school who is not in sympathy with the Women's Hostel, his objection seeming to be chiefly that it would increase the number of students as more men as well as more women might be expected to study in Athens as a consequence of the opening of the Hostel.

Thomas was here parroting Capps's version of Hill, whom she refers to as "the former Director" even though the managing committee had not yet

---

74. A. Winsor Weld, secretary of the ASCSA trustees, "Vote of the Trustees of the American School of Classical Studies at Athens," 9 February 1926, submitted with other documents to Abraham Flexner on 4 March 1927 to supplement Capps's 17 December 1926 application for ASCSA endowment funds. International Education Board records, series 1.2, box 35, folder 493, Rockefeller Archive.

ratified Hill's termination as director at its December 27 meeting. Flexner included a mild protest in his reply to Capps: "I wonder if Miss Thomas is quite fair to Mr. Hill. In discussing the project with me, Mr. Hill made no objection to women students. He did object, however, to having so large a Hostel exclusively for women."[75]

Thomas was a personal friend of Flexner, whose brother Simon had married her sister Helen, and she met with him in January to discuss the hostel appeal. At his request she traveled to Princeton in February and again in March to meet with Capps "in order that any remaining difficulty may be completely cleared up." Capps assured her that there were no differences, that they were "in complete accord. . . . He repeated that he knew of nothing and said that he could only suppose that Mr. Hill, or Miss Richter [Gisela Richter, curator of Greek and Roman art at the Metropolitan Museum], were again at work fomenting trouble." On March 4, 1927, Thomas, Gildersleeve, and Pendleton sent Flexner a formal appeal supported by a large number of documents relating to the women's hostel. This was presented as an adjunct to the application for ASCSA endowment funds submitted in December by Capps and Flexner accepted it as part of that application, though Capps had not indicated in his application that the Women's Hostel Committee would be sending these additional documents. Flexner explained to Thomas that he was not aware of any differences between her and Capps: "I simply wanted to make sure that you are in entire agreement. Since writing you I have seen Professor Capps, and I have put the same question to him, and he tells me, as you do, that you are in complete accord."[76]

What Thomas did not know, since Capps had never sent her a copy of his application, was that Capps had omitted the paragraph they had agreed upon referring to the formal appeal that would be sent by the Women's Hostel Committee presenting further details of the hostel. More significantly, he had not mentioned this committee at all, ignoring their role in purchasing the lot and securing the option for the British portion. The application asked for $200,000 for "a Hostel or dormitory for students, building and equipment" with the following note:

75. Edward Capps, "Memorandum for Mr. Flexner on the Present Needs of the School at Athens," 17 December 1926; Edward Capps to Abraham Flexner, 24 December 1926; M. Carey Thomas, "Statement concerning the Women's Hostel to be inserted in the general statement of the needs of the American School"; Abraham Flexner to Edward Capps, 27 December 1926, International Education Board records, series 1.2, box 35, folder 492, Rockefeller Archive.

76. M. Carey Thomas to Abraham Flexner, 4 and 25 March 1927; Abraham Flexner to M. Carey Thomas, 28 February and 28 March 1927, International Education Board records, series 1.2, box 35, folder 493, Rockefeller Archive.

The Women's Colleges began to agitate twelve years ago for proper provision for our women students, and money was raised for the purchase of a plot of land for a small building to house about eight women, but the money for the building was not raised. Meantime the number of students and visiting teachers has increased, so that the present need is for a building to house at least twenty students (men and women); and an option has been obtained on a lot adjoining our own now owned by the British School. The representatives of the Women's Colleges are willing to make common cause and see such a building erected on the two lots, and this is urgently needed. Dining accomodations [*sic*] will be provided for the entire clientelle [*sic*] of the School in this building.[77]

On May 27, 1927, the International Education Board, to which the appeal had been transferred because the General Education Board could not make grants abroad, agreed to appropriate to the American School of Classical Studies at Athens a sum of $500,000 for endowment, construction and equipment, and a revolving publication fund, with the understanding that ASCSA would raise the additional $250,000 needed to execute the program outlined in Capps's appeal within a reasonable amount of time. Thomas had left the United States in June 1927 to spend two years abroad writing her autobiography. On July 16, Capps wrote her from Athens about the grant, congratulating her on "the outcome of our application" and suggesting that they work together to raise the $67,000 needed to complete the school's portion of the $200,000 for the hostel: "It ought not to be very difficult, in spite of the handicap of the recent dissension over Mr Hill. As I look over the situation here I am more and more satisfied, not only that Mr. Hill's removal was absolutely indispensable for the good of the School, but also that in Carpenter and Meritt we have a staff very decidedly superior to Hill and Blegen."[78]

Thomas's joy soon turned to wrath, however, for Capps had already secured his endowment funds and ousted Hill and Blegen; he no longer needed to court the good opinion of representatives of the women's colleges. In October and November, he sent letters to Gildersleeve and Thomas indicating that the grant had changed both the status of the hostel and of the Women's Hostel Committee. Capps claimed that the committee's appeal on March 4, 1927, had

---

77. Capps, "Memorandum for Mr. Flexner." See also M. Carey Thomas to William C. Loring, 29 January 1928, International Education Board records, series 1.2, box 35, folder 495, Rockefeller Archive.

78. Edward Capps to M. Carey Thomas, 16 July 1927, International Education Board records, series 1.2, box 35, folder 494, Rockefeller Archive.

constituted a different application for funding separate from his application submitted on December 17, 1926. His application had been funded; theirs had not. This was blatantly untrue, since Capps had sent Flexner Thomas's statement about the Women's Hostel on December 24, 1926, and asked him to insert it in his application. In his meetings with Thomas, they had written a paragraph stating that her committee would be sending further documents in support of the women's hostel, though Capps did not include this paragraph in his application. Thomas finally saw the exact wording Capps had used in his application, "a building to house at least twenty students (men and women)." Next to this he had written in the margin, "This was also understood to be acceptable to Miss Thomas and the Hostel Com.," which was manifestly false since this wording had never been presented to the committee.[79] In response to these developments, a meeting of the Women's Hostel Committee was held on November 22. Grace reported to Ida that Thomas had sent several cables, "one quite incoherent with rage," instructing the committee not to approve Capps's plans but to wait for a letter from Thomas that would follow. As Grace reported to Ida, "I quite chuckled when I heard of her and Capps falling out and Miss Gildersleeve seemed to see the point of my mirth. I remarked that I thought every statement of his ought to be checked up and examined and Miss G. said she agreed perfectly."[80]

The committee met again on January 31, 1928, to discuss Thomas's letter, which maintained that they should insist on their prerogatives:

> I am quite sure that there is not—and cannot be—any misunderstanding about our Women's Hostel. The action of the Trustees stands unreversed and certainly held good when we made the application to the General Board. Mr. Capps used the same wording we used in our petition which accompanied the request sent by Mr. Capps. . . . If he plays us false now it will justify all that has been said about his double-faced methods but this seems to me inconceivable. . . . I am convinced that we have only to be firm. Professor Capps could not have given his solemn word to me to pass on to Mr. Flexner before the gift was made that he and I were "in entire agreement" in regard to the Hostel and not stand by it. Such a thing is unthinkable. . . . I know how busy you all are. But this Hostel under our management will mean so

---

79. Copy of letter from Edward Capps to Virginia Gildersleeve, 20 October 1927, International Education Board records, series 1.2, box 35, folder 495, Rockefeller Archive.

80. Grace H. Macurdy to Ida T. Hill, 25 December 1927, Ida Thallon Hill Papers, box 2, folder 5, Blegen Library.

much for women's culture and scholarship we cannot let it be taken away from our Committee.[81]

Thomas also had personal reasons for wanting to keep the hostel under the management of the committee, for she expressed an interest in "running" the hostel herself after her autobiography was finished. She also offered to advance the money to purchase the British lot herself. In her reports to President MacCracken on these meetings, Grace noted that Thomas's passionate interest in building a women's hostel was not shared by the rest of the committee: "Personally I do not object to having the Hostel used for both men and women and I should be glad to see foreign women of high scholarship admitted to it as well as Americans. This was also the feeling of the rest of the Committee in our last meeting." She also sent MacCracken a letter from Julia Caverno that concluded, "I really have no doubt that Mr. Capps will get that Hostel in any form he wants. But I honestly don't feel bound to fight as I did in Mr. Hill's case."[82] Knowing Ida's interest in anything to do with Capps, Grace sent her a more colorful account of the meeting:

Now be discreet about the following information, for it will not do for me to hand out in general the information gleaned at these private meetings. So tell only the *Four* about it. Capps wants to chuck and annihilate our Hostel Committee altogether. Miss Thomas will not be chucked. So though I do not care a farthing about the whole business I am with Miss T in wishing to hold the Trustees to the agreement that WE are the HOSTEL COMMITTEE forever and amen! We have a long document to that effect and Misses Pendleton, Gildersleeve, and Morris[s] are going to meet Judge Loring and get his opinion of the legality of this former agreement with US. Capps' view is that he having got the money for the Hostel our committee has no more excuse for being. But 1) the Land does not belong to him and 2) the money is not all raised yet and the Hostel Committee has tentatively agreed to raise $30,000. . . . Many choice things that pleased me were said at the Meeting. I must not quote individuals too much, but one distinguished lady, president of a college [Ellen Pendleton], said Capps did not know when he was telling the

81. Copy of letter of M. Carey Thomas to Virginia Gildersleeve, Ellen Pendleton, and Ada Comstock, 10 November 1927, MacCracken Papers, box 82, folder 31, Vassar Archives.

82. Grace H. Macurdy to Henry N. MacCracken, 28 November 1927, Julia H. Caverno to Grace H. Macurdy, 27 November 1927, MacCracken Papers, box 82, folder 31, Vassar Archives.

truth and when not and that he got every thing he touched into a muddle. *Do not repeat that* in general for obvious reasons.[83]

On January 29, 1928, Thomas sent a long letter to Judge Loring with many supporting documents laying out her case in preparation for the meeting he and Frederick Fish, representing the ASCSA trustees, were to have with Ellen Pendleton, Virginia Gildersleeve, and Margaret Morriss, representing the Women's Hostel Committee, on February 11. She also sent him a copy of a letter she had written to Abraham Flexner on February 5 "about the serious misunderstandings that have suddenly developed between Professor Capps and our Women's Hostel Committee in regard to the gift that you obtained for the building equipment of the Hostel." She wished to explain why she had not paid sufficient attention to his warnings to make sure that she and Capps were in agreement about the hostel:

> I felt that it was impossible to insist further with Professor Capps because of the very pleasant relations between him and our Women's Hostel Committee. . . . I could not doubt his word formally given that we were in perfect agreement. There was another reason why I was not as much alarmed by your warning as I should have been. I recognized as everyone who works with Professor Capps must, a certain instability in his character and I thought that perhaps your warnings referred to this. He has the defects of his qualities. He is fertile in ideas and is always thinking of new plans. In the fascination of new ideas he sometimes forgets old ones—I had admired him for his initiative and vision. I have always defended him when people emphasized this side of his character. This whole matter has been a great shock and a very great surprise to me.[84]

Flexner wrote to both Thomas and Loring stating that the International Education Board had given the money to the ASCSA trustees and it was up to them to decide how it would be used. Although Thomas thought that her evidence, particularly the trustees' own resolutions of February 9, 1926, would win the day, she seriously underestimated the power of the money Capps had raised and his control over the trustees. Grace described the outcome

---

83. Grace H. Macurdy to Ida T. Hill, 4 February 1928, Ida Thallon Hill Papers, box 2, folder 5, Blegen Library.

84. M. Carey Thomas to Abraham Flexner, 5 February 1928, Copy of letter of M. Carey Thomas to William C. Loring, 29 January 1928, International Education Board records, series 1.2, box 35, folder 495, Rockefeller Archive.

in her report to MacCracken of the March 21 meeting of the Women's Hostel
Committee:

> The subject discussed was the letter of Judge Loring to Miss Pendleton after
> the conference of Feb. 11. . . . The letter states that a dormitory for both men
> and women, not a hostel for women, will be erected by the Trustees and that
> it shall also have a restaurant and dining hall; shall be administered by the
> Director of the School and not by the Women's Hostel Committee, and shall
> be entirely under the control of the Managing Committee of the Ameri-
> can School. . . . Miss Thomas and Professor Capps have been at variance
> about the proposed Hostel and she is not included on any [of] the suggested
> committees in Judge Loring's letter. She will doubtless be disappointed that
> the Hostel for which she has worked so long is not to be built, but there
> appeared no other course open to the Committee under the circumstances
> but to acquiesce and dissolve, leaving our colleges unpledged to do anything
> further. I think that Miss Thomas's efforts have not been wasted as otherwise
> the dormitory to be built would probably not have included women at all.
> . . . It was the sense of the committee present yesterday that the dormitory
> for men and women is better than the proposed Women's Hostel, but that
> there is no longer any reason for our continuing to function as a committee.
> . . . I am sorry for Miss Thomas, but think the result inevitable and one that
> might have been foreseen by her.[85]

Although Capps wrote in his annual report that the hostel committee
"expressed themselves as entirely satisfied with the dispositions which had
been made by Judge Loring and his Committee in consultation with their
Committee," Ellen Pendleton's letter to Loring on behalf of the committee did
nothing of the sort. She enclosed a copy of the minutes stating the details of
the agreement in a very cold and noncommittal fashion, including the committee's withdrawal of its offer to raise any money for the building, concluding, "I believe I do not need to add anything to the minutes of the meeting
beyond the assurance that the action was taken after careful consideration."[86]
In Athens, the Four were not surprised at Capps's victory, and Hill wrote
about it to Prentice, Bassett, and Caskey with an apt analogy:

---

85. Grace H. Macurdy to Henry N. MacCracken, 22 March 1928; William C. Loring to
Ellen F. Pendleton, 20 February 1928, MacCracken Papers, box 82, folder 31, Vassar Archives.

86. Copy of letter of Ellen F. Pendleton to William C. Loring, 23 March 1928, International
Education Board records, series 1.2, box 35, folder 495, Rockefeller Archive. Edward Capps,
"Forty-Seventh Annual Report," 19.

I have been interested to learn the EC has decided to try staging a tragedy with the cast: Jehu, EC; Jezebel, MCT; Eunuchs of Jezebel, friendly to Jehu, ASC Trustees. Miss Thomas will doubtless learn,—what we have known these four years, actually or prophetically—that all doublecrossing of her Hostel Committee is the work of the MC Chairman.[87]

Grace sent Ida the final word on the hostel in her report on the "very dull" managing committee held on May 11, 1929:

The Trustees have named the Hostel "The William Caleb Loring Hall" because of the astuteness which Judge L. showed in dealing with the women! As Capps was the principal in that I do not see why it is not called the *Edward Capps Hall*. I wish it were just to see what Miss Thomas would do. Lily [Ross Taylor, at this time professor at Bryn Mawr] says that Miss Donnelly [Lucy Martin Donnelly, Bryn Mawr professor of English] says that Miss T. cannot hear Capps's name mentioned in her presence without turning pale with rage or something of that sort. He certainly queered her plans.[88]

In the end, the coeducational dormitory was much more useful to ASCSA than a hostel for women would have been, but it was a painful personal defeat for Thomas. Capps had manipulated her for his own purposes and then discarded her when he no longer needed her. Thomas's biographer, Helen Lefkowitz Horowitz, inaccurately cites this incident as a triumph for Thomas:

Launching the women's hostel at Athens proved to be exceedingly difficult. . . . In the process she had to best the director of the American School and a Princeton classicist in their efforts to turn the women's project into a coeducational residence hall. Throughout the successful effort Thomas managed to stay informed and in control. Letters and minutes demonstrate that she had not lost her touch. In the mid-1920s—when she summoned it—Carey Thomas could have the command over detail and the negotiating skills of 1905.[89]

---

87. Bert H. Hill to William Prentice, Samuel Bassett, and Lacey Caskey, 17 April 1928, Bert Hodge Hill Papers, box 11, folder 2, Blegen Library. In this story from the Old Testament 2 *Kings*, the pagan queen Jezebel is thrown out of her tower window by her own eunuchs at the behest of the Israelite commander Jehu, who then drives his chariot over her.

88. Grace H. Macurdy to Ida T. Hill, 19 May 1929, Ida Thallon Hill Papers, box 2, folder 5, Blegen Library.

89. Horowitz, *The Power and Passion*, 446.

As the documents clearly reveal, this was not a successful effort. The women's hostel was never built, and Thomas herself was excluded from any further participation in the affairs of the American School in Athens.

Grace Macurdy's active participation in these two controversies, which absorbed much of her time and energy during the period from 1925 to 1929, taught her two important lessons. She realized that she could overcome her aversion to public confrontation and speak out for her beliefs, despite the emotional strain she felt and the difficulties caused by her deafness. More significantly, she now recognized more clearly than ever before the marginalized position of women in the academic world. Most of the women associated with ASCSA thought Hill had been treated unjustly and were willing to go on record in his support. Situated outside the customary academic network of rewards and sanctions, they were less susceptible to the influence of a man like Capps. However, there were simply too few of them to make a real difference, especially on the managing committee, and many men found it easy to dismiss their voices as the protests of "excited ladies." Grace was correct when she observed that Capps and others would not have been unduly disturbed if several of the women's colleges had left ASCSA, particularly since they already thought that there were too many women students at the school. There was scarcely a ripple when the first female ASCSA trustee, Sarah Choate Sears, wife of J. Montgomery Sears, resigned in 1927 in protest at the treatment of Hill. Grace would profit from both of these lessons as she sought a new direction in her scholarship.

CHAPTER 10

༺ ⊚ ༻

Redefining the Classical Scholar as a Woman

G race made a dramatic change in her scholarly focus even before *Troy and Paeonia* was published, turning away from Greek literature and prehistoric influences on Greek civilization and culture to concentrate on Hellenistic history. Striking as this shift was, its most startling aspect was her decision to spotlight the lives of queens within the dynasties from Philip II of Macedon to Cleopatra VII of Egypt (359–30 BCE). No classical scholar, male or female, had ever attempted to recover and document the lives of individual Greek women whose names are part of recorded history. The small number of publications that had dealt with ancient women up to this time had all been written by men, in articles and monographs that treated women (or "Woman") as a special problem, a category to be considered in isolation from history. Many of these studies were intended for nonspecialist audiences and employed a light, popularizing tone quite foreign to professional classical scholarship.[1] Grace's serious scholarly focus on individual Greek women was completely unprecedented. Although she never explicitly wrote about what prompted this new turn in her scholarship, it is likely that several interconnected factors contributed to her motivation.

---

1. For more information on early writing about ancient women, see Barbara F. McManus, *Classics and Feminism: Gendering the Classics,* The Impact of Feminism on the Arts and Sciences (New York: Twayne Publishers, 1997), 5–14.

In his tribute upon her retirement. President MacCracken attributed her new scholarly focus to Grace's feminism:

> Her deep interest in the achievements of women and in their opportunities both for political and for social equality has led her studies of late into the history of Greek women. She has made known to us the story of the famous women of the Macedonian line and of other great women of the classical period, which helps us to understand the paradox of Greek literature with its long series of famous heroines existing side by side with the historical record from which women are conspicuous by their absence.[2]

Grace had marched and campaigned for women's suffrage, particularly in advance of the 1917 bill that gave women the right to vote in New York State. She declared in an interview that the passage of the suffrage amendment was the greatest political change to affect Vassar students, who were now much more interested in economics and politics, a development which was "all to the good and unavoidable."[3] Her years at Vassar had led to a fervent belief in education's capacity to empower women. For example, she once gave a former student from a very wealthy family, Henriette Blanding, a card of introduction to Gilbert Murray, hoping that he might influence her to continue her studies: "I have always wished for her that she might come to Oxford to study and to avoid the society life in San Francisco, which her mother desires for her."[4] Grace's new scholarly project would create an important educational resource for modern women, one that demonstrated through reliable and unbiased research that some ancient women did play a significant role in government and politics despite the tremendous odds against them. By highlighting the achievements of some ancient women, Grace hoped that she could encourage a sense of independent agency in young women faced with what seemed to be socially preordained limits.

Although Grace had embarked on her study of ancient queens before she became involved in the two controversies at the American School of Classi-

---

2. Henry Noble MacCracken, "Annual Report 1937," 14, Vassariana, 378.7V C, Vassar Archives.

3. "Vassar Girls Unchanged, Declares Miss Macurdy," *Vassar Miscellany News*, 14 April 1937, 1. According to family tradition, Grace was once jailed overnight for her participation in a suffrage parade (interview with Caroline Skinner O'Neil by Barbara F. McManus, 13 May 2005), but I have been unable to document this.

4. Grace H. Macurdy to Gilbert Murray, 24 February 1914, MSS Gilbert Murray 157, fols. 52–57, Bodleian. Henriette de Saussure Blanding had published a volume of poems in 1911, which Grace sent Murray as proof of her potential, but apparently Grace's scheme did not work, since Blanding married a scion of San Francisco society later in 1914.

cal Studies at Athens, this experience strengthened her determination to give credit to the ancient women who had carved out some influence within a system that gave all collective and institutional power to males. From first-hand experience, Grace had seen that women could draw only on their own personal, individual power in such a situation, an insight as illuminating for the queens of Hellenistic times as it was for academic women in the early twentieth century.

Another motivation stemmed from Grace's compulsion to speak out against injustice. Whenever she perceived unfair treatment, Grace immediately felt the need to protest even if personally uninvolved, and she sprang to the defense of men as well as women. In one instance, for example, she wrote MacCracken on behalf of an assistant professor of history at Vassar, John Perry Pritchett, who was being forced out of the department because his method of teaching did not conform to long-established patterns in the department:

> I should like to express to you my very strong feeling of the injustice that may be done to an individual when his or her academic career is brought to a close either by the arbitrary decision of a chairman of a department or by a majority vote of the voting members of a department. I know from very bitter experience the suffering and danger that may come from a prejudice against a member of a department on the part of the chairman. . . . As almost the oldest member of the present faculty I base my own dislike of tyrannical action by individuals on a long experience and observation of departmental procedures. I think it peculiarly unfortunate if young men who come here (or young women either) are checked in their teaching aims and aspirations by those of an older generation.[5]

Her compulsion to challenge biased and discriminatory assertions was evident in her 1923 reply to Charlotte Cowdroy's article in the *Pall Mall Gazette* arguing that women should give up paid employment when they marry. Though single herself, Grace's indignation was galvanized by Cowdroy's call for "a return to a healthy state of public opinion which will cry shame on a man and wife alike when an able-bodied man is not the sole breadwinner," as shown by the rapidity of her response, only two days after the original article.[6] The core of her argument in her reply to Cowdroy foreshadows an essential feature of the new approach Grace would pioneer in the study of

5. Grace H. Macurdy to Henry N. MacCracken, 5 February 1937, MacCracken Papers, box 43, folder 46, Vassar Archives.

6. Charlotte Cowdroy, "A Study of Mrs. Thompson," *Pall Mall Gazette*, 9 January 1923, 9.

ancient women: "This is all very primitive, treating women as a species and not as individuals. It is very notable in the, as a whole anti-feminist, Greek literature that the expression 'race' or 'tribe' of women begins to be used very early. I have yet to see the same expression applied to men in that literature."[7] Ancient Greece was never far from Grace's thoughts, even when dealing with contemporary issues, and she pointed out the injustice—and absurdity—of setting principles or passing laws that lumped together all women into a single category. In an article a few years later, "Blame of Women," she demonstrated how generalizing women as a race apart played out in the history of bitter invective against women in literary works from Hesiod to Strindberg.[8]

It was a small step from defending contemporary women to defending ancient ones. Modern studies of ancient women had been marred by the same bias as that found in the writings of the ancient Greeks, in which women were treated as a species rather than as individuals affected by differences of socio-economic class, culture, and time. Grace chose to counter this bias by studying the lives of individual women in a context where there was enough evidence to permit meticulous research—ancient monarchies. When she sent Gilbert Murray a copy of her book *Hellenistic Queens*, she mentioned her intention to liberate these queens from the negative evaluations of earlier scholars: "[John Pentland] Mahaffy is still quoted in his insane judgments of them by many scholars and I have always felt that [Edwyn Robert] Bevan also, though so much more sensible than Mahaffy, is too generalizing and hard on them."[9]

Grace's motivations were not all altruistic, however. Chief among them was her desire to win distinction as a classical scholar. Grace had never hidden her ambition; indeed, frankness and knowledge of her own motivations were among Grace's most notable characteristics, as explained by Polyxenie Kambouropoulou, a Greek refugee who had graduated from Vassar in 1922 and later returned to teach in the psychology department:

> [Grace Macurdy] was very interested in learning from Miss K. about the ideas of Freud, and wanted to know why so many people strongly disagreed with him. . . . Once Miss K. was telling Miss Macurdy about Freud's theories on motives, that men often attribute to themselves motives which they don't

---

7. "Shall the Married Woman Work?," *Pall Mall Gazette*, 11 January 1923, 9.

8. Grace H. Macurdy, "Blame of Women," *Vassar Quarterly* 2 (1926): 190–98.

9. Grace H. Macurdy to Gilbert Murray, 26 March 1932, MSS Gilbert Murray 157, fol. 151, Bodleian. Mahaffy was Professor of Ancient History at Trinity College Dublin; his extensive works on the Hellenistic era include many condemnations of various queens—e.g., *Empire of the Ptolemies* (1895) and *History of Egypt under the Ptolemaic Dynasty* (1899). Bevan was a Hellenistic historian at King's College London; his works include *The House of Seleucus* (1902) and *The House of Ptolemy: A History of Hellenistic Egypt under the Ptolemaic Dynasty* (1927).

really have. To that Miss Macurdy answered, "I know my own motives." And she did. She was a good natural psychologist, because she was so frank. She was intellectually alive until her death.[10]

Grace's desire for scholarly recognition had been altered by her years at Vassar and her constantly strengthening feminism. Her ambition now was to win distinction as a scholar who spoke with authority as a woman. She had first thought she could achieve this by following in the footsteps of Jane Ellen Harrison, but after *Troy and Paeonia* Grace had come to realize that Harrison's model was not sufficient for the kind of recognition she sought. Harrison's field of study as well as her authorial voice did not conform to the established parameters of classical scholarship. Harrison wrote "as a woman" to the extent that she used a more enthusiastic, affective voice than was typical of scholarly writing, but she did not write about women, and that affective voice tended to alienate many traditional scholars. Harrison had won a place on the periphery of the scholarly community, but Grace was seeking a place at the center. At Harvard and Berlin, Grace had been trained as a careful and exacting philologist, and she was determined to demonstrate that she could effectively use these skills without suppressing or downplaying her gender. She concluded that she could best accomplish this by turning to the study of ancient women.

Hellenistic Queens

J. A. K. Thomson supported Grace in this ambition; in fact, he offered her the first opportunity to present her new area of research to an audience by inviting her to speak on "Great Macedonian Women" in May 1925 as part of his public lecture series at King's College London (see chapter 1). The positive reception to her lecture encouraged her to continue work on this topic, which required a great deal of painstaking research. Her primary training had been in philology, the study of language and literature, not in history, and her previous concentration on myth and ritual, prehistoric tribes, and ethnography had no relation to the complexities of Hellenistic monarchies or to teasing out the scanty and scattered references to women within them. Grace was an indefatigable researcher, however, and she welcomed the challenge. In contrast to the emotionally draining struggles within the ASCSA managing committee, the

---

10. Polyxenie Kambouropoulou, inteview by Catherine Germann, 1969. *Notable American Women* files, MC 230, box 54, Schlesinger.

reading rooms at the British Library and the Cambridge University Library must have appeared quiet havens where she could focus on what she did best.

As she researched and wrote, Grace recognized the need to move beyond the confines of traditional, text-based scholarship. It was clear that women's lives could not be reconstructed from historical and literary texts alone, particularly since these were all written by males and skewed by various types of bias and stereotypical thinking. Grace had to supplement texts with material evidence, especially coins and inscriptions, but also sculpture, vases, and papyri. Her summer travels now included visits to museum collections in a number of European countries and consultations with numismatists and archaeologists.

Grace published her first article on the subject of Hellenistic queens in 1927, "Queen Eurydice and the Evidence for Woman Power in Early Macedonia."[11] The initial response to this article encouraged Grace to continue with this line of research. As she wrote Ida, "I am working on my Women. I must send you a reprint of Macedonian Women from AJP. I got very nice letters about it from Myers [*sic*], Casson (!) and Tarn."[12] John Linton Myres, the Wykeham Professor in Ancient History at Oxford University, wrote Grace, "It is a difficult but very interesting subject, and your collection of materials will be most useful."[13] William Woodthorpe Tarn was a Scottish barrister who became a noted independent scholar specializing in Hellenistic history after ill health forced him to retire from the practice of law. Stanley Casson was a classical archaeologist associated with the British School in Athens and New College, Oxford University. Grace's exclamation point underlines his change of opinion toward her work, since he had criticized *Troy and Paeonia* rather harshly (see chapter 7).

Besides seeking to bring together and analyze "the chief facts that have been preserved" about each of the Hellenistic queens, Grace had two specific goals in this book, both of which were responses to approaches to these women by earlier and contemporary scholars. Her preface contains a straightforward declaration of these goals:

11. Grace H. Macurdy, "Queen Eurydice and the Evidence for Woman Power in Early Macedonia," *American Journal of Philology* 48 (1927): 201–14.

12. Grace H. Macurdy to Ida T. Hill, 25 December 1927, Ida Thallon Hill Papers, box 2, folder 5, Blegen Library.

13. J. L. Myres to Grace H. Macurdy, 13 December 1927, Biographical Files: Macurdy, Grace Harriet, folder 2, Vassar Archives. One wonders how much Myres really appreciated the uniqueness of what Grace was doing, since he goes on to say "You have made the essential point when you quote and amplify [Johann Gustav] Droysen's observation about Macedonian society as a prosaic version of Homeric," and then expounds his own theory that there was no historical connection between the Homeric Achaeans and the Macedonians. Grace's reference to Droysen is actually a very minor point in her article, not at all "essential" to her main argument about women's participation in politics.

In the following investigation of woman-power in the Hellenistic centuries I have confined my study to the three chief dynasties, Macedonia, Seleucid Syria, and Ptolemaic Egypt. Since the statement is so generally made with regard to the queens of these royal houses that in them a woman is the equal of a man, it has seemed to me desirable to attempt to arrive at a clear idea of what is meant by this equality and to discover whether it prevailed alike in all three dynasties. . . . I have also discussed the question of the character of these queens, who are generally reputed to have been wicked. This reputation rests, as does the statement that they possessed power equal to that of the men, on the acts of a few of the many who were queens in the Hellenistic centuries. Of these few it may be said that if they were in nature and character the counterparts of the men, they should be judged by the same standard.[14]

In her book Grace conclusively demonstrates that queens never achieved independent power equal to that of the kings in Macedonia and very rarely did so in Seleucid Syria. In Egypt, it was not until Cleopatra II (ca. 183–116 BCE) that Ptolemaic queens attained coregency with kings, and only Cleopatra VII, with the help of Rome, achieved sole political power in her own right. At first glance this may seem like a negative view of "woman power," but in Grace's hands it is actually strongly feminist. By showing that women, unlike men, never attained the throne purely by right of birth, she focuses attention on the individual qualities and strength of character that enabled some of these queens to wrest political influence and actual power from an overwhelmingly patriarchal dynastic system.[15] Women, Grace contends, must be

---

14. Grace H. Macurdy, *Hellenistic Queens: A Study of Woman-Power in Macedonia, Seleucid Syria, and Ptolemaic Egypt*, Johns Hopkins University Studies in Archaeology 14 (Baltimore: John Hopkins Press, 1932), ix–x.

15. In his website on "The Genealogy of the Seleucids," Alex McAuley criticizes Grace's "minimalist view of female power": "Macurdy considers female power almost exclusively in the same terms as male influence, considering them less influential if their power does not match that of male royals. I find such consideration of feminine influence *vis-à-vis* male influence to be ultimately misleading because it undermines the vastly different expectations and spheres of influence of both genders, making for a paradigm whose equality was neither present nor possible" ("Appendix I: Seleucid Royal Women," 5, accessed on 20 February 2015, http://www .seleucid-genealogy.com/Extras_files/Appendix%20I.pdf). McAuley then praises Elizabeth Carney for advancing the notion that "power did not automatically come with a woman's status: 'being a *basilissa* did not in itself convey any specific power, but it did offer a potential which might be realized by royal women bold enough to try.' Power is thus not institutional but highly personal, determined more by the gumption and charisma of a particular royal woman than by her status" (6; quoting Elizabeth Carney, "'What's in a Name?': The Emergence of a Title for Royal Women in the Hellenistic Period," in *Women's History and Ancient History*, ed. Sarah B. Pomeroy [Chapel Hill: University of North Carolina Press, 1991], 164). However, this is exactly

viewed as individuals, not as a "species"; hence her book relates the individual stories of each queen sequentially throughout each of the three dynasties. Although this structure entails some repetition, it effectively counteracts such sweeping generalizations as the following statement by J. P. Mahaffy: "[Cleopatra VII] was of a race in which almost every reigning princess for the last two hundred years had been swayed by like storms of passion, or had been guilty of like violations of common humanity."[16]

In case after case, Grace shows how some women achieved political power "through the doorway of marriage, which often afforded them opportunity to act as regent for an absent husband, or for a minor child, or as co-regent with a husband whose weakness of character allowed a queen of strong nature to come forward as co-ruler."[17] For example, Cleopatra II, daughter of Ptolemy V and the Seleucid princess Cleopatra I, was "the first of the Macedonian queens in Egypt to achieve a political equality with her husband."[18] Following the Pharaonic custom of brother-sister marriage, she married her brother Ptolemy VI. When he was defeated in battle and fled, she ruled in Alexandria with her younger brother Ptolemy VIII, who styled himself Euergetes II (meaning "benefactor"). Through her efforts, the brothers were reconciled and her husband returned, after which for five years she ruled jointly with her husband and his brother until Ptolemy VIII was sent to rule Cyrenaica. She then was coruler with Ptolemy VI until he died in 145 BCE, after which she was sole regent for their young son for about a year until she married her younger brother Ptolemy VIII, who then killed her son. Despite this, they ruled jointly until Ptolemy VIII married Cleopatra II's daughter Cleopatra III, after which the rulers were known as "king Ptolemy and queen Cleopatra the Sister and queen Cleopatra the Wife." Cleopatra II drove Ptolemy VIII and Cleopatra III out of Alexandria and claimed sole rule of Egypt from 130 to 127 BCE, though civil war soon broke out between her supporters and those of Ptolemy VIII. After a brief exile in Syria, Cleopatra II returned to Egypt in 124 BCE and reconciled with her second husband and her daughter, ruling again with them

---

the point that Grace's entire book is designed to convey, that some individual queens acquired power equal or nearly equal to that of kings, but only through their own personal qualities.

16. Macurdy, *Hellenistic Queens*, 3, quoting J. P. Mahaffy, *The Empire of the Ptolemies* (London: Macmillan, 1895), 445.

17. Macurdy, *Hellenistic Queens*, 1.

18. See Macurdy, *Hellenistic Queens*, 147–61 for a full discussion of the life and accomplishments of Cleopatra II. Grace calls her younger brother Ptolemy VII Euergetes II, though I have followed modern scholars in numbering him Ptolemy VIII. Grace gives no number to Cleopatra's son Ptolemy Neos Philopator since it is doubtful whether he ever reigned, but contemporary scholars term him Ptolemy VII and adjust the numbers of all later Ptolemies accordingly.

until his death in 116 BCE, after which she ruled with her daughter and her young grandson until her own death a few months later.

Grace presents a cogent explanation for Cleopatra's remarkable accession and retention of power, based on a combination of circumstances which she was able to turn to her own advantage repeatedly through her "good sense and brains," plus "a tough unyielding nature which did not know how to acknowledge defeat."[19] As the only daughter of Ptolemy V and Cleopatra I, she had an assured position in the dynasty, in contrast with her two brothers who were rivals for power and needed her to consolidate their position. Her "strong will and political sense" enabled her to negotiate the sharing of power when this was necessary, even when this meant accepting her own daughter as the second wife of her husband, although Grace laments that we have no way of knowing what this meant "actually and psychologically in the daily life of the Palace and of the government." Commenting on the amnesty decrees of 118 BCE, issued in the names of king Ptolemy and queen Cleopatra the Sister and queen Cleopatra the Wife, Grace sees evidence of the sound judgment and political shrewdness of Cleopatra II rather than any qualities of her cruel and self-indulgent husband: "If the arrangements were composed by the rulers themselves and not by their advisers, I strongly incline to the view that Cleopatra II, the first of the line to be co-regent with her husband, a woman of extraordinary ability, character, and nerve, had more to do with framing the decrees than Euergetes II."

In keeping with her goal of presenting a more judicious and balanced account of the characters of individual Hellenistic queens and counteracting the condemnation of them as a group, Grace frequently employs a moralizing tone that was very common in her time but is not typical of modern scholarship. She does, however, insist that queens and kings be evaluated by the same norms:

As for the character of the queens, I have repeatedly said that they must be judged by the standards of the men of their times, for the striking phenomenon with these women is the fact that so many of them approached more nearly than women in any other period to the character and achievements of the men of their race. It has been said of them that "It is only in the intensity and recklessness with which they pursue their ends that we see any trace of womanhood left in them." It would be truer to say that some of them approach masculine intensity and recklessness in pursuing their ends, for it

---

19. All the quotations in this paragraph are taken from Macurdy, *Hellenistic Queens*, 151–61.

is, in general, in the ranks of men rather than among women that reckless adventurers on the grand scale are to be found.[20]

For example, while deploring the cruelty of the Seleucid queen Cleopatra Thea, daughter of Cleopatra II of Egypt, Grace notes that she had herself endured cruelty and was following an established pattern of dynastic murders: "Her life had trained her to be exactly what she appears to have become—an egotist, made for power and stopping at nothing to get it." She adds that the worst stories about her may have been invented by her son Antiochus Grypus, who had poisoned her to prevent her from poisoning him. Grace emphasizes the importance of discussing these ancient women in the context of the specific social conventions of their culture and time, remarking that modern concepts of humility and altruism "would have seemed imbecility" to the Hellenistic rulers and that a "Macedonian queen would never have thought of demanding fidelity in the modern sense of the word from her husband." Arsinoe II, full sister and wife of Ptolemy II Philadelphus (meaning "sister-loving"), was not troubled by her husband's many mistresses: "She had won an impregnable position in the government of Egypt and had a mind and political sense far above that of the usual woman. She infinitely preferred her part as her husband's directing power to that of his mistress Bilistiche." Grace is critical of the reasoning behind W. W. Tarn's dismissal of the claim that Arsinoe had attempted to seduce her stepson Agathocles; according to Tarn, "The flaw in Arsinoe was not perhaps immorality but ambition . . . and it is not necessary to suppose her a bad woman merely because she became a great ruler." She points out that "this judgment implies that a woman can have but one vice and that breaking the moral law for her means breaking her marriage vows," observing that Arsinoe was certainly the instigator of dynastic murders, which were "regarded as only a safe, natural, and essential precaution for any king."[21]

Although Grace's primary aim in this book is comprehensiveness rather than originality, she does not hesitate to present her own reasoning and conclusions on controversial details. In a number of cases she draws upon her philological expertise to verify her position. For example, she argues against the consensus of modern scholars that Phila I, the first wife of king Demetrius I Poliorcetes (meaning "besieger") of Macedon, was on the island of Salamis when it was captured by Ptolemy I, who then safely returned her and her

---

20. Macurdy, *Hellenistic Queens*, 233–34; the quotation is from Edwyn Bevan, *The House of Seleucus* (London: Edward Arnold, 1902), 2:280.

21. Macurdy, *Hellenistic Queens*, 100, 234, 63, 124, 129–30; the quotation is from W. W. Tarn, *Antigonos Gonatas* (Oxford: Clarendon Press, 1913), 123.

children to Macedonia. After pointing out that Phila's two children by Demetrius were both grown at that time and living elsewhere, Grace demonstrates that the Greek of the ancient historian Diodorus Siculus must mean "his children and his mother," not "his children and their mother," indicating that the woman on Salamis was Demetrius's mother Stratonice, who was probably looking after his small children by another of his wives, rather than Phila.[22] In supporting her conclusions about matters of detail, Grace also calls upon various other forms of evidence, including one unusual example based on female experience. Cleopatra V Selene, daughter of Cleopatra III and Ptolemy VIII, was briefly the sister-wife of Ptolemy IX and later married to three kings of Syria. Cicero states that two sons of Selene and King Antiochus of Syria came to Rome to seek help in claiming the Egyptian throne, and Grace argues that their mother was Cleopatra V Selene:

> A doubt has been expressed of the likelihood of Selene's being young enough in 90 BC when she would be about forty, to bear the two sons of whom we hear from Cicero, and it has been suggested that a younger Selene was their mother. Bevan says, "One must remember that women age more quickly in the south. It is not impossible that Selene might have borne children when over forty, but highly improbable." I do not know what the statistics are for southern nations, but the bearing of children by women over forty is such a common phenomenon in England and America that it appears not improbable in a woman of such vigor and vitality as Selene's life shows her to have been.

A footnote shows that Grace pursued the matter further: "Dr. Constantine Kalamara of Athens has kindly sent me statistics of a considerable number of births in his obstetric clinic, in which the women bearing the children have been forty years old or over."[23]

In passages like these and many others, it is clear that Grace is speaking as a woman scholar discrediting prejudices about women, although she never explicitly mentions her own sex. In general, Grace uses a traditionally

---

22. Macurdy, *Hellenistic Queens,* 64–65. A more detailed and complex example of Grace's philological argumentation can be found in her article "Roxane and Alexander IV in Epirus," *Journal of Hellenic Studies* 52 (1932): 256–61. Here she convincingly demonstrates that the modern conviction that Alexander the Great's widow and son spent time in Epirus under the protection of his mother Olympias is based on a misreading of the Greek sources: "I submit, therefore, that historians in repeating the story until it has become part of the current account of the life of Roxane and her child have not sufficiently examined the evidence for it" (261).

23. Macurdy, *Hellenistic Queens,* 172 and n. 204. The quotation is from Edwyn Bevan, *The House of Ptolemy,* 334, n. 4.

objective, scholarly tone based on voluminous research and citation, but she occasionally speaks in a more personal voice, as for example when discussing the dynastic murders perpetrated by Laodice I, wife of the Seleucid king Antiochus II: "Without wishing to condone the crimes of Laodice, I find it a refreshing change from the sentiments of other historians that Beloch actually mentions the fact that 'Alexander at the time when he became king committed much worse deeds, or let them occur.'"[24] Grace's perspective as a scholar whose authoritative reading of the evidence is enhanced by her experience and understanding as a woman is particularly evident in her discussion of Cleopatra VII, the last of the Ptolemaic queens of Egypt. She is equally contemptuous of negative and positive feminine stereotypes that interfere with a judicious interpretation of the facts:

> [John P. Mahaffy's] views about the psychology of female love, in which he thinks nothing is more frequent than "a strong passion co-existing with self-ish ambition, so that a woman embraces with keener transports the lover whom she has betrayed than one whom she has not thought of betraying," must surely have been gathered from an extensive reading of melodrama rather than from an experience of the facts of life. It is as foolish to condemn her and all the women of her line, as Mahaffy in an unguarded moment does . . . for crimes condoned in the case of the men, as to present her as a "sympathetic" heroine, "a dainty little queen with her fat baby at her breast," "a lonely and sorely-tried woman who fought all her life for the fulfillment of a patriotic and splendid ambition."[25]

Grace's own summation, while acknowledging Cleopatra's fascination for later ages, sets the Egyptian queen firmly in her own time and circumstances:

> The accusation of lust is not justified by the facts of her life. She was faithful in her relation to the two Romans, Julius Caesar and Antony; she hoped to be the wife of the first and was actually the wife of the second. . . . She cheated Octavian of his triumph over her, and her splendid immortality of fame he could not take from her, though he got her emeralds and pearls and

---

24. Macurdy, *Hellenistic Queens*, 85, quoting K. J. Beloch, *Griechische Geschichte*, 2nd ed. (Berlin and Leipzig: Walter de Gruyter, 1925–27), 4.1:676.

25. Macurdy, *Hellenistic Queens*, 221, quoting Mahaffy, *Empire of the Ptolemies*, 477. The second set of quotations is from Arthur E. P. B. Weigall, *The Life and Times of Cleopatra, Queen of Egypt: A Study in the Origin of the Roman Empire* (Edinburgh and London: Blackwood, 1914), 11, 410. The first Weigall quotation is actually a paraphrase; the exact wording is even more sentimental: "Can this dainty little woman, we ask, who soothes at her breast the cries of her fat baby, while three sturdy youngsters play around her, be the sensuous Queen of the East?"

frankincense to pay his soldiers and his debts in Italy. More than any other Macedonian except Alexander the Great, to whom she is akin in her brilliance, her intellectual power, and her ambition, she has exercised the spell of her magic over those of her time and every generation since. She was not a pattern of virtue, nor a monster of wickedness, nor a good bourgeois wife, nor a great and splendid patriot, but a Ptolemy with the virtues and vices of her race.[26]

Grace was very pleased with the reviews for *Hellenistic Queens* and particularly delighted that the book had been reviewed in the *Times Literary Supplement*. Reviewers almost universally praised the quality and thoroughness of Grace's scholarship and the book's comprehensiveness:

Professor Macurdy has avoided every form of sensationalism and instead has presented a scholarly and decidedly welcome study of Hellenistic queens in which she evaluates without prejudice their personality, influence, and importance.[27]

This is an attractive and well-illustrated book and a work of sound scholarship and historical research at the same time.[28]

In her book, Hellenistic Queens, Professor Macurdy has assembled all the available material pertaining to the lives and the careers of the queens of Macedonia, Seleucid Syria, and Ptolemaic Egypt. The result is a highly satisfactory and illuminating study of woman-power during the Hellenistic Age. . . . Every source of information is carefully tapped. In addition to the literary texts there are generous citations from inscriptions, papyri, and coins.[29]

This book is a very solid and painstaking compilation, and should be a useful work of reference for students of the Hellenistic period; it is well documented and contains a number of attractive plates.[30]

---

26. Macurdy, *Hellenistic Queens*, 220–22.

27. Jakob A. O. Larsen, review of *Hellenistic Queens*, *Classical Philology* 27 (1932): 315.

28. M. C. [Max Cary], review of *Hellenistic Queens, Journal of Hellenic Studies* 52 (1932): 315. I am grateful to Christopher Stray for the identification of this reviewer.

29. Sterling Tracy, review of *Hellenistic Queens, Classical Weekly* 26 (1933): 207.

30. R. W. Moore, review of *Hellenistic Queens, Times Literary Supplement,* 9 June 1932, 430. I am grateful to Christopher Stray for finding the name of this reviewer. Ralph Westwood Moore, future headmaster of Harrow, was a young man of twenty-six at the time of this review.

A few reviewers, however, turned the praise of comprehensiveness into a somewhat dismissive relegation of the book to that of "encyclopedic reference" with little that is new. In one of only two generally negative reviews, Casper Kraemer states, "Miss Macurdy is a diligent collector rather than a historian. . . . [The book] is frankly encyclopaedic. . . . As a work of reference, therefore, her book has real value."[31] However, all the reviewers, especially those who maintained that the book did not make an original contribution to scholarship, were oblivious to the groundbreaking nature of Grace's whole project. She was not just collecting information about women in the Hellenistic monarchies; she was making the women the *subjects* of her investigation. By studying Hellenistic monarchies from the perspective of the queens, by focusing on the women as agents and discussing the men in relation to them, she was turning historical scholarship on its head. It makes a great deal of difference, for example, to present Olympias as the subject of discourse and to bring Alexander the Great into the discussion as her son, rather than to focus on Alexander and then mention Olympias as his mother, which was the heretofore universal practice of scholars. None of the reviewers recognized the revolutionary nature of the book from this perspective, and only two commented on Grace's own sex: William Woodthorpe Tarn ("It is interesting to have a woman's judgment on this remarkable series of women.") and Herbert William Parke ("Professor Macurdy has done a great service to the memory of many of her sex.").[32]

Most of the reviewers lamented the absence of genealogical or even chronological tables. Noting that Grace "moved with ease" among the many Hellenistic kings and queens with the same names and with multiple and complicated marital arrangements, they observed that such tables would have helped the average reader follow the narrative more comfortably. In the text,

---

31. Casper J. Kraemer Jr., review of *Hellenistic Queens, American Journal of Archaeology* 39 (1935): 157. Kraemer, a papyrologist at New York University, employs a noticeably patronizing tone in his review, objecting to Grace's "unpleasantly bookish" style and "continuous moral judgment." His inaccurate and misleading summary of Grace's conclusion does not inspire confidence in the review: "The resultant conclusion is that, by and large, these 'masterful' women were merely good wives and mothers to masterful men" (157). The other negative review was by Fritz Geyer, review of *Hellenistic Queens, Historische Zeitschrift* 150 (1934): 121–22. Geyer's main objection was that Grace had not cited his book on early Macedonia or his articles in *Realencyclopädie der classischen Altertumswissenschaft*. Since his book was not published until 1930 and at least one of his articles not until 1931, they were rather late for Grace to include, since she refers in her book to the fact that she did not receive a 1931 article by W. W. Tarn until her book was in page proofs.

32. W. W. Tarn, review of *Hellenistic Queens, Classical Review* 46 (1932): 167; H. W. P. [Herbert William Parke], review of *Hellenistic Queens, Hermathena* 22 (1932): 292. I am grateful to Christopher Stray for identifying this reviewer.

Grace often refers to various rulers by their nicknames rather than their numbers, apparently for stylistic purposes. This can be confusing, although her index does list the numbers and nicknames of all the rulers mentioned in the text.

Grace sent Gilbert Murray a copy of *Hellenistic Queens* soon after it was published, but the excessive name-dropping in her accompanying letter suggests that she was nervous about his response to this new direction in her scholarship:

> I have sent you a copy of my book on Hellenistic Queens with some misgivings, as I do not know that you will interested [sic] in my study of these ladies. I have been working on them for a good many years now and yet I feel that I should like to write the book over again. I have had some pleasant letters about it from [Michael Ivanovich] Rostovtzeff and other scholars in America and England. They seem to think that, as [William Scott] Ferguson wrote me, it was high time that some one should present such a dossier. . . . [William W.] Tarn agrees with me about Cleopatra VII, on whom and Antony he has been working for two years for the CAH [*Cambridge Ancient History*] in its next volume. That is, he agrees with me that she not [sic] licentious and in some other particulars.[33]

Murray politely reassured her of his interest, but subsequent statements in her letters indicate that Grace was never confident that he fully understood or appreciated this turn in her scholarship. By this time, however, she no longer needed his approbation, and she forged ahead with her pioneering studies of women.

Vassal-Queens

Grace was gratified by the generally positive reviews of *Hellenistic Queens* and immediately began work on a sequel, as she noted in her department report of 1933: "My book on *Hellenistic Queens* has received favorable notice in reviews by American, English, German, French and Italian scholars. . . . I am engaged on a companion study on the *Vassal Queens of the Roman Empire*."[34] Vassal-queens and vassal-kings were pro-Roman monarchs who ruled semi-autono-

33. Grace H. Macurdy to Gilbert Murray, 26 March 1932, MSS Gilbert Murray 157, fol. 151, Bodleian.

34. Grace H. Macurdy, Report of the Greek Department 1932–33, 11 May 1933, Annual Reports R.36 S.5, Vassar Archives.

mous client kingdoms that Rome controlled but had not annexed as provinces directly governed by Roman magistrates; these monarchs had considerable power over economic, cultural, and religious internal affairs in their kingdoms as long as they did not conflict with Roman interests. However, they ruled at the behest of Rome, were expected to supply troops to fight on Rome's behalf whenever called upon, and could be removed from power at any time by the emperor. Writing this book proved a more complicated and occasionally frustrating project for Grace, since she had to comb through obscure publications and museum collections because many of these women were known only through coins or inscriptions. In order to present a substantial account, she expanded her criteria to include the women of the Herodian court in Judaea (only two of whom, Julia Berenice and Salome, daughter of Herodias, were actually vassal-queens) and two queens who challenged the authority of Rome through war (Boudicca of Britain and Zenobia of Palmyra).

Grace's purpose in this book is not the same as the goals of her earlier book, despite the claim of W. W. Tarn that "this book is a continuation of Dr. Macurdy's *Hellenistic Queens*, which appeared in 1932, and presumably has the same object, to define as far as possible 'the kind and extent of power possessed by the women'; she is really vindicating woman's place in the then world."[35] Grace is quite clear that the power of client monarchs, male as well as female, was severely circumscribed by the control of Rome and had little or nothing to do with their gender. Since male rulers who could lead armies on Rome's behalf were perceived as more valuable than females, however, the fact that any of the client rulers were women was due to the earlier tradition that had allowed some women to achieve positions of power in Hellenistic kingdoms of the east. Instead of trying to "vindicate" women's place in the ancient world, Grace is seeking in this book to recover the names and lives of women in these client kingdoms, to reveal their agency, and to demonstrate once again the difference it makes to view history from the perspective of women. As she states in her conclusion:

> The names of most of the vassal-queens are familiar only to the numismatist, the epigraphist, and to those who have made a special study of their little principalities. . . . The phenomenon of their appearance as rulers and the fact that Rome entrusted to some of them the privileges of the client-kings testify to the survival in them, in spite of their restricted power, of the competence, energy, and intelligence which queens of the Hellenistic dynasties possessed in so high a degree. . . . The power of the vassal-queens in the first

35. W. W. Tarn, review of *Vassal-Queens*, *Journal of Roman Studies* 28 (1938): 77.

century A. D. . . . was a survival of the tradition of the Hellenistic queens, who had ruled from time to time in Macedonia, Syria, and Egypt. . . . Since their names have reached us in such meagre and accidental transmissions, it seems altogether likely that in the strong and turbulent houses to which these queens belonged, there were other notable women, of whom history has kept no trace, and of whom no "médaille austère" has been upturned, to make its revelation.[36]

Grace notes that the well-known Russian ancient historian Michael Ivanovitch Rostovtzeff had devoted a lengthy article to one of the vassal-queens, Dynamis of Bosporus, declaring that he had made her "live again, an adventurous, fierce, and bold south-Russian queen."[37] However, Rostovtzeff's article, originally written for a publication in honor of a woman, Countess P. S. Uvaroff, has as its avowed purpose the identification of the queen whose portrait is preserved in a small bronze bust found in the ruins of an ancient building in a Russian city on the Black Sea; Grace's book includes this bust as its frontispiece. Far from evoking the personality of Dynamis, Rostovtzeff's reconstruction of her life, based on a thorough study of all available sources and including much information about the men with whom she was associated, is presented rather as a "suggested reconstruction of the history of the kingdom of Bosporus in the period of transition."[38] Though he relates Dynamis to the Hellenistic queens who preceded her, he does so in the generalizing way deplored by Grace in her earlier book: "Her history reminds us to a great extent of the history of the clever, energetic, enduring, and ambitious women, wicked wives of many husbands, who appeared at the Hellenistic courts after Alexander."[39] He is also rather dismissive in discussing the connections between some of the vassal-queens and women in the imperial families at Rome:

> In the historical struggle for the throne of Bosporus, no less than in the general history of the East at that time, a striking part was played by a number of eminent women with powerful connexions at the court of Rome, where such personal influences worked often in conjunction with political consid-

---

36. Grace H. Macurdy, *Vassal-Queens and Some Contemporary Women in the Roman Empire*, Johns Hopkins University Studies in Archaeology 22 (Baltimore: Johns Hopkins University Press, 1937), 129–33.

37. Macurdy, *Vassal-Queens*, 2.

38. M. Rostovtzeff, "Queen Dynamis of Bosporus," *Journal of Hellenic Studies* 39 (1919): 109.

39. Rostovtzeff, "Queen Dynamis," 98.

erations, creating at times some rather odd combinations. . . . The cunning
Levantines were especially successful in influencing the women who often
accompanied the political rulers of Rome, especially on their journeys to
the charming East.[40]

In contrast, Grace takes seriously the ties of friendship and support
between Roman women and vassal-queens. She points out that Livia's correspondence with Herod the Great's sister Salome was so well known that
one of his sons, Antipater, tried to blacken Salome's name through a forged
letter to Livia. Grace speculates that Dynamis, who erected a statue to Livia
in the Temple of Aphrodite, might also have corresponded with the empress,
and she uses these two women to draw an astute contrast between the public
powers that could be granted to women in the eastern kingdoms and the lack
of such powers in Rome: "Dynamis, queen of Bosporus, ruled in a *condo-
minium* [coregency] with her various husbands, or independently, and issued
gold coins with her own head and title, while her "benefactress," Livia, a much
greater personage and the wife of Augustus, had no such acknowledged power
and privilege."[41]

Using primarily coins and inscriptions, Grace makes a strong case for
the importance of the little-known Antonia Tryphaena, great-granddaughter
of Mark Antony, a vassal-queen herself, ruling in the kingdom of Pontus as
regent for her young son Polemo after the murder of her husband King Cotys
of Thrace, and mother of three vassal-kings and two vassal-queens. The only
ancient historians who refer to her, Tacitus and Strabo, do not even give her
name, but Grace points out her courage in going to Rome to accuse the mur-
derer of her husband. She further demonstrates the political recognition a
woman could achieve for herself and her children through holding a public
priesthood (she was priestess of Livia) and through major civic benefactions
(Tryphaena cleared choked-up channels in the harbor and rebuilt the market
place of Cyzicus).[42]

In her discussion of Cleopatra Selene, daughter of Mark Antony and
Cleopatra VII and coruler with Juba, client-king of Mauretania, Grace adds a
section composed at her request by her colleague Maud Worcester Makemson,
professor of astronomy at Vassar.[43] An epigram of the Greek poet Crinagoras
had connected the death of Selene with a lunar eclipse, and Makemson furnishes astronomical data that identify this eclipse as occurring on March 23,

40. Rostovtzeff, "Queen Dynamis," 97.

41. Macurdy, *Vassal-Queens,* 131.

42. Macurdy, *Vassal-Queens,* 41–48.

43. Maud Worcester Makemson, "A Note on Eclipses," in Macurdy, *Vassal-Queens,* 60–62.

5 BCE. Although Grace could have written this section herself and simply cited Makemson's research, she gives full credit to her colleague by having Makemson present this section in her own words.

Despite the sparseness and ambiguous or biased nature of the evidence, Grace maintains a woman-centered focus throughout the book. Even when fuller sources are available, they permit only fleeting and sometimes misleading glimpses of the women's personalities. In the case of Julia Berenice, daughter of Herod Agrippa I who became the mistress of the future Roman emperor Titus, Grace argues that Berenice, titled *basilissa* in Greek and *regina* in Latin, was coruler of the kingdom of Chalcis with her brother Herod Agrippa II. While modern historians almost universally claim that she had an incestuous relationship with Agrippa II, Grace points out the bias in the two ancient sources for this conclusion, a passage in Juvenal's highly exaggerated sixth satire against women (VI. 156–60) and a section of the *Antiquities* of Josephus (XX. 145–46) which reflects his anger at Berenice's and Agrippa's support for Josephus's enemy Justus of Tiberias. Thus Grace does not accept this evidence as conclusive:

> The fact that Agrippa never married gave color to the report that his sister, who presided over his court and shared his power, also lived with him as a wife. The case against her rests on such prejudiced evidence, that of the disgruntled Josephus and that of Juvenal, hater of all things Jewish, that I cannot regard it as proved. . . . Like Cleopatra [Berenice] is always vital and in action, subduing the hearts of men by her charm and cherishing the ambition to be the greatest in the great world. We do not know anything of her life after the final frustration of her hopes of marrying Titus. . . . I attach the greatest importance to the fact that Tacitus mentions her among the vassal allies of Vespasian and Titus and to her title *regina* in the Latin inscription from Beyrout, as well as to the recurring phrase "Their Majesties" in Josephus.[44]

The reviews of *Vassal-Queens* were again positive, with most praise given to the collection of difficult-to-find information:

> No one has ever before brought together the available evidence for all the vassal queens of Rome.[45]

---

44. Macurdy, *Vassal-Queens*, 89–91.
45. Lily Ross Taylor, review of *Vassal-Queens*, *American Journal of Archaeology* 43 (1939): 173.

Professor Macurdy has done a real service in collecting the evidence about these women, many of whom are probably more or less unknown to the average classicist.[46]

To sum up: the book is thorough and detailed, comprehensive and careful, with a useful appendix upon the eclipse that helps to fix the date of Cleopatra Selene's death.[47]

As before, reviewers did not perceive the revolutionary nature of presenting women as the focus of historical narrative. In fact, one reviewer completely misconstrued the purpose of Grace's emphasis on women as individuals, lamenting the scantier sources that made this volume less of a contribution "to the study of the eternal feminine" than *Hellenistic Queens* had been.[48] The German ancient historian Thomas Lenschau came closest to an appreciation of the uniqueness of Grace's contribution: "Both works, the *Hellenistic Queens* as well as the *Vassal-Queens*, have the indisputable merit of treating with scholarly thoroughness a side of history that in most other presentations gets short shrift. For this reason, it is welcome."[49]

One review, however, caused considerable consternation at Vassar—that of M. I. Finkelstein in the *American Historical Review*. Finkelstein's tone in this brief review is highly condescending; clearly he considers the entire topic trivial and unworthy of serious consideration:

Since we know next to nothing about these women, and since that little comes either from coins, from dedicatory inscriptions, or from odd sentences by various sycophantic writers of the Roman Empire, Professor Macurdy achieves a work of 148 pages by the simple technique of introducing details about the lives of fathers, sons, and brothers. All of which makes a long list of births, deaths, wars, and adulteries but nothing more.[50]

Scholars must be prepared to encounter such negative reviews of their work, but Finkelstein's concluding comment deeply distressed Grace and outraged her colleagues: "Professor Macurdy's racialism—these vassal-queens

---

46. John V. A. Fine, review of *Vassal-Queens*, *Classical Weekly* 31 (1938): 77.

47. M. P. Charlesworth, review of *Vassal-Queens*, *Classical Review* 52 (1938): 189.

48. C. Bradford Welles, review of *Vassal-Queens*, *American Journal of Philology* 59 (1938): 379.

49. Thomas Lenschau, review of *Vassal-Queens*, *Philologische Wochenschrift* 58 (1938): 533; my translation.

50. M. I. Finkelstein, review of *Vassal-Queens*, *American Historical Review* 44 (1939): 683.

lacked 'the potent drop that ran in the conquering blood of the Macedonians and produced a Cleopatra'—is particularly unfortunate at the present moment." President MacCracken asked Grace's successor as chair of the Greek Department, Philip Haldane Davis, to compose a letter of protest that MacCracken sent to the journal's editor under his own name. This letter, subsequently published along with Finkelstein's reply, concludes:

> I am writing to you not simply to point out that the reviewer is ill-natured—that is his own business—but that he makes a serious charge when he accuses the author of "racialism . . . particularly unfortunate at the present time." Anyone who knows Professor Macurdy even slightly can tell the reviewer how free she is of any prejudice of that sort, and Mr. Finkelstein is going very far indeed when he bases such a charge on a casual reference which she makes to Cleopatra's Macedonian blood. "Racialism" is indeed unfortunate at any time. So is the kind of irresponsible accusation here made by Mr. Finkelstein. In the interests of truth and the author's good name, I ask you to print this letter in your journal.[51]

Finkelstein's reply begins with the same dismissive tone he had employed in the review: "Frankly, I do not think that Professor Macurdy's book merits further discussion in the *American Historical Review*, but President MacCracken has raised one issue which does. When I commented on Professor Macurdy's racism, I was not interested in her personal views or prejudices (and I am quite willing to believe that she is free from 'racial' prejudice) but in a tendency among historians of which her book is symptomatic." He states that ancient historians tend to "offer 'racial' explanations of historical phenomena," which ignore modern scientific conceptions of race that indicate only physical, not psychological or cultural, inheritance, and which therefore could dangerously enhance Nazi propaganda. His letter concludes, "It is regrettable that the issue has become personalized in this case. I should like to repeat that I intended no reflection on Professor Macurdy's good name. My one concern is in the elimination of an unscientific view which has such frightful implications in our contemporary world." At the time of this review, Moses Isaac Finkelstein was instructor in history at City College of New York and involved in a number of left-wing political organizations.[52] In 1946 he changed his sur-

---

51. Letters of H. N. MacCracken and M. I. Finkelstein, "Historical News," *American Historical Review* 45 (1939): 268. Correspondence between Davis and MacCracken about this issue can be found in the MacCracken Papers, box 43, folder 48, Vassar Archives.

52. For more information about this period in M. I. Finley's life, see Daniel P. Tompkins, "The World of Moses Finkelstein: The Year 1939 in M. I. Finley's Development as a Historian,"

name to Finley, and he was fired by Rutgers University in 1952 because he refused to answer questions posed by the Senate Internal Security Subcommittee about possible communist affiliations; he subsequently emigrated to England, where he had a distinguished career as a historian of ancient society and economics at Cambridge University and was knighted in 1979.

In this case, however, Finkelstein/Finley was indeed writing "irresponsibly." Although Grace was using a rather naive, poetic/romantic terminology, she was not proffering a racial explanation for historical phenomena. The full passage at issue states, "Very few of these vassal-queens could lay claim to any Macedonian or Greek blood. They were mostly Asiatic, Bithynian, Pontic, Cappadocian, Jewish, Iranian, Syrian. They lacked, on the whole, both opportunity to emulate the greatness of past queens and also the potent drop that ran in the conquering blood of the Macedonians and produced a Cleopatra even in the last degenerate days of the Ptolemaic dynasty."[53] Her point is that the vassal-queens differed from the Hellenistic queens because the power they could exercise was severely curtailed by Roman control of their kingdoms and because they could not claim ancestral connections with Alexander the Great or the successor generals. When discussing Zenobia of Palmyra, for whom some ancient writers alleged distant descent from Cleopatra VII, Grace makes her position on inheritance very clear:

> It is not absolutely impossible that a drop of Seleucid or Ptolemaic blood might have run in the veins of Zenobia, but it is not probable. But there is no need of bringing in the theory of such an inheritance to account for the energy and ability of the Palmyrene Zenobia. She was of the dominant type of woman which occasionally appears in any energetic, successful, and ambitious community, and her chance to show what her quality was came to her, as to every Hellenistic queen or client-queen, when the kingdom fell to her charge on the death of her husband, when she was left as regent for her young son. It is probable that she was as courageous, as intellectual, and as competent as she is represented to be in the *Historia Augusta*.[54]

Despite his protestations to the contrary, in his review Finkelstein/Finley did charge Grace with "racialism," a charge exacerbated by his reference to "the present moment." If he really wished to challenge historians' tendency to offer racial explanations of historical phenomena, he should have precisely

---

in *Classical Antiquity and the Politics of America: From George Washington to George W. Bush*, ed. Michael Meckler (Waco, Tex.: Baylor University Press, 2006), 95–125.

53. Macurdy, *Vassal-Queens*, 5.

54. Macurdy, *Vassal-Queens*, 124.

defined this objective. The last sentence of his review is far more "casual" and "unscientific" than anything in Grace's book.

"The constantly expanding horizon of Greek studies"

As Grace entered her seventh decade she continued to expand her own horizons, not only with a new scholarly focus on ancient women, but also with interdisciplinary courses and team-teaching, active mentoring, energetic travel, and even a new religious affiliation (see figures 23–24 for photos of Grace in the 1930s). When she was asked to write about the Greek department for *Vassar Quarterly* in 1934, she began with an anecdote that exemplified her forward-looking attitude:

> Some years ago a young instructor from the college, who was playing cards in my house with my nephew, asked him what his aunt was doing in her study upstairs. My nephew, accustomed to studying aunts, replied, "I suppose she is studying." The young lady cried out in horrified commiseration— "How perfectly terrible! To have to study at her time of life!" She thought that I must long ago have learned all that there is to know about Greek. But she was quite wrong. It would indeed be terrible ever to reach a time of life when the impulse to study or the desire to learn more should be gone. . . . I may say that the Greek Department has an endless source of delight and satisfaction in the constantly expanding horizon of Greek studies. Whether abroad or at home, in the library or in the class room, we are dealing with very precious stuff—the stuff on which the spirit of man is nurtured.[55]

As soon as Grace became head of the Greek department, she completely reorganized Abby Leach's course Ancient Greek Life, renaming it Ancient Greek Life and Civilization and eventually Ancient Greek Civilization. In her hands it became a study of the development of Greek art, thought, and social and political institutions from the Homeric to Hellenistic periods and the largest and most popular course in the department. Grace encouraged students to pursue special research topics in this class with notable success and proudly informed President MacCracken that two of these student articles were accepted for publication in the Archaeological Institute of America's

---

55. Grace H. Macurdy, "Some Remarks from the Greek Department," *Vassar Quarterly* 19 (1934): 137.

popular journal *Art and Archaeology*.[56] In 1935 Grace sent him a letter from "a good average girl" as an indication of this course's ongoing value to students. As Grace explained in an accompanying letter, "I hope that you will not think that I have labored in vain. At least I have labored with great joy in bringing the fruit of my Greek studies to a larger audience than our small classes in the Greek language." The student, Mary Ann Littick, had written:

> I'm sorry that I did not have the opportunity of speaking to you after class to tell you how much I have enjoyed "Greek Civilization." I must admit to having taken the course merely as a fill-in and because Miss Greenfield and other friends spoke so much of you. I came into it with practically no background and feeling that it was a poor choice because it would correlate with nothing except "Blake to Keats." But now, it seems to correlate with everything, and in the most unexpected places. I do feel that it has been one of the real experiences of my three years here. You have not only opened up a new field to me, but you've made that field vital and living by your own splendid enthusiasm for it. I did appreciate your comparisons with familiar things, and, especially, your nice sense of humor.[57]

The strongest accolade for this course, however, came in a spontaneous tribute to Grace Macurdy included in a 1959 letter to Dorothy Plum of the Vassar library by Barbara Neville Parker, who had majored in English and French, graduated from Vassar in 1927, and gone on to become a museum curator at the Boston Museum of Fine Arts and author of a book on the painter John Singleton Copley. Parker wrote that her most vivid memory of Vassar was Grace's civilization course, which she and her roommate had taken in their senior year because they needed a "snap course" and they had heard that Grace was an easy grader:

> So Ellen and I took the course. I shall never forget the first day. . . . Miss MacCurdy stood up and we saw her for the first time as a lecturer. Her white hair was flying all around; she had a kind of loose attractive dress on, and a beautiful blue chain of stones around her neck which exactly matched her eyes (not that she had planned this, for she never thought about herself as far as we could see). Then she started to talk to us about Greek Art. Well, all I can say is that I spent more time on my long paper for Miss MacCurdy

---

56. Grace H. Macurdy to Henry N. MacCracken, 13 December 1924 and 14 November 1927, MacCracken Papers, box 30, folder 44 and box 32, folder 9, Vassar Archives.

57. Grace H. Macurdy to Henry N. MacCracken, 28 May 1935; and Mary Ann Littick to Grace H. Macurdy, undated, MacCracken Papers, box 39, folder 69, Vassar Archives.

than all my other papers put together! I well remember the subject, it was *Fibulae*, which means safety-pin in Greek I believe. You know, origins of, and so forth. I spent hours and hours in the Vassar Library over this paper, and whatever scholarship I have done since, I believe stems from the enthusiasm which I got direct from Miss MacCurdy.[58]

Grace kept Vassar in step with the constantly expanding horizons of Greek studies by broadening her department's offerings in cultural courses, including the courses Greek Religion (added in 1927), Late Greek Civilization (added in 1929) covering the Hellenistic period, Hellenistic Sculpture (added in 1931 and renamed Hellenistic Art in 1932), and a major in Classical Archaeology offered in conjunction with the Latin department. As she noted in her 1934 department report:

> A department of Greek must not confine itself to literature, but must endeavor to spread knowledge of the whole of the civilization and art. This breadth of interest is a vital necessity for the teacher. What we hope that we are doing is to make some students so deeply interested in the Greek language and literature that they will become specially expert and carry on the torch of Greek learning. We also desire to bring the meaning and knowledge of Greek achievement to a greater number who have little or no knowledge of Greek and in the best sense to "popularize" and diffuse the most valuable things inherent in the Greek civilization.[59]

In her last years as chair of the department, Grace initiated more dramatic changes, including interdisciplinary collaboration with other departments and team teaching. In 1935 she introduced two literature courses for which knowledge of the Greek language was not required—Greek Literature in Translation and Greek Theater and Drama. Both of these were taught by Grace and Philip Davis, with some additional lectures by Irene Ringwood Arnold. In 1936, Grace and Oliver Tonks of the art department created a course in Greek and Roman art, team taught by Grace, Philip Davis, and several members of the art department. The most innovative new course was created by Winifred Smith of the English Department in conjunction with Grace, a comparative literature course, Tragedy: Greek, Renaissance, and Modern, taught by Grace,

---

58. Barbara Neville Parker to Dorothy A. Plum, 3 February 1959, Biographical Files: Macurdy, Grace Harriet, folder 3, Vassar Archives; Barbara Neville Parker and Anne Bolling Wheeler, *John Singleton Copley: American Portraits* (Boston: Museum of Fine Arts, 1938).

59. Grace H. Macurdy, Report of the Greek Department 1933–34, 5 May 1934, Annual Reports R.36 S.5, Vassar Archives.

Davis, and Smith. Grace wrote enthusiastically about this course in her final
department report:

> This course has been an extraordinarily interesting experience for me. Miss
> Smith is a brilliant and incisive teacher and the teaching of the class by a
> "committee" of three has been such a successful experiment that it should, in
> my opinion, be extended to other subjects. It has been good for the students
> to realize that no one teacher is infallible and they have gained from hearing
> discussion among their instructors. I have never seen a class more alive and
> keen. It has been a great intellectual pleasure for me to have had a share in it.
> . . . In our present curriculum there is so little elasticity and so little recogni-
> tion for a "major" in any one department of the work in another field that,
> as it seems to me, we have fallen prey to false syntheses and have erected
> unnatural barriers between fields of knowledge that should lie open.[60]

This interdisciplinary work led Grace to participate in a project of the
National Council of Teachers of English to gather and summarize information on proposals for the correlation of English with other disciplines at the
secondary and college levels, resulting in an article on "The Living Legacy of
Greece and Rome" in *A Correlated Curriculum*.[61]

Grace also inspired students in her Greek language courses during this
period, particularly Elizabeth Bishop, an English major at Vassar who studied
Greek for four years and decided to write an English translation of Aristophanes' comedy *The Birds* as her senior project under Grace's supervision in
1933–34. Bishop became Poet Laureate of the United States from 1949 to 1950
and won the Pulitzer Prize for Poetry in 1956. Bishop's notebook from Grace's
1932 course in Euripides reveals Grace's repeated efforts to connect the ancient
texts with modern poetry, careful analysis of meter, attention to literary interpretation of the plays, and continued devotion to Gilbert Murray. On the first
day of class, Grace recommended that the class read T. S. Eliot's essay "Euripides and Gilbert Murray," but Bishop commented, "<u>She</u> thinks Eliot's unfair—
'Murry [*sic*] has brought E. back to the modern world.'" (Bishop always refers
to Grace in her notebook as "<u>She</u>.")[62]

---

60. Grace H. Macurdy, Report of the Greek Department 1936–37, 26 May 1937, Annual
Reports R.36 S.5, Vassar Archives.

61. Grace H. Macurdy and Ruth Mary Weeks, "The Living Legacy of Greece and Rome,"
in *A Correlated Curriculum*, National Council of Teachers of English Monograph No. 5, comp.
Ruth Mary Weeks. (New York: Appleton-Century, 1936), 138–47.

62. Elizabeth Bishop, College notes: Greek 310a: Euripides [1932], Elizabeth Bishop Papers,
series VII, folder 69A.5, Vassar Archives. For more information on Bishop's translation of Aristophanes, see Mariana Machová, "Elizabeth Bishop: Translation as Poetics," PhD diss., Charles

Near the end of her career, hearing-aid technology finally improved to the point that it could somewhat ease Grace's disability, with the smaller bone-conduction hearing aid that could be attached to a headband and wired to a battery carried in the pocket. As Grace wrote to Gilbert Murray during her last year of full-time teaching, "I am well and strong for my work after all these years. I have had a wonderful new lease of hearing from the Sonotone, which enables me to forget my deafness in the classroom and in ordinary conversation. I often feel that I have had more than I deserve of the really good things of life and the kindness and friendship of my colleagues and pupils."[63]

Although Vassar, like everywhere else in the United States, was struggling with financial problems in the 1930s, the trustees voted in 1931 to raise the maximum salary for full professors from $5,000 to $6,000, and Grace was one of the few professors whose salary was raised immediately. As MacCracken informed her, "In recognition of your special value to the college as a scholar and teacher and representative of classical learning, your salary has been voted to be $6,000 hereafter. I take this occasion to express my own pleasure in this vote, and my increasing senes [sic] of the importance of what you have contributed to the college in so many ways."[64] In this time of budgetary constraints, Grace found that she needed to fight for the salaries and even the retention of her younger colleagues. Philip Haldane Davis, with a bachelor of arts and a master of arts from Princeton, had been hired in 1924 as instructor in Latin and Greek on the Matthew Vassar Jr. endowment, which specified a male in the position. Since attracting male scholars to Vassar was difficult because of its low salary scale, his position was relatively secure, although Grace and Hazel Haight had to make a strong case for promoting him to full professor after he received his doctorate from Princeton in 1930 to prevent him from accepting an offer from Brown University at a much higher salary. In 1921, Grace hired a former student, Irene C. Ringwood (Vassar BA 1915, Columbia MA 1916) as acting instructor, securing Ringwood as her sabbatical replacement for the following year when her plan to hire J. A. K. Thomson failed. Grace subsequently took on the role of mentor and champion of Ringwood's career, helping her to gain the Drisler Fellowship for graduate study at Columbia, where she earned her doctorate in 1927, supporting her scholarship in Greek inscriptions in connection with festivals, and fighting hard for her

University in Prague, 2011, 33–45, accessed on 4 March 2015, https://is.cuni.cz/webapps/zzp/download/140004159/?lang=en.

63. Grace H. Macurdy to Gilbert Murray, 30 October 1936, MSS Gilbert Murray 157, fol. 155, Bodleian.

64. Henry N. MacCracken to Grace H. Macurdy, 11 February 1931, MacCracken Papers, box 30, folder 44 and box 35, folder 68, Vassar Archives.

retention and promotion at Vassar. When Ringwood became engaged to Herbert Arnold, teacher of Latin and Greek at the Choate School in Connecticut, Grace informed her colleagues through a warm and witty announcement she made at a 1931 meeting of the Journal Club:

The departments of Greek and Latin in this college are held together by many bonds of friendship and common interest. Yet there is an honorable rivalry between them . . . that leads the one department to keep its eye warily on the other in order to see that it is itself not left behind in the race. In the presentation of the Hippolytus we may say that honors were even, as we can match Miss Tappan and Miss Ringwood against each other, and Mr. Davis happily belongs to both departments. In the realm of literature the rivalry has, we hope, good results. Miss Saunders writes a book on *Vergil's Primitive Italy*. The Greek Department responds with *Hellenistic Queens*. The sporting blood of Miss Haight is raised, so that she hastens to get *Romance in the Latin Poets* out close on the heels of the Queens. For some time, however, the Head of the Greek Department has been uneasy, since the Latin Department distinctly seems to have scored by securing a fine young bio-chemist as a son-in-law and having a hyphenated name [Inez Scott-Ryberg] in their list in the catalogue. Feeling that this could not continue unrivalled, and with full approbation of the chairman, Assistant Professor Ringwood has secured a son-in-law for the Greek Department—we will never say a better son-in-law than the one attained by the Latin Department, but one more deeply imbued with Greek. I wish he were here to reply as he well could and would in the Greek language to my congratulatory announcement of the plighting of H. P. Arnold and Irene C. Ringwood. Homer in a very beautiful passage known to you all has named *esthlen homophrosunen* [splendid like-mindedness] as the thing that makes the life together of man and wife the most beautiful thing in the world—a joy for their friends, a bitterness to their enemies, but what it is they [know] the best themselves *malista de t' ekluon autoi*. That oneness of spirit we know our new son-in-law and our beloved Irene have, and I ask you to join with me in congratulating them both and wishing them long years of Greek together.[65]

Another romance was brewing in the department between Philip Davis, a widower with three young children who had played the role of Hippolytus in

---

65. Minutes of the Journal Club, 15 December 1931, Multiple Collections, box 1, Vassar Archives. Grace here paraphrases a famous passage in the *Odyssey* (6.181–85) in which Odysseus wishes that Nausicaa may have a marriage and home founded on "like-mindedness," the greatest boon in marriage.

the Greek production of Euripides's play, and Hallie Flanagan, director of the Vassar Experimental Theatre. Grace announced this in a clever postscript to her 1934 *Vassar Quarterly* article on the Greek Department:

> Mr. T. S. Eliot in his most recent book of essays tells us to make no sharp distinction between "romantic" and "classic." Professor Haight has written on "Romance in the Latin Elegiac Poets" and we now announce a romance in the classical departments in the marriage in Athens of Professor Philip Davis, member of the Departments of Greek and Latin, to Professor Hallie Flanagan, Head of the Experimental Theatre.[66]

Despite many strongly worded letters recommending the promotion of Irene Ringwood Arnold to associate professor in the 1930s, arguing that "she has a field in which no other woman in this country is working and one that is increasingly important for the study of history," Grace could not persuade MacCracken, who had reservations about "her possession of personality sufficiently commanding to warrant promotion to the associate professorship in a department with numbers no larger than those in Greek." Grace was deeply distressed when MacCracken told her in February 1935 that Arnold's contract would not be renewed, and she entreated that she be retained even if it meant a salary reduction. Arnold accepted a half-time position for 1935–36, but the following year, when Davis was made a full-time member of the Greek Department in preparation for Grace's retirement in 1937, Arnold was dismissed. Grace did everything in her power to find another position for Arnold, though the Depression complicated the search. In May 1936, Grace paid tribute to Arnold, announcing her appointment as head of the classics department of the Bennett School and Junior College in Millbrook, New York.[67]

During her annual summer in England in 1929, Grace was delighted to attend many of the events celebrating the centenary of King's College London as a guest of J. A. K. Thomson. However, when MacCracken asked her to serve as Vassar's delegate to Radcliffe's fiftieth anniversary celebration in May of the same year, she demurred:

> I hope that you will not disapprove of my decision not to attend. If Radcliffe had indicated in its invitation of me that the presence of one of their

---

66. Macurdy, "Some Remarks," 138.

67. Grace H. Macurdy to Henry N. MacCracken, 11 January 1930; Henry N. MacCracken to Grace H. Macurdy, 20 January 1930, MacCracken Papers, box 33, folder 91, Vassar Archives. "Dr. Arnold Appointed Teacher at Bennett," *Poughkeepsie Eagle-News*, 14 May 1936, 8.

ancient, and I hope honorable, graduates was in any way especially desired, or would add in any way to their celebration, I should have felt it my duty to attend. But I received only the ordinary invitation and no suggestion of any thing else. . . . I write thus at length to try to explain to you that it is not, I trust, pettiness that makes me feel that Radcliffe might have made an effort to secure the presence of a graduate of early date whose name is known to some extent in her specialty. . . . I hope that you will not think that I harbor any real resentment against my Alma Mater for not urging me officially to come.[68]

Grace was undoubtedly thinking of the honor paid to Abby Leach at Radcliffe's twenty-fifth anniversary, when Leach had been lauded as "the Commencement of Radcliffe" and had been selected to deliver the commencement address. Grace was the first Harvard Annex graduate to earn a doctorate and the first to make a career as a college professor (Leach was a special student at the Annex and did not earn a degree); moreover, she had the most distinguished record of scholarly publications of all the early graduates. Grace was clearly offended, though she couched her annoyance in polite phrases. MacCracken, however, pressed her to attend, though Dean Mildred Thompson would be Vassar's official delegate, and she did agree to go to the May 31 celebration. Her feathers were smoothed somewhat when Radcliffe president Ada Comstock wrote her, "It would have been a great disappointment to me if you had been absent. The significance of the occasion really depends upon its bringing together the alumnae and friends of the College to review its past and to consider its future; and we need very much the participation which you can give."[69]

During this period Grace was also expanding the horizons of her travel abroad, partly in search of information and artifacts relating to her research on queens, but also as a benefit of her ever increasing contacts with international scholars. Grace took full advantage of her second sabbatical in the spring of 1930, as she later wrote in an article for the *Miscellany News*: "My own province, study of ancient civilization, art, and literature brought me to Greece, England, Germany and France, in which countries I renewed my acquaintance with the sites of old cultures and with foreign museums and libraries, and met scholars and investigators whose discoveries and interpretations of history are doing much to illuminate the past achievement of humanity and to explain

---

68. Grace H. Macurdy to Henry N. MacCracken, 23 April 1929, MacCracken Papers, box 32, folder 9, Vassar Archives.

69. Ada L. Comstock to Grace H. Macurdy, 7 May 1929, Ada Louise Comstock Records of the President, RGII, series 2, folder 84, box 9, Radcliffe College Archives, Schlesinger.

the present."[70] Although Ida Thallon Hill and Lib Pierce Blegen had urged her to come to Athens earlier, she delayed her trip until J. A. K. Thomson had his spring vacation and could travel with her. During their visit they attended the celebration of the Greek Republic's hundredth anniversary of independence, socialized with distinguished archaeologists such as Sir Arthur Evans, Georg Karo, and Wilhelm Dörpfeld, enjoyed a private visit to the National Archaeological Museum in Athens guided by Carl Blegen, and traveled through the Peloponnese and northern Greece viewing archaeological sites. In Berlin, Grace relished a private tour of the Pergamon Museum, which had not yet opened to the public. Back in London, Gilbert Murray took her to a League of Nations luncheon, where she sat at the table of the speaker, the British politician and diplomat Philip Kerr, and she also attended the Royal Literary Society's dinner in honor of Sir James Barrie's seventieth birthday, where she dined with the novelist John Galsworthy and the poet John Masefield.

In contrast to her attitude toward Radcliffe's anniversary, Grace was delighted to serve as Vassar's representative at the centenary of the University of London in 1936, as she wrote MacCracken:

> I have greatly enjoyed being delegate of Vassar College to the Centenary of the University of London. Invitations have showered on me. I have chiefly attended those cap-and-gown functions at which Vassar was publicly represented by me, such as the great Reception to Delegates in the Imperial Institute, where the names of the Universities and Colleges were proclaimed as we were presented to the Earl of Athlone and the other dignitaries, and the Service at St. Paul's. I felt very solemn and in the spirit of a great tradition while walking in the splendid procession up Ludgate Hill to the Cathedral. The Luncheon in the Guildhall was also very delightful and impressive and every one was most kind and interesting. There were very few women delegates—Bryn Mawr, Wellesley, and Smith besides Vassar were almost the only women's colleges represented. I omitted such festivities as the Draper's Ball.[71]

Though reveling in her participation in these time-honored academic traditions, Grace could not help but notice how few other women had the same privilege. As she looked at the program, she realized that the British academic establishment did not really understand the American system of women's colleges. London had invited colleges, universities, and learned societies from

---

70. G. H. Macurdy, "Prof. Macurdy Writes of Semester Spent Abroad," *Vassar Miscellany News*, 18 October 1930, 1.

71. Grace H. Macurdy to Henry N. MacCracken, 4 July 1936, MacCracken Papers, box 41, folder 23, Vassar Archives.

around the world to send delegates to the centenary celebrations; these were
listed on the official program by country. Under the heading United States, she
saw a list of institutions whose order was presumably determined by prestige:
first universities, then liberal arts colleges, then several institutes of technology. Instead of including Bryn Mawr, Smith, Vassar, and Wellesley among the
liberal arts colleges, where they belonged, the program listed them under a
separate, italicized heading, *Women's Colleges*, making the United States the
only country to have two separate headings for institutions of higher education. Grace was not the only American to wonder why other women's colleges
were not included. After the festivities were over, Bertha Putnam, a delegate
for a learned society who happened to be a professor at Mount Holyoke College, wrote Sir Edwin Deller, Principal of the University of London, to ask why
Mount Holyoke had not been invited to send a delegate to the centenary. Was
this, she wondered, an aspersion on the quality of Mount Holyoke degrees?
A memo from Deller to his assistant asked, "I take it that the omission (& it
was omitted) of Holyoke from the Centenary Celebration was 'pure inadver-
tence'?" The assistant's reply was, "Yes—coupled with the grossest ignorance."[72]

On these trips Grace frequently purchased Greek artifacts for the classical
museum at Vassar and for her private collection with Thomson. Grace was
particularly proud of her ability to find bargains and to save shipping costs
by transporting the vases and bronzes herself on her return voyages. When
she attended an auction sale of duplicate objects at the Metropolitan Museum
of Art in New York, she engaged in some modest boasting in her report to
MacCracken:

> Mr. Ringling must have spent one hundred thousand dollars in the three ses-
> sions. . . . The prices of the vases were astounding to me and it made me real-
> ize the value of our collection small as it is. We have for instance a Roman
> winejar propped up against the wall in room 56. Mr. Ringling gave three
> hundred and ninety dollars for two similar jars. I have purchased in England
> for the college several Cyprian vases for from a pound to two pounds ten,
> such as were sold for prices varying from forty to sixty dollars in this sale
> and in particular three false necked vases belong to us, purchased by me in
> Oxford Street, London, and two similar ones together with a piriform vase

---

72. Bertha Putnam to Edwin Deller, 3 July 1936; memo of Edwin Deller to McNaughton
with response, 6 July 1936, CF 1/36/718, Senate House Library, University of London, The University Archives.

fetched one hundred and fifty dollars at this sale. Ours cost about fifteen dollars for our three.[73]

Grace was not above a spot of intimidation when bringing these objects into the United States. Her nephew, Bradford Skinner, who always met and brought her home from the ship, related an amusing anecdote: "One day a customs agent questioned her about the artifacts. She drew herself up and said, 'Young man, nobody knows the value of these better than I do. You have no idea. Now let me pass,' and she marched away, leaving the agent nonplussed."[74] Grace's expert eye enabled her to discover a Proto-Corinthian pitcher dating from the seventh century BCE in an antique shop in Poughkeepsie.[75]

As she grew older, Grace began to feel the need of a religious affiliation, and she found the non-doctrinaire, intellectual approach of the Quakers congenial, as she wrote Lady Mary Murray in 1929: "I have been thinking of joining the Quakers, as I have had for many years no definite church connections and a statement sent me by Roscoe Pound of Harvard and some others about their aims and lack of theological creed seemed to me to suit my ideas of religion." Accordingly she joined the Haverford Meeting of Friends in Pennsylvania, though she rarely took part in their activities. After her death their newsletter included a brief obituary: "She joined Haverford Meeting about sixteen years ago and though unable to attend meeting she greatly prized her membership with Friends. She was a distinguished scholar, and beautiful in life and character."[76]

This time of expanding horizons for Grace was also touched by personal sorrows. In November of 1932, her brother William died of Parkinson's disease, and in April 1933 her sister Theodosia died after a long illness. Grace had always been very close to Theodosia; they shared the summer house on Cape Cod built by the carpenter who had proposed to Grace so many years ago, and they had both dedicated their lives to intellectual careers. After Theodosia retired from her position as head of the ordering department at the Boston Public Library, Grace invited her to share her apartment at Williams Hall, and the two sisters lived together from 1929 to 1931, when Theodosia's deteriorating health forced her to move to a sanatorium in Framingham, Massachusetts.

---

73. Grace H. Macurdy to Henry N. MacCracken, April 1928. MacCracken Papers, box 32, folder 9, Vassar Archives.

74. Caroline Skinner O'Neil, interview by Barbara F. McManus, 13 May 2005.

75. Ida T. Hill to Bert H. Hill, 22 June 1941, Bert Hodge Hill Papers, box 8, folder 1, Blegen Library.

76. Grace H. Macurdy to Mary Murray, 24 December 1929, MSS Gilbert Murray 542, fols. 238–39, Bodleian; "Death Notices," *The Meeting* 93 (1946): 3, Biographical Files: Macurdy, Grace Harriet, folder 3. Vassar Archives.

Grace was able to be with her when she died and mourned her loss deeply. As she wrote MacCracken, "My dear sister was happy that I could be with her. She died on Wednesday night, the end of a singularly noble and beautiful life. It has been a great gift to have lived near to her."[77]

Grace herself experienced two memorable mishaps at Vassar during this period. As she started to cross Raymond Avenue on the afternoon of January 18, 1935, she was struck by a slow-moving laundry truck. She sustained a three-inch scalp wound and numerous contusions and sprains, requiring several weeks in the college infirmary to recover. She declined to press charges against the driver, explaining that she had been preoccupied and was unable to hear the driver's warning blast on his horn because of her deafness.[78] Less serious but more bizarre was an accident in January of the following year. Alice Howe, a student living in Raymond Hall, was melting wax to coat her skis. She carelessly tossed the hot wax in her metal wastebasket, igniting the papers in the basket. Panicking, she threw the flaming wastebasket out her window, hitting Grace on the head as she walked by the building. Grace was saved by her large hat, which was burned beyond recognition, and abundant gray hair, some of which was scorched and had to be cut off; she suffered only dizziness and a large bruise on her forehead.[79] The story of this incident became notorious on the Vassar campus, and Grace's reaction was later recounted by two observers with some embellishment and inaccuracy, though reflecting the essential personality of the woman they remembered:

When I asked our classicist what she thought at the time, she said: "I just said to myself, the revolution has come. Be calm. Sophrosunë!" Classical training has its merits. (Henry Noble MacCracken)[80]

Her tremendous sense of humor never deserted her. In one week, she was knocked down by a slow-moving milk truck and hit on the head by a waste basket filled with flaming paper. . . . She dismissed these two accidents with: "What can the gods have against me? It was bad enough for them to hit me with a milk truck . . . but now they are flinging flaming pots from the heav-

---

77. Grace H. Macurdy to Henry N. MacCracken, 10 April 1933, MacCracken Papers, box 38, folder 16, Vassar Archives.

78. "Professor Macurdy Struck by Truck in Raymond Avenue," *Poughkeepsie Eagle-News,* 19 January 1935, 1; and "Professor Macurdy Making Steady Gain," 6 February, 1935, 3.

79. Jane N. Baldwin, MD, to Henry N. MacCracken, 28 January 1936, MacCracken Papers, box 38, folder 16, Vassar Archives.

80. Henry Noble MacCracken, *The Hickory Limb* (New York: Scribner, 1950), 101. The Greek word *sophrosune* is untranslatable; it refers to a self-restraint and inner harmony based on wisdom and self-knowledge.

ens." Her humor, her gaiety and her eloquence made her seem always young to me. (Edward Linner)[81]

"Surprising to Be Seventy"[82]

When he learned that Grace was planning to retire in June of 1937, Philip Davis, her designated successor as department chair, sent an urgent plea to MacCracken to prevent this "disaster," noting particularly the two collaborative courses in art and comparative literature that she had just begun:

> Miss Macurdy is the soul of these two courses, and I feel that the chances of building them up into what they should be, depend to a large measure, on her remaining. The retirement of a distinguished Hellenist like Miss Macurdy will in itself be a heavy loss to the college. I know that you feel this yourself. The college and the department will be much poorer without her rich personality, and I cannot express to you too strongly my personal desire to have her with us just as long as possible.[83]

Grace, however, had determined to retire. She had completed her books on ancient queens and launched several new initiatives in the Greek Department. Her "children" were established with their own families or careers, and she was ready for new opportunities and challenges. Her financial situation was a concern, since she had never been able to save very much, but she was eligible for a pension from the Carnegie Foundation for the advancement of teaching, endowed by Andrew Carnegie in 1905. Although the program of "free pensions" had been discontinued in 1915 because of lack of resources to meet the huge liability the foundation had assumed, a reduced pension was still granted to faculty who had begun teaching at associated institutions before 1915. Grace was notified that her pension would be $1,600 annually.[84] More crucially, friends and former students established a Grace Harriet Macurdy Fund in 1937, donating $33,450, augmented by a grant of $10,500 from the

---

81. Edward R. Linner, "As I Remember Them," *Vassar Alumnae Magazine* 55 (1969): 17.

82. Grace H. Macurdy to Henry N. MacCracken, 26 October 1936, MacCracken Papers, box 43, folder 46, Vassar Archives. Grace is echoing Gilbert Murray in this sentiment about her retirement.

83. Philip H. Davis to Henry N. MacCracken, 29 October 1936, MacCracken Papers, box 43, folder 46, Vassar Archives.

84. Reduction of Carnegie Foundation Pensions for Vassar College Teachers, 1915, box 7, folder 12; Henry N. MacCracken to Grace H. Macurdy, 14 May 1937, MacCracken Papers, box 43, folder 46, Vassar Archives.

Rockefeller Foundation, "the income to be for her own use during her lifetime and after her death to revert to the Department of Greek to further the pursuit of classical studies." A second Macurdy fund was established by Mabel Stanwood Duncan (Vassar BA 1904, MA 1907) in 1940.[85]

Grace planned to move into a smaller apartment at Williams with a lower rent after spending her first year of retirement abroad, so she pared down her possessions, donating to Vassar 547 volumes from her personal library, "including many fine old Greek books in vellum bindings."[86] Although systematic in her scholarship, Grace was not particularly organized in regard to personal items, but she sorted through her papers and correspondence and gave to the library letters from scholars and eminent individuals, including early letters from Gilbert Murray and John Masefield as well as the highly prized letter she had received from Theodore Roosevelt complimenting her on an article she had written: "I must give myself the pleasure of saying how much I have enjoyed your article on 'The Passing of the Classics.' Perhaps I especially appreciated your criticism of ex-President Elliott's [*sic*] position! If you come to New York at any time, I do wish you would give me the chance to see you."[87] Significantly, she did not donate any letters from J. A. K. Thomson.

The alumnae amply expressed their appreciation of Grace through their generous donations to the Grace Harriet Macurdy Fund; the current Vassar students did so in an editorial praising Grace and Aaron L. Treadwell, a professor of zoology who was retiring in the same year, "two of our best known and most loved professors":

> We do not need to be "A" students in advanced science nor Greek majors reading Aeschylus to regret the retirement of Dr. Treadwell and Professor Macurdy. While such groups may miss them keenly, far greater numbers of us whose freshman notebooks are filled with Zoology 101 drawings or whose small Latin and less Greek were enriched by rare and memorable lectures on Hellenism, are glad that we once came into contact with a distinguished scientist and a distinguished classicist. There are many teachers of note who have devoted their lives to a college. Yet people who possess brilliance with wide humanism and youth of spirit are few. It is this happy combination of qualities which makes the slightest acquaintance with Dr. Treadwell or Miss

---

85. "Rush to Colleges Upheld at Vassar," *New York Times*, 8 June 1937, 26; "Grace Macurdy, Professor Emeritus of Greek, Dies; Funds Left to V. C.," *Vassar Chronicle*, 26 October 1946, 2.

86. Biographical Files: Macurdy, Grace Harriet, folder 3, Vassar Archives.

87. Theodore Roosevelt to Grace H. Macurdy, 19 December 1917, Autograph Files, Vassar Archives. Grace H. Macurdy, "The Passing of the Classics," *Educational Review* 54 (1917): 439–50.

Macurdy something to remember at once as a delightful experience and as a basis for judging what fine teaching should be. Their contribution to us needs no editorial watering to keep it green. Instead, we express our thanks to them and our hopes that unofficially we may continue to enjoy it.[88]

Desiring a more professional retirement tribute for Grace, Philip Davis wrote Ida Hill, Gilbert Murray, and J. A. K. Thomson asking them to submit brief testimonials honoring Grace on her retirement. Murray wrote Thomson asking to see a copy of his testimonial, but Thomson replied that he had already mailed his piece and did not have a copy, though he summarized its content, describing it as a "more or less impartial appreciation of her work in scholarship."[89] The three international tributes, along with one by Davis himself, were published in the fall 1937 issue of the *Vassar Alumnae Magazine* along with Hazel Haight's photograph of Grace with her cat Jason (see figure 21).[90]

The tribute by Davis is relatively informal, stressing the void Grace's departure leaves at Vassar and her role as an ambassador of Greek studies: "She has been all her life a Hellene, without being any less an American, at the busy center of a large family. She carries her hellenism about this world with her, having fun with it, doing good with it, and teaching others to do the same." Ida characterizes Grace as "both a great teacher and a creative power": "Seldom does one find a more satisfying combination of profound scholarship and versatility. In the broad field of Greek literature—in prose or in verse— Miss Macurdy has always been as much at home as in her mother tongue. . . . But it is not only in the classics that her knowledge is so wide. She is indeed *docta multarum linguarum* [learned in many languages], for in addition to a remarkable facility with German, her knowledge of English literature is truly astonishing."

Murray's tribute begins with an odd statement: "Soon after my own retirement from the Chair of Greek in Oxford I hear that a much younger scholar, Miss Grace Macurdy, is about to retire from the Chair at Vassar." Since Grace was born in September 1866, only eight months after Murray, the "much younger scholar" is clearly a slip on his part, one that perhaps suggests that he is still thinking of her as a protégée rather than as an equal. However, the substance of his encomium greatly pleased Grace. Terming her "in the fullest

---

88. "In Parting," *Vassar Miscellany News*, 14 April 1937, 2

89. Gilbert Murray to J. A. K. Thomson, 27 March 1937; J. A. K. Thomson to Gilbert Murray, 29 March 1937, MSS Gilbert Murray 173, fols. 188–91, Bodleian.

90. Davis, Philip H., and Ida Thallon Hill, Gilbert Murray, J. A. K. Thomson, "Tribute to Miss Macurdy," *Vassar Alumnae Magazine* 23 (1937): 8–9.

sense of the word a true 'scholar', of a kind which is rare in America and by no means common in Europe," he specifies exactly what he means by this term:

> There have been in my time two main tendencies in Greek study: the dogged pursuit of erudition and research by which Germany has produced so many works of monumental learning, and the sensitive appreciation of language and the habitual familiarity with the great masterpieces of Greek literature which made Greek poetry and philosophy an integral part of our traditional culture in England. Miss Macurdy seemed to me, like the great scholars of both countries, most happily to unite the two methods, while she added to them her own special gifts of sympathy and imagination and her readiness to face new facts and understand new ideas.

Murray's tribute, however, reveals no sense that he has understood Grace's effort to redefine the classical scholar as a woman. He places her in the top ranks of the long procession of male scholars with no acknowledgment that she was tailoring the academic cap and gown to the female form. Thomson's tribute, the only one of the four that even mentions Grace's sex, begins with a strong statement of the international recognition that Grace has achieved as a woman scholar, one who has not suppressed her gender to earn acceptance as a scholar:

> I think that on this side of the ocean it is the general impression that Miss Macurdy was the first American woman to meet the Greek scholars of Europe and America on something like equal terms. She has reached that position by a combination, too rarely found, of exact linguistic knowledge with learning and historical imagination. The ancient world is alive for her, and whatever she writes is full of her personality.

In contrast to Murray's description of *Hellenistic Queens* as "a valuable collection of material," Thomson maintains, "Her work on the queens of Hellenistic and Roman times—most of them, with the startling exception of Cleopatra, quite forgotten—is a really important contribution to history." Thomson concludes by noting the lack of popular recognition for scholarship: "Anyone who chooses to spend a life-time in the study of ancient Greek must be content to do without fame. If Miss Macurdy had reached the same eminence in some popular subject as she has done in her own, she would be a famous woman."

But Grace had never sought acclaim outside the scholarly community. Thomson understood her highest aspirations; Murray praised her for scholarship like his own; Grace was content.

CHAPTER 11

༄༅

Retirement

"Now Begin the Folio"

Grace viewed retirement from teaching as an opportunity to engage in more scholarship and writing on new subjects. As late as 1945, when she answered an alumnae questionnaire from Radcliffe, she was looking forward and making plans for additional projects, despite seriously compromised vision due to cataracts: "My life has been very full of various duties since I gave up my chairmanship of the Department of Greek, and I have plans for future writing if my vision permits. Was it R. L. Stevenson who said 'Now begin the folio'?"[1] Grace here refers to a line from Robert Louis Stevenson's 1878 essay "Aes Triplex": "By all means begin your folio; even if the doctor does not give you a year, even if he hesitates about a month, make one brave push and see what can be accomplished in a week."[2]

After enjoying her retirement celebrations, Grace immediately sailed for England with plans to stay abroad for fifteen months. Her home base was a flat in Lexham Gardens next to that of Thomson, but she intended to travel in Europe despite the threatening political situation in 1937. As she wrote Gilbert Murray, "I shall spend some time in Europe if the explosives of the Infamous

---

1. "News from the Classes," *Radcliffe Quarterly* 29 (1945): 28.
2. Robert Louis Stevenson, *Aes Triplex and Other Essays*, 2nd ed. (Portland, Maine: Thomas B. Mosher, 1903), 22.

Pair of Dictators *leave* any Europe."³ On August 8, Grace traveled by train to Switzerland, where she joined Murray and J. A. K. Thomson on their annual summer vacation hiking in the Alps. Thomson's niece Margaret was also part of the group, and when Murray returned to England the three traveled together in Italy for several weeks. Thomson later wrote Murray that when he and Grace were on the train to Genoa, they were joined in their compartment by a man from Liberia and his daughter. The man was in some distress, since he had discovered that all his cash had been packed in his forwarded luggage; Thomson lent him the equivalent of a pound in French and Italian currency and was surprised later to receive a letter from the man containing an English pound: "This experience has put up my opinion of human nature, and especially of Liberia, which I take to be the worst-governed country in the world. Lots of white people, knowing they would never see me again, would not have bothered to repay me."⁴

Back in England, Grace and Thomson socialized with friends, including Ida Hill and Gilbert Murray, and added to their collection of Greek artifacts. Grace started research for a new book on the concept of pity in Greek literature. She and Thomson had originally planned to write this book together, but he was now busy with other projects. They spent long hours discussing the nature of this book and decided that it would be a timely response to the current political situation and should be written for a less scholarly audience than Grace's other works. In the spring of 1938, Grace spent some time in France, informing Murray: "I am on the point of going to France for a time, as the six months allowed for an alien's stay in England are up. I never feel like an alien!"⁵ The final months of her period abroad were complicated by illness, caused by a painful bout of shingles and some bad dentistry that landed her in a nursing home in England for several days. She had a stormy crossing in September, arriving in New York only four days after the great hurricane of 1938, but she recovered her health and spirits soon after settling back in Vassar, which she called "my spiritual and intellectual home."⁶

---

3. Grace H. Macurdy to Gilbert Murray, 23 June 1937, MSS Gilbert Murray 157, fols. 165–66, Bodleian.

4. J. A. K. Thomson to Gilbert Murray, 21 September 1937, MSS Gilbert Murray 173, fols. 201–2, Bodleian.

5. Grace H. Macurdy to Gilbert Murray, 19 February 1938, MSS Gilbert Murray 157, fols. 169–70, Bodleian.

6. Grace H. Macurdy to Henry N. MacCracken, 12 February 1937, MacCracken Papers, box 43, folder 46, Vassar Archives.

War Work

Unlike many of her classical colleagues in the United States, Grace was not enamored of Benito Mussolini nor beguiled by his propaganda about reviving the grandeur of ancient Rome. In 1935, when Hazel Haight was on sabbatical leave in Italy, she prevailed upon Vassar's president to request for her an audience with Mussolini so she could present several volumes from Vassar in honor of the bimillenaries of Horace and Augustus. All the books were related to Italy except *Hellenistic Queens*, which Grace reluctantly agreed to include in the donation. Hazel wrote an effusive account of her June 4 audience to MacCracken:

> His Excellency read your letter, partly aloud, in my presence. He expressed great pleasure in the interest shown in Italy by the gift of the books. . . . The books, he said, would eventually be placed in the Library of the Royal Academy of Italy. All this sounds very formal, but the interview soon changed from rather stiff English to a most informal conversation in Italian about the new archaeological zones in Rome, plans for others, the latest discovery of a great frescoed tomb at Ostia. I was there for about twenty minutes and was deeply impressed by the honor of having the *Capo del Governo* in these troubled days lay aside all affairs of state and journey with me back to the ancient Italy which he knows well.[7]

In the same month, Grace wrote Murray, "The world is so full of horrors now—fascists and despots and other terrible things. Miss [Gertrude] Hirst often says to me that she and I will never visit Germany again, for Hitler will probably outlast our time and we cannot bring ourselves to go while he remains. And Mussolini is cleverer, but just as bad, worse perhaps for not being such an unmitigated fool as Hitler."[8] As with other types of injustice, Grace saw the "horrors" that were happening in Europe as a personal challenge. She believed that she must do anything in her power to alleviate the sufferings caused by "such monsters of stupidity and ignorance as Hitler, Goehring [*sic*], and Mussolini," whether it was something small and personal like sending Gillette razor blades to Thomson and needles to his sister Mary,

---

7. Elizabeth H. Haight to Henry N. MacCracken, 7 June 1935, MacCracken Papers, box 39, folder 80, Vassar Archives.

8. Grace H. Macurdy to Gilbert Murray, 13 June 1935, MSS Gilbert Murray 157, fol. 152, Bodleian.

or co-sponsoring a full-page advertisement in behalf of Greek war relief in the *Poughkeepsie Eagle-News*.[9]

Soon after Britain declared war on Germany, Grace founded and chaired a faculty branch of the British War Relief Society (BWRS), and she was the driving force behind Vassar's participation in collecting clothing and raising funds for this cause throughout the war. Along with more than fifty other Vassar faculty, she signed a petition sent to President Roosevelt in 1940 urging "all possible aid to the Allies, short of war." Grace even contributed a revolver plus at least twenty rounds of ammunition to the first shipment of donated weapons made by the "American committee for defense of British homes." This shipment was delivered to a home guard unit in Bournemouth in 1940, and the participation of a female college professor was considered noteworthy enough to be included in a newspaper announcement of the event.[10]

After the war, the BWRS conferred on Grace a pin "for meritorious service." The pin is gold-plated silver with blue and white enamel; it depicts the British royal family's coat of arms and motto. More significantly, the BWRS formally nominated Grace for a special British award initiated to recognize civilians of Allied countries who gave outstanding aid of various kinds to the British Commonwealth during World War II. Although ill at the time, Grace was thrilled when she received a letter from the British ambassador to the United States, Archibald Clark Kerr, Lord Inverchapel, that she had been selected to receive the King's Medal for Service in the Cause of Freedom. This medal, a heavy silver disk suspended from a white ribbon (a bow in the case of women) with a central red stripe flanked by two blue stripes, bore a portrait of King George VI on the obverse and a knight receiving a drink from a woman on the reverse. It was awarded to only 1,277 Americans and 2,539 individuals worldwide. Unfortunately, Grace did not live to attend the ceremony in Manhattan on December 10, 1946 when the actual medals were distributed.[11]

---

9. Grace H. Macurdy to Gilbert Murray, 30 October 1936 and 29 May 1941, MSS Gilbert Murray 157, fols. 155 and 183–84, Bodleian; "That *Greece . . .* and *Freedom . . .* May Live!" *Poughkeepsie Eagle-News*, 8 February 1941, 10.

10. Grace H. Macurdy to Gilbert Murray, 1 March 1941, MSS Gilbert Murray 157, fols. 180–81, Bodleian; "Fifty at Vassar Urge All Aid to Allies Short of War," *Poughkeepsie Eagle-News*, 5 June 1940, 1, 9; "Americans Privately Assist the British," *The Times Recorder* (Zanesville, Ohio), 14 November 1940, 4.

11. Treasury: Ceremonial Branch: King's Medal for Service (KMS Series) Records T339, The National Archives of the UK; "Professor Macurdy, Mrs. Becker Decorated By the British for Their War Relief Activities," *Poughkeepsie New Yorker*, 15 July 1946, Biographical Files: Macurdy, Grace Harriet, folder 3, Vassar Archives; "Britain Honors 187 in City Area," *New York Times*, 11 December 1946, 34.

The Quality of Mercy

Repelled by the horrors of the Holocaust and the carnage of the war, Grace was not satisfied with her many efforts in behalf of war relief; she wanted to create a more lasting intellectual counterweight to the forces of inhumanity that were sweeping the world. As always, she turned to the Greeks, reviving and expanding her older idea of writing a history of pity in Greek literature. This book, *The Quality of Mercy: The Gentler Virtues in Greek Literature*, was published in 1940.[12] It is very different from her other books, clearly intended for a broader, less scholarly audience. There is no bibliography, and her many footnotes draw heavily on English-language sources, though German works are still in evidence. She transliterates Greek words in the text and includes much background information that classical scholars would not need. She chose to dedicate the book to Gilbert Murray and J. A. K. Thomson, whose work (particularly Thomson's) this book resembles more than anything else she wrote. She clearly recognized this when she wrote Murray about the book's dedication: "I wish very much to dedicate the book to you and to J. A. K. Thomson. I hope that it has something of the spirit of you both and all your books have been my constant companions for so many years and I have used them so constantly in class and out that I cannot conceive of my intellectual life without them."[13]

Her stated aim in the preface is to disprove the view "that the Greeks were 'not humane by instinct' and that their feeling for mercy and pity was greatly inferior to that of modern man."[14] Although she does not mention the current world situation in connection with this aim, she explicitly invokes contemporary issues in several passages in the book:

> **Western ideals of mercy, right, and justice:** These ideals are now darkened by the influence of ignorance and cruelty, but we may still say of them what Antigone in face of death said of her Unwritten Laws: "Their life is not of today alone, nor yet of yesterday, but it goes on forever."
>
> **Refugees:** In the early play, the *Suppliants* [of Aeschylus], the violence of the Egyptian suitors is for the moment checked, and the question of the expediency for Argos of receiving the refugees—a question that often

---

12. Grace H. Macurdy, *The Quality of Mercy: The Gentler Virtues in Greek Literature* (New Haven: Yale University Press, 1940).

13. Grace H. Macurdy to Gilbert Murray, 16 December 1939, MSS Gilbert Murray 157, fols. 173–74, Bodleian.

14. Macurdy, *Quality of Mercy*, vii.

faced Athens as it faces every civilized country in the world today—is settled in favor of the suppliant girls.

Persecution of dissenters: Persecution for opinions about questions of morality and religion has been a frequent phenomenon in history, and now that thought and mercy are forbidden in countries which have been centres of light and learning, it is easier to understand why, even in the time of Enlightenment in Athens, the poet [Euripides] who hated cruelty and said that pity could not live among the ignorant was finally obliged to leave a city which, after long years of war, was forgetting what pity and what wisdom meant.

Cruelty toward children (re death of Astyanax in Euripides's *Trojan Women*): A countless number of little Astyanaxes have been killed but lately and are still being slaughtered for the glory of the war lords and their undying shame.[15]

The scope of this book is very wide, beginning with Homer and Hesiod and ranging through the elegiac and lyric poets, the three great tragedians Aeschylus, Sophocles and Euripides, the historians Herodotus and Thucydides, the Attic Orators, the comic poet Menander, and the philosophers Socrates and Plato. It covers a time span of approximately a millennium and encompasses diverse genres, all connected through Grace's focus on the Greek writers' treatment of "the gentler virtues," justice, pity, mercy, wisdom, and self-control. She frequently refers to later writers such as Shakespeare, Shelley, Matthew Arnold, Hegel, and Nietzsche, even pointing out some startling contemporary correspondences between Menander and P. G. Wodehouse and between Herodotus and the modern art of filmmaking ("Herodotus from his first page sets before our eyes a motion-picture of interesting men, women, and children."[16]).

Grace's focus occasionally slips as she allows herself to be drawn into scholarly controversies that temporarily distract from her main theme and are not likely to interest the general audience she hopes to reach. She also cannot resist discussing various authors' treatment of women, particularly Euripides, whom she defends against the charge of misogyny by emphasizing that he presented women as individuals with the same potential as men: "Women were one of the poet's 'causes'; he was interested in their psychology, not from malice, but because he realized that they, as well as men, had minds, and were potent for good or evil." Her indignation is especially roused by Gilbert Nor-

---

15. Macurdy, *Quality of Mercy*, xiii, 93, 121, 132.
16. Macurdy, *Quality of Mercy*, 142.

wood's use of a contemporary feminine stereotype to criticize the character of Alcestis, a characterization which Grace terms "extraordinary to the point of being ludicrous": "[Norwood] personally finds her frigid, unimaginative, ungenerous, and basely narrow, . . . 'that frightful figure, the thoroughly good woman.'"[17]

In regard to the treatment of women, Grace praises Herodotus, unlike Thucydides, for viewing women's actions as worthy of commemoration:

> His pages are sprinkled with the names of women, some of whose stories he tells at length, while merely mentioning the tragic deeds of others. He is aware of the part that women have often played in making history, and his sympathetic picture of Artemisia, the fighting queen of his native Halicarnassus, indicates his appreciation of women who do not conform to the ideal of his friend Pericles [i.e., "to be talked about as little as possible, for good or evil, among men"].[18]

Grace also discusses two orations that deal with women, Lysias's *On the Murder of Eratosthenes*, a tale of seduction and exposed adultery which "hardly differs from stories that are told today in modern courtrooms or in the newspapers," and Pseudo-Demosthenes' *Against Neaera*, "important for the light which it throws on marriage and concubinage in Athens, and on the position of the class of women called *hetaerae* [companions, high-class prostitutes]." She justifies the inclusion of these orations by their links with New Comedy, but it is their connection with women that chiefly interests her.[19]

An advertising letter addressed "to those interested in the Ancient World" sent with the brochure of new publications by Yale University Press singled out Grace's book for special comment: "While we believe that all of the volumes described in the enclosed circular will be of interest to you, we wish to call your particular attention to THE QUALITY OF MERCY, by Grace Macurdy."[20] Despite such attention, the book was not as widely reviewed as Grace's previous works, perhaps because of its more popular approach, or possibly because of the exigencies of wartime. Reviewers universally complimented the book on its theme and relationship to the contemporary situation, as for example William Greene in *Classical Philology*: "This is one of the comparatively

---

17. Macurdy, *Quality of Mercy*, 137, 133, quoting Gilbert Norwood, *Greek Tragedy* (London: Methuen, 1920), 190.

18. Macurdy, *Quality of Mercy*, 145.

19. Macurdy, *Quality of Mercy*, 158, 162.

20. Janet L. Marshall, Education Department, Yale University Press, 20 January 1941, Biographical Files: Macurdy, Grace Harriet, folder 1, Vassar Archives.

few books, important in substance and eloquent in expression, that are the best justification of classical scholarship; and in a world that at the moment seems so lacking in the gentler virtues Professor Macurdy's study is doubly welcome."[21] All but one of the five reviews in classical journals were very positive, praising the book's wide-ranging scope yet meticulous detail:

> Like all her work, this study is characterized by Professor Macurdy's careful and thorough scholarship and her wide familiarity both with Greek and other literature, and with the discussions of scholars and commentators. Its great interest lies in the following of the subject through the masterpieces of Greek literature and in the bringing together of the illustrations found in the various authors.[22]

Although David Robinson opens his review by calling the book an "eloquent and substantial volume on a timely and appropriate subject," he is more critical than the other reviewers. Oddly, even though he notes that the book "is meant to be popular," the core of Robinson's objections is concerned with scholarly citation. He complains that Grace has cited mostly Anglophone secondary sources and more British than American scholars, and almost half of his review is devoted to a list of works he thinks Grace should have cited.[23]

Grace was very pleased with Gilbert Murray's response to the book, which the chair of Vassar's seventy-fifth anniversary committee passed on to Yale University Press to use in their publicity:

> I was delighted to find your book waiting for me. It is a subject that urgently needed treating. People have missed the importance of "The Quality of Mercy" in Greek Civilization. I have just been studying, for instance, the way the Romans tried to push gladiatorial games and how the Greeks alone kicked against them. . . . I need hardly add that you seem to me to treat the subject with your usual delicacy of observation and scrupulous accuracy.[24]

In their private correspondence, both Thomson and Murray reiterated their praise of the book. Thomson wrote, "I was afraid it might be sentimental, but it is not that. It has real beauty of spirit and unassuming scholarship," and

---

21. William C. Greene, review of *The Quality of Mercy, Classical Philology* 37 (1942): 227.

22. Emily H. Dutton, review of *The Quality of Mercy, Classical Journal* 38 (1943): 233.

23. David M. Robinson, review of *The Quality of Mercy, American Journal of Philology* 64 (1943): 371–73.

24. Gilbert Murray to Grace H. Macurdy, 24 June 1940, MSS Gilbert Murray 157, fol. 177, Bodleian.

Murray responded, "Yes, I thought Miss Macurdy's book very good indeed. She has imagination and is, at the same time, very exact in her scholarship." Later he wrote, "The Vassar people asked leave to quote some sentences of a letter I wrote to Miss Macurdy about her book 'The Quality of Mercy,' which I gladly gave. I think she has a fair amount of honour in her own country, but certainly deserves it."[25]

Although Grace was elated by the reception of this book, she received the most satisfaction from a letter sent to her by an American army officer just returned from the war, since he represented the audience that she was hoping to reach:

> Of all the work done by American scholars in the field of Classics I had rather been the author of *The Quality of Mercy* than of any other book I know. What impressed me most was the fact that pursuit of the gentler virtues in Classical literature had breathed into your pages their spirit.[26]

Soon after Grace had completed this book, Vassar's Greek Department was stunned by the sudden death of Philip Davis due to a cerebral hemorrhage on February 20, 1940. Theodore Erck, who had been hired as assistant professor of Greek when Grace retired, was appointed acting chair of the department, and Grace immediately offered to teach Davis's courses, earning an "especial debt of gratitude" in Erck's department report:

> Professor Grace Macurdy . . . came to the rescue at once with her great knowledge and experience and took over a large share of Mr. Davis's work. She has conducted two of his important classes with her customary brilliance and success, as I learn from reports of students on every hand. Her advice and encouragement in a difficult situation were invaluable.[27]

Along with all her activities for war relief, this additional teaching drained Grace's energy, and the Vassar physician Dr. Jane North Baldwin was concerned that Grace's health was deteriorating. This concern was justified in the summer of 1941 when Dr. Baldwin found a lump in Grace's breast that proved to be cancerous. Although she was seventy-five and some doctors advised her

25. J. A. K. Thomson to Gilbert Murray, 2 July 1940; Gilbert Murray to J. A. K. Thomson, 8 July and 31 December 1940, MSS Gilbert Murray 174, fols. 13–15 and 48, Bodleian.

26. Quoted in Evalyn A. Clark et al., "A Minute of the Faculty in Memory of Grace Harriet Macurdy," 1946, Biographical Files: Macurdy, Grace Harriet, folder 3, Vassar Archives.

27. Theodore Erck, Report of the Greek Department 1939–40, 9 May 1940, Annual Reports R.36 S.5, Vassar Archives.

to let the disease take its course, Grace was a fighter, so she entered Vassar Brothers Hospital in September for a radical mastectomy. Despite the punishing nature of this surgery, Grace recovered well, as she exulted in a 1942 letter to Murray: "I had a serious operation last September, from which I rebounded so quickly that my doctors regard me as a miracle for a woman of my years."[28]

In September 1939, Ida Hill came to the United States for an indefinite stay because of the war while Bert Hill remained in Greece. Vassar's Alumnae House, next to Williams Hall where Grace lived, became her residence. Lib and Carl Blegen also spent the war years in America, with Lib living some of the time at Alumnae House and some with Carl. Ida's proximity was a great boon for Grace, for the two women dined together frequently and spent many hours in conversation. Ida read Grace's articles, and Grace helped Ida as she attempted to revive a manuscript on *The Ancient City of Athens: Its Topography and Monuments* that she had begun some years earlier.

Grace did not abate her scholarly efforts after finishing *The Quality of Mercy* (see figure 25 for a photo of Grace in the 1940s). In the spring of 1943, she wrote a former student and good friend, the psychologist Luella Cole Lowie (Vassar BA 1916), "I am writing various articles—*Classical Philology* has just accepted one and one was printed in the last *Journal of Biblical Literature*. I have had six published or accepted in the last year and a half and have written several 'duds' besides. I wish mine paid in a pecuniary way, but that is a sordid thought."[29]

Grace's last comment was prompted by her increasing financial worries. Her mastectomy and hospital stay had strained her limited resources, and her eyesight was worsening due to the growth of cataracts in both eyes. Nevertheless, she continued her research and writing, which for her were as necessary as breathing and eating. Two of her last published articles dealt with the topic of women in Greek tragedy. Authors who had published an article or review in the very first issue of *Classical Weekly* were asked to submit a brief note for that journal's thousandth issue in 1944. Grace chose to comment on one of the earliest known authors of Greek tragedies, Phrynichus, traditionally named as the first to bring female characters on the stage. Grace discussed how this innovation added pathos, a deeper emotional component, to tragedy:

> I suggest that the great discovery which Phrynicus [*sic*] made for the development of tragedy was the emotional value of women under the impact

---

28. Grace H. Macurdy to Gilbert Murray, 13 June 1942, MSS Gilbert Murray 157, fols. 185–86, Bodleian.

29. Grace H. Macurdy to Luella C. Lowie, 21 April 1943, Robert Harry Lowie Papers, BANC MSS C-B 927, box 15, folder 15, The Bancroft Library, University of California, Berkeley.

of terror, massed in a chorus. . . . From the group of collective heroines of
such a chorus a single heroine is projected, as Hypermnestra is projected in
the Danaid trilogy from the original group of Danaids. . . . Nietzsche said
that when God created women he put an end to boredom. When Phrynicus
formed choruses of women and introduced heroines, he created a new *genre*,
which finally replaced in favor the old dithyramb, with which audiences were
beginning to be bored.[30]

In a lengthier article, "Had the Danaid Trilogy a Social Problem?," Grace
challenges a number of male scholars on their reading of female psychology in Aeschylus's play *Supplices* (*The Suppliant Women*). Grace's thesis is that
George Thomson's sociological analysis of the theme of the *Supplices* in his
book *Aeschylus and Athens* is "evasive and mistaken."[31] Thomson argues that
the play's theme is the status of women in contemporary Athenian society
and that Aeschylus advocates the subjugation of women in the interests of
private property. In his view, the chorus of Danaid girls represent Athenian
heiresses (*epikleroi*) seeking to avoid their legal obligation to marry their next
of kin when they reject the suit of their Egyptian cousins. After conclusively
demonstrating that Thomson's interpretation of Athenian law is faulty because
Danaos, the girls' father, is still alive and therefore has the legal right to marry
his daughters to any men he chooses, Grace argues insightfully that the theme
of the play is essentially dramatic, not social:

> In this drama Aeschylus is doing something far greater than expounding
> the theme of the social status of women. He is putting on the stage, for the
> first time in our knowledge of drama, women throbbing with life, with their
> wild outbursts of emotion, their passionate determination, desperate cun-
> ning, and power over men in their helplessness. . . . I maintain, then, that
> the problem of the Danaid trilogy is dramatic and not a social problem, and
> that the question is "What happened to the Danaids?" not that of the con-
> temporary (with Aeschylus) social status of Athenian women. In the Greek
> drama women played a great part, and the titles of many of Aeschylus' dra-
> mas show how often they were his theme. The men in the audiences must

---

30. Grace H. Macurdy, "Prologue to a Study of the Tragic Heroine," *Classical Weekly* 37
(1944): 239–40.

31. Grace H. Macurdy, "Had the Danaid Trilogy a Social Problem?" *Classical Philology* 39
(1944): 95; George Derwent Thomson, *Aeschylus and Athens: A Study in the Social Origins of
Drama* (London: Lawrence and Wishart, 1940).

have reflected on the women in their own homes when they saw the stage heroines and heard the comments on women's character that were uttered.[32]

In discussing the character of the Danaid girls, Grace disputes the German scholar Wilhelm Schmid and even Gilbert Murray, both of whom claim that the Danaids were "actuated by a natural frigidity and hatred of men." In contrast, Grace draws upon her own perceptions as a woman to interpret the Danaids' behavior, calling them Aristotelian heroines 'like ourselves,' which may be the first time that this phrase of Aristotle, characterizing the tragic hero as neither excessively perfect nor extremely base, was applied to a female character by a woman scholar:

Aeschylus . . . is writing a drama, not about heiresses, but about tragic girls, caught in the net of circumstance and brought by dreadful suffering to commit dreadful deeds. In the second play of the trilogy they are murderesses; in the one which we have they are girls driven to desperation by the brutality of their would-be lovers. They have the sympathy of everyone in the drama (except the Egyptian herald), and they must have had the sympathy of the audiences before whom the play was performed. They do not secure the sympathy of W. Schmid, who believes that Aeschylus could not have known such women from his experience and that he has made them still more unwomanly and abnormal than they were in the legend, in order to give psychological motivation for their deeds. . . . But the women of Greece were not all of the "feminine" type commended by Pericles, and Aeschylus may well have known, even in Athens, women of bolder impulses. . . . The Danaids, too, in the *Supplices* express the single terrified state of mind of girls who have undergone the horrid experience of being attacked by men whom they hate. This state of mind is neither unwomanly nor abnormal— rather, indeed, both womanly and normal.[33]

Pioneer Ancestors and *Encyclopaedia Britannica*

Despite the progression of her cataracts, when Grace's Seattle relative Horace Winslow McCurdy asked her to conduct research on the history of the McCurdy branch of their family, she agreed to take on the project, throwing

---

32. Macurdy, "Had the Danaid Trilogy," 98, 99–100.
33. Macurdy, "Had the Danaid Trilogy," 98–99.

herself into the work with her usual thoroughness and attention to detail. As she wrote Gilbert Murray:

> For some months now I have left Greek research to write a history of the pioneer ancestors of my family for a rich young shipbuilder cousin of mine in Seattle, who wishes to preserve our records for his children. Just now I am deep in the Sophists and anti-Sophists of New England and the closely allied Nova Scotia, almost part of New England, in the time of the American Revolution. It is an extraordinarily interesting period of conflicting loyalties.[34]

Horace McCurdy was Grace's first cousin once removed, the grandson of her uncle William Augustus McCurdy Jr., who had emigrated from Canada to the frontier Territory of Washington. Grace had visited with young Horace many times when she was teaching at Columbia during the summers and he was warrant officer on the transport ship *Henry R. Mallory* during World War I. Back in Seattle, Horace had risen to become president and general manager of the Puget Sound Bridge and Dredging Company, which did a booming business in shipbuilding and related construction during World War II.[35] Grace's far-ranging research about the family brought her into contact with many prominent distant relatives, including George Grant MacCurdy, prehistoric archaeologist and anthropologist of Yale University; Edward MacCurdy of Surrey, author of *The Notebooks of Leonardo da Vinci*; Fleming Blanchard McCurdy, member of the Canadian Parliament for Nova Scotia; and Judge John B. M. Baxter, Chief Justice of the province of New Brunswick. Given her own humble origins, Grace was proud that this research connected her and her family with distinguished ancestors and contemporary individuals. She wrote that Edward MacCurdy had "told me that I had the Mc Curdy [*sic*] aspect, in shape of face etc. resembling his father. I wish I could lay claim to all their good qualities! One, that of persistence, I am sure I have had."[36] In discussing her family's descent from Mayflower passenger Richard Warren, she noted, "It is an interesting coincidence that the two most powerful men in

---

34. Grace H. Macurdy to Gilbert Murray, 24 October 1943, MSS Gilbert Murray 157, fols. 188–89, Bodleian.

35. For more information on Horace McCurdy, see the online HistoryLink essay "McCurdy, H. W. (1899–1989)," accessed 16 March 2015, http://www.historylink.org/index.cfm?DisplayPage=output.cfm&file_id=7181.

36. Grace H. Macurdy to F. B. McCurdy, 14 June 1943, private collection of James Griffith McCurdy.

the world at this moment, Winston Churchill and Franklin Delano Roosevelt are descendants in the eighth generation of Richard and Elizabeth Warren."[37]

Although Grace collected as much information as she could find to document genealogical details, she became absorbed in the historical events in which her ancestors played a part, as the above letter to Murray indicates. She eventually composed a lengthy manuscript (163 typed pages plus appended copies of documents) that she entitled *Pioneer Ancestors of an American Family, 1620–1857*, and mailed this to Horace in June 1944. She included in her manuscript a passage sent to her by Horace indicating that he would dedicate the book to his father and acknowledge her as its author: "It is with pleasure and pride that I dedicate to my father's memory the publication of the genealogy of Clan McCurdy compiled by his cousin Grace."[38] She continued to pursue some genealogical research even after mailing the manuscript, because Horace wanted to prove that their ancestor Neil McCurdy "was a *Scot*." However, despite her best efforts, she was unable to find documentary confirmation of the parents of Neil McCurdy or of his birth on Rathlin Island, off the northernmost coast of Ireland. As she confided to her nephew Ernest Macurdy of Watertown (see figure 17), son of her older brother William, she was not sure that Horace shared her interest in the broader history:

> I hope Horace will have our genealogy etc. printed, as it is full of interesting
> & valuable history for your children. It deals with the McCurdys, but my
> mother's side is equally interesting & I wish I might be spared to write that
> out. We have all been brought up in great ignorance of our ancestors & the
> part they played in the early history & making of America. Horace is interested chiefly in the McCurdy Scotch line, but Everett McCurdy [his cousin]
> appreciates the historical value of the research.[39]

Grace did not live to see the printed book, which was very different from what she had envisaged, though she never regretted devoting so much of her time and energy to research on her family. Horace did not publish the book until 1963, in a privately printed limited edition of two hundred copies, as the

37. Grace H. Macurdy, *Pioneer Ancestors of an American Family, 1620–1857*, Unpublished manuscript, 1944, Seattle Public Library, R929.2 M139Mg, 99. As Grace wrote her nephew Ernest, however, the connection was very distant: "Through Richard Warren we are 8th, 9th or 10th (according to generation) cousins of F. D. R. & Churchill and of Roosevelt in several other lines." Grace H. Macurdy to Ernest Macurdy, 15 September 1943, private collection of June Macurdy Landin.

38. Quoted in Macurdy, *Pioneer Ancestors*, 157.

39. Grace H. Macurdy to Ernest Macurdy, 14 March and 10 September 1945, private collection of June Macurdy Landin.

Genealogical History of James Winslow McCurdy and Neil Barclay McCurdy, with himself as author, Gordon Newell as editor, and Brian Llewellyn Young as genealogical researcher. Grace is mentioned only in the foreword, where she is thanked as one of five people who provided "invaluable assistance" in his research.[40] However, large sections of text in the book are taken verbatim from Grace's manuscript, and almost all the documents quoted or referenced are ones that she found for him. Horace admits in a footnote the lack of documentary proof regarding the parentage of Neil McCurdy but nevertheless claims that "a diligent search has turned up strong circumstantial evidence" that his parents were Daniel McCurdy and Mary Butler of Rathlin Island.[41] As Grace had feared, Horace eliminates much of the historical background that she believed was so valuable. To give one small example, Horace devotes a little over two pages to the family background of Ruth Avery, wife of Neil McCurdy. Much of this consists of lists of people with births and marriages; all the descriptive text is taken directly from Grace's manuscript. Grace's section on the Averys, on the other hand, comprises sixty-nine pages and begins by setting the marriage of Ruth and Neil in historical context:

> The marriage of Neil McCurdy, my great-grandfather, with my great-grandmother, Ruth Avery, was a result of the meeting of two racial movements; one the great Scotch-Irish immigration of the eighteenth century into Canada and the New England states, Maine above all, and the movement northwest from New England of traders and settlers seeking lands in the Province of Maine and beyond.[42]

As she was completing *Pioneer Ancestors*, Grace received a request from Mary Ritter Beard, a suffragist and historian particularly interested in the role of women, to write eleven short biographies of women for the new edition of the *Encyclopaedia Britannica*. In 1941, Beard had been asked by Walter Yust, editor-in-chief of the encyclopedia, to conduct an in-depth study of *Britannica*'s coverage of women and women's issues. Beard, assisted by Dora Edinger, Janet Selig, and Marjorie White, spent eighteen months examining the encyclopedia and submitted "A Study of the *Encylopaedia Britannica* in Relation to Its Treatment of Women" to Yust in November 1942.[43] Yust asked Beard to

---

40. H. W. McCurdy, *Genealogical History of James Winslow McCurdy and Neil Barclay McCurdy* (Seattle: Superior Publishing Company, 1963), 6.

41. McCurdy, *Genealogical History*, 37.

42. Macurdy, *Pioneer Ancestors*, 27.

43. For more information on this project plus excerpts from the report, see Ann J. Lane, ed., *Making Women's History: The Essential Mary Ritter Beard* (New York: Feminist Press, 2000), 215–24.

solicit women to write new pieces and to rewrite existing articles in response to her critique. Believing strongly that women's presence in the encyclopedia should be enlarged, Grace agreed to prepare the eleven biographical sketches she had been asked to write, although she struggled to complete the library research that this entailed because of her failing eyesight. It was with great relief that she announced to Gilbert Murray in 1945 that she had submitted the biographies:

> My task of writing eleven biographies of women for the new edition of the *Encyclopoedia Britannica* [*sic*] has happily been completed now. I have sent these Lives off and feel greatly relieved that my sight has lasted out for this interesting task. I am told by the Editor that it is intended to lay emphasis on the part that woman [*sic*] have played in history and civilization (in the new edition). I was assigned several empresses (two of them saints!), some literary women, and one or two Roman ladies of some intellectual distinction.[44]

Grace noted in several letters and in her 1945 alumna report to *Radcliffe Quarterly* that she had completed these biographies, but *Britannica* never published any of them, and Grace was never listed among its contributors. An inquiry to *Britannica* produced the following response:

> Prof. Macurdy appears to have submitted material as part of a project to compile a list of biographies of women for inclusion in the encyclopaedia as needed. We have no record, however, of any of those biographies having been received or subsequently added to the encyclopaedia. Our records on this project are, unfortunately, not complete. A list dated 22 May 1945 identifies a "Macurdy" as a "prospective author" for entries on Julia Mamaea, Moero (Myro), Nossis, Olympias, and Pamphila. . . . The project was apparently headed by Ms. Marjorie White. What few records we have, however, do not indicate whether she was a member of the Britannica staff or was hired specifically for that project.[45]

In the end, Yust and *Britannica* did not follow through on the project; the report and critiques of Beard and her staff, plus the contributions she solicited, were never incorporated in the encyclopedia. From the message quoted

---

44. Grace H. Macurdy to Gilbert Murray, 11 January 1945, MSS Gilbert Murray 157, fols. 190–91, Bodleian.

45. Lars Mahinske, editorial staff of the *Encylopaedia Britannica,* to Barbara F. McManus (e-mail), 17 and 25 October 1997.

above, it appears that all the contributions were simply discarded. In 1947 Mary Beard wrote to a friend, "Mr. Yust has never kept me in touch with one of the numerous sketches or anything else which he authorized me to collect for this compendium. . . . I am asking no more women to write."[46] Fortunately, Grace was spared the knowledge of the failure of this project and the disposal of the biographies she had fought so hard to complete.

Illness and Death

By the time Grace finished the *Britannica* biographies her vision was so poor that she could no longer read, and her handwriting in the few letters she wrote in the summer of 1945 is nearly illegible. The cataract in one of her eyes was opaque and the other was steadily worsening. Nevertheless, she was planning further research projects, as she wrote Murray, "My own reading is limited, but I hope I may be helped by an operation on one eye this summer. I have various themes that I desire to follow up in that happy contingency."[47] Grace was disappointed in her hope of an imminent operation on her sightless eye, since she had to wait until the cataract was fully "ripe"; she did not have the surgery until the end of the year. At that time cataract surgery was expensive and dangerous. The lens had to be hard and opaque so that it could be removed without breaking. The surgeon made a large incision halfway around the cornea; because fine sutures were not available, sandbags were placed around the patient's head to keep it immobile until the incision healed. The patient risked loss of the eye or even death if there were problems during the operation or recovery period.

Without the ability to read and write, Grace found the waiting both tedious and distressing, though she downplayed her misery in a letter to Murray:

> Your gift of the "Arbitration" [Murray's translation of the *Epitrepontes* of Menander] brought very great pleasure to me and to Ida Thallon Hill, who read it aloud to me in three sessions. . . . Mrs. Hill was my pupil long ago and her familiarity with modern Greek from her years of residence in Athens is added to her love of ancient Greek literature. She has kept me from brooding

---

46. Quoted in Lane, *Making Women's History*, 216.

47. Grace H. Macurdy to Gilbert Murray, 18 June 1945, MSS Gilbert Murray 157, fols. 192–93, Bodleian.

over my diminished sight by reading to me for hours in her beautiful voice
every evening. We have had a wide range from Shakespeare to Santayana.[48]

Ida's devoted care certainly helped Grace through this period, but the
combination of impaired vision and hearing weighed heavily on Grace,
increasingly closing her off from contact with the world outside herself. Her
Sonotone hearing aid had improved her hearing to the point that she could
enjoy Ida's reading aloud in her quiet room, but it was frightening to ven-
ture outside with her double disability. In the words of another friend, Hazel
Haight, "Between fear of the operation and many months of lack of eyesight
she became a very nervous invalid."[49] Hazel was probably unaware that Grace
was worried about more than the outcome of the operation, since she did
not have the funds to cover the $1,000 it would cost. She could not sched-
ule the operation without the money in the bank, but without the operation
she would never be able to read and write again. After weighing all possible
options, she reluctantly concluded that she would have to sell her summer
house, so she wrote her nephew Ernest with a proposal:

> Would you consider buying my cottage at North Falmouth for one thousand
> dollars? When you wrote me last summer I felt that it would be unfair to
> Fid and Carl who had looked after the place so long if I should sell it. Now I
> am compelled to raise money for a very expensive operation on my eye for
> cataract. . . . I have been working on the McCurdy genealogy for Horace,
> who pays for the investigation only (not me) that is for the fees for copying
> records etc. I shall have to stop that.[50]

Grace had bequeathed the summer house to her niece Fid in her will and was
loath to renege on her promise, but she could see no other way to finance the
operation; Fid and Carl did not want to buy the cottage themselves because
they lived too far away to make regular use of it. The house was appraised at
$3,800 for tax purposes, but Grace was willing to sell it plus all the furniture
to Ernest for only as much as she needed for the surgery. She was delighted
when Ernest agreed to these terms:

---

48. Grace H. Macurdy to Gilbert Murray, 18 June 1945, MSS Gilbert Murray 157, fols. 192–
93, Bodleian.

49. Elizabeth H. Haight to Lady Mary Murray, 17 March 1946, MSS Gilbert Murray 544,
fols. 136–37, Bodleian.

50. Grace H. Macurdy to Ernest Macurdy, 14 March 1945, private collection of June Macurdy Landin.

It is a great relief to me to have the money in the bank for my operation and I hope that you are liking the place. . . . I hear from Horace McCurdy now & then. He finally offered to help with expenses of my operation and I was glad to be able to tell him that I did not need his help. He emphasized that he had an enormous number of requests (he did not get one from me!) for aid. He is evidently a very successful man and doubtless, as he says, is the victim of "spongers."[51]

While awaiting her operation, Grace received the news that her younger brother John Ordway Macurdy, whom the family called Dick, had died of cancer of the bladder on July 27, 1945, and she remembered him fondly in a letter to Ernest: "Dick was so witty and realy [*sic*] had many gifts that were not developed. When he was little, I used to read to him by the hour Scott's *Marmion* and Macaulay's *Lays of Ancient Rome*, and he could repeat long passages of them."[52] With the possible exception of her youngest brother, Leigh, who had disappeared nearly forty years earlier, Grace was the only one of the Macurdy siblings still alive.

After the long ordeal of her cataract surgery and recuperation, Grace was still unable to read by the end of January 1946, as she wrote her friend Luella: "I have had a long, expensive & tiresome convalescence and have not yet got proper reading & writing glasses—the distance ones serve me very well, but I am to get others in due time."[53] By March she was wearing the thick, heavy glasses used at that time after cataract surgery. Never troubled by personal vanity, Grace cared nothing about the appearance of the glasses; she was simply overjoyed to be able to read and write again, as Hazel Haight reported to Lady Mary Murray, "You will be glad to know that Miss Macurdy's operation was a success and, now that she is able to read again, she seems like her old self."[54]

Sadly, Grace was not able to pursue any of the "various themes" that she desired to research when her eyesight was restored, for her breast cancer had metastasized and spread. On July 24, 1946, a short time after receiving the letter announcing that she would be awarded the King's Medal for Service in the Cause of Freedom, Grace entered Vassar Brothers Hospital, and she drew

51. Grace H. Macurdy to Ernest Macurdy, 31 May 1945, private collection of June Macurdy Landin.

52. Grace H. Macurdy to Ernest Macurdy, 10 September 1945, private collection of June Macurdy Landin.

53. Grace H. Macurdy to Luella C. Lowie, 31 January 1946, Robert Harry Lowie Papers, BANC MSS C-B 927, box 15, folder 15, The Bancroft Library, University of California, Berkeley.

54. Elizabeth H. Haight to Lady Mary Murray, 17 March 1946, MSS Gilbert Murray 544, fols. 136–37, Bodleian.

her last breath at 4:20 p.m. on October 23.[55] After a funeral service in Poughkeepsie, she was buried in the Macurdy family plot in Watertown's Common
Street Cemetery. Grace's niece Fid was executrix and sole legatee of her will.
Since Grace's summer house had already been sold, Fid inherited only $579.34
in cash and savings bonds, plus personal effects valued at $300, the total legal
residue of a life that had been rich in everything but money.[56]

J. A. K. Thomson immediately informed Gilbert Murray of Grace's death,
though his letter is not extant. It is clear from Murray's reply, however, that
Grace had confided to Thomson all the difficulties of her last year, though she
had kept these from most people: "I a[m] very sorry about Miss Macurdy,
not so much for her death as for the long troubled time that came before it.
I had heard a little about her loss of sight, but I did not know of the financial
trouble. She was a very attractive and able woman."[57]

Epilogue

On April 6, 1949, the Vassar Classical Museum held a celebration in honor
of Grace and the two hundred Greek artifacts from their joint collection that
J. A. K. Thomson had sent to Vassar after Oxford's Ashmolean Museum had
selected the pieces they wanted. After various solemn tributes, Grace's dear
friend Henry Noble MacCracken closed the evening in a manner befitting the
scholarly, humane, and humorous woman he knew so well:

> In a mood of happy reminiscence [he] seemed to restore her to us all. It is
> impossible to quote the lively, entertaining anecdotes which he recounted,
> but some of his phrases are memorable. "She was centric, a center of people
> always." "It is fitting that half this collection should be at Oxford for she was
> as much British, or rather *Scotch*, as American." "Her books about Greek
> Queens were the scholar's answer to the oft repeated statement that women
> held an inferior position in the ancient world." . . ."She wore her scholarship
> like a beautiful garment and it fitted her."[58]

---

55. Certified copy of death certificate for Grace H. Macurdy, certificate no. 57133, district
no. 1302, registered no. 458, signed by Dr. Jane North Baldwin, 23 October 1946, *Notable American Women* files, MC 230, box 54, Schlesinger.

56. Probate documents of Grace Harriet Macurdy, box 42189, Surrogate's Court, Dutchess
County, New York.

57. Gilbert Murray to J. A. K. Thomson, 25 October 1946, MSS Gilbert Murray 174, fol. 226,
Bodleian.

58. Elizabeth Hazelton Haight, "The Macurdy Collection," *Vassar Alumnae Magazine* 34
(1949): 12.

Grace Harriet Macurdy's scholarly achievements were truly formidable, both in quality and quantity: five scholarly books, including four with university presses; fifty-seven scholarly articles in all the major American and British classical journals of her time; sixteen reviews of scholarly books; and several poems and articles in more popular venues (see appendix 2 for a chronological list of her publications). In her own lifetime, she successfully broadened the definition of a classical scholar. Despite her working-class background and her deafness, despite all the contrasts and anomalies of her life, she achieved international recognition as a scholar of Greek. Most significantly, she earned this distinction as "a woman and a scholar" in such a way that neither side of the equation diminished the other, as happened with two other outstanding female classicists of the era. In the case of her early role model, Jane Ellen Harrison, gender was accentuated at the expense of recognition as a "sound scholar," while the womanhood of Macurdy's younger colleague Lily Ross Taylor was ignored in her achievement of scholarly status as an "honorary male."[59]

When Grace graduated from high school, she had composed a poem in which she imagined herself continually weaving "the busy threads" of learning, working toward "the perfect Cloth of Gold." By the time of her death, she had fulfilled the promise of that early poem; after donning the garment of scholarship, she tailored her research and writing and the manner of her life until that garment fit her, a woman, perfectly. But her life also provides a model for the future, for other women scholars who do not wish to repress their gender. Grace's last poem, on the Attic black-figured vase depicting women at a well, was not the retrospective epitaph perceived by her colleagues but rather was as forward-looking as Grace herself. Like the artist in that poem, Grace's model "shapes still new visions" of how to study and honor the role women have played in history and culture and of what it means to achieve recognition as a distinguished scholar while living fully as a woman. Though her name and the pattern of her life were eclipsed in the decades after her death, she prefigures the dramatic changes for the study of women in history and for the lives of academic women that began in the 1970s and are still evolving today.

---

59. For more information about Lily Ross Taylor, see Barbara F. McManus, *Classics and Feminism: Gendering the Classics,* The Impact of Feminism on the Arts and Sciences (New York: Twayne Publishers, 1997), 32–35.

POSTSCRIPT

Since Barbara McManus's death, amid the celebrations and commemorations of her life and work, I have offered further reflections comparing her impact upon the field of classics with that of Grace Harriet Macurdy. At a meeting of the New York Classical Club in November 2015, I also contrasted the impact of these two pioneering feminist scholars with the influence of Macurdy's contemporary Edith Hamilton (1867–1963), who also wrote about classical antiquity. My presentation, entitled "Redefining the Woman Classicist: Edith Hamilton, Grace Harriet Macurdy and Barbara McManus in New York (1901–2015)," focused on the scholarly and professional contributions as well as the teaching careers of all three.

Barbara concludes chapter 10 of this book with remarks about Macurdy made by Macurdy's longtime companion J. A. K. Thomson, at the time of her retirement from Vassar in 1937. These remarks proved particularly relevant to the contrast between Hamilton on the one hand, and Macurdy and Barbara on the other. Thomson first comments on the international recognition that Macurdy achieved as a woman scholar who did not suppress her gender in order to earn acceptance by her academic peers, and declares her studies on the queens of Hellenistic and Roman times "a really important contribution to history." But Thomson then notes the lack of popular recognition accorded to scholarship. In this context, he observes, "Anyone who chooses to spend a lifetime in the study of ancient Greek must be content to do without fame. If

Miss Macurdy had reached the same eminence in some popular subject as she has done in her own, she would be a famous woman." Here Barbara adds, "But Grace had never sought acclaim outside the scholarly community. Thomson understood her higher aspirations."

Edith Hamilton enjoyed fame and acclaim outside the scholarly community. Her best-selling books and essays on classical, and particularly Greek, antiquity—among them *The Greek Way* (1930), *The Roman Way* (1932), *Three Greek Plays* (1937) and *Mythology* (1942)—made her virtually and justifiably a household name throughout the United States for several decades. By reimagining the classical world and its legacy for a wide reading public, Hamilton helped reauthorize Greco-Roman antiquity as a source of cultural and intellectual prestige among mid-twentieth-century middlebrow Americans. Although her academic attainments fell far short of Macurdy's, she drew on a solid educational background. After earning bachelor-of-arts and master-of-arts degrees in Latin and Greek from Bryn Mawr College, Hamilton spent the 1895–96 academic year studying classics in Germany at the Universities of Leipzig and Munich before assuming the position of headmistress at the Bryn Mawr School in Baltimore. As soon as she retired from that post twenty-six years later, she began reacquainting herself with several Greek and Latin authors, primarily the Attic tragedians and the poet Catullus. Shortly thereafter, in 1927, she launched her remarkably successful career as a popular writer.[1]

Hamilton first made her literary mark by penning relatively specialized articles about the Greek theater that two well-positioned friends in New York literary circles—the critics John Mason Brown and Rosamund Gilder—helped place in *Theatre Arts Monthly*, a venue for drama enthusiasts. Yet as soon as Elling Aannestad, an editor at the publishing house of Norton, "discovered" the sixty-two-year-old Hamilton as an emerging talent, commissioning *The Greek Way* and indeed nearly all of her books, Hamilton abandoned serious scholarly investigations in favor of pursuing popular, and lucrative, success. At the age of seventy-five, she and Doris Fielding Reid, her lover and life partner, moved to Washington, DC, where she attracted many public figures as disciples. Most notable among them was Robert F. Kennedy (Democratic senator from New York), who included two quotes from Hamilton's writings in an impromptu speech he delivered on April 4, 1968, upon learning that the Reverend Martin Luther King Jr. had been assassinated. Hamilton con-

---

1. For these and other details of Hamilton's life, see Doris Fielding Reid, *Edith Hamilton: An Intimate Portrait* (New York: W. W. Norton, 1967) and Judith P. Hallett, "Greek (and Roman) Ways and Thoroughfares: The Routing of Edith Hamilton's Classical Antiquity," in *Unsealing the Fountain: Pioneering Female Classical Scholars from the Renaissance to the Twentieth Century*, ed. Rosie Wyles and Edith Hall (Oxford: Oxford University Press, 2016) 216–42.

tinued to achieve renown up until her death at age ninety-five, and for years thereafter. In 1957 her translation of Aeschylus's *Prometheus* was performed in Athens at the ancient theater of Herodes Atticus, where she was named an honorary citizen of Athens on the occasion of her ninetieth birthday. The Greek director Michael Cacoyannis used her translation of Euripides' *Trojan Women* when he staged the play on Broadway in 1963, a few months after she died, and filmed it in 1973.

Scholars often point out Hamilton's shortcomings as a responsible researcher on classical antiquity, and a translator of classical texts. But from the early 1930s—when Norton issued *The Greek Way* and *The Roman Way* for popular consumption, at the same time that Johns Hopkins University Press published Macurdy's magisterial, erudite study of *Hellenistic Queens*—Hamilton's writing was rarely held accountable to scholarly standards or even factual accuracy. In addition, Hamilton rarely acknowledged the existence of scholars who had published learned studies on the topics she treated. She did not seek to be, or be regarded as, a classical scholar or university-level classics teacher like Grace Harriet Macurdy or Barbara McManus.

Indeed, Hamilton single-handedly redefined the term *classicist* as one who represents classical antiquity to the world at large without necessarily acquiring such standard credentials as a doctoral degree or secondary-school teaching certificate; without holding a full-time academic position that entails participating in planning and assessing student performances at multiple levels of learning; and without undertaking, presenting, or publishing original research in a documented scholarly format. Hers was authority on Greco-Roman antiquity largely assumed and achieved without the ordinary processes of authorization—authority translated into celebrity.

In an affectionate and reverential memoir that appeared in 1967, four years after Hamilton's death, Doris Fielding Reid attempts to explain Hamilton's lack of interest in serious classical scholarship and academic professionalism, so different from the fierce commitment to both displayed by Grace Harriet Macurdy and Barbara McManus. Reid does so when describing Hamilton's disappointing experience studying classics in Germany. Whereas Macurdy immensely enjoyed and profited from the year she spent in Berlin, Hamilton claimed, "The lectures were very thorough linguistically but most uninspiring. Instead of the grandeur and beauty of Aeschylus and Sophocles, it seemed that the important thing was their use of the second aorist." Reid concludes, "It seems that by that time Edith had realized what was and was not important to her in her exhaustive study of the Greek language and the Greeks. The reasons for her lifetime convictions of the importance of ancient Greece were by then formulated. They had nothing to do with the use of the second aorist or the subjunctive, and the glamor and authority of the famous classicists at the University of Leipzig affected her not at all."[2]

Reid, therefore, claims that by the time Hamilton had completed some graduate work at Bryn Mawr College—work that Reid, who had not formally studied classics, or even graduated from high school, characterizes as "exhaustive study of the Greek language and the Greeks"—Hamilton did not need further academic training thereafter, or to strive for accountability in her assertions about classical antiquity. She thereby characterizes Hamilton's "exhaustive study" as a privileged endeavor for rare beings instinctively aware of what mattered about ancient Greece, and therefore superior to the professionally licensed mode of classical learning pursued and influentially imparted by scholars such as Grace Harriet Macurdy and Barbara McManus. Their academic way of earning and confirming credentials in the study of classical philology, literature, and history was, in the opinion of Reid and presumably Hamilton herself, a grammatically obsessed endeavor overseen by self-regarding control freaks.

Which brings us back to Thomson's statement that if Grace Harriet Macurdy "reached the same eminence in some popular subject as she has in her own, she would be a famous woman." At the time he made this observation, and for decades thereafter, Edith Hamilton pursued and achieved such external acclaim by reinventing ancient Greece as a popular subject. Her redefinition of the classicist, and in her case specifically the female classicist, as an authority self-ordained, able to command veneration for classical antiquity through detachment from the demands and constraints of serious scholarship and professionalism, brought classics to wide attention and appreciation in our country.

Yet the less heralded efforts of Grace Harriet Macurdy and Barbara McManus, consummate scholars and professionals both, to redefine the professional classical scholar as well as the classicist have given study of the classical world its staying power. In evaluating Macurdy's career, Barbara rightly emphasizes that she availed herself of opportunities provided by the American classical community while drawing inspiration and support from British classicists, thereby expanding the definition of classical scholar to include a woman of working-class background who spoke authoritatively in her own voice and focused her most enduring work on the lives of ancient women. Barbara McManus herself expanded the definition of classical scholar even further. For this category now embraces a woman who taught for her entire career at a small, all-female, Catholic, undergraduate liberal-arts institution, made

---

2. Reid, *Edith Hamilton*, 36.

groundbreaking contributions to classical studies through her efforts at integrating technology into teaching and research as well as through her interdisciplinary, cutting-edge feminist scholarship, and who immensely enriched the classics profession itself by gathering, interpreting, and sharing information about its current and past practitioners, such as Grace Harriet Macurdy.

These efforts to situate the achievements of Grace Harriet Macurdy in the realm of classics, by comparing Macurdy not only with her contemporary Edith Hamilton, but also with her biographer Barbara McManus, respond to recommendations made by the two Ohio State University Press reviewers, Donald Lateiner and Elizabeth Carney, for improving this manuscript. Donald Lateiner's report, for example, stated "greater contextualization of women in American Classics" would be welcome, "so readers know at once why her long story is worth reading," adding, "The picture is so focused on [Abby Leach, Macurdy] and Vassar that one does not detect the growing role of women in teaching and research in American academe, the women's colleges, and Classics." While Carney recommended the inclusion of "a bit more about Vassar's history and . . . its students at the time," she, too, would have appreciated more on "other women's colleges." I hope that my cursory comparison between Macurdy and Hamilton furnishes some sense of how one of Macurdy's contemporaries, who held two academic degrees in classics from another American women's college, took advantage of professional opportunities available to her at that time, although Hamilton pursued secondary school administration and a career in writing rather than college teaching and specialized scholarship.

Lateiner, who has published several articles on Macurdy's Vassar colleague Elizabeth Hazelton Haight, also remarked on the absence of an "introduction to [Haight], this nearly lifelong Latinist colleague who lived somewhat in [Macurdy's] shadow."[3] So, too, he was eager "to hear more of Abby Leach's complaints about Macurdy"; "the personalities of [the two Vassar presidents] involved in the conflict between Leach and Macurdy", and "whether their interference in this departmental dispute was typical or unique"; and "the significance of Macurdy's publications" other than two books (especially her work on Euripides). I hope that the questions posed by Lateiner, and the evidence required to address these questions, will attract careful attention by future researchers on classics at Vassar.

---

3. Lateiner, whose publications on Haight include a 1993 article about her correspondence with renowned Columbia classicist Gilbert Highet, also asked "Did Macurdy have any noteworthy relationship with this Columbia eminence" and "significant participant" in World War II intelligence?

In a letter written a few days before her death, Barbara voiced her belief that greater contextualization "is not a necessary or appropriate part of this biography," as it "devolves into contextual areas that . . . are too specific and would not be essential to my book." I honor her belief. I would submit, too, that this book itself, in its entirety, clearly states the significance of Grace Harriet Macurdy to the study of classical antiquity in America, and to the history of women's contributions to our field. As befits the complexity of Macurdy's long life, it makes a complex statement, with powerful narrative clarity, gradually and at some length. It is a statement that the impressive research and insightful writing of Barbara McManus have made eminently worth reading.

Judith P. Hallett

APPENDIX 1

Descendants of Adam Duncan Thomson and William Augustus McCurdy

Note: Second and third generations are detailed only for individuals in contact with Grace Macurdy.

Adam Duncan Thomson and Lydia Russell Bradford

FIRST GENERATION

1. Adam Duncan Thomson, son of **Dugald Thomson** and **Experience Wescott**, was born on 7 Aug 1800 in St. Andrews, New Brunswick, died on 10 Sep 1870 in Bayside, New Brunswick, at age 70, and was buried in Sep 1870 in Sandy Point Cemetery in New Brunswick. The cause of his death was dropsy.

Adam married **Lydia Russell Bradford**, daughter of **Benjamin Bradford** and **Lucy Russell**, in 1828 in New Brunswick. Lydia was born in Dec 1808 in New Brunswick, died on 2 Aug 1889 in Calais, Maine, at age 80, and was buried in Aug 1889 in Sandy Point Cemetery. On 22 Sep 1871 she next married **Samuel Kelly** in St. Stephen, New Brunswick, and went to live in Calais until her death.

Children from this marriage were:

2   M i.   **Dugald S. Thomson** was born about 1828 in St. Andrews, New Brunswick, and died on 24 Mar 1874 in St Stephen, New Brunswick, about age 46.

              Dugald married **Sarah Augusta Hill** (d. 1892).

3   F ii.   **Ann (Nancy) Thomson** was born about 1831 in St. Andrews, New Brunswick, died there on 14 Jan 1858 about age 27, and was buried in 1858 in Sandy Point Cemetery.

              Ann married **Joshua Hanson** (d. 1907).

4   F iii.   **Eliza Thomson** was born about 1833 in St. Andrews, New Brunswick.

+ 5   F iv.   **Rebecca Manning Thomson** (see below).

6   F v.   **Adelia Ann Thomson** was born about 1839 in St. Andrews, New Brunswick, died there on 27 Mar 1864 about age 25, and was buried in 1864 in Sandy Point Cemetery. The cause of her death was diphtheria.

7   F vi.   **Elizabeth Thomson** was born about 1848 in St. Andrews, New Brunswick.

8   M vii.   **William Carey Thomson** was born about 1851 in St. Andrews, New Brunswick, died there on 9 Mar 1864 about age 13, and was buried in 1864 in Sandy Point Cemetery. The cause of his death was diphtheria.

SECOND GENERATION (CHILDREN)

5. Rebecca Manning Thomson was born in Mar 1837 in St. Andrews, New Brunswick, died on 22 Sep 1895 in Watertown, Massachusetts, at age 58, and was buried in 1895 in Common Street Cemetery in Watertown. The cause of her death was chronic disease of the kidney.

Rebecca married **Simon Angus McCurdy/Macurdy** (see below **Person 44**) between 1854 and 1855 in Bayside, New Brunswick.

Children from this marriage were:

9   F   i.   **Eliza McCurdy** was born in 1856 in St. Andrews, New Brunswick, and died there in at age 4.

10   F   ii.   **Theodosia E. Macurdy** was born in 1858 in St. Andrews, New Brunswick, and died on 5 Apr 1933 in Framingham, Massachusetts, at age 75. She never married and had no children. [According to Grace, her middle name was **Ernest**, but Theodosia herself used the middle name **Endicott**.]

11   F   iii.   **Maria Hayes Macurdy** was born Jan 1860 in St. Andrews, New Brunswick, died on 6 Sep 1903 in Watertown, Massachusetts, at age 43, and was buried in Common Street Cemetery. The cause of her death was sarcoma.

Maria married **George Herbert Tarleton** (d. 1936) on 4 Oct 1886 in Watertown. The couple had two surviving children.

+   12   F   iv.   **Edith St. Clair Macurdy** (see below).

+   13   M   v.   **William Thomson Macurdy** (see below).

14   F   vi.   **Grace Harriet Macurdy** was born on 12 Sep 1866 in Robbinston, Maine, and died on 23 Oct 1946 in Poughkeepsie, New York, at age 80. The cause of her death was breast cancer and dropsy. She never married and had no children.

+   15   M   vii.   **John Ordway Macurdy** (see below).

16   M   viii.   **Leigh Theodore Macurdy** was born on 27 Jul 1876 in Watertown, Massachusetts.

Leigh married **Eva McVey** sometime before 1911, apparently in West Virginia, and changed his name, possibly to Hugh McVey.

17   M   ix.   **Ronald Thomson Macurdy** was born on 30 May 1879 in Watertown, Massachusetts, died there on 7 Oct 1879, and was buried in Common Street Cemetery. The cause of his death was cholera.

THIRD GENERATION (GRANDCHILDREN)

12. Edith St. Clair Macurdy was born on 5 Mar 1862 in St. Andrews, New Brunswick, died on 23 Jun 1918 in Boston, Massachusetts, at age 56, and was buried in Common Street Cemetery. The cause of her death was acute appendicitis.

Edith married **Henry Reuben Skinner**, son of **Hiram D. Skinner** and **Eliza Ann Swanton**, on 6 Oct 1892 in Watertown, Massachusetts. Henry was born on 8 May 1860 in Foxboro, Massachusetts, died on 11 Aug 1912 in Watertown at age 52, and was buried in Common Street Cemetery. The cause of his death was cerebral hemorrhage and arteriosclerosis.

Children from this marriage were:

21 F i.   **Rebecca Elizabeth Skinner** was born on 4 Nov 1893 in Watertown, Massachusetts, and died there on 15 Sep 1898 at age 4. The cause of her death was sarcoma of the left kidney.

22 F ii.   **Theodosia Frances Skinner** was born on 1 Aug 1895 in Watertown, Massachusetts, and died in Dec 1982 in Chula Vista, Mexico, at age 87.

Theodosia married **Carl Peter Immekus** (d. 13 May 1967) on 16 Sep 1920 in Poughkeepsie, New York. The couple had no children

Theodosia next married **William Reading Webb Jr.** (d. 7 Dec 1993) after 1967 in Flushing, New York. The couple had no children.

23 M iii.   **Richard Henry Leigh Skinner** was born on 27 Feb 1900 in Watertown, Massachusetts, and died on 3 Aug 1971 in New York, New York, at age 71. He never married and had no children.

24 M iv.   **Bradford Swanton Skinner** was born on 9 Oct 1905 in Watertown, Massachusetts, and died on 9 Feb 1973 in Springfield, Massachusetts, at age 67.

Bradford married **Dorothy Fitzgerald** (d. 19 Mar 1999) on 3 Sep 1929 in Dayton, Ohio. The couple had two children.

13. William Thomson Macurdy was born Jul 1864 in St. Andrews, New Brunswick, died on 25 Nov 1932 in Watertown, Massachusetts, at age 68, and was buried on 27 Nov 1932 in Common Street Cemetery. The cause of his death was arteriosclerosis and Parkinson's disease.

William married **Anna Louise Richardson**, daughter of **Henry Richardson** and **Eleanor Safford**, on 31 Aug 1886 in Cambridge, Massachusetts. Anna was born in Sep 1865 in Belmont, Massachusetts, died on 29 Oct 1929 in Watertown, Massachusetts, at age 64, and was buried on 1 Nov 1929 in Common Street Cemetery. The cause of her death was arteriosclerosis with cerebral hemorrhage.

Children from this marriage were:

> 25   F   i.   **Edith Richardson Macurdy** was born on 9 Mar 1887 in Watertown, Massachusetts, and died in Mar 1968 in Belmont, Massachusetts, at age 81.
>
> Edith married **George Miller Hosmer** on 27 Jun 1917 in Watertown, Massachusetts. The couple had no children.

> 26   F   ii.   **Louise Bradford Macurdy** was born on 12 Apr 1889 in Watertown, Massachusetts, and died in Mar 1969 in Belmont, Massachusetts, at age 79.
>
> Louise married **James Grant** (d. 1955). The couple had no children.

> 27   F   iii. **Harriet Thomson Macurdy** was born in Aug 1891 in Watertown, Massachusetts, and died there on 16 Dec 1907 at age 16.

> 28   F   iv.   **Eleanor Fuller Macurdy** was born on 6 Sep 1893 in Watertown, Massachusetts, and died in Jun 1975 in Tucson, Arizona, at age 81.
>
> Eleanor married **Phillips Brooks Quinsler** (d. Jul 1964) on 11 Jun 1919 in Watertown, Massachusetts. The couple had four children.

> 29   M   v.   **Ernest Hayes Macurdy** was born on 1 Jan 1899 in Watertown, Massachusetts, died on 22 Dec 1981 in Bedford, Massachusetts, at age 82, and was buried on 26 Dec 1981 in Common Street Cemetery. The cause of his death was gastritis, complicated by stress and chronic psychotic depression.

Ernest married **Helen Sarah Ramsdell** (d. 3 Nov 1995) on 24 Sep 1932 in Haverhill, Massachusetts. The couple had three children.

15. John Ordway Macurdy was born on 25 Jul 1873 in Watertown, Massachusetts, died on 27 Jul 1945 in Wheeling, West Virginia, at age 72, and was buried on 30 Jul 1945 in Cadiz Union Cemetery in Cadiz, Ohio. The cause of his death was carcinoma of the bladder.

John married **Mary Frances Monahan**, daughter of **James F. Monahan** and **Bridget McConnell**, on 7 Jun 1910 in Everett, Massachusetts. Mary was born on 2 Nov 1875 in Everett.

The child from this marriage was:

> 30 M i. **John Ordway Macurdy** was born on 17 Nov 1911 and died on 28 Oct 1983 in New York, New York, at age 71.
>
> John married **Carolyne Anders** (d. 21 Mar 1995) in 1935 in New York, New York. The marriage had ended in divorce by 1942.

William Augustus   cCurdy and Harriet Hayes

FIRST GENERATION

40. William Augustus McCurdy, son of **Neil McCurdy** and **Ruth Avery**, was born in Mar 1793 in St. Andrews, New Brunswick, and died on 14 Oct 1878 in Watertown, Massachusetts, at age 85. The cause of his death was old age.

William married **Harriet Hayes**, daughter of **John Cook Hayes** and **Dorothy Baxter**, on 12 Sep 1820 in All Saints Church, St. Andrews, New Brunswick. Harriet was born in Jul 1798 in Norton, New Brunswick, and died on 15 May 1886 in Watertown, Massachusetts, at age 87. The cause of her death was old age.

Children from this marriage were:

> 41 M i. **James McCurdy** was born in 1821 in St. Andrews, New Brunswick, and died on 4 Oct 1846 on his ship *Everton*, sailing from Honduras to Boston, at age 25.

James married **Mary Poor** on 18 Jul 1846 in Eastport, Maine. The couple had no children.

42 F ii. **Mary Ann McCurdy** was born on 6 Aug 1823 in St. Andrews, New Brunswick, and died on 23 Mar 1914 in Bayside, New Brunswick, at age 90.

Mary married **Henry Rigby** (d. 1 Jan 1894) on 16 Dec 1841 in St. Andrews, New Brunswick. The couple had eleven children, not all of whom survived.

+ 43 M iii. **Hayes Warren McCurdy/Macurdy** (see below).

44 M iv. **Simon Angus McCurdy/Macurdy** was born in Jan 1830 in St. Andrews, New Brunswick, died on 12 May 1905 at the Westborough Insane Hospital in Westborough, Massachusetts, at age 75, and was buried on 26 May 1905 in Common Street Cemetery. The cause of his death was lobar pneumonia and senile dementia.

Simon Angus married **Rebecca Manning Thomson** (d. 22 Sep 1895) between 1854 and 1855 in Bayside, Charlotte, New Brunswick (for information on this couple's descendants, see above, **Person 5**).

45 F v. **Harriet Augusta McCurdy** was born on 14 Mar 1833 in St. Andrews, New Brunswick.

Harriet married **James Turner** on 13 Apr 1865. The couple had one biological and one adopted son. They moved to Malden, Massachusetts, sometime before 1910.

+ 46 M vi. **William Augustus McCurdy** (see below).

47 F vii. **Susan McCurdy** was born about 1827 in St. Andrews, New Brunswick, and died after 1911 in McAdam, New Brunswick.

Susan married **Asa Mitchell** (d. 24 Apr 1893) on 9 Dec 1847 in St. Andrews, New Brunswick. The couple had seven children.

48 M viii. **Theodore Harding McCurdy** was born in 1838 in St. Andrews, New Brunswick, died there on 6 Jul 1849 at age 11, and was buried

in Bayside Baptist Cemetery, New Brunswick. The cause of death was drowning.

SECOND GENERATION (CHILDREN)

43. Hayes Warren McCurdy/Macurdy was born on 13 May 1826 in St. Andrews, New Brunswick, died on 9 Feb 1905 in Watertown, Massachusetts, at age 78, and was buried on 12 Feb 1905 in Common Street Cemetery. The cause of his death was senile debility and general decay.

Hayes Warren married **Maria Foy Kent** about 1859. Maria was born on 4 Jul 1834 in Vassalboro, Maine, and died on 23 Jan 1912 in Watertown, Massachusetts, at age 77.

Their adopted child was:

    49 M i.   **Arthur James Macurdy** was born on 7 Nov 1876 in Massachusetts and died in 1954 at age 78.

                    Arthur married **Sarah Maybelle Kenrick** on 20 May 1903 in Brookline, Massachusetts. The couple had one child.

46. William Augustus McCurdy was born on 14 Mar 1833 in St. Andrews, New Brunswick, and died on 20 Jan 1890 in Port Townsend, Washington, at age 56.

William married **Johanna Caroline Ebinger** on 3 Mar 1867 in Portland, Oregon. Johanna was born on 21 Feb 1850 in Wisconsin and died on 31 Aug 1880 in Portland, Oregon, at age 30.

Children from this marriage were:

    51 M i.   **William Horace McCurdy** was born on 21 Dec 1868 in Victoria, British Columbia, and died on 16 Apr 1911 in Port Townsend, Washington, at age 42.

    52 M ii.   **Francis Pettygrove McCurdy** was born on 21 Feb 1870 in Vallejo, California, and died on 1 Apr 1947 in Roseburg, Oregon, at age 77.

+ 53 M iii. **James Griffith McCurdy** (see below).

54   M iv.   **Winslow Morgan McCurdy** was born on 10 Oct 1877 in Port Townsend, Washington, and died there on 14 Jul 1928 at age 50.

THIRD GENERATION (GRANDCHILDREN)

53. James Griffith McCurdy was born on 15 Mar 1872 in Port Townsend, Washington, and died there on 24 Nov 1942 at age 70.

James married **Anna Tobina Laursen** on 10 Jun 1893 in Port Townsend, Washington. Anna was born on 6 Jan 1875 in Vejle, Denmark, and died on 25 Feb 1962 in Port Townsend, Washington, at age 87.

The child from this marriage was:

56   M i.   **Horace Winslow McCurdy** was born on 30 Jul 1899 in Port Townsend, Washington, and died on 13 Nov 1989 in Seattle, Washington, at age 90.

Horace married **Sarah Catharine McManus** on 3 Jun 1922 in Marblehead, Massachusetts. The couple had two children.

APPENDIX 2

❧

Chronological List of Scholarly Publications of Grace H. Macurdy

1905. *The Chronology of the Extant Plays of Euripides*. Lancaster, Pennsylvania: New Era Printing Company.

1905. Review of *An Abridged History of Greek Literature*, by Alfred and Maurice Croiset. *Educational Review* 29: 314–17.

1907. "*The Heraclidae* of Euripides. Has Our Text of This Play Been Mutilated or Revised?" *Classical Quarterly* 1: 299–303.

1907. Review of *Euripides and the Spirit of His Dramas*, by Paul Decharme. *Classical Weekly* 1: 5–6.

1909. "Alcibiades: a Study of a Greek Statesman from the Pages of His Contemporaries." *Classical Weekly* 2: 138–40, 145–48.

1909. "The Simple Past Condition with Potential Indicative in Apodosis." *Classical Philology* 4: 313–15.

1910. "The Classical Element in Gray's Poetry." *Classical Weekly* 4: 58–62.

1910. "The Fifth Book of Thucydides and Three Plays of Euripides." *Classical Review* 24: 205–7.

1910. Review of *Plato's Doctrine of Ideas*, by J. A. Stewart. *Classical Weekly* 4: 21–22.

1910. Review of *Aristotle's Criticism of Plato*, by J. M. Watson. *Classical Weekly* 4: 30–31.

1910. "Traces of the Influence of Plato's Eschatological Myths in Parts of the Book of Revelation and the Book of Enoch." *Transactions of the American Philological Association* 41: 65–70.

1910. "Virgil's Use of Märchen from the *Odyssey*." In *Studies in English and Comparative Literature by Former and Present Students at Radcliffe College, Presented to Agnes Irwin, Dean of Radcliffe College, 1894–1909*. Radcliffe College Monographs 15, 3–12. Boston and London: Ginn and Company.

1911. "The *Andromache* and the *Trachinians*." *Classical Review* 25: 97–101.

1912. "A Note on the Vocative in Herodotus and in Homer." *Classical Philology* 7: 77–78.

1912. "The Connection of Paean with Paeonia." *Classical Review* 26: 249–51.

1912. "The Origin of a Herodotean Tale in Connection with the Cult of the Spinning Goddess." *Transactions of the American Philological Association* 43: 73–80.

1913. "Klodones, Mimallones and Dionysus Pseudanor." *Classical Review* 27: 191–92.

1913. Review of *The Wars of Greece and Rome. Selections from Herodotus in Attic Greek*, ed. W. D. Lowe. *Classical Weekly* 6: 190.

1913. Review of *An Elementary Greek Grammar*, by E. E. Bryant and E. D. Lake. *Classical Weekly* 6: 190–91.

1914. "Rainbow, Sky, and Stars in the *Iliad* and the *Odyssey*: A Chorizontic Argument." *Classical Quarterly* 8: 212–15.

1915. "The *Odunephata Pharmaka* of *Iliad* V. 900, and Their Bearing on the Prehistoric Culture of Old Servia." *Classical Quarterly* 9: 67–71.

1915. "The Water Gods and Aeneas in the Twentieth and Twenty-First Books of the *Iliad*." *Classical Review* 29: 70–75.

1915. "The Wanderings of Dardanus and the Dardani." *Transactions of the American Philological Association* 46: 119–28.

1916. "The Hyperboreans." *Classical Review* 30: 180–83.

1917. "The Significance of the Myrmidons and Other Close Fighters in the *Iliad*." *Classical Journal* 12: 589–92.

1917. "The Passing of the Classics." *Educational Review* 54: 439–50.

1917. "Sun Myths and Resurrection Myths." *Journal of Hellenic Studies* 37: 160–67.

1918. "The Derivation and Significance of the Greek Word for 'Cock.'" *Classical Philology* 13: 310–11.

1919. "The Blackbird in Early Literature." *The Nation* 108: 689–90.

1919. "Aleuas and Alea." *Classical Quarterly* 13: 170–71.

1919. "The Diaphragm and the Greek Ideal or the Treachery of Translations." *Classical Philology* 14: 389–93.

1919. "The North Greek Affiliations of Certain Groups of Trojan Names." *Journal of Hellenic Studies* 39: 62–68.

1920. "The Meaning of *Aphatein* in a Spartan Inscription." *Classical Review* 34: 98–99.

1920. "The Hyperboreans Again, Abaris, and Helixoia." *Classical Review* 34: 137–41.

1921. "Hermes *Chthonios* as Eponym of the Skopadae." *Journal of Hellenic Studies* 41: 179–82.

1921. "The Word 'Sorex' in C. I. L. I² 1988, 1989." *Journal of Roman Studies* 11: 108–10.

1922. Review of *Greeks and Barbarians*, by J. A. K. Thomson. *The Freeman* 6: 259–60.

1923. "The Horse-Taming Trojans." *Classical Quarterly* 17: 50–52.

1925. *Troy and Paeonia, with Glimpses of Ancient Balkan History and Religion*. New York: Columbia University Press.

1925. "Atreus and Agamemnon." *American Journal of Archaeology* 29: 32–33.

1926. "Blame of Women." *Vassar Quarterly* 2: 190–98.

1926. "Hektor in Boeotia." *Classical Quarterly* 20: 179–80.

1927. "Queen Eurydice and the Evidence for Woman Power in Early Macedonia." *American Journal of Philology* 48: 201–14.

1928. "Basilinna and Basilissa, the Alleged Title of the 'Queen Archon' in Athens." *American Journal of Philology* 49: 276–82.

1928. "A Debt of Catullus to Euripides." *Classical Weekly* 21: 129–30.

1928. "Review of *Magic Staff or Rod in Graeco-Italic Antiquity*, by F. M. J. De Waele. *American Journal of Archaeology* 32: 541–42.

1929. "The Defeated Contestant in Pindar." *Classical Weekly* 22: 208.

1929. "Homeric Names in -tor and Some Other Names of the Short Form Occurring in Homer." *Classical Quarterly* 23: 23–27.

1929. "The Political Activities and the Name of Cratesipolis." *American Journal of Philology* 50: 273–78.

1930. "The Name *Poseidaon* and Other Names Ending in -*aon* in the *Iliad*." *American Journal of Philology* 51: 286–88.

1930. "The Refusal of Callisthenes to Drink the Health of Alexander." *Journal of Hellenic Studies* 50: 294–97.

1930. "The Derivation of the Greek Word *Paean*." *Language* 6: 297–303.

1931. Review of *Greek Life and Thought*, by LaRue Van Hook. *American Journal of Archaeology* 35: 494–95.

1932. *Hellenistic Queens: A Study of Woman-Power in Macedonia, Seleucid Syria, and Ptolemaic Egypt*. Johns Hopkins University Studies in Archaeology 14. Baltimore: Johns Hopkins University Press.

1932. "The Grammar of Drinking Healths." *American Journal of Philology* 53: 168–71.

1932. "Lida Shaw King and Her Classical Work." In *Exercises Commemorative of Lida Shaw King, Dean of Pembroke 1905–1922*, 7–14. Providence: Brown University Press.

1932. "A Note on the Jewellery of Demetrius the Besieger." *American Journal of Archaeology* 36: 27–28.

1932. Review of *The Divinity of the Roman Emperors*, by L. R. Taylor. *Vassar Quarterly* 17: 156–58.

1932. "Roxane and Alexander IV in Epirus." *Journal of Hellenic Studies* 52: 256–61.

1933. Review of *Romance in the Latin Elegaic Poets*, by E. H. Haight. *Vassar Quarterly* 18: 58–60.

1933. Review of *The Legacy of Alexander: A History of the Greek World from 323 to 146 BC*, by M. Cary. *American Historical Review* 38: 725–26.

1933. Review of *The Early Age of Greece* Vol. II, by Sir William Ridgeway. *American Journal of Archaeology* 37: 178–79.

1934. Review of *Old Age Among the Ancient Greeks: The Greek Portrayal of Old Age in Literature, Art, and Inscriptions*, by Bessie Ellen Richardson. *American Journal of Archaeology* 38: 497–98.

1935. "Julia Berenice." *American Journal of Philology* 56: 246–53.

1936. "Iotape." *Journal of Roman Studies* 26: 40–42.

1936. "The Living Legacy of Greece and Rome," with Ruth Mary Weeks. In *A Correlated Curriculum*, National Council of Teachers of English Monograph 5, comp. Ruth Mary Weeks, 138–47. New York: Appleton-Century.

1937. *Vassal-Queens and Some Contemporary Women in the Roman Empire*. Johns Hopkins University Studies in Archaeology 22. Baltimore: Johns Hopkins University Press.

1938. "Aeschylus, *Agamemnon* 1327 ff." *Classical Review* 52: 4–5.

1940. *The Quality of Mercy: The Gentler Virtues in Greek Literature*. Vassar College 75th Anniversary Publications. New Haven: Yale University Press.

1940. Review of *Barnard College: The First Fifty Years*, by Alice Duer Miller and Susan Myers. *New York History* 21: 220.

1942. "Apollodorus and the Speech Against Neaera (Pseudo-Dem. LIX)." *American Journal of Philology* 63: 257–71.

1942. "Platonic Orphism in the Testament of Abraham." *Journal of Biblical Literature* 61: 213–26.

1942. "References to Thucydides, Son of Melesias, and to Pericles in Sophocles *OT* 863–910." *Classical Philology*, 37: 307–10.

1942. "Sophoclean Irony in *Oedipus Tyrannus* 219–21." *Philological Quarterly* 21: 244–47.

1943. "The Dawn Songs in *Rhesus* (527–56) and in the Parodos of *Phaethon*." *American Journal of Philology* 64: 408–16.

1943. Review of "The Use of Fire in Greek and Roman Love Magic," by E. Tavenner, in *Studies in Honor of Frederick W. Shipley, by His Colleagues. American Journal of Archaeology* 47: 361–62.

1944. "Prologue to a Study of the Tragic Heroine." *Classical Weekly* 37: 239–40.

1944. "Had the Danaid Trilogy a Social Problem?" *Classical Philology* 39: 95–100.

1946. "Blood and Tears in *Antigone* 526–30." *Classical Philology* 41: 163–64.

Reprints

[1905] 1966. *The Chronology of the Extant Plays of Euripides.* New York: Haskell House.

[1932] 1975. *Hellenistic Queens: A Study of Woman-Power in Macedonia, Seleucid Syria, and Ptolemaic Egypt.* Westport, Connecticut: Greenwood Press.

[1932] 1977. *Hellenistic Queens: A Study of Woman-Power in Macedonia, Seleucid Syria, and Ptolemaic Egypt.* New York: AMS Press.

[1932] 1985. *Hellenistic Queens: A Study of Woman-Power in Macedonia, Seleucid Syria, and Ptolemaic Egypt.* Chicago: Ares Publishers.

[1937] 1993. *Vassal-Queens and Some Contemporary Women in the Roman Empire.* In *Two Studies on Women in Antiquity.* Chicago: Ares Publishers.

BIBLIOGRAPHY

Abbott, Frank Frost, and Allan Chester Johnson. *Municipal Administration in the Roman Empire.* Princeton, New Jersey: Princeton University Press, 1926.

Ackerman, Robert. *The Myth and Ritual School: J. G. Frazer and the Cambridge Ritualists.* New York: Garland, 1991.

"Address of the Committee of Twelve." *Transactions and Proceedings of the American Philological Association* 26 (1895): xxxiv–xxxvii.

Aeschylus, *Agamemnon, with Introduction and Notes by A. Sidgewick.* Oxford: Clarendon Press, 1881.

"Archaeological Discussions: Summaries of Original Articles Chiefly in Current Periodicals." *American Journal of Archaeology* 7 (1903): 230, 452.

Banner, Lois W. *Intertwined Lives: Margaret Mead, Ruth Benedict, and Their Circle.* New York: Knopf, 2003.

Bassett, Samuel E. Review of *Troy and Paeonia*, by Grace H. Macurdy. *Classical Weekly* 19 (1926): 202–6.

Baxter, John B. M. *Simon Baxter: The First United Empire Loyalist to Settle in New Brunswick: His Ancestry and Descendants.* St. John, New Brunswick: The New Brunswick Museum, 1943.

Beard, Mary. *The Invention of Jane Harrison.* Cambridge, Mass.: Harvard University Press, 2000.

Bellinger, Alfred R. Review of *Hellenistic Queens*, by Grace H. Macurdy. *American Historical Review* 38 (1933): 359.

Beloch, K. J. *Griechische Geschichte.* 2nd ed. 4 vols. Berlin and Leipzig: Walter de Gruyter, 1913–27.

Bevan, Edwyn. *The House of Ptolemy: A History of Hellenistic Egypt under the Ptolemaic Dynasty.* London: Methuen, 1927.

———. *The House of Seleucus.* 2 vols. London: Edward Arnold, 1902.

Bill, I. E. *Fifty Years with the Baptist Ministers and Churches in the Maritime Provinces of Canada.* St. John, New Brunswick: Barnes and Company, 1880.

Blegen, Carl W. "Necrology: Bert Hodge Hill." *American Journal of Archaeology* 63 (1959): 193–94.

Bonner, Campbell. Review of *Troy and Paeonia*, by Grace H. Macurdy. *Classical Philology* 22 (1927): 438–39.

Briggs, Ward W. "Abby Leach (1855–1918)." *Classical World* 90 (1996–97): 97–107.

Brooks, Robert C. "Penobscot Loyalists." *Downeast Ancestry* 7 (1983): 134–37. Accessed 22 January 2011. http://freepages.genealogy.rootsweb.ancestry.com/~aek740/penobscot_loyalists.htm.

Burke, Charles T. *Watertown: Town on the Charles*. Watertown, Mass.: Town of Watertown 350th Anniversary Celebration Committee, 1980.

C., M. [Max Cary]. Review of *Hellenistic Queens*, by Grace H. Macurdy. *Journal of Hellenic Studies* 52 (1932): 315.

C., S. [Stanley Casson]. Review of *Troy and Paeonia*, by Grace H. Macurdy. *Journal of Hellenic Studies* 46 (1926): 276–78.

Calder III, William M. "CAPPS, Edward." In *Biographical Dictionary of North American Classicists*, edited by Ward W. Briggs, 84–85. Westport, Conn., and London: Greenwood Press, 1994.

Capps, Edward. "Forty-First Annual Report of the American School of Classical Studies at Athens, 1921–1922." Extract from the *Bulletin of the Archaeological Institute of America*, 9–40. Accessed 22 January 2015. http://www.ascsa.edu.gr/pdf/uploads/AR_41_1921–22.pdf.

———. "Forty-Sixth Annual Report of the American School of Classical Studies at Athens, 1926–1927." Extract from the *Bulletin of the Archaeological Institute of America*, 9–24. Accessed 22 January 2015. http://www.ascsa.edu.gr/pdf/uploads/AR_46_1926–27.pdf.

———. "Forty-Seventh Annual Report of the American School of Classical Studies at Athens, 1927–1928," Extract from the *Bulletin of the Archaeological Institute of America*, 9–29. Accessed 2 February 2015. http://www.ascsa.edu.gr/pdf/uploads/AR_47_1927–28.pdf.

Carney, Elizabeth. "'What's in a Name?': The Emergence of a Title for Royal women in the Hellenistic Period." In *Women's History and Ancient History*, edited by Sarah B. Pomeroy, 154–72. Chapel Hill: University of North Carolina Press, 1991.

Castle, C. F. Review of *The Chronology of the Extant Plays of Euripides*, by Grace Harriet Macurdy. *Classical Journal* 2 (1907): 185–86.

Charlesworth, M. P. Review of *Vassal-Queens*, by Grace H. Macurdy. *Classical Review* 52 (1938): 188–89.

Cowdroy, Charlotte. "A Study of Mrs. Thompson." *Pall Mall Gazette*, 9 January 1923, 9.

Davis, Jack L. "The Birth of *Hesperia*: A View from the Archives." *Hesperia* 76 (2007): 21–35.

———. "Blegen and the Palace of Nestor: What Took So Long?" In *Carl W. Blegen: Personal and Archaeological Narratives*, edited by Natalia Vogeikoff-Brogan, Jack L. Davis, Vasiliki Florou, 209–29. Atlanta, Ga.: Lockwood Press, 2015.

Davis, Jack L. and Evi Gorogianni. "Embedding Aegean Prehistory in Institutional Practice: A View from One of Its North American Centers." In *Prehistorians Round the Pond: Reflections on Aegean Prehistory as a Discipline*, edited by J. F. Cherry, D. Margomenou, and L. E. Talalay, 93–113. Ann Arbor, Mich.: Kelsey Museum Publication 2, 2005.

Davis, Jack L., and Natalia Vogeikoff-Brogan. "'On His Feet and Ready to Dig': Carl William Blegen." In *Carl W. Blegen: Personal and Archaeological Narratives*, edited by Natalia Vogeikoff-Brogan, Jack L. Davis, Vasiliki Florou, 1–15. Atlanta, Ga.: Lockwood Press, 2015.

Davis, Philip H., and Ida Thallon Hill, Gilbert Murray, J. A. K. Thomson. "Tribute to Miss Macurdy." *Vassar Alumnae Magazine* 23 (1937): 8–9.

Directions and Helpful Suggestions for the Use of the Acousticon. New York: Dictograph Products Corporation, 1920.

Dutton, Emily H. Review of *The Quality of Mercy*, by Grace H. Macurdy. *Classical Journal* 38 (1943): 233–36.

Dwelley, George R. "Superintendent's Report." In *Forty-Sixth Annual Report of the School Committee of Watertown for 1883–84*, by the Watertown School Committee, 11–31. Watertown, Mass.: Fred G. Barker, 1884.

———. "Superintendent's Report." In *Forty-Seventh Annual Report of the School Committee of Watertown*, by the Watertown School Committee, 9–29. Watertown, Mass.: Fred G. Barker, 1885.

———. "Superintendent's Report." In *Fiftieth Annual Report of the School Committee of Watertown*, by the Watertown School Committee, 9–28. Watertown, Mass.: Fred G. Barker, 1888.

Earle, Mortimer Lamson, ed. *The Medea of Euripides*. New York, Cincinnati, Chicago: American Book Company, 1904.

Enßlin, W. Review of *Vassal-Queens*, by Grace H. Macurdy. *Historische Zeitschrift* 158 (1938): 168.

Erck, Theodore H. "MACURDY, Grace Harriet." In *Notable American Women, 1607–1950: A Biographical Dictionary*. Ed. Edward T. James. Cambridge, Mass.: Belknap Press, 1971, Vol. II, 480–81.

Fine, John V. A. Review of *Vassal-Queens*, by Grace H. Macurdy. *Classical Weekly* 31 (1938): 77.

Finkelstein, M. I. Review of *Vassal-Queens*, by Grace H. Macurdy. *American Historical Review* 44 (1939): 683.

Forster, Edward. Review of *The Quality of Mercy*, by Grace H. Macurdy. *Classical Review* 55 (1941): 31–32.

Geyer, Fritz. Review of *Hellenistic Queens*, by Grace H. Macurdy. *Historische Zeitschrift* 150 (1934): 121–22.

Gilman, Arthur. "Secretary's Annual Report, Sixth Year." In *Reports of the Treasurer and Secretary*, by The Society for the Collegiate Instruction of Women, 5–14. Cambridge, Mass.: William H. Wheeler, 1885. Accessed 20 May 2000. http://pds.lib.harvard.edu/pds/view/2573644?n=17&s=4&printThumbnails=no.

Greene, William C. Review of *The Quality of Mercy*, by Grace H. Macurdy. *Classical Philology* 37 (1942): 227–29.

Haight, Elizabeth Hazelton. "The Macurdy Collection." *Vassar Alumnae Magazine* 34 (1949): 11–12.

Hale, R. Wallace. *Early New Brunswick Probate Records, 1785–1835*. Westminster, Md.: Heritage Books, 1989.

Hallett, Judith P. "Greek (and Roman) Ways and Thoroughfares: The Routing of Edith Hamilton's Classical Antiquity," in Rosie Wyles and Edith Hall, eds., *Unsealing the Fountain: Pioneering Female Classical Scholars from the Renaissance to the Twentieth Century*. Oxford: Oxford University Press, 2016.

Halporn, J. W. "Women and Classical Archaeology at the Turn of the Century: Abby Leach of Vassar College." In *Assembling the Past: Studies in the Professionalism of Archaeology*, edited by A. B. Kehoe and M. B. Emmerichs, 121–32. Albuquerque: University of New Mexico Press, 1999.

Hammond, Isaac W., ed. *Town Papers: Documents Relating to Towns in New Hampshire, "A" to "F" Inclusive*. Vol. 11. Concord, N.H.: Parsons B. Cogswell, 1882.

Harrison, Jane Ellen. "Greek Religion and Mythology." *The Year's Work in Classical Studies* 10 (1915): 71–80.

———. *Prolegomena to the Study of Greek Religion*. Cambridge: Cambridge University Press, 1903.

———. *Themis: A Study of the Social Origins of Greek Religion*. Cambridge: Cambridge University Press, 1912.

Heidel, W. A. "American Doctoral Dissertations in Classical Philology." *Classical Quarterly* 1 (1907): 242–48.

Heilbrun, Carolyn G. *When Men Were the Only Models We Had: My Teachers Barzun, Fadiman, Trilling*. Philadelphia: University of Pennsylvania Press, 2002.

Hill, B. H. "Excavations at Corinth 1925: Preliminary Report." *American Journal of Archaeology* 30 (1926): 44–49.

———. "Excavations at Corinth 1926." *American Journal of Archaeology* 31 (1927): 70–79.

Hill, Ida Thallon. *The Ancient City of Athens: Its Topography and Monuments*. Cambridge, Mass.: Harvard University Press, 1953.

Hill, Ida Thallon, and Lida Shaw King. *Decorated Architectural Terracottas*. Corinth 4.1. Cambridge, Mass.: Harvard University Press, 1929.

Hirst, G. M. "The Cults of Olbia." *Journal of Hellenic Studies* 21 (1902): 245–67; 22 (1903): 24–53.

Hohl, Ernst. Review of *Vassal-Queens*, by Grace H. Macurdy. *Gnomon* 14 (1938): 172.

Horowitz, Helen Lefkowitz. *Alma Mater: Design and Experience in the Women's Colleges from Their Nineteenth Century Beginnings to the 1930's*, 2nd ed. Amherst: University of Massachusetts Press, 1993.

———. *The Power and Passion of M. Carey Thomas*. 1994. Reprint, Urbana and Chicago: University of Illinois Press, 1999.

Jebb, Richard Claverhouse. *The Growth and Influence of Classical Greek Poetry: Lectures Delivered in 1892 on the Percy Turnbull Memorial Foundation in the Johns Hopkins University*. Boston: Houghton Mifflin, 1893.

Johnson, Daniel Fred. *Vital Statistics from New Brunswick Newspapers*. Accessed 15 July 2009. http://archives.gnb.ca/APPS/NewspaperVitalStats/Default.aspx?Culture=en-CA.

Johnston, John. *A History of the Towns of Bristol and Bremen in the State of Maine, including the Pemaquid Settlement*. 2 vols. Albany, N.Y.: Joel Munsell, 1873.

Kahrstedt, U. Review of *Hellenistic Queens*, by Grace H. Macurdy. *Gnomon* 9 (1933): 278–79.

Knapp, Charles. "Doctoral Dissertations in Classics, Columbia University, 1885–1933." *Classical Weekly* 27 (1934): 164–68.

Kraemer, Casper J., Jr. Review of *Hellenistic Queens*, by Grace H. Macurdy. *American Journal of Archaeology* 39 (1935): 156–58.

Lane, Ann J., ed. *Making Women's History: The Essential Mary Ritter Beard*. New York: Feminist Press, 2000.

Langridge-Noti, Elizabeth. "Elizabeth Pierce Blegen (1888–1966)." *Breaking Ground: Women in Old World Archaeology*. Accessed 22 January 2015. http://www.brown.edu/Research/Breaking _Ground/results.php?d=1&first=Elizabeth%20Pierce&last=Blegen.

Larsen, Jakob A. O. Review of *Hellenistic Queens*, by Grace H. Macurdy. *Classical Philology* 27 (1932): 315–16.

Lateiner, Donald. "Gilbert Highet to E. H. Haight, a letter from Post-war Germany." *Quaderni di Storia* 38 (1993): 131–41.

———. "Elizabeth Hazelton Haight, a Biography." *Classical World* 90 (1996): 153–66.

Leach, Abby. "The Athenian Democracy in the Light of Greek Literature." *American Journal of Philology* 21 (1900): 361–77.

———. "Fatalism of the Greeks." *American Journal of Philology* 36 (1915): 373–401.

Lenschau, Thomas. Review of *Vassal-Queens*, by Grace H. Macurdy. *Philologische Wochenschrift* 58 (1938): 532–33.

Linner, Edward R. "As I Remember Them." *Vassar Alumnae Magazine* 55 (1969): 14–19.

Lloyd-Jones, Hugh. "Harrison, Jane Ellen." In *The Oxford Dictionary of National Biography*, edited by H. C. G. Matthew and B. Harrison, 25: 504–7. Oxford: Oxford University Press, 2004.

Lord, Louis E. *A History of the American School of Classical Studies at Athens, 1882–1942: An Intercollegiate Project*. Cambridge, Mass.: Harvard University Press, 1947.

MacCracken, Henry Noble. *The Hickory Limb*. New York: Scribner, 1950.

MacCracken, H. N., and M. I. Finkelstein, letters to the editor. "Historical News." *American Historical Review* 45 (1939): 268.

Machová, Mariana. "Elizabeth Bishop: Translation as Poetics." PhD diss., Charles University in Prague, 2011. Accessed 4 March 2015. https://is.cuni.cz/webapps/zzp/download/140004159/?lang=en.

Macurdy, Grace Harriet. (See appendix 2 for all scholarly publications.)

———. "Correspondence." *Classical Review* 41 (1927): 157–58.

———. "Gilbert Murray in War Work." *Radcliffe Quarterly* 3 (1918): 4–9.

———. *Pioneer Ancestors of an American Family, 1620–1857*. Unpublished manuscript, 1944. Seattle Public Library, R929.2 M139Mg.

———. [signed "an American Woman"]. "Shall the Married Woman Work?" *Pall Mall Gazette*, 11 January 1923, 9.

———. "Some Remarks from the Greek Department." *Vassar Quarterly* 19 (1934): 137–38.

———. "Women at the University of Berlin." *The Radcliffe Magazine* 2 (1900): 135–38.

Mahaffy, J. P. *The Empire of the Ptolemies*. London: Macmillan, 1895.

———. *History of Egypt under the Ptolemaic Dynasty*. London: Methuen, 1899.

Maine Register or State Year-Book and Legislative Manual. Portland, Maine: G. M. Donham, 1891.

Manual of the Cambridge School for Girls. Cambridge, Mass., 1898.

McCarthy, Mary. *How I Grew*. New York: Harcourt Brace Jovanovich, 1987.

McCarty's Annual Statistician. San Francisco: L. P. McCarty, 1885.

McCurdy, H. W. *Genealogical History of James Winslow McCurdy and Neil Barclay McCurdy*. Seattle: Superior Publishing Company, 1963.

McCurdy, H. W., with Gordon Newell. *Don't Leave Any Holidays*. 2 vols. Portland, Ore.: Graphic Arts Center, 1981.

McManus, Barbara F. *Classics and Feminism: Gendering the Classics*. The Impact of Feminism on the Arts and Sciences. New York: Twayne Publishers, 1997.

———. "J. A. K. Thomson and Classical Reception Studies: American Influences and 'Classical Influences.'" In *British Classics outside England: The Academy and Beyond*, edited by Judith P. Hallett and Christopher Stray, 129–48. Waco, Texas: Baylor University Press, 2008.

———. "'*Macte nova virtute, puer!*': Gilbert Murray as Mentor and Friend to J. A. K. Thomson." In *Gilbert Murray Reassessed*, edited by Christopher Stray, 181–99. Oxford: Oxford University Press, 2007.

Mills, Mara. "When Mobile Communication Technologies Were New." *Endeavour* 33 (2009): 140–46.

Moore, Frank Gardner. "A History of the American Philological Association." *Transactions and Proceedings of the American Philological Association* 50 (1919): 5–32.

Moore, R. W. Review of *Hellenistic Queens*, by Grace H. Macurdy. *Times Literary Supplement*, June 9, 1932, 430.

Murray, Gilbert. *The Trojan Women of Euripides, Translated into English Rhyming Verse with Explanatory Notes.* London: George Allen, 1905.

Nicholson, Virginia. *Singled Out: How Two Million British Women Survived without Men after the First World War.* New York: Oxford University Press, 2008.

Norcross, Rev. James E. *A Memorial History of the First Baptist Church, Watertown, Massachusetts 1830–1930.* Cambridge, Mass.: Hampshire Press, 1930.

Norwood, Gilbert. *Greek Tragedy.* London: Methuen, 1920.

P., H. W. [Herbert William Parke]. Review of *Hellenistic Queens*, by Grace H. Macurdy. *Hermathena* 22 (1932): 292–93.

Palmieri, Patricia Ann. *In Adamless Eden: The Community of Women Faculty at Wellesley.* New Haven, Conn.: Yale University Press, 1995.

Parker, Barbara Neville, and Anne Bolling Wheeler. *John Singleton Copley: American Portraits.* Boston: Museum of Fine Arts, 1938.

Pounder, Robert L. "The Blegens and the Hills: A Family Affair." In *Carl W. Blegen: Personal and Archaeological Narratives*, edited by Natalia Vogeikoff-Brogan, Jack L. Davis, Vasiliki Florou, 85–98. Atlanta, Ga.: Lockwood Press, 2015.

Raymond, W. O. "At Portland Point," *New Brunswick Magazine* 2 (1899): 311–25.

———. "New Brunswick General History, 1758–1867." In *Atlantic Provinces.* Vol. 13 of *Canada and Its Provinces: A History of the Canadian People and Their Institutions by One Hundred Associates*, edited by Adam Shortt and Arthur G. Doughty, 127–210. Toronto: Publishers Association of Canada, 1914.

Reid, Doris Fielding. *Edith Hamilton: An Intimate Portrait.* New York: W. W. Norton, 1967.

Robinson, Annabel. *The Life and Work of Jane Ellen Harrison.* Oxford: Oxford University Press, 2002.

Robinson, David M. Review of *The Quality of Mercy*, by Grace H. Macurdy. *American Journal of Philology* 64 (1943): 371–73.

Robinson, G. Frederick, and Ruth Robinson Wheeler. *Great Little Watertown: A Tercentenary History.* Cambridge, Mass.: Riverside Press, 1930.

M Rostovtzeff, M. "Queen Dynamis of Bosporus." *Journal of Hellenic Studies* 39 (1919): 88–109.

Rupp, David W. "Mutually Antagonistic Philhellenes: Edward Capps and Bert Hodge Hill at the American School of Classical Studies and Athens College." *Hesperia* 82 (2013): 67–99.

Schwager, Sally. "'Harvard Women': A History of the Founding of Radcliffe College." EdD diss., Harvard University, 1982.

Scott, John A. "Origins and Etymologies." *The Nation* 122 (1926): 614.

Shewan, A. Review of *Troy and Paeonia*, by Grace H. Macurdy. *Classical Review* 41 (1927): 37.

Singer, Sandra L. *Adventures Abroad: North American Women at German-Speaking Universities, 1868–1915.* Contributions in Women's Studies 201. Westport, Conn.: Praeger Publishers, 2003.

Stevenson, Robert Louis. *Aes Triplex and Other Essays.* 2nd ed. Portland, Maine: Thomas B. Mosher, 1903.

Stray, Christopher. "Murray, (George) Gilbert Aimé (1866–1957)." In *The Oxford Dictionary of National Biography,* edited by H. C. G. Matthew and B. Harrison, 39: 912–18. Oxford: Oxford University Press, 2004.

Stuart, Jessie. *Jane Ellen Harrison: A Portrait from Letters.* London: Merlin Press, 1959.

Sturtevant, E. H. Review of *Troy and Paeonia,* by Grace H. Macurdy. *American Journal of Archaeology* 30 (1926): 94–95.

Tarn, W. W. *Antigonos Gonatas.* Oxford: Clarendon Press, 1913.

———. Review of *Hellenistic Queens,* by Grace H. Macurdy. *Classical Review* 46 (1932): 167.

———. Review of *Vassal-Queens,* by Grace H. Macurdy. *Journal of Roman Studies* 28 (1938): 77–78.

Taylor, James Monroe and Elizabeth Hazelton Haight. *Vassar,* American College and University Series (New York: Oxford University Press, 1915).

Taylor, Lily Ross. Review of *Vassal-Queens,* by Grace H. Macurdy. *American Journal of Archaeology* 43 (1939): 173.

Thomson, J. A. K. "Tribute to Miss Macurdy." *Vassar Alumnae Magazine* 23 (1937), 9.

Tompkins, Daniel P. "The World of Moses Finkelstein: The Year 1939 in M. I. Finley's Development as a Historian." In *Classical Antiquity and the Politics of America: From George Washington to George W. Bush,* edited by Michael Meckler, 95–125. Waco, Texas: Baylor University Press, 2006.

Tracy, Sterling. Review of *Hellenistic Queens,* by Grace H. Macurdy. *Classical Weekly* 26 (1933): 207.

Vogeikoff, Natalia. "Ida Thallon Hill (1875–1954)." *Breaking Ground: Women in Old World Archaeology.* Accessed 22 January 2015. http://www.brown.edu/Research/Breaking_Ground/results .php?d=1&first=Ida%20Thallon&last=Hill.

Vogeikoff-Brogan, Natalia. "Loring Hall: Could It Have Been 'Thomas Hall'?" *Akoue: Newsletter of the American School of Classical Studies at Athens* 62 (2010): 17, 25–26. Accessed 3 February 2015. http://www.ascsa.edu.gr/pdf/uploads/akoue-spr2010web.pdf.

Vogeikoff-Brogan, Natalia, and Jack L. Davis, Vasiliki Florou, eds. *Carl W. Blegen: Personal and Archaeological Narratives.* Atlanta, Ga.: Lockwood Press, 2015.

W., T. B. L. [Thomas Bertram Lonsdale Webster]. Review of *The Quality of Mercy,* by Grace H. Macurdy. *Journal of Hellenic Studies* 62 (1942): 93.

Watertown Assessors, *The Taxable Valuation of the Real and Personal Estates with the Amount of Tax in the Town of Watertown.* Watertown, Mass.: Fred G. Barker, 1898–1917.

Weigall, E. P. B. *The Life and Times of Cleopatra, Queen of Egypt: A Study in the Origin of the Roman Empire.* Edinburgh and London: Blackwood, 1914.

Welles, C. Bradford. Review of *Vassal-Queens,* by Grace H. Macurdy. *American Journal of Philology* 59 (1938): 379–80.

Wells, Walter. *Provisional Report upon the Water-Power of Maine.* Augusta, Maine: Stevens & Sayward, 1868.

Westbrook, H. T. Review of *Troy and Paeonia,* by Grace H. Macurdy. *Journal of Philosophy* 23 (1926): 361–62.

Whitney, Solon F. "Watertown." In *History of Middlesex County, Massachusetts, with Biographical Sketches of Many of its Pioneers and Prominent Men*, edited by E. Hamilton Hurd, 317–431. Philadelphia: J. W. Lewis & Co., 1890.

Winter, J. G. Review of *Troy and Paeonia*, by Grace H. Macurdy. *Classical Journal* 22 (1927): 696–98.

Zwart, Ann Townsend. "LEACH, Abby." In *Notable American Women, 1607–1950: A Biographical Dictionary*, edited by Edward T. James, 2: 379–80. Cambridge, Mass.: Belknap Press, 1971.

INDEX